Sixth Edition

D0077584

TRAINING IN
INTERPERSONAL SKILLS

TIPS FOR MANAGING PEOPLE AT WORK

Stephen P. Robbins

San Diego State University

Phillip L. Hunsaker

University of San Diego

Prentice Hall

Boston   Columbus   Indianapolis   New York   San Francisco   Upper Saddle River
Amsterdam   Cape Town   Dubai   London   Madrid   Milan   Munich   Paris   Montreal   Toronto
Delhi   Mexico City   São Paulo   Sydney   Hong Kong   Seoul   Singapore   Taipei   Tokyo

Editorial Director: Sally Yagan	**Production Manager:** Meghan DeMaio
Editor in Chief: Eric Svendsen	**Creative Art Director:** Jayne Conte
Director of Editorial Services: Ashley Santora	**Cover Designer:** Bruce Kenselaar
Editorial Project Manager: Meg O'Rourke	**Cover Art:** Fotolia
Editorial Assistant: Carter Anderson	**Full-Service Project Management/Composition:**
Director of Marketing: Patrice Lumumba Jones	Kalpana Venkatramani/PreMediaGlobal
Marketing Manager: Nikki Ayana Jones	
Marketing Assistant: Ian Gold	**Text Font:** Times
Senior Managing Editor: Judy Leale	

Library of Congress Cataloging-in-Publication Data

Robbins, Stephen P., 1943–
   Training in interpersonal skills: tips for managing people at work / Stephen P. Robbins, Phillip L. Hunsaker. — 6th ed.
    p. cm.
   Includes index.
   ISBN-13: 978-0-13-255174-8
   ISBN-10: 0-13-255174-8
   1. Supervision of employees.   2. Interpersonal communication.   I. Hunsaker, Phillip L.   II. Title.
   HF5549.12.R63 2011
   658.3'02—dc22

        2010050141

Prentice Hall
is an imprint of

www.pearsonhighered.com

ISBN-10: 0-13-255174-8
ISBN-13: 978-0-13-255174-8

"For our interpersonal partners in life, Laura and Jo."

BRIEF CONTENTS

CONTENTS

PREFACE

Training in Interpersonal Skills (TIPS) was one of the first interpersonal skills training packages for management students. Since the book's original publication, college and university management faculty have increasingly come to recognize the importance of developing interpersonal skill competencies in their students. Dr. Milton Blood, a former professor and executive with the International Association for Management Education, has explained why management skills training has gained in popularity over more traditional theory-building courses:

> Leadership sounds like an applied topic, but its classroom presentation can leave students no better prepared to lead. . . . The business school graduate needs to lead, not trace the history of leadership research. [Similarly] the graduate needs to motivate, not compare and contrast six different theories of motivation.[i]

By developing and practicing the interpersonal skills in this book, students can learn how to build productive relationships with others in any situation. They will also master skills vital to personal and organizational effectiveness such as self-management, communication, teaming, and problem solving. In addition, they will master the interpersonal skills necessary for effective leadership, including persuading, politicking, goal setting, motivating, coaching, and managing change.

THE SIXTH EDITION

The content of the sixth edition has been revised according to the feedback from reviewers and current research on the emerging interpersonal skills needed for organizational managers. The majority of reviewers of the fifth edition used all of the chapters and agreed that the relevant material was well covered and supported by current academic research. Consequently, we have maintained the same coverage of concepts and skills, although research references and examples have been updated throughout the book and some chapters have been reorganized to present more meaningful topic progressions (e.g., discussion on personal mission statements was moved in front of personal goal setting in Chapter 3). We have also modified the *Behavioral Checklists* and the *Observer's Rating Sheets* in each chapter so that they specifically focus on observable behaviors and allow more relevant feedback for role-play and exercise participants. PowerPoint slides covering the content and exercises in each chapter are now available.

With the addition of chapters on applying emotional intelligence and communicating across cultures, the text now contains 21 chapters. Skills for running meetings have been incorporated into the second Integrating Exercise. Several new topics have been added and many pedagogical tools, including role-plays, cases, self-assessments, and exercises have been added, replaced, and revised to improve the chapters. Some specific changes to enhance the teaching of interpersonal skills include the following:

- New *Self-Assessment Questionnaires* on locus of control; type A personality; passive/assertive/aggressive behavior.
- The addition of Manager's Application Tips boxes that describe how to apply the results of each Self-Assessment Questionnaire.

---

[i] M. R. Blood, "The Role of Organizational Behavior in the Business School Curriculum," in J. Greenberg (ed.), *Organizational Behavior: The State of Science* (Hillsdale, NJ: Lawrence Erlbaum Erlbaum, 1994), p. 216.

- New *Reinforcement Exercises* on strategic planning for personal mission achievement; giving and receiving feedback while protecting self-image; avoiding diversity problems by learning from *The Office*: *Diversity Day*; promoting ethical leadership.
- New sections on applying persuasive skills in formal presentations; online language differences of males and females; training programs that work best; avoiding gaffes.
- New concepts including social networking; impression management; persuasion tactics of social proof and ingratiation; group process loss; facilitating stages of team development.
- Coverage of ethics has been expanded to include new material on principles for ethical decision making; ethical decisions in cross-cultural contexts; encouraging ethical behavior in others; tests for ethical actions.

THE BEHAVIORAL SKILLS LEARNING MODEL

Each chapter in *Training in Interpersonal Skills* is organized around the social learning model which has proven to be a major pedagogical aid. It contains 10 components: (1) assessment of basic skill levels; (2) review of key concepts relevant to applying the skills; (3) test of conceptual knowledge; (4) identification of the specific behavioral dimensions needed for each skill; (5) observation of how to apply the skill through modeling exercises; (6) skill practice in small groups; (7) summary checklist self-assessment to identify deficiencies; (8) application questions to cement practical understanding of the concepts; (9) reinforcement exercises outside of the classroom; and (10) development of an action plan for ongoing skill improvement. This model is explained in detail in Chapter 1.

WHAT THE REVIEWERS SAY

Reviewers of recent editions have been professors who use *Training in Interpersonal Skills* in various management, organizational behavior, human relations, interpersonal skills, teams, and communication courses. In overall quality, the vast majority of users have assigned the book an "A" for meeting student needs. The book has been praised for its ability to address theory without becoming overwhelming and for its practical role-play exercises. With respect to writing style, reviewers have complemented each chapter's stand-alone independence, allowing chapters to be rearranged at the professor's discretion.

When asked how they would describe this text to a colleague, reviewers responded:

"This text brings considerable academically researched topics to the student in a concise format. It becomes a practicum for the students discovering their strengths and weaknesses and provides opportunities to practice enhancing the strengths and overcoming the weaknesses in areas critical to long term career success."

"I really like the applied approach of this textbook. It complements management theory textbooks and helps the student receive real-life examples on each concept. It is "a good source of in-class group exercises that supplement the theory lectures." The text is "focused on application, helps to increase self-awareness, covers current topics in OB well, focused on doing and applying rather than memorizing. It is filled with application exercises making it a hands-on text for learning in the college classroom."

APPLICATIONS FOR THE BOOK

Training in Interpersonal Skills is widely used as a skills-training supplement in courses such as Interpersonal Relations, Organizational Behavior, Management, Human Relations, Supervision, and Organizational Development. It is also successfully used as a complete training package for practicing managers in executive development programs. The recent more comprehensive editions of the book are frequently utilized as the primary text for university courses on interpersonal relations and management training programs.

NOTE TO INSTRUCTORS

The *Instructor's Manual* is more than the typical instructor's manual made up of outline summaries of chapter contents and examination questions. Instead, it is a valuable teaching aid consisting of additional exercises, different teaching options, suggestions and ideas from our own experiences, and discussion questions for each chapter to enhance learning in various settings.

While many adopters find the instructor's manual has improved with each edition of the text, and like the extra activities and ideas for tying skills together, others didn't know there was one, or say that they seldom refer to an instructor's manual for any text. We are happy to learn that the majority of adopters feel that it can be a significant guide for facilitating skills learning; we urge you to take advantage of this valuable learning tool.

For each skill chapter, the manual provides a content summary, how to integrate the material with other management/organizational behavior topics, answers to the questions for class discussion, comments on the exercises, exercise materials, supplemental exercises, and suggested references. At the end of the manual are appendices on student journals, multiple-choice questions, written assignment examples, and behavioral examination exercises with instructor rating guides. New for this addition are PowerPoint slides covering the content and exercises in each chapter.

We welcome any comments or suggestions that you may have for improving the skill sets, role-plays, and exercises to enhance forthcoming editions. Please send your ideas to Phil Hunsaker at philmail@sandiego.edu.

The Instructor's Manual and PowerPoints are available to adopting instructors online at www.pearsonhighered.com. Registration is simple and gives you immediate access to new titles and new editions.

If you ever need assistance, our dedicated technical support team is ready to help with the media supplements that accompany this text. Visit http://247.pearsoned.com/ for answers to frequently asked questions and toll-free user support phone numbers.

CourseSmart Textbooks Online

CourseSmart Textbooks Online is an exciting new choice for students looking to save money. As an alternative to purchasing the print textbook, students can subscribe to the same content online for less than the suggested list price of the print text. With a CourseSmart eTextbook, students can search the text, make notes online, print out reading assignments that incorporate lecture notes, and bookmark important passages for later review. For more information, or to subscribe to the CourseSmart eTextbook, visit www.coursesmart.com.

ACKNOWLEDGMENTS

We are grateful to our students who offered us open and honest feedback about what worked best for them in the previous editions of *TIPS*. They also contributed many ideas for improvements. The same is true for the many professors who have utilized the text over the years.

We owe a lot to our wives, Laura Ospanik and Jo Hunsaker, for agreeing to let us take the time away from usual family activities to complete the multiple editions of *TIPS*. We acknowledge this debt and are certain that they will collect what they believe is owed to them many times over, still with our undying gratitude. Special thanks go to Jo Hunsaker for allowing this madness to continue during this current revision.

We also want to thank the Prentice Hall book representatives and our editor-in-chief, Eric Svendsen, for encouraging us to complete the sixth edition. We are especially grateful to Ashley Santora, our director of editorial services, for keeping everything organized throughout the revision process and Meg O'Rouke, our Project Manager, for obtaining the helpful reviews. We want to thank Kalpana Venkatramani for guiding this revision through its production stage.

Finally, we want to acknowledge the reviewers who provided substantive and helpful feedback that definitely strengthened this edition. Our special thanks to:

John M. Zink
Transylvania University

Robert H. Blanchard
Salem State College

Kimberly Johnson
Auburn University Montgomery

Deborah L. Saks
Purdue University

Jennifer Morton
Ivy Tech Community College

Stephen P. Robbins

Phillip L. Hunsaker

1

■ ■ ■

Skills: An Introduction

Today's business graduates have an abundance of technical knowledge.
They can do linear programming problems, calculate a discounted rate
of return, develop a sophisticated marketing plan, and crunch numbers
on a computer spreadsheet. They're technically solid, but most lack the
interpersonal and social skills necessary to manage people. If there is
an area where business schools need to improve, it's in developing the
"people skills" of their graduates.

—A CORPORATE RECRUITER

This is not an isolated criticism of business programs. In recent years, industry recruiters,[1] the business media,[2] management faculty,[3] and the accrediting agencies of business programs[4] have noted the weakness in interpersonal skills among recent business graduates. Unfortunately, the same can be said about our society in general. With all of the advances in technology, we have learned how to generate more information and products better, faster, and cheaper but at the cost of more stress, shallow relationships, and less satisfying lives. "We have learned how to make a living but not a life."[5]

Actually, the interpersonal skills necessary to produce happy, productive, and satisfying relationships have pretty much remained the same today as they have been over time. They are just overlooked in our frenzy to try to keep up with and cope with accelerating technological change. The irony is that these interpersonal skills are now needed more than ever to cope with the stress of information overload in both our professional and personal lives. Although quantitative and technological skills may be more emphasized in many business curriculums, the importance of interpersonal skills has not been overlooked by all business educators, as evidenced by work on emotional intelligence by Daniel Goleman and others,[6] and a variety of course offerings in leading universities on interpersonal dynamics, coaching and mentoring, and team building.

The purpose of this book is to provide you with the interpersonal skills to help you not only develop successful careers as leaders and team members, but also productively manage your personal relationships to produce a meaningful and satisfying life. The interpersonal skills presented in the following chapters have been found to be vital ingredients for managerial success. As you debrief the chapter exercises and complete the application questions and reinforcement exercises, however, you will quickly discover how you can apply these same skills to productively manage relationships in all areas of your life. So what are these crucial interpersonal skills and what are the best ways to learn them?

INTERPERSONAL SKILLS AND EFFECTIVE MANAGEMENT BEHAVIOR

Studies seeking to identify what differentiates effective managers from ineffective ones have determined that successful managers engage in 51 behaviors. Managers must be motivated to engage in these behaviors, and they must have the requisite skills to effectively implement them.

Behaviors

Through aggregation, researchers condensed the 51 behaviors of effective managers into six role sets[7] that can be summarized as follows:

1. *Controlling the organization's environment and its resources.*   This set of behaviors includes the ability to be proactive and stay ahead of environmental changes in long-range planning and on-the-spot decision making. It also involves basing resource decisions on clear, up-to-date, accurate knowledge of the organization's objectives.
2. *Organizing and coordinating.*   In this role, the manager organizes subordinates' behaviors around tasks and then coordinates interdependent relationships to accomplish common goals.
3. *Information handling.*   This set of behaviors comprises using information and communication channels for identifying problems, understanding a changing environment, and making effective decisions.
4. *Providing for growth and development.*   Managers must provide for their own personal growth and development—as well as for the personal growth and development of subordinates—through continual learning on the job.
5. *Motivating employees and handling conflict.*   In this role, the manager enhances the positive aspects of motivation—so that employees feel compelled to perform their work—while concurrently eliminating those conflicts that might inhibit employee motivation.
6. *Strategic problem solving.*   Managers must take responsibility for their own decisions and ensure that subordinates effectively use decision-making skills.

The researchers found that these six sets of behaviors account for more than 50 percent of a manager's effectiveness. Even if managers understand the necessity of these specific behaviors, they will not engage in them unless they are motivated to do so.

Motivation

The desire to be a manager is another factor that influences managerial effectiveness. Researchers have found the following seven subcategories that make up the motivation to manage:[8]

1. *Authority acceptance.*   A desire to accept the authority of superiors.
2. *Competitive games.*   A desire to engage in competition with peers involving games or sports.
3. *Competitive situations.*   A desire to engage in competition with peers involving occupational or work activities.
4. *Assertiveness.*   A desire to behave in an active and assertive manner.

5. *Imposing wishes.*   A desire to tell others what to do and to utilize sanctions in influencing others.
6. *Distinctiveness.*   A desire to stand out from the group in a unique and highly visible way.
7. *Routine functions.*   A desire to carry out routine day-to-day activities often associated with managerial work.

Research has demonstrated that successful managers tend to achieve higher motivation-to-manage scores on inventories measuring these desires. If these seven factors are things that you enjoy and are willing to do, they are a fairly good predictor of your willingness to engage in effective managerial behaviors.

Skills

Even if you know the behaviors that effective managers engage in and have the motivation to apply them, you still need the appropriate skills to implement them effectively. The most popular approach to managerial effectiveness has been to break the manager's job down into critical roles or skills.[9] Such efforts generally conclude that the effective manager must be competent in four different skill areas:[10]

1. *Conceptual skills.*   The mental ability to coordinate all of the organization's interests and activities.
2. *Human skills.*   The ability to work with, understand, and motivate other people, both individually and in groups.
3. *Technical skills.*   The ability to use the tools, procedures, and techniques of a specialized field.
4. *Political skills.*   The ability to enhance one's position, build a power base, and establish the right connections.

Do managers need competence in all of these skills to be successful? The answer is a qualified yes. All four sets of skills were found to be important for managerial success.[11] Research has indicated, however, that conceptual skills are required to a greater extent at the chief executive level than at lower levels. It has also been found that human skills—such as the ability to listen, communicate verbally, show patience, and understand subordinates' needs—are most important for success at any managerial level.

These conclusions have been supported by a survey of 100 business leaders about which management skills are required for success in the 21st century. Responses revealed that the effective 21st-century manager is likely to be a transformational leader, that is, a masterful change agent who, through the use of outstanding interpersonal skills and analytical application, is able to motivate others by sharing a strategic vision, while at the same time adhering to a rigorous ethical code.[12] The most important skills or attributes for 21st-century managers to possess were thought to be:

- Communication and interpersonal skills
- An ethical or spiritual orientation
- The ability to manage change
- The ability to motivate
- Analytic and problem solving skills

The Need for Skills Training

Of the three components of managerial effectiveness—appropriate behaviors, motivations, and skills—this book concentrates on developing the interpersonal skills component of managerial success. In terms of effective managerial behaviors, communicating, developing employees, motivating others, and handling conflicts all involve interpersonal skills. Individuals who have a high motivation to manage manifest this desire through the application of their interpersonal skills in competitive activities with peers, by taking charge in groups, and by exercising power over others. Finally, the human and political skills needed at all levels of management are clearly interpersonal in nature.

Given that competent interpersonal skills are an important, if not the most important, attribute for managerial effectiveness, it is clear why constituencies such as human resource personnel, business media, management professors, and business accrediting bodies are disturbed by the number of business graduates who are deficient in these skills. College graduates who aspire to a career in management might have the motivation to manage as well as a conceptual understanding of the behaviors required to be effective, but if they have poorly developed interpersonal skills, they are ill-equipped for the future. Sending motivated business school graduates into the workplace with only a cognitive grasp of the behaviors necessary for managerial success allows them to talk a good game but does not prepare them to be proficient players.[13]

DEFINING THE KEY INTERPERSONAL SKILLS

Given the general agreement that interpersonal skills are necessary for managerial success, what specific skills are required? A number of studies have sought to identify these necessary interpersonal skills,[14] and despite the widely varying terminology, certain skills tend to surface on most lists. For instance, leadership skills such as the ability to handle conflicts, run meetings, coach, practice team building, and promote change are regarded as key interpersonal skills by most studies. The elements of effective communication that appear in most studies are sending messages, listening, and providing feedback. More recently, communicating across cultures has emerged as being crucial for many people in today's international organizations. Motivating employees is included in most lists, although it's rarely stated as simply "motivation"; rather, it's broken down into parts, such as goal setting, clarifying expectations, persuading and empowering people, and providing feedback.

Table 1.1 represents a synthesis of what these studies have found to be the interpersonal skills required for effective managerial performance. Although the table might omit some important

---

TABLE 1.1   Interpersonal Skills of Effective Managers

Key Interpersonal Skills

Self-awareness	Sending messages
Listening	Persuading
Setting goals	Politicking
Providing feedback	Running meetings
Empowering	Resolving conflicts
Leading	Negotiating
Managing change	Working with diverse groups of people
Coaching	Working with teams
Ethical decision making	Creative problem solving
Cross-cultural communicating	Applying emotional intelligence

skills, it represents our best selection of the skills that research and practice suggest are important for success in managing people. Given our current state of knowledge, these are the interpersonal skills that most experts believe effective managers have and prospective managers need to develop.

LEARNING THE SKILLS

Can interpersonal skills be taught? If so, what teaching methods should be used? Any objective discussion of skills must eventually—either explicitly or implicitly—deal with these complex issues.[15] This section summarizes our current knowledge regarding these questions.

Can Interpersonal Skills Be Taught?

Some social scientists view interpersonal skills as personality traits that are deeply entrenched and not amenable to change.[16] Just as some people are naturally quiet and others are outgoing, the anti-training side argues that some people can work well with others, but many people simply cannot; that is, it's a talent you either have or don't have. Most of their evidence is of an anecdotal variety but can be intuitively appealing when they single out individuals with highly abrasive interpersonal styles and propose that no amount of training is likely to convert them into people-oriented types.

On the other hand, skills advocates have an increasing body of empirical research to support their case. Evidence suggests that training programs that focus on the human-relations problems of leadership, supervision, attitudes toward employees, communication, and self-awareness produce improvements in managerial performance.[17] This research has convinced business and public-sector organizations to spend tens of millions—maybe hundreds of millions—of dollars each year on development programs to improve their managers' interpersonal skills.

Nothing in the research suggests that skills training can magically transform every interpersonally incompetent manager into a highly effective leader, but that should not be the test of whether interpersonal skills can be taught. The evidence strongly demonstrates that these skills can be learned. Although people differ in their baseline abilities, the research shows that training can result in better skills for most people who want to improve.

The Importance of Teaching Skills

In universities, instruction in human behavior runs the gamut from highly theoretical, research-based reviews of the behavioral literature to entirely experientially based courses in which students learn about workgroup behavior by experiencing it. Textbooks reflect this diversity.[18] Skill building—through case studies, role-plays, structured exercises, work simulations, and the like—has become an accepted added dimension of many college and university courses in human behavior.

Why is this important? You wouldn't want to submit yourself to an appendectomy if your surgeon had read everything available on the appendix and its removal but had never actually removed one before. You'd also be apprehensive if your surgeon had years of experience operating but had never studied the sciences of physiology and anatomy. Just as competent surgeons need a sound understanding of how the body works as well as surgical skills that have been finely honed through practice and experience, college and university instructors have come to believe that competent managers need a sound understanding of human behavior and the opportunity to hone their people skills through practice and experience.

If these skills are not taught in college and university programs that are designed to prepare people for managerial careers, where will they be taught? They are too important to be left to on-the-job learning. As a recent report from the American Assembly of Collegiate Schools of Business concluded:

> business curricula should begin to address [interpersonal skills and personal charac-teristics] in a manner more nearly approximating the same explicit and systematic approach that characterizes the cognitive category if students are to be comprehen-sively prepared at the point of graduation for the managerial challenges ahead.[19]

How Do You Teach Skills?

"I hear and I forget. I see and I remember. I do and I understand." This famous quote, attributed to Confucius, is frequently used to support the value of learning through experience. The saying has some truth to it, but contemporary research on learning suggests that a more accurate re-phrasing would be "I understand best when I hear, see, and do!"

The lecture format continues to be the most popular method of teaching. It's a proven, ef-fective means for increasing student awareness and understanding of concepts. As such, it prob-ably should be part of any comprehensive system for learning skills. However, it should be only a part. A skill, by definition, is "the ability to demonstrate a system and sequence of behavior that is functionally related to attaining a performance goal."[20] No single action constitutes a skill. For example, the ability to write clear communications is a skill. People who have this skill know the particular sequence of actions to be taken to propose a project or summarize a report. They can separate primary from secondary ideas. They can organize their thoughts in a logical manner. They can simplify convoluted ideas. But none of these acts is by itself a skill. A skill is a system of behavior that can be applied in a wide range of situations.

To become competent at any skill, people need to understand the skill conceptually and be-haviorally, have opportunities to practice the skill, get feedback on how well they are performing the skill, and use the skill often enough to integrate it into their behavioral repertories.[21] Kolb[22] has developed a model that encompasses most of these learning dimensions, as shown in Figure 1.1.

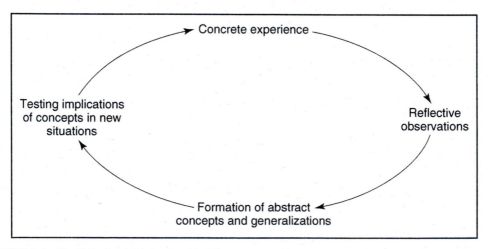

FIGURE 1.1 The Experiential Learning Model

Source: Osland, Joyce S., David A. Kolb, Irwin M. Rubin, and Marlene E. Turner, *Organizational Behavior: An Experiential Approach, 8th ed.* (Upper Saddle River, N.J.: Prentice Hall, 2007), p. 58.

Ten-Step TIPS Learning Model

1. Self-Assessment Exercise
2. Skill Concepts
3. Concept Quiz
4. Behavioral Checklist
5. Modeling Exercise
6. Group Exercises
7. Summary Checklist
8. Application Questions
9. Reinforcement Exercises
10. Action Plan

FIGURE 1.2   TIPS Learning Model

This figure illustrates Kolb's experiential learning model. Consistent with social learning theory,[23] it emphasizes that the development of behavioral skills comes from observation and practice.

According to the Kolb model, comprehensive learning encompasses four elements: (1) active participation in a new experience (concrete experience); (2) examination of that experience (reflective observation); (3) integration of conclusions into workable theories based on the new experience (abstract conceptualization); and (4) application of the theories to new situations (active experimentation). If this model is taken as a guide, the learning of skills is maximized when students get the opportunity to combine watching, thinking, and doing.[24]

Using Kolb's model and well-known learning principles, we propose the 10-step TIPS learning model for acquiring interpersonal skills, as illustrated in Figure 1.2. First, individuals need to assess their baseline skills. Carl Rogers[25] would call this step self-discovery. Each skill chapter in this book begins with a self-assessment questionnaire, followed by a scoring key and an interpretation. The self-assessment quiz is not meant to be a refined or highly valid measurement device. Rather, it is intended to give individuals insights into how much they already know about the skill in question. Second, individuals need to learn the basic concepts underlying the skill. This is achieved by reviewing the published materials available on the skill. The third step is providing feedback to ensure that the basic concepts are understood. In our model, this is accomplished with a short quiz. The fourth step is the identification of specific skill behaviors that the individual wants to learn. This behavioral checklist, derived from the skill concepts, clarifies the specific behaviors the individual needs to acquire and it is also used by others for evaluating how well the individual has learned the behaviors in question. Because research on decision making tells us that people have difficulty working with more than about seven pieces of information at one time,[26] the number of these specific behaviors needs to be limited. The importance of this behavioral checklist can't be overstated. It contains the sole criteria by which actual behavioral performance will be judged. By keeping evaluation focused only on the behaviors identified in the checklist, we reduce the likelihood that appraisals will veer off to include personality variables, personal styles, or similar extraneous factors.

The fifth step is a modeling exercise that allows the learner to observe others who are exhibiting the desired skill behaviors. In the sixth step, students form small groups and practice their newly acquired skills. Individuals not actively involved in a group exercise learn and contribute through observation and evaluation. The seventh step—completing a summary checklist—requires learners to identify which, if any, behaviors they are deficient in. This appraisal comes both from self-assessment and from evaluations made by others. Deficiency feedback should be used to focus on where further practice is needed. Application questions provide opportunities to check understanding of how skill behaviors relate, and reinforcement exercises facilitate the transfer of classroom learning to real-life situations. Finally, the action plan provides specific changes to implement.

Guidelines for Participating in Chapter Exercises

The modeling and group exercises in the skill chapters include case discussions, experiential exercises, and role-plays. Modeling exercises are performed by a few students in front of the class. They provide an opportunity to observe participants performing specific skill behaviors and to learn from these observations. Two class members volunteer or are selected to be the actors in the following role-play. The rest of the class serves as observers and provides feedback when the exercise is completed. Group exercises are performed in trios or small groups. They allow everyone to participate in trying out the behavioral skills being studied. Specific instructions are provided for each of the different cases and experiential exercises. The majority of both the modeling and the group exercises are role-plays, however, so some overall guidelines will help clarify your participation in them as actors and observers.

ACTOR GUIDELINES   Actors in a role-play should read the background information on the exercise and their own role. They should not read the other actors' roles—doing so will lessen the effectiveness of the exercise. The role description establishes your character. Follow the guidelines it establishes. Don't change or omit the facts you're given, but feel free to behave in ways that you feel would be relevant. Remember that role-playing is acting, so you need to project yourself into the character you are portraying and act out your thoughts and feelings as if you were in the real situation.

OBSERVER GUIDELINES   During the 5 minutes when the role-players plan and organize, class observers should review the behavioral criteria and think about how they would perform the exercise if they were in the actor's role that is demonstrating the skills. During the role-play, observers evaluate the actor's skills using the *Observer's Rating Sheet*. Observers should make notes of examples of particularly good behaviors—as well as those that need improvement—to share during the debriefing. After a modeling exercise has been completed, the actor first evaluates his or her performance of the relevant skills on the *Observer's Rating Sheet*. Then the class observers compare their ratings and discuss the participants' performance, starting with the strong points and followed by areas that could be improved.

DEBRIEFING INSTRUCTIONS   After the role-play exercise is completed, the debriefing starts by having the role-players evaluate their own behavior on the *Observer's Rating Sheet* that follows the exercise. The observers respond with their ratings of each role-player's skill behaviors. This will confirm or provide feedback about discrepancies regarding self-perceptions. After the first role-player has shared and received feedback, the process is repeated for other role-players if they are also applying relevant behavioral skills.

STUDENT-CREATED SCRIPTS   As an option to any of the group exercises in the skill chapters, students can create their own scenario and scripts for a 5-minute role-play demonstrating application of relevant chapter skills. Another alternative is to have half of the class create and demonstrate role-plays in which actors demonstrate the right way to apply skills and the other half of the class demonstrate the wrong way. While actors in one group are demonstrating either the right or wrong way, the other groups can act as observers and identify which of the behaviors in that skill are correctly or incorrectly applied for debriefing.

Summary and Coming Attractions

This text has been developed to help college and university programs teach their students the interpersonal skills necessary for successful careers in organizations and management. Today, general agreement exists about what the most important interpersonal skills are. Furthermore, our knowledge about how people learn provides us with a solid basis for designing interpersonal skill-learning modules. We have used this knowledge to create an interpersonal skills book—TIPS—that can be used alone or as a supplement to more research- and theory-based textbooks on organizational behavior, human relations, applied psychology, principles of supervision, or similar courses that aim at improving students' people skills.

Because we believe that before you can understand others you need to know yourself, Chapter 2 provides a battery of self-assessment tests. After you've completed and scored the tests, you'll have a realistic evaluation of your own assets and liabilities, including insights into your values, needs, assertiveness level, and interpersonal style in dealing with others. Many skill programs stress the importance of such self-objectivity as an essential part of an individual's interpersonal skills development.[27] With this self-awareness, you are now primed to assess your own values and develop a personal mission statement in Chapter 3.

Chapters 4 through 21 cover the additional 17 interpersonal skills identified in Table 1.1. For the most part, you'll find that the chapters follow our 10-step skill development model. The last section gives you an opportunity to integrate the skills you have learned. It includes two comprehensive exercises that tie together many of the skills that you'll have practiced already.

Endnotes

1. AACSB, "The Cultivation of Tomorrow's Leaders: Industry's Fundamental Challenge to Management Education," *Newsline*, Vol. 23, No. 3 (Spring 1993), pp. 1–3.
2. *Business Week*, "The Battle of the B-Schools Is Getting Bloodier" (March 24, 1986), pp. 61–70.
3. L. L. Cummings, "Reflections on Management Education and Development: Drift or Thrust Into the 21st Century?" *Academy of Management Review*, Vol. 15, No. 4 (October 1990), pp. 694–696.
4. AACSB, "Accreditation Research Project: Report on Phase I," *AACSB Bulletin* (Winter 1980), pp. 1–46.
5. B. Moorehead, *Words Aptly Spoken* (Kirkland, WA: Overlake Christian Press, 1995), pp. 197–198.
6. See, for example, D. Goleman, "Leadership That Gets Results," *Harvard Business Review*, Vol. 78, No. 2 (2000), pp. 78–90; D. Goleman, R. Boyatzis, and A. McKee, *Primal Leadership: Realizing the Power of Emotional Intelligence* (Boston, MA: Harvard Business School, 2002), pp. 12–18.
7. J. J. Morse and F. R. Wagner, "Measuring the Process of Managerial Effectiveness," *Academy of Management Journal* (March 1978), pp. 23–35.
8. J. B. Miner and N. R. Smith, "Decline and Stabilization of Managerial Motivation over a 20-Year Period," *Journal of Applied Psychology* (June 1982), pp. 297–305.
9. R. L. Katz, "Skills of an Effective Administrator," *Harvard Business Review* (September–October 1974), pp. 90–102.
10. C. M. Pavett and A. W. Lau, "Managerial Work: The Influence of Hierarchical Level and Functional Specialty," *Academy of Management Journal* (March 1983), pp. 170–177.
11. Ibid.
12. M. Mallinger, "Management Skills for the 21st Century: Communication and Interpersonal Skills

Rank First," *Graziadio Business Report,* Vol. 1, Issue 2 (1998), pp. 7–10.

13. D. D. Bowen, "Developing a Personal Theory of Experiential Learning," *Simulation & Games*, Vol. 18, No. 2 (June 1987), pp. 192–206.

14. AACSB, "Outcome Measurement Project of the Accreditation Research Committee, Phase II: An Interim Report," American Assembly of Collegiate Schools of Business (December 1984); AACSB, "Outcome Measurement Project: Phase III Report," American Assembly of Collegiate Schools of Business (May 1987); AACSB, "The Cultivation of Tomorrow's Leaders: Industry's Fundamental Challenge to Management Education," *Newsline*, Vol. 23, No. 3 (Spring 1993), pp. 1–3; Richard E. Boyatzis, *The Competent Manager: A Model for Effective Performance* (New York: John Wiley & Sons, 1982); H. B. Clark, R. Wood, T. Kuchnel, S. Flanagan, M. Mosk, and J. T. Northrup, "Preliminary Validation and Training of Supervisory Interactional Skills," *Journal of Organizational Behavior Management* (Spring/Summer 1985), pp. 95–115; H. Z. Levine, "Supervisory Training," *Personnel* (November–December 1982), pp. 4–12; B. D. Lewis, Jr., "The Supervisor in 1975," *Personnel Journal* (September 1973), pp. 815–818; J. Porras and B. Anderson, "Improving Managerial Effectiveness Through Modeling-Based Training," *Organizational Dynamics* (Spring 1981), pp. 60–77.

15. L. W. Porter, "Teaching Managerial Competencies: An Overview," *Exchange: The Organizational Behavior Teaching Journal*, Vol. 8, No. 2 (1983), pp. 8–9.

16. F. E. Fiedler, *A Theory of Leadership Effectiveness* (New York: McGraw-Hill, 1967).

17. M. J. Burke and R. R. Day, "A Cumulative Study of the Effectiveness of Management Training," *Journal of Applied Psychology* (May 1986), pp. 232–245.

18. Randall B. Dunham, *Organizational Behavior: People and Processes in Management* (Homewood, IL: Richard D. Irwin, 1984); Joyce S. Osland, David A. Kolb, and Irwin M. Rubin, *Organizational Behavior: An Experiential Approach,* 7th ed. (Upper Saddle River, NJ: Prentice Hall, 2001), pp. 11–26.

19. AACSB, "Outcome Measurement Project of the Accreditation Research Committee, Phase II: An Interim Report," American Assembly of Collegiate Schools of Business (December 1984).

20. Richard E. Boyatzis, *The Competent Manager: A Model for Effective Performance* (New York: John Wiley & Sons, 1982), p. 33.

21. David W. Johnson and Frank P. Johnson, *Joining Together: Group Theory and Group Skills,* 5th ed. (Boston, MA: Allyn & Bacon, 1994).

22. David A. Kolb, *Experiential Learning: Experience as the Source of Learning and Development* (Englewood Cliffs, NJ: Prentice Hall, 1984).

23. Albert Bandura, *Social Learning Theory* (Englewood Cliffs, NJ: Prentice Hall, 1977).

24. G. P. Latham and L. M. Saari, "Application of Social Learning Theory to Training Supervisors Through Behavioral Modeling," *Journal of Applied Psychology* (June 1979b), pp. 239–246; C. C. Manz and H. P. Sims, Jr., "Vicarious Learning: The Influence of Modeling on Organizational Behavior," *Academy of Management Review* (January 1981), pp. 105–113; P. J. Decker, "The Enhancement of Behavioral Modeling Training of Supervisory Skills by the Inclusion of Retention Processes," *Personnel Psychology* (Summer 1982), pp. 323–332; H. B. Clark, R. Wood, T. Kuchnel, S. Flanagan, M. Mosk, and J. T. Northrup, "Preliminary Validation and Training of Supervisory Interactional Skills," *Journal of Organizational Behavior Management* (Spring/Summer 1985), pp. 95–115.

25. Carl R. Rogers, *On Becoming a Person* (Boston, MA: Houghton Mifflin, 1961).

26. G. A. Miller, "The Magical Number Seven, Plus or Minus Two: Some Limits on Our Capacity for Processing Information," *Psychological Review* (March 1956), pp. 81–97.

27. AACSB, "Outcome Measurement Project of the Accreditation Research Committee, Phase II: An Interim Report," American Assembly of Collegiate Schools of Business (December 1984); Kathleen S. Verderber and Rudolph F. Verderber, *Inter-Act: Using Interpersonal Communication Skills,* 4th ed. (Belmont, CA: Wadsworth, 1986).

2

■ ■ ■

Self-Awareness:
A Point of Departure

SELF-ASSESSMENT EXERCISE: ASSESSING YOUR SELF-AWARENESS[1]

For each of the following questions, enter the number that best describes you. Choose a number from the following scale:

Strongly Agree	Agree	Neutral	Disagree	Strongly Disagree
1	2	3	4	5

_____ **1.** I am aware of my strengths and weaknesses.
_____ **2.** I have a plan for developing new skills and improving in other areas.
_____ **3.** I regularly engage in self-assessment exercises.
_____ **4.** I understand what motivates my behavior and choices in life.
_____ **5.** I know what my core values are and how they affect the choices I make.
_____ **6.** I am satisfied with the quality of my interactions with others.
_____ **7.** I control my emotions in difficult situations.
_____ **8.** I have realistically appraised my core abilities as well as my limitations.
_____ **9.** I am satisfied with the way in which I communicate with others.
_____**10.** I understand how I best process information.
_____**11.** I weigh alternatives before selecting a course of action.
_____**12.** I work well in team situations.
_____**13.** I am comfortable in large groups.
_____**14.** I understand the strong points and the disadvantages of my personality.
_____**15.** I understand whether I am extroverted or introverted and know how this impacts my ability to work with others.
_____**16.** I am an agreeable person at work or in school.
_____**17.** Others would describe me as conscientious.
_____**18.** I am open to and seek new experiences.
_____**19.** I am skilled at monitoring my own behavior, reading others' views of me accurately, and taking in but not relying exclusively on the opinions others have about me.

_____ **20.** I consciously work at developing and displaying a positive attitude.
_____ **21.** I check my perceptions with others.
_____ **22.** I move beyond stereotypes when getting to know others.
_____ **23.** I am open to things that don't immediately interest me.
_____ **24.** I limit the degree to which I project my beliefs and values onto others.
_____ **25.** I come to new situations and people without preconceived expectations.
_____ **26.** I have a realistic view of how I am perceived by others.
_____ **27.** I am comfortable sharing my thoughts and feelings with others.
_____ **28.** I am open to being with and learning from people who are different from me.
_____ **29.** I use my emotions appropriately in business settings as well as in personal life.
_____ **30.** I relate to others' problems and am a source of help and support to others.
_____   Total

Scoring and Interpretation

Add up your numbers for the 30 questions you just answered. Each of the questions represents factors that enhance self-awareness. The numerical ratings are in reverse correlation to degree of agreement, however. The lower your total, the better your self-awareness skills. The higher your total score, the more improvement you need in acting to enhance your self-awareness. In general, if you scored more than 90, the medium score possible, you should create a plan for improving your self-awareness.

SKILL CONCEPTS

This chapter is about knowing yourself. Centuries ago, Socrates pronounced the edict, "Know thyself." More recently, management gurus such as Peter Drucker have advised that "Success in the knowledge economy comes to those who know themselves—their strengths, their values, and how they best perform."[2] In this chapter you learn why it is important to increase your self-awareness, as well as techniques for getting to know yourself better. You will actually begin the process by completing self-assessment questionnaires and discussing the ramifications with your colleagues.

Why Increase Your Self-Awareness?

Many of us avoid self-awareness. We want to protect, maintain, and enhance our self-concepts and the images others have of us. We have fears, inadequacies, self-doubt, and insecurities that we don't want to reveal to others, or even admit to ourselves. If we open ourselves up to honest self-appraisal, we might see things we don't want to see. We are also afraid to tell people who we really are because we fear they're going to reject us. The feeling is, "If you knew I was a klutz as an athlete or that I came from a poor family or that I was gay—if you knew this, if you knew that—you wouldn't care about me anymore; you might reject me. So I'm going to try to pretend to be something else, even to myself." We build protection around our inner core to hide our vulnerabilities because we're so afraid that we'll be taken advantage of.

But maintaining that facade is exhausting and unsustainable. As reasoning and complex human beings, we balance the "need to know" with the "fear of knowing." No one is perfect, and knowledge of our strengths and weaknesses can help us gain insights into areas we want to change and improve.

To improve your interpersonal skills, you need to know yourself. Self-awareness is absolutely fundamental. According to Bill George, author of *Authentic Leadership and True North,* you can't have the qualities of emotional intelligence (to be discussed in Chapter 4) unless you have self-awareness. You can't be in touch with your motivations and you'll lack empathy. You can't be authentic without it.[3]

The more you know about yourself, the better you'll be able to understand how you're perceived by others and why they respond to you the way they do. The more you know about your unique personal characteristics, the more insight you'll have into your basic behavioral tendencies and inclinations for dealing with others.

These self-insights have been found to be determinates of career and personal success. It is often said that individuals cannot effectively lead others unless they are able to effectively lead themselves first. It is difficult, if not impossible, to lead yourself if you do not really know and understand yourself. Self-awareness—knowing your motivations, emotions, and personality, what you enjoy and dislike, what comes easy and what poses challenges, and so on—is therefore a key precursor in developing effective leadership ability.[4]

For example, leaders with more accurate self-awareness of their own performance are also more likely to adopt more suitable leadership styles for a given organizational context. Empathy, or external self-awareness, allows leaders to be sensitive to the effectiveness of their current leadership style with others. Their internal or emotional self-awareness allows them to challenge their own underlying assumptions and emotions to change their current style to a more appropriate one.

The intention of the self-assessments in this chapter is not to psychoanalyze you but to help you become more aware of your behaviors and their impact on others. Given this information, you can choose to drop ineffective behaviors and try out new ones, if you wish. Nothing in this chapter is meant to suggest that you need to change. Its contents are designed only to help you gain expanded insight into yourself. However, it is important to be self-aware so that you can make appropriate decisions.

How to Increase Your Self-Awareness

The first step in increasing your self-awareness is to emphasize your need to know more than your fear of knowing. The good news is that most of us are less defensive about deficits in skills, which can be improved through practice than about deficits in personality which are usually thought of as relatively permanent. If we can reduce our fear of knowing our skills deficits enough to satisfy our need to grow and improve these skills, what are some of the ways that we can gain insight into our behaviors? Some ways to increase our self-awareness are described in this section.

Many self-evaluation techniques can facilitate self-analysis. The techniques described here are based on learning from experiences and completing self-assessment inventories. Exhibit 2.1 summarizes additional techniques that can be used to gain greater self-awareness from experiences.

SOLICIT FEEDBACK   Getting honest feedback is perhaps the best way to gain self-awareness.[5] It helps to have at least one person in your life who will give you honest, gut-level feedback, particularly when you're being inauthentic. This should be someone you trust enough to go to when you have real problems and ask, "Am I off base here? Am I crazy?" It could be your spouse or your significant other, it might be a mentor or a best friend, or you could hire a therapist or personal coach. But you need to select someone you can be really honest with.

While formal and informal feedback processes have always provided a useful opportunity for individuals to self-reflect, many organizations are providing their managers with 360-degree

- **Self-written interviews, life story, autobiographical story**—This technique requires an individual to write an autobiography that describes his or her life. It is a written narrative of personal history. Specific content statements would describe life events, education, hobbies, major changes that have occurred in the past; consequences of the described events; and the individual's feelings about these events. Also included is a description of turning points in one's life and the pros and cons of past career decisions.
- **Daily or weekly logs**—As individuals pass through a particular time period, they write down events and decisions made, and the time devoted to these activities. When constructing such a diary, it is desirable to include both workdays and non-workdays.
- **Written daydreams**—The individual first stimulates a fantasy or vision about the future or a currently preferred surrounding. For future analysis, individuals then record what they have visualized.
- **Written future obituaries or retirement speeches**—Individuals write personal obituaries or retirement speeches that might be given at the time of their death or retirement. The individual describes what he or she would be remembered for and the comments made by coworkers and acquaintances.
- **Ranking of significant work values**—The individual lists what he or she believes are important or relevant values and then ranks them in terms of appropriateness or desirability. Listed values may relate to the following general categories: money, financial security, material gain; helping people, social contribution; power over self, self-improvement; security, stability, predictability; mental challenge, and mental stimulation.
- **Assets and liabilities balance sheet**—The individual makes two lists. The first list articulates assets or strengths; the second articulates liabilities or weaknesses. When using this technique, it is desirable to have individuals describe specific situations and behaviors to help ensure accurate and complete assessments of personal assets and liabilities.
- **Lifestyle representation**—Individuals describe their current lifestyle in either written or pictorial form. When using this technique, individuals are encouraged to be as behaviorally specific as possible.

EXHIBIT 2.1   Individual Self-Assessment Techniques

Source: Adapted from Mealiea, L.W., and G. P. Latham, *Skills for Managerial Success* (Chicago: Irwin, 1996), p. 34.

feedback, allowing them to receive insights about their strengths and weaknesses from their superiors, peers, and subordinates. These 360-degree feedback programs are increasing in popularity because, by collating impressions from multiple individuals both up and down the hierarchy chain, they can provide a significantly richer source of reflection data than that received from just one or two individuals.[6]

Another source of authentic feedback is support groups. Men's, women's, or couple's therapy or task or student groups are examples. Support groups made up of other people you've never met before can also be sources of authentic feedback about yourself. This is especially true if they are very diverse geographically and racially. Diverse stranger support groups that only meet together to enhance each other's self-awareness often share deep secrets and provide riskier feedback than they would with their best friends or coworkers.

With all of these sources of feedback, other people can tell how you come across, how others see you, and the effect you're having that you may not know about. Once you own those characteristics—once you see them and accept them—you can really be empowered and use your strengths.

REFLECTION   Reflection is the act of reviewing data—experiences, situations, and actions—in order to better understand and learn from them. The importance and value of reflection has been gaining sizable acceptance in business literature and organizations, but it is difficult for many managers to fit regular reflective activities into their hectic schedules. Eastern-based contemplative practices such as meditation and yoga are growing in popularity as activities to facilitate personal reflection.[7]

Self-awareness reflections can take many forms, some private and some involving other individuals or groups. A private way to learn from experience is to seek out solitude to reflect on your experiences and learn from them. It helps to set aside reflection time at regularly scheduled intervals at the beginning or end of a workday, when the stress of daily action has either not begun or has subsided.

Solitude means being out of human contact and being alone—and remaining this way for a significant period of time. Silence is an essential part of solitude. Silence means escaping from sounds and noises, other than those of nature. Solitude is especially important for people with heavy interaction demands who don't usually have much time alone.

What you do during your time alone—walking, meditating, or just relaxing—really does not matter as long as you are achieving solitude. The amount of solitude you need for rejuvenation and reflection will vary with the demands of your environment. The benefits of solitude are many, including a chance to contemplate who you are, the nature of your relationships with other people, and what your goals will be. Solitude also fosters creativity because it gives you a chance to speculate without the censorship and evaluation that come with putting forth new ideas in public.[8]

WRITE IN A JOURNAL   Another way to learn from experiences by reflecting is to keep a journal. Journals are similar to diaries, but they are more than just accounts of a day's events. A journal should include entries that address critical aspects of your interpersonal experiences. Journal entries might include comments about insightful or interesting quotations, anecdotes, newspaper articles, or even humorous cartoons. They might also include reflections on personal events, such as interactions with bosses, coaches, teachers, students, employees, teammates, roommates, and so on. Such entries can describe a good (or bad) way somebody handled a situation; a problem in the making; the different ways people react to situations; or people in the news, a book, or a film. You can also use your journal to "think on paper" about readings from textbooks or examples from your own experience of concepts presented in readings.[9] If you want to solicit feedback from others, post your journal as an online blog and see what other people think.

At least three good reasons support keeping a journal. First, the very process of writing increases the likelihood that you will be able to look at an event from a different perspective or learn something from it. Putting an experience into words can be a step toward taking a more objective look at it. Second, you can (and should) reread earlier entries. Earlier entries provide an interesting and valuable autobiography of your evolving thinking about interpersonal relations and particular events in your life. Third, good journal entries can provide a repository of ideas that you may later want to use more formally for papers, pep talks, or speeches. You can find examples of journal entries related to leadership skills in the Appendix, which also provides more instructions and ideas for creating useful journals.

KEEP A BLOG   With the invention of e-technologies, journals can become blogs. A blog is a website where you post entries in chronological order and commonly display them in reverse chronological order. The modern blog evolved from the online diary where people keep a running account of their personal lives.[10] If you are seeking to learn about yourself from the feedback and opinions of others, blogs have the option of allowing others to read your entries and leave comments in an interactive format. "Open Diary," launched in October 1998, innovated the reader comment and was the first blog community (which has thousands of online diaries) where readers could add comments to other writers' blog entries.[11]

SELF-PERFORMANCE APPRAISAL   Another way to learn about yourself is by analyzing your goal achievement performance. Whenever you make a key decision or take a key action, write down what you expect will happen. Then compare the actual results with your expectations every 3 or 4 months. If you practice this method consistently, it will show you your strengths and weaknesses. It will also indicate what you are doing, or failing to do, that deprives you of the full benefits of your strengths. Finally, it will demonstrate areas in which you are not particularly competent or where you have no strengths at all and cannot perform adequately.[12]

Several useful implications for action typically follow from experience–goal matching analysis. First, you will know what you are good at so that you can concentrate on your strengths to do what you do best to produce important results. Second, you will know where you need to work on improving your strengths and which skills you need to acquire. Third, you will discover areas in which you need to acquire additional knowledge to fully realize your strengths. Fourth, you will discover your bad habits—the things you do or fail to do that inhibit your effectiveness and performance. For example, perhaps you are a great planner, but lax at implementation. Or, your bad habit may be failing to practice the good manners and common courtesies that are the "lubricating oil" of an organization. Finally, you will be confronted with areas in which you have no talent or interest whatsoever. You should probably not waste any effort on improving areas of low competence because it takes far more energy and work to improve from incompetence to mediocrity than it takes to improve an area of strength from first-rate to excellent performance.[13]

SELF-ASSESSMENT INVENTORIES   Another method to increase self-awareness is taking and interpreting self-assessment questionnaires. They have the advantage of being private and under the control of the individual using them. These same advantages are disadvantages because self-assessments are subject to individual perspectives, which can at times be biased or defensive. Consequently, the results of self-assessments should always be checked out by soliciting feedback from relevant others to verify their validity from multiple perspectives.

Each of the following chapters in this book starts off with a self-assessment inventory to establish your baseline ability in the skills that are the focus of that specific chapter. Each chapter concludes with feedback from peers and self-evaluation to assess your level of skill development after reading the concepts and completion of the exercises in that skill chapter. The self-assessment inventories presented in this section were chosen because they provide feedback on general skills that influence your overall interpersonal competence and application of the specific skills presented in the other chapters of this book.

The six self-assessment questionnaires that follow provide feedback on characteristics found to be associated with interpersonal competence and offer you important insights.[14] You may want to check out additional characteristics to get a more complete understanding of yourself. One source of additional information is the Prentice Hall Self-Assessment Library CD-ROM. Other sources of self-assessment instruments are campus counseling centers, professional counselors, and career search organizations.

SELF-AWARENESS QUESTIONNAIRES (SAQ)

Which of your many personal characteristics are most likely to affect the way you deal with others? We have picked seven measures that are related to effective interpersonal relations and improving your interpersonal skills. Learning style refers to your preferred way of learning based on your relative emphasis of four different learning modes. Interpersonal needs indicate what you want from your interactions with others. Your level of assertiveness indicates how you go about getting what you want. The big five personality factors indicate your levels of adjustment, sociability, openness, agreeableness, and conscientiousness. Cognitive style refers to the general way you approach and attempt to solve problems. Locus of control refers to whether you believe you are or are not in control of what happens to you. The Type A personality test indicates the degree that you feel under time pressure to accomplish several things at once, making you competitive and aggressive, versus taking things more slowly and enjoying non-work-oriented activities.

The following questionnaires have been designed to measure each of these characteristics. Take the time now to complete them. When you're finished, you'll find directions for scoring each of the questionnaires and a discussion of what the results say about you and your interpersonal skills.

SAQ 1: Learning Style[15]

Assess your learning style by ranking the following eight statements describing different ways of learning. Circle the number along each scale that best describes your behavior from the extremes of 1, "This does not describe me at all," to 5, "This describes me perfectly." Circling 3 would be an uncommitted position to either extreme. Circling 2 means the statement is rarely how you behave, and 4 indicates that the statement is often how you behave.

1. I enjoy venturing into new experiences and relationships to see what I can learn.
   This does not describe me at all 1 2 3 4 5 This describes me perfectly

2. I actively participate in "here-and-now" experiences that enable me to become aware of how I affect my environment and others.
   This does not describe me at all 1 2 3 4 5 This describes me perfectly

3. I am a careful observer of events and people, and find myself reflecting on what I see and hear from what goes on around me.
   This does not describe me at all 1 2 3 4 5 This describes me perfectly

4. I find myself talking with others about our recent experiences so that I can make sense of what people say and do and why events turn out as they do.
   This does not describe me at all 1 2 3 4 5 This describes me perfectly

5. I like to manipulate abstract ideas and symbols to visualize how concepts and things are related.
   This does not describe me at all 1 2 3 4 5 This describes me perfectly

6. I find myself engaging in "what if" forms of reasoning and synthesizing ideas into hypotheses and models for future testing.
   This does not describe me at all 1 2 3 4 5 This describes me perfectly

7. I enjoy taking risks by testing my ideas on others or in actions to see if they work.
   This does not describe me at all 1 2 3 4 5 This describes me perfectly

8. I am a decisive and practical problem solver who enjoys putting plans into action.
   This does not describe me at all 1 2 3 4 5 This describes me perfectly

Scoring SAQ 1: Learning Style

There are no right or wrong answers to the above questions. They are only designed to provide insights into how you think and behave when you are learning. To determine your learning style preferences, add your "scores" for each sequential pair of questions (1 + 2, 3 + 4, etc.) in the following table.

Scores from Questions	Learning Processes
1 _____ + 2 _____ = _____	Concrete Experience
3 _____ + 4 _____ = _____	Reflective Observation
5 _____ + 6 _____ = _____	Abstract Conceptualization
7 _____ + 8 _____ = _____	Active Experimentation

Your highest scores suggest the learning processes that you tend to favor. The lower the scores, the less inclined you are to use these processes when learning. Write your scores on each of the four learning processes in the circle with the appropriate label in Exhibit 2.2. Mark where your scores

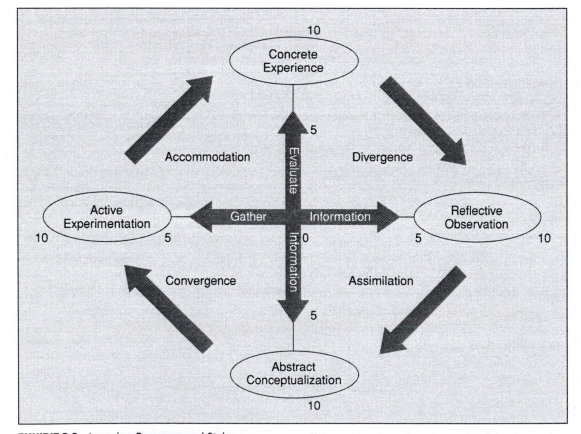

EXHIBIT 2.2   Learning Processes and Styles

Source: Adapted from David A. Kolb, "Management and the Learning Process," *California Management Review* 18 (Spring 1976), pp. 21–31.

fall on the vertical and horizontal axes for gathering and evaluating information in Exhibit 2.2. Then connect these points to form a rectangle. The largest quadrant in the rectangle is your learning style. If your scores were 10 on concrete experience (CE), 9 on reflective observation (RO), 3 on abstract conceptualization (AC), and 5 on active experimentation (AE), your largest area would be in the upper right hand quadrant, and your learning style indicated would be Divergence. Read the following descriptions of the four learning processes and the four learning styles and reflect on whether your self-selected style appropriately describes how you learn. Then compare your scores with others and reflect on the ramifications.

Interpreting SAQ 1: Learning Style Scores

Exhibit 2.2 represents a visualization of the experiential learning model that is based on four different learning processes that combine to form four distinct learning styles.[16] The horizontal axis represents two opposing ways of gathering information through either the mode of RO or AE. RO consists of passively observing others involved in experiences and making sense of what is observed by reflecting on what happens from different perspectives. When learning through AE, on the other hand, people jump right into whatever is happening and initiate activities to see what happens.

The vertical axis represents two opposing ways of evaluating information for learning through either CE or AC. CE generates learning through experiencing your feelings while you are dealing with a concrete reality. AC generates meaning through thinking about and analyzing new information to form abstract concepts, generalizations, hypotheses, models, or plans.

These alternative ways of learning from experience and transforming this learning into action represent four different *learning styles.* Adult learners must constantly choose which abilities to use as learning situations change, but over time a preferred dominant pattern emerges.[17] Most people predominantly focus on one or two learning processes rather than all four and a dominant learning style emerges. Characteristics of the four dominant learning styles of diverging, assimilating, converging, and accommodating are shown in Exhibit 2.3.

Diverging Style

People who learn through a blend of the CE and RO have the diverging learning style. They prefer to learn by reflecting on specific experiences and drawing new inferences from them rather than making decisions and taking action. Diverging learners tend to be highly imaginative, excel at brainstorming, like to gather information, and like group involvement in the generation of creative ideas. They view specific events or situations from many perspectives and listen with an open mind. Such learners often are interested in the arts, humanities, or liberal arts. They are frequently found in human resource management or service roles in organizations.

Assimilating Style

Preferences for combining RO with AC enable assimilating learners to understand a wide range of information, put it into concise form, and create theoretical models to explain what they observe. Engaging the world of abstract ideas and theory, assimilators prefer learning through lectures, reading, and research, more so than experiential exercises that require interacting with others. People who develop this style are attracted to careers in areas such as science, information technology, or strategic planning.

Converging Style

Individuals with a converging style of learning use abstract concepts as the basis for AE. They find practical uses for theories and concepts, and enjoy solving problems. Like those who use assimilation, individuals with a converging emphasis prefer working with technical tasks and

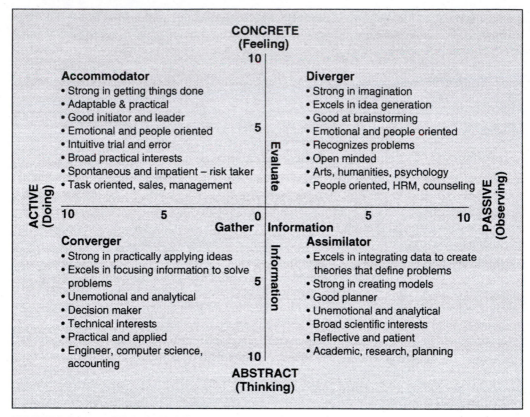

EXHIBIT 2.3   Learning Style Characteristics

Source: Adapted from Joyce S. Osland, David A. Kolb, Irwin M. Rubin, and Marlene E. Turner, *Organizational Behavior: An Experiential Approach, 8th ed.* (Upper Saddle River, N.J.: Prentice Hall, 2007), p. 56.

problems more than working with people. Converging styles prefer careers in the physical sciences, engineering, and technology careers.

Accommodating Style

AE and carrying out plans that produce CEs is the domain of the accommodating style. This style focuses on doing and "hands-on" experience. Such people enjoy engaging new challenges, adapt quickly to new situations, and are willing to take risks. A theory that doesn't fit the facts is quickly discarded, for this style tends to act spontaneously on "gut" feelings more than analysis. Although they are at ease with others, people with the accommodating style tend to be impatient, assertive, and task oriented. They prefer to learn through group assignments or field work. Accommodation is often the dominant style of people trained for action-oriented jobs in business sales and management.

Balanced Styles

Nearly 2,000 studies on learning styles research have generated two major implications: one for individual learners and one for organizations.[18] For individuals, strengthening your non-dominant learning abilities will increase your adaptive flexibility and facilitate your learning in a wider variety of experiences. Learning styles are dynamic, not fixed, and people should allocate time to expand lesser used capabilities.[19] People with balanced learning profiles (i.e., relative equal scores on all dimensions) are more adaptively flexible learners.[20]

MANAGERS' APPLICATION TIPS

Team and organizational leaders need to value and draw on the differing capabilities of people with diverse learning styles. Many managers tend to be strongest on the accommodating style of learning, focused on active experimentation and concrete experiences. Managers with an accommodating style tend to make fewer inferences from data and are less consistent in their actions than, say, researchers with the assimilating style. Collectively, the four styles are complimentary and all are needed to optimize performance throughout an organization.

SAQ 2: Interpersonal Needs Questionnaire (FIRO-B)[21]

For each of the following statements, decide which answer best applies to you. Place the number of the answer at the left of the statement.

Usually	Often	Sometimes	Occasionally	Rarely	Never
1	2	3	4	5	6

_____ **1.** I try to be with people.
_____ **2.** I let other people decide what to do.
_____ **3.** I join social groups.
_____ **4.** I try to have close relationships with people.
_____ **5.** I tend to join social organizations when I have an opportunity.
_____ **6.** I let other people strongly influence my actions.
_____ **7.** I try to be included in informal social activities.
_____ **8.** I try to have close, personal relationships with people.
_____ **9.** I try to include other people in my plans.
_____**10.** I let other people control my actions.
_____**11.** I try to have people around me.
_____**12.** I try to get close and personal with people.
_____**13.** When people are doing things together, I tend to join them.
_____**14.** I am easily led by people.
_____**15.** I try to avoid being alone.
_____**16.** I try to participate in group activities.

For each of the next group of statements, choose one of the following answers:

Most People	Many People	Some People	A Few People	One or Two People	Nobody
1	2	3	4	5	6

_____**17.** I try to be friendly to people.
_____**18.** I let other people decide what to do.

_____**19.** My personal relationships with people are cool and distant.
_____**20.** I let other people take charge of things.
_____**21.** I try to have close relationships with people.
_____**22.** I let other people strongly influence my actions.
_____**23.** I try to get close and personal with people.
_____**24.** I let other people control my actions.
_____**25.** I act cool and distant with people.
_____**26.** I am easily led by people.
_____**27.** I try to have close, personal relationships with people.

For each of the next group of statements, choose one of the following answers:

Most People	Many People	Some People	A Few People	One or Two People	Nobody
1	2	3	4	5	6

_____**28.** I like people to invite me to things.
_____**29.** I like people to act close and personal with me.
_____**30.** I try to influence strongly other people's actions.
_____**31.** I like people to invite me to join in their activities.
_____**32.** I like people to act close toward me.
_____**33.** I try to take charge of things when I am with people.
_____**34.** I like people to include me in their activities.
_____**35.** I like people to act cool and distant toward me.
_____**36.** I try to have other people do things the way I want them done.
_____**37.** I like people to ask me to participate in their discussions.
_____**38.** I like people to act friendly toward me.
_____**39.** I like people to invite me to participate in their activities.
_____**40.** I like people to act distant toward me.

For each of the next group of statements, choose one of the following answers:

Usually	Often	Sometimes	Occasionally	Rarely	Never
1	2	3	4	5	6

_____**41.** I try to be the dominant person when I am with people.
_____**42.** I like people to invite me to things.
_____**43.** I like people to act close toward me.
_____**44.** I try to have other people do things I want done.
_____**45.** I like people to invite me to join their activities.
_____**46.** I like people to act cool and distant toward me.
_____**47.** I try to influence strongly other people's actions.
_____**48.** I like people to include me in their activities.
_____**49.** I like people to act close and personal with me.
_____**50.** I try to take charge of things when I'm with people.
_____**51.** I like people to invite me to participate in their activities.
_____**52.** I like people to act distant toward me.
_____**53.** I try to have other people do things the way I want them done.
_____**54.** I take charge of things when I'm with people.

Scoring SAQ 2: FIRO-B

SAQ 2 is known as the Fundamental Interpersonal Relations Orientation—Behavior (FIRO-B) questionnaire.[22] The theory underlying this questionnaire is that there are three interpersonal needs that vary among individuals. The first is inclusion—the need to establish and maintain a relationship with other people. Inclusion concerns how you balance the desire to be part of a group against the desire for solitude. The second is control—the need to maintain a satisfactory balance of power and influence in relationships. Control concerns the trade-offs we have to make between the desire for structure and authority and the desire for freedom. Finally, there is the need for affection— the need to form close and personal relationships with others. Affection concerns how you balance the desire for warmth and commitment against the desire to maintain distance and independence.

Each of these three needs has two subdimensions: the expressed desire to give the need and the wanted desire to receive the need from others. So, for instance, the questionnaire measures your need to include others and your need to be included by others. The result is that SAQ 2 generates six separate scores. To calculate your scores, refer to Table 2.1. The term *Item* in the column refers to question numbers on the SAQ 2 questionnaire; *Key* refers to answers on each of those items. If you answered an item using any of the alternatives in the corresponding key column, circle the item number below. When you have circled all of the items for a single column, count up the number of circled items and place that number in the corresponding box at the bottom of the column. These numbers tell you the strength of your interpersonal need in each of the six areas. Your score in each box will range between 0 and 9. Your total interpersonal needs score is calculated by summing up the numbers in all six total column boxes. Place your overall summation score in the total FIRO-B score box.

TABLE 2.1 FIRO-B Scoring Key

Expressed Inclusion		Wanted Inclusion		Expressed Control		Wanted Control		Expressed Affection		Wanted Affection	
Item	Key	Item	Key	Item	Key	Item	Key	Item	Key	Item	Key
1	1-2-3	28	1-2	30	1-2-3	2	1-2-3-4	4	1-2	29	1-2
3	1-2-3-4	31	1-2	33	1-2-3	6	1-2-3-4	8	1-2	32	1-2
5	1-2-3-4	34	1-2	36	1-2	10	1-2-3	12	1	35	5-6
7	1-2-3	37	1	41	1-2-3-4	14	1-2-3	17	1-2	38	1-2
9	1-2	39	1	44	1-2-3	18	1-2-3	19	4-5-6	40	5-6
11	1-2	42	1-2	47	1-2-3	20	1-2-3	21	1-2	43	1
13	1-2	45	1-2	50	1-2	22	1-2-3-4	23	1-2	46	5-6
15	1	48	1-2	53	1-2	24	1-2-3	25	4-5-6	49	1-2
16	1	51	1-2	54	1-2	26	1-2-3	27	1-2	52	5-6
□		□		□		□		□		□	Maximum is 9 for each needs score
Total		Total		Total		Total		Total		Total	

□ Total FIRO-B score (54 is the maximum possible for the sum of the six needs scores)

Interpreting FIRO-B Scores

Your total interpersonal needs score is the sum of your individual needs scores. Your total interpersonal needs score will fall somewhere between 0 and 54. According to national studies, the average person scores 29.3, and 50 percent of adult respondents' scores fell between 20 and 38.[23] A high score indicates that you have strong interpersonal needs. You have a strong desire to interact with others and are probably outgoing and gregarious. A low score means you don't mind being alone a lot of the time and are more reserved around others.

What is the significance of your score? Business school students have been found to have different scores depending on their majors.[24] Marketing and human resource majors had above-average scores, and accounting and systems analysis students had lower-than-average scores. These findings indicate that students with higher interpersonal needs tend to select people-oriented careers and those with low interpersonal needs prefer more technical careers where interacting with others is not required. However, these findings do not necessarily predict your success as a manager, because that depends to a large degree on the types of work and people you are supervising.

There is no right score. The value of this information is that it lets you know your own interpersonal tendencies and inclinations. Your scores are also good indicators of how others are likely to see you. If you are not happy with the result of some of the inventories, pay special attention to the skills that will improve your behavior in those areas in the following chapters, and, check out the Managers' Application Tips for ideas about how you can better apply your interpersonal skills.

One way to know yourself better is to examine your scores on each need category as they relate to each other. Your highest individual scores, for example, indicate which interpersonal needs are least satisfied and probably dominate your relationships with others. The range of scores for each need is 0 to 9, so 4.5 is the median, which roughly equates to the average of national scores, although they do vary for each category. You might look to see if you are significantly higher or lower than average on the six different interpersonal needs scores. If so, how are these differences probably perceived by others, and do you behave in ways you want to change?

Another valuable use of your scores is to compare them to the scores of persons with whom you relate. Are you compatible? That is, does one person want what the other expresses? Or are you incompatible? That is, does one person express something another does not want? Other problems can arise when both parties want to express the same thing, such as control, or when neither wants to express something that is necessary, such as control. Finally, what do you think happens when two people emphasize the same need, such as affection, as opposed to situations in which they emphasize different needs, such as control versus affection?

As you probably have surmised, incompatible interpersonal needs can be responsible for a host of problems, from seeing interactions from different points of view, to conflict and lack of needs satisfaction. On the other hand, research has confirmed that compatible individuals usually like each other more and work better together.[25]

MANAGERS' APPLICATION TIPS

By being aware of your interpersonal needs and those of others, you can increase your interpersonal effectiveness by redefining issues, letting others have opportunities to satisfy their needs, and adapting your own behaviors to be more consistent with the needs of others.

SAQ 3: Assertiveness Questionnaire[26]

For each of the following statements, decide which answer best applies to you. Place the number of the answer to the left of the statement.

Never True	Sometimes True	Often True	Always True
1	2	3	4

_____ **1.** I respond with more modesty than I really feel when my work is complimented.

_____ **2.** If people are rude, I will be rude right back.

_____ **3.** Other people find me interesting.

_____ **4.** I find it difficult to speak up in a group of strangers.

_____ **5.** I don't mind using sarcasm if it helps me make a point.

_____ **6.** I ask for a raise when I feel I really deserve it.

_____ **7.** If others interrupt me when I am talking, I suffer in silence.

_____ **8.** If people criticize my work, I find a way to make them back down.

_____ **9.** I can express pride in my accomplishments without being boastful.

_____**10.** People take advantage of me.

_____**11.** I tell people what they want to hear if it helps me get what I want.

_____**12.** I find it easy to ask for help.

_____**13.** I lend things to others even when I don't really want to.

_____**14.** I win arguments by dominating the discussion.

_____**15.** I can express my true feelings to someone I really care for.

_____**16.** When I feel angry with other people, I bottle it up rather than express it.

_____**17.** When I criticize someone else's work, they get mad.

_____**18.** I feel confident in my ability to stand up for my rights.

Scoring SAQ 3: Assertiveness

SAQ 3 evaluates your basic interpersonal style in terms of the emphasis you place on passive, aggressive, and assertive behaviors.[27] Passive behavior is inhibited and submissive. Individuals who score high in passive behavior seek to avoid conflicts and tend to sublimate their own needs and feelings in order to satisfy other people. Aggressive behavior is the opposite of passiveness: it is domineering, pushy, self-centered, and without regard for the feelings or rights of others. People who score high in assertiveness express their ideas and feelings openly, stand up for their rights, and do so in a way that makes it easier for others to do the same. The assertive person, therefore, is straightforward yet sensitive to the needs of others.

To calculate your assertiveness style scores, refer back to the responses you gave on SAQ 3. Sum up your answers to items 1, 4, 7, 10, 13, and 16. That is your Passive score. Put that number in the appropriate box at the end of this section. Your Aggressive score is the total of your answers to items 2, 5, 8, 11, 14, and 17. Your Assertive score is the total of your answers to items 3, 6, 9, 12, 15, and 18. Put these scores in the appropriate boxes that follow. Your score in each box will range between 6 and 24.

Interpreting SAQ 3: Assertiveness Scores

SAQ 3 assessed your assertiveness level. You might wonder if you are too passive or too aggressive, or whether you are assertive enough in your interpersonal relations. A high Passive score indicates an unwillingness to confront problems. Your desire to please other people could cause others to perceive you as an easy mark who can easily be bullied by others. There may be times, however, when passive behavior is useful or appropriate. Examples could be if a situation or issue is not a priority, if you want to defer to someone else's expertise, or if you are trying to keep a low profile in a particular situation.

A high Aggressiveness score can also cause problems. Aggressive behavior involves forceful thoughts or feelings expressed in a way that does not consider the needs or rights of others. In this case, you're likely to be seen as "the little dictator." Your desire to take command and dominate others could be interpreted as pushiness and selfishness. Aggressive behavior tends to cut off communication and can eventually end relationships if the people you are interacting with feel overwhelmed and become defensive and angry. Aggressive behavior, however, can at times be useful or appropriate. Examples would be when you are dealing with people who have histories of treating you with disrespect and trying to take advantage of you, or if you decide that the stakes are so high that you must be understood and your points must be accepted.

The higher your Assertiveness score is, the more open and self-expressive you are. You confront issues in a straightforward manner. You say what you mean, but you're not rude or thoughtless. You're sensitive to the needs of others and receptive to what they have to say. Generally speaking, assertiveness is a desirable quality, in that it tends to facilitate effective interpersonal relations. Bowen[28] argues that passive and aggressive behaviors hinder effective interpersonal relations because neither facilitates openness and receptiveness. The preferred style, according to Bowen, is assertive behavior. Assertiveness improves interpersonal communication because the more assertive you are, the more assertive you encourage others to be. Assertiveness facilitates more effective interactions because it lessens defensiveness, domination, putting down other people, wishy-washiness, and similar dysfunctional behaviors.

We skipped over passive/aggressive behavior earlier because it's never an appropriate style to engage in. But is it helpful to look at it within the context of the full range of assertiveness styles? Passive/aggressive behavior is initially deferential—there is no argument or disagreement. However, a passive/aggressive person follows the initial passive response with an aggressive action. Sometimes a person who acts in a passive/aggressive manner does not feel strong enough to confront another openly. Or the person may think his or her own position or job might be compromised with an honest response. A passive aggressive person might agree to do a presentation for you (which they really do not want to do), for example, then "forget" to show up and you get reprimanded for failing to do your job. By comparing words with actions, you can discern discrepancies between someone's statements and behavior. If the actions are harmful, damaging or detrimental, the person is probably engaging in passive/aggressive behavior and seeking to undermine you while pretending not to.[29]

MANAGERS' APPLICATION TIPS

Part of choosing behavior and being in control of it is developing a repertoire of responses and understanding the relative effectiveness of each in any given situation. The reality is that all of these behaviors may be legitimate and effective at some point, for some reasons, and in some circumstances. You need to be aware of your preferred habitual response, and also what your options are, so that you can alter your response for specific situations and contexts.

SAQ 4: The Big Five Personality Questionnaire[30]

Below are ten sets of personality traits that may or may not apply to you. Please write a number next to each statement to indicate the extent to which you agree or disagree with that statement. You should rate the extent to which the pair of traits applies to you, even if one characteristic applies more strongly than the other. Use the following number scale:

1 = Disagree strongly; 2 = Disagree moderately; 3 = Disagree a little; 4 = Neither agree nor disagree; 5 = Agree a little; 6 = Agree moderately; 7 = Agree strongly

I see myself as:

_____ **1.** Extraverted, enthusiastic.
_____ **2.** Critical, quarrelsome.
_____ **3.** Dependable, self-disciplined.
_____ **4.** Anxious, easily upset.
_____ **5.** Open to new experiences, complex.
_____ **6.** Reserved, quiet.
_____ **7.** Sympathetic, warm.
_____ **8.** Disorganized, careless.
_____ **9.** Calm, emotionally stable.
_____ **10.** Conventional, uncreative.

Scoring the Big Five Personality Scale

Your scores for each of the Big Five personality dimensions are the average of two sets of adjectives. One set of adjectives is reversed scored for each pair. The questions relating to each personal dimension are below. "R" denotes reverse-scored items.

Extraversion: 1, 6R; Agreeableness: 2R, 7; Conscientiousness; 3, 8R; Emotional Stability: 4R, 9; Openness: 5, 10R. To obtain your Big Five Personality scores:[31]

1. **Recode** the reverse-scored items 2, 4, 6, 8, and 10 (i.e., recode a 7 with a 1, a 6 with a 2, a 5 with a 3, etc.).
2. Take the **average** of the two items (the standard item and the recoded reverse-scored item) that make up each two-item scale.
   Example using the Extraversion scale: A participant has scores of 5 on item 1 (Extraverted, enthusiastic) and 2 on item 6 (Reserved, quiet). First, recode the reverse-scored item (i.e., item 6), replacing the 2 with a 6. Second, take the average of the score for item 1 and the (recoded) score for item 6. So the TIPI Extraversion scale score would be $(5 + 6)/2 = 5.5$.
3. Enter your scores for each of the Big Five personality dimensions on the appropriate scales on the Big Five Interpretation Sheet.

Interpreting SAQ 4: Big Five Personality Scores

Personality describes a person's relatively stable set of behavioral, emotional, and cognitive characteristics that have been inherited and acquired through social and environmental interactions.[32] Personality traits are relatively stable over time and in different situations: A person who is shy in the classroom is also probably shy at work. Although there are a very large number of personality traits—for example, extroversion, introversion, locus of control, agreeableness, assertiveness, shyness, and confidence—researchers have determined that five characteristics determine the basic structure of human personality. Although some of the traits in the "Big Five" model are inherited, most of the time they can be modified through training, experience, and a conscious attempt to change. Read the following brief descriptions of each characteristic and compare your scores to the norms in the Big Five Interpretation Sheet.

Big Five Interpretation Sheet

Personality Dimension	Score	Norm	TRAITS	
			Above Norm	**Below Norm**
Emotional stability	_____	4.44	secure, guilt free	high strung, anxious
Extraversion	_____	5.23	assertive, sociable	private, reserved
Openness	_____	5.40	curious, broad interests	conservative, cautious
Agreeableness	_____	4.83	altruistic, trusting	skeptical, questioning
Conscientiousness	_____	5.38	dependable, organized	spontaneous, adaptable

These norms are based on a sample of 1813 respondents.[33]

Extraversion represents the degree to which an individual is social or antisocial, outgoing or shy, assertive or passive, active or inactive, and talkative or quiet. A person rating high on these dimensions is extroverted, while the opposite end of the scale is introverted.

Agreeableness measures the degree to which a person is friendly or reserved, cooperative or guarded, flexible or inflexible, trusting or cautious, good-natured or moody, soft-hearted or tough, and tolerant or judgmental. Those scoring high on these dimensions are viewed as agreeable and easy to work with, while those rating low are viewed as more disagreeable and difficult to work with.

Emotional stability refers to a person's degree of emotional stability. It characterizes whether a person is consistent or inconsistent in how he or she reacts to certain events, reacts impulsively or weighs options before acting, and takes things personally or looks at situations objectively. Those who rate high on emotional stability are viewed as generally calm, stable, having a positive attitude, able to manage their anger, secure, happy, and objective. Those who rate low are more likely to be anxious, depressed, angry, insecure, worried, and emotional.

Conscientiousness represents the degree to which an individual is dependable or inconsistent, can be counted on or is unreliable, follows through on commitments or reneges, and keeps promises or breaks them. Those who rate high on conscientiousness are generally perceived to be careful, thorough, organized, persistent, achievement-oriented, hardworking, and persevering. Those with low scores are seen as inattentive to detail, uncaring, disrespectful, unmotivated, unorganized, and apt to give up easily.

Openness characterizes the degree a person is interested in broadening horizons or limiting them, learning new things or sticking with what is already known, meeting new people or associating with current friends, and going to new places or staying in known places. Individuals who score high on this factor tend to be seen as intellectual, broad-minded, curious, imaginative, and cultured. Those with low scores are seen as narrow-minded, less interested in the outside world, and uncomfortable in unfamiliar situations.

MANAGERS' APPLICATION TIPS

By indentifying subordinates' personality dimensions you can better understand why they behave as they do. This understanding can help you assemble compatible teams, assign appropriate responsibilities, provide effective rewards for motivating performance.

SAQ 5: Cognitive Style[34]

For each item, circle either "a" or "b." If you feel both "a" and "b" are true, decide which one is more like you, even if it is only slightly more true.

1. I would rather
   a. Solve a new and complicated problem
   b. Work on something I have done before

2. I like to
   a. Work alone in a quiet place
   b. Be where "the action" is

3. I want a boss who
   a. Establishes and applies criteria in decisions
   b. Considers individual needs and makes exceptions

4. When I work on a project, I
   a. Like to finish it and get some closure
   b. Often leave it open for possible change

5. When making a decision, the most important considerations are
   a. Rational thoughts, ideas, and data
   b. Peoples' feelings and values

6. On a project, I tend to
   a. Think it over and over before deciding how to proceed
   b. Start working on it right away, thinking about it as I go along

7. When working on a project, I prefer to
   a. Maintain as much control as possible
   b. Explore various options

8. In my work, I prefer to
   a. Work on several projects at a time, and learn as much as possible about each one
   b. Have one project that is challenging and keeps me busy

9. I often
   a. Make lists and plans whenever I start something and may hate to seriously alter my plans
   b. Avoid plans and just let things progress as I work on them

10. When discussing a problem with colleagues, it is easy for me
    a. To see "the big picture"
    b. To grasp the specifics of the situation

11. When the phone rings in my office or at home, I usually
    a. Consider it an interruption
    b. Don't mind answering it

12. Which word describes you better?
    a. Analytical
    b. Empathetic

13. When I am working on an assignment, I tend to
    a. Work steadily and consistently
    b. Work in bursts of energy with "down time" in between

14. When I listen to someone talk on a subject, I usually try to
    a. Relate it to my own experience and see if it fits
    b. Assess and analyze the message

15. When I come up with new ideas, I generally
    a. "Go for it"
    b. Like to contemplate the ideas some more

16. When working on a project, I prefer to
    a. Narrow the scope so that it is clearly defined
    b. Broaden the scope to include related aspects

17. When I read something, I usually
    a. Confine my thoughts to what is written there
    b. Read between the lines and relate the words to other ideas

18. When I have to make a decision in a hurry, I often
    a. Feel uncomfortable and wish I had more information
    b. Am able to do so with available data

19. In a meeting, I tend to
    a. Continue formulating my ideas as I talk about them
    b. Only speak out after I have carefully thought the issue through

20. In work, I prefer spending a great deal of time on issues of
    a. Ideas
    b. People

21. In meetings, I am most often annoyed with people who
    a. Come up with many sketchy ideas
    b. Lengthen meetings with many practical details

22. Are you a
    a. Morning person?
    b. Night owl?

23. What is your style in preparing for a meeting?
    a. I am willing to go in and be responsive
    b. I like to be fully prepared and usually sketch an outline of the meeting

24. In a meeting, would you prefer for people to
    a. Display a fuller range of emotions
    b. Be more task oriented

25. I would rather work for an organization where
    a. My job was intellectually stimulating
    b. I was committed to its goals and mission

26. On weekends, I tend to
    a. Plan what I will do
    b. Just see what happens and decide as I go along

27. I am more
    a. Outgoing
    b. Contemplative

28. I would rather work for a boss who is
    a. Full of new ideas
    b. Practical

In the following, choose the word in each pair that appeals to you more:

29. a. Social
    b. Theoretical

30. a. Ingenuity
    b. Practicality

31. a. Organized
    b. Adaptable

32. a. Active
    b. Concentration

Scoring SAQ 5: Cognitive Style

Count one point for each item listed in the following table that you circled in the inventory.

SCORE FOR **I**	SCORE FOR **E**	SCORE FOR **S**	SCORE FOR **N**
2a	2b	1b	1a
6a	6b	10b	10a
11a	11b	13a	13b
15b	15a	16a	16b
19b	19a	17a	17b
22a	22b	21a	21b
27b	27a	28b	28a
32b	32a	30b	30a
Total I _____	**Total E** _____	**Total S** _____	**Total N** _____

Circle the one with more points: I or E   Circle the one with more points: S or N

SCORE FOR **T**	SCORE FOR **F**	SCORE FOR **J**	SCORE FOR **P**
3a	3b	4a	4b
5a	5b	7a	7b
12a	12b	8b	8a
14b	14a	9a	9b
20a	20b	18b	18a
24b	24a	23b	23a
25a	25b	26a	26b
29b	29a	31a	31b
Total T _____	**Total F** _____	**Total J** _____	**Total P** _____

Circle the one with more points: T or F   Circle the one with more points: J or P

Your four-letter cognitive style score is:

I or E _____   S or N _____   T or F _____   J or P _____

Interpreting SAQ 5: Cognitive Style Scores

Interpretation: Cognitive Style.[35]   Carl Jung's personality typology was the model for the Myers-Briggs Type Indicator (MBTI), which was the basis of the cognitive style inventory you just completed. Jung's typology classified preferences in four different areas of cognitive functioning. The first is focusing energy. Extroverts focus on the outer world whereas introverts focus on their inner world. The second is perceiving information. The comparison is between external sensing and internal intuition. Third is making judgments based on either thinking or feeling. Fourth is structuring, which refers to preference for being adaptable or being organized. These dimensions are summarized in Exhibit 2.4, and explained in more detail in this section.

Each person has a way of working and living that is influenced considerably by his or her preferences in cognitive functioning. Although these are not by any means the only factors, they are very influential in the way a person relates to others. Preferences in energy focus, perceiving information, making decisions, and structure are summarized as the end points on the continuum that follows. In actuality, a person's preferences can be at any point on a continuum between the two end points.

E = Extrovert Preference   or   **I = Introvert Preference**
Prefers to live in contact with others and things   Prefers to be more self-contained and work things out personally

S = Sensing Preference   or   **N = Intuition Preference**
Puts emphasis on facts, details, and concrete knowledge   Puts emphasis on possibilities, imagination, creativity, and seeing things as a whole

T = Thinking Preference   or   **F = Feeling Preference**
Puts emphasis on analysis using logic and rationality   Puts emphasis on human values, establishing personal friendships; makes decisions mainly on beliefs and dislikes

J = Judging Preference   or   **P = Perceiving Preference**
Puts emphasis on order through reaching decisions and resolving issues   Puts emphasis on gathering information and obtaining as much data as possible

EXHIBIT 2.4   Different Preferences in the Four Areas of Cognitive Functioning

As indicated in the comparisons in Exhibit 2.4, the initial letter of each preference provides a shorthand reference to the factor for understanding and discussion except for intuition, which is coded N, so that it does not conflict with I for introvert. These letters are used in the text that follows to describe the 16 combinations of preference alternatives and discuss the implications for interpersonal relations.

Introversion versus Extroversion.   ***Introverts*** prefer exploring and analyzing their own inner world. They are introspective and preoccupied with personal thoughts and reflections.[36] Introverts often appear awkward and inhibited because their best qualities are shared with only a few close people. Introverts' best work is done by self-initiative without interference from others. They are not influenced by majority views or public opinion. In work situations, introverts like quiet for concentration, are careful with details, think a lot before they act, and work contentedly alone.

The ***extrovert***, on the other hand, is characterized by a dominant interest in the outer world: a need to join in with others, constant attention to environment, the cultivation of friends and ac-quaintances, concern about the image projected to others. At work, extroverts like variety and action, tend to be fast-paced, dislike complicated procedures, are often impatient with long, slow jobs, are interested in the results of their job, often act quickly (sometimes without thinking), and usually "communicate well."[37]

No one is a "pure" type. We are all in a state of balance between extroversion (E) and in-troversion (I), but we use one type more naturally and more frequently. Since interpersonal skills are about interacting with others, some extroversion is useful. But too much can be counterpro-ductive, with the threat of becoming too other-directed, losing personal identity, and becoming submerged in conformist herd psychology.

Perceiving Information.   This dimension relates to the ways a person becomes aware of ideas, facts, and occurrences. When using ***sensing***, perception occurs literally through the use of the five senses. As a result, sensors are very much present-oriented, interested in practical matters, and prefer things to be orderly, precise, and unambiguous. They typically work steadily, like es-tablished routine, seldom make errors of fact, and rarely trust their inspirations.

Perceiving by ***intuition***, alternatively, cannot be traced back to a conscious sensory experi-ence but is instead a subconscious process, with ideas or hunches coming "out of the blue," yielding the hidden possibilities of a situation. The intuitive is future-oriented, always looking ahead and inspiring others with innovations. By the time everyone else catches up, the intuitive is off on another idea. In fact, the intuitive finds it difficult to tolerate performance of routine tasks; as soon as one is mastered, another is started. Intuitives also like solving new problems, work in bursts of energy, frequently jump to conclusions, are impatient with complicated situa-tions, dislike taking time for precision, and follow their inspirations, good or bad.

Making Judgments.   Just as there are two ways of perceiving information, there are two ways of making decisions about one's perceptions: by thinking or by feeling. ***Thinking*** is a logical and analytical process, searching for the impersonal, true versus false, correct versus incorrect. Principles are more important to the thinker than people, and the thinker often has a difficult time adapting to situations that cannot be understood intellectually.[38] Thinkers like analysis and put-ting things into logical order. They are relatively unemotional and uninterested in people's feelings. Thinkers may even hurt people's feelings without knowing it. They are able to repri-mand people or fire them when necessary and may seem hard-hearted. Although they need to be treated fairly, thinkers can get along without harmony.

Alternatively, ***feeling*** is a personal, subjective process, seeking a good versus bad—or like versus dislike—judgment. Thinking uses objective criteria but feeling is based on personal values.

It is different from emotion because feeling judgments are mental evaluations and not emotional reactions. Feelers live according to such subjective judgments based on a value system that is related to either society's values, as in the case of the extrovert, or personal values, as in the introvert.

Structuring.   This dimension refers to whether the preference is for being adaptable by keeping open to perceiving new information or getting organized and making quicker decisions. When a person follows explanations open-mindedly, for example, perception (adaptability) is preferred. On the other hand, if one's mind is rather quickly made up as to agreement or disagreement, then judging (organization) is preferred.

A fundamental difference in these two preferences is manifested in terms of which process is turned off or ignored. For judging to take place, perception must stop; all the facts need to be in so that a decision can be made. On the other hand, for perception to continue, judgments need to be put off for the time being because there is not enough data and new developments may occur.

The perceptive types live their lives, as opposed to the judging types who run theirs. Each preference is useful, but they both work better if a person can switch modes when necessary. A pure perceptive type is like a ship with all sail and no rudder, while a pure judging type is all form and no content.

To see the effects of the combination of all four of Jung's Personality Preference scores, find your four-letter type in Exhibit 2.5. Descriptions of typical personality characteristics of people that have each of the 16 different combinations are described after the four-letter classifications.

The Cognitive Style questionnaire classified you as extroverted or introverted (E or I), sensing or intuitive (S or N), thinking or feeling (T or F), and perceiving or judging (P or J). These classifications can be combined into 16 cognitive style types (e.g., INTJ, ENTP). Find your cognitive style type and interpretation from the following:

ISTJ.	You're organized, compulsive, private, trustworthy, and practical.
ISFJ.	You're loyal, amiable, and willing to make sacrifices for the greater good.
INFJ.	You're reflective, introspective, creative, and contemplative.
INTJ.	You're skeptical, critical, independent, determined, and often stubborn.
ISTP.	You're observant, cool, unpretentious, and highly pragmatic.
ISFP.	You're warm, sensitive, unassuming, and artistic.
INFP.	You're reserved, creative, and highly idealistic.
INTP.	You're socially cautious, enjoy problem solving, and are highly conceptual.
ESTP.	You're outgoing, live for the moment, unconventional, and spontaneous.
ESFP.	You're sociable, fun-loving, spontaneous, and very generous.
ENFP.	You're people-oriented, creative, and highly optimistic.
ENTP.	You're innovative, individualistic, versatile, and entrepreneurial.
ESTJ.	You're realistic, logical, analytical, decisive, and have a natural head for business or mechanics. You like to organize and run things.
ESFJ.	You're gracious, have good interpersonal skills, and are eager to please.
ENFJ.	You're charismatic, compassionate, and highly persuasive.
ENTJ.	You're outgoing, visionary, argumentative, have a low tolerance for incompetence, and are often seen as a natural leader.

EXHIBIT 2.5   Characteristics of Different Cognitive Styles

MANAGERS' APPLICATION TIPS

The MBTI offers managers guidance for making decisions about hiring, placement, and firing. Insights about personality type also can be applied to team building and promoting employee development. Armed with knowledge of the employees' personality type, managers can ascertain how to most effectively delegate to specific employees and what types of assignments would be most appropriate.

SAQ 6: Locus of Control[39]

Circle the letter next to the statement that best describes what you believe.

1. a. Many of the unhappy things in people's lives are partly due to bad luck.
   b. People's misfortunes result from the mistakes they make.

2. a. One reason we have wars is because people don't take enough interest in politics.
   b. There will always be wars, no matter how hard people try to prevent them.

3. a. In the long run, people get the respect they deserve in this world.
   b. An individual's worth is often unrecognized no matter how hard he tries.

4. a. The idea that teachers are unfair to students is nonsense.
   b. Students don't realize the extent accidental happenings influence their grades.

5. a. Without the right breaks, one cannot be an effective leader.
   b. Capable people can become leaders if opportunities exist.

6. a. No matter how hard you try, some people just don't like you.
   b. If you understand how to get along with others, most people will like you.

7. a. What is going to happen will happen.
   b. Trusting to fate does not turn out as well as taking a definite course of action.

8. a. If a student is prepared, there is rarely, if ever, such a thing as an unfair test.
   b. Many exam questions are so unrelated to course work that studying is useless.

9. a. Becoming a success is a matter of hard work; luck has little to do with it.
   b. Getting a good job depends mainly on being in the right place at the right time.

10. a. The average citizen can have an influence in government decisions.
    b. People in power run the world and there is not much the little guy can do about it.

11. a. When I make plans, I am almost certain that I can make them work.
    b. It is not wise to plan ahead because things turn out to be a matter of luck anyway.

12. a. In my case, getting what I want has little or nothing to do with luck.
    b. Many times we might just as well decide what to do by flipping a coin.

13. a. What happens to me is my own doing.
    b. I don't have enough control over the direction my life is taking.

Scoring and Interpreting SAQ 6: Locus of Control

Count one point for each "b" circled in questions 2, 3, 4, 8, 9, 10, 11, 12, 13, and one point for each "a" circled in questions 1, 5, 6, 7. Total scores of six or less indicate that you have an internal locus of control, i.e., you generally believe that you are responsible for what happens to you. Scores of seven or more indicate that you have an external locus of control, i.e., you generally believe that forces beyond your control are responsible for what happens to you. Scores are on a continuum ranging from 0 to 13. The more extreme scores in either direction indicate more firm beliefs that you either are or are not in control of what happens to you. Scores toward the middle indicate more vacillation between the two possibilities.

Research has shown that internals tend to be more in control of their own behavior, are more motivated to achieve, and are more involved in social activities than externals. Internals are also more likely than externals to seek leadership opportunities where they can influence others. Externals generally prefer structured work that requires compliance to established operating procedures. They prefer direction from others over being in charge themselves.[40]

MANAGERS' APPLICATION TIPS

If you are a manager (or seek to be one), the odds are that you have an internal locus of control, and it may be hard for you to imagine that others don't have much confidence in their abilities to influence what happens to them. You need to recognize that many externals exist and you need to deal with them differently than with externals like yourself. For example, you should delegate to internals by explaining the objective and letting them manage themselves and determine how to best achieve their tasks. With externals, on the other hand, delegation should be very structured and detailed with frequent benchmarks built in for them to check in, ask for clarification, and be reassured.

SAQ 7: Type "A" Personality[41]

Check "yes" or "no" to the response that most often, though not always, applies to you.

Yes   No

_____ _____ 1. When you are under pressure, do you usually do something about it immediately?

_____ _____ 2. Has anyone ever told you that you eat too fast?

_____ _____ 3. When someone takes too long to come to the point in a conversation, do you often "put words in his or her mouth" in order to speed things up?

_____ _____ 4. Do you often find yourself doing more than one thing at a time, such as working while eating, reading while dressing, figuring out problems while driving?

_____ _____ 5. Do you feel irritated if someone interrupts you while you are in the middle of something important?

_____ _____ 6. Are you always on time or a little bit early for appointments?

_____ _____ 7. Do you feel impatient or restless when forced to wait in line, such as at a restaurant, store, or post office?

_____ _____ 8. Do you find competition on the job or outside activities enjoyable and stimulating?

_____ _____ 9. Do you consider yourself to be definitely hard driving and competitive?

_____ _____ 10. Would people who know you rate your general level of activity as "too active" and advise you to "slow down"?

_____ _____ 11. Would people who know you well agree that you tend to get irritated easily?

_____ _____ 12. Would people who know you agree that you tend to do most things in a hurry?

_____ _____ **13.** Would people who know you agree that you have more energy than most people?

_____ _____ **14.** Do you enjoy competition and try hard to win?

_____ _____ **15.** Is it very difficult for you to relax after a hard day?

_____ _____ **16.** Do you think top executives usually reach their high positions through hard work rather than social skills and the luck of "being in the right place at the right time"?

_____ _____ **17.** During the average busy week, do you usually spend over 50 hours working or studying?

_____ _____ **18.** Do you usually work or study when you are not expected to (e.g., evenings or weekends) at least once a week?

_____ _____ **19.** Do you bring work home or study at night and weekends more than once a week?

_____ _____ **20.** Do you often stay up later than you prefer or get up early in order to get more work done?

_____ _____ **21.** Do you regularly keep two or more tasks moving forward at the same time by shifting back and forth rapidly from one to another?

_____ _____ **22.** Do you often set deadlines or quotas for yourself at work or at home?

_____ _____ **23.** Is it hard for you to take a vacation without doing at least a little work while you're away?

_____ _____ **24.** In the past three years, have you ever taken less than your allotted number of vacation days from work or completed term papers during vacation time?

_____ _____ **25.** Did you ever hold more than one job simultaneously or work while taking a full load in school?

Scoring

Add up the number of checks you have in the "yes" column to obtain your Type A personality score. All of the questions in this questionnaire represent characteristics of Type A personalities. Scores of 20–25 indicate that you are an extreme Type A possessing most of the Type A traits; scores of 10–20 indicate that you are a moderate Type A possessing many of the Type A traits; scores of 1–10 indicate that you are a low Type A possessing a few of the Type A traits. If you scored 0, you are a type B who does not possess any of the Type A trait.

Interpretation of Type A Scores

People with Type A personalities are typically impatient, restless, competitive, aggressive, under intense perceived time pressure, and always attempting to accomplish several things at once. Type B's, on the other hand, do not feel under pressure; they take things much more slowly and enjoy a variety of non-work-oriented activities.

Because Type A's thrive in an environment of tight deadlines and devote long hours to accomplishing volumes of work, they often achieve rapid promotions through the middle level of management. In most organizations, 61 to 76 percent of managers are Type A's.[42] If they perceive a high degree of control over their job environment, Type A's experience high job satisfaction and performance.[43]

Unfortunately Type A's report high incidents of health complaints and seldom manage to remain in good health for their entire careers. Hostility and anger are the most "toxic" Type A characteristics and the main contributors to coronary heart disease for both men and women[44] which is one of the reasons only a few Type A's obtain top-level management positions. Another part of the problem is that Type A's don't slow down enough to make thoughtful analyses of complex issues. Their impatience and hostility produce stress and discomfort among those with whom they work. Consequently, most successful top executives are type B individuals, who have the patience and more amiable interpersonal style required to maintain organizational harmony.[45]

MANAGERS' APPLICATION TIPS

Most Type A individuals are unaware of or refuse to acknowledge their problems, or their need to change. Many attribute their past successes to Type A behaviors and others they fear that seeking help to change their behavior will be viewed as a sign of weakness. If extreme Type A's continue in this manner, their behavior could become a major social problem. Since hostility and anger are the most "toxic" contributors to coronary heart disease for both men and women, Type A managers need to be open to feedback that they are hostile, and then do something to improve. Suggestions include reducing cynical mistrust of the motives of others; reducing the frequency and intensity of their anger, frustration, and rage; and learning to treat others with kindness and consideration.

SUMMARIZING YOUR SELF-AWARENESS PROFILE

You now have calculated your scores for learning style, interpersonal needs, assertiveness, the Big Five personality factors, and cognitive style. Together they make up your Self-Awareness Profile. The interpretation sections for each characteristic have allowed you to analyze your scores and interpret what they say about you. Summarize your self-assessment profile in the spaces in the following table for future class discussion.

Learning Style Scores from page 18:

Learning Style _____

Concrete Experience _____

Reflective Observation _____

Abstract Conceptualization _____

Active Experimentation _____

Interpersonal Needs Scores from Table 2.1 on page 23:
Total interpersonal needs score: _____.
Enter your scores from Table 2.1 on page 23:

Need	Expressed	Wanted
Inclusion	_____	_____
Control	_____	_____
Affection	_____	_____

Assertiveness Scores from page 25:

Passive _____

Aggressive _____

Assertive _____

Big Five Personality Scores from page 31:

Emotional stability _____

Extraversion_____

Openness_____

Agreeableness _____

Conscientiousness _____

Cognitive Style Scores from page 33:

_____ E [Extrovert] or I [Introvert]

_____ S [Sensing] or N [Intuition]

_____ T [Thinking] or F [Feeling]

_____ J [Judging] or P [Perceiving]

Locus of Control Score

_____ Internal (6–0)

_____ External (7–10)

Type "A" Personality Score

____ 20–25	Extreme Type A
____ 10–20	Moderate Type A
____ 1–10	Low Type A
____ 0	Type B

All of these personality characteristics impact the nature of your interpersonal relationships and job performance.[46] Understanding the meaning of these factors and being aware of your own scores can help you determine areas for personal growth, professional development, and compatible person/job fit.

CONCEPT QUIZ

Take the following 10-question, true–false quiz concerning self-awareness. Answers are at the end of the quiz. If you miss any, go back through the text and find out why you got them wrong.

Circle the right answer.

True   **False**   1. To increase self-awareness, your need to know needs to be stronger than your fear of knowing.

True   **False**   2. Comparing actual results with your expectations will show your strengths and weaknesses.

True   **False**   3. Writing down your thoughts about significant experiences increases the likelihood of learning from them.

True	False	4.	To be most productive, you should go into solitude with a list of things to accomplish.

True   False   4. To be most productive, you should go into solitude with a list of things to accomplish.

True   False   5. Self-assessments should always be verified by soliciting feedback from relevant others.

True   False   6. Learning style is based on four very different learning processes.

True   False   7. Interpersonal needs have two subdimensions: the expressed desire to give the need and the wanted desire to receive the need from others.

True   False   8. Aggressive behaviors are more effective in interpersonal relations than either passive or assertive behaviors.

True   False   9. Personality traits are relatively stable over time and in different situations.

True   False   10. Cognitive style affects how you think about relating to others, not how you actually behave.

Answers: (1) True; (2) True; (3) True; (4) False; (5) True; (6) True; (7) True; (8) False; (9) True; (10) False

BEHAVIORAL CHECKLIST

The following behaviors are important for enhancing self-awareness. Refer to them when evaluating your own and others' skills in these areas.

To Increase Your Self-Awareness:

- Compare actual experiences with previously set goals.
- Keep a journal.
- Create time to find solitude and reflect.
- Complete self-assessment questionnaires.
- Solicit feedback from others.

GROUP EXERCISES

Exercise 1: Checking Self-Assessments with Feedback from Others

Meet in established learning groups or form small groups with three to five class members. The following activities take approximately 40 minutes to complete and should be conducted within these groups.

1. Each group member spends 3–5 minutes introducing himself or herself. Highlight your background, career goals, and most important accomplishments to date, and briefly describe what you believe are your interpersonal strengths and limitations.
2. After all group members have completed their introductions, discuss this statement: "First impressions can provide a lot of insight into people."
3. Then, one person volunteers to be the focus.
4. Based on their first impressions of the focus person's behaviors exhibited in steps 1 and 2 of this exercise, group members give the focus feedback about how they perceive his or her scores on the self-assessment questionnaires in this chapter: Learning Style, FIRO,

Assertiveness, the Big Five Personality Factors, and Cognitive Style. Use the Summary that follows for a framework.

5. Then the focus shares his or her scores on the self-assessment questionnaires and feelings about their accuracy.
6. The group discusses how the group assessments corresponded with the focus's individual assessment profile scores: How different or similar were the assessments? Why? What does this imply?
7. Finally, based on these assessments and discussion, the group members help the focus develop an action plan for becoming an effective group member, including what the focus should do and how other group members can help the focus.
8. After the first focus clarifies this feedback, another person volunteers to be the focus, and steps 4–8 are repeated. The process continues until all group members have shared and received feedback.

Time. 40 minutes to complete steps 1–8.

Exercise 2: Developing a Team Resumé

1. Meet with your learning team, or form teams of five to six people.
2. Develop a team resumé that includes the results of every team member's self-assessments and members' other skills, experience, and attributes.
3. Each team presents its resumé to the class.
4. The rest of the class provides feedback on what they see as the team's strengths and areas they need to enhance.

Time. 60 minutes

Summary Checklist

Take a few minutes to reflect on your self-assessment results and the feedback you have received from others. Now assess yourself on each of the following key self-awareness behaviors. Make a check (✓) next to those behaviors in which you need improvement.

I compare actual experiences with previously set goals.   _____

I keep a journal.   _____

I create time to find solitude and reflect.   _____

I complete self-assessment questionnaires and
verify results with relevant others.   _____

I solicit feedback from others.   _____

APPLICATION QUESTIONS

1. How do you describe your personality? How could you improve it to enhance your interpersonal competence?
2. What are your interpersonal strengths and weaknesses? How can you find out more about them?
3. Think of people you know who are high and low in self-awareness. What are the differences in their interpersonal styles? What are the consequences?

4. How can your self-awareness from completing each of the self-assessment questionnaires in this chapter help you interact effectively with others?
   a. Learning Style
   b. Interpersonal Needs
   c. Assertiveness
   d. Big Five Personality
   e. Cognitive Style
   f. Locus of Control
   g. Type A Personality

REINFORCEMENT EXERCISES

The following suggestions are activities you can do to reinforce the self-assessment and self-awareness techniques in this chapter. You may want to adapt them to the Action Plan you will develop next, or try them independently.

1. Read the Appendix and review the section on journals in this chapter. Keep a daily journal for the remainder of this semester. Record significant events and insights that will enhance your self-awareness. At the beginning of each new week, study your journal entries from the previous week to see what you can learn about yourself.
2. Share your self-assessment inventory scores with a significant other. Explain their meaning. Discuss their implications and see what you can learn from the other person's reactions and experiences with you.
3. Visit your campus counseling center. Ask which self-assessment inventories are available.
4. Ask a good friend to share with you his or her perceptions of your strengths and weaknesses as a friend.
5. Practice finding solitude for 30 minutes a day for a week.

ACTION PLAN

1. In what areas do I most need to improve my self-awareness?

2. Why? What will be my payoff?

3. What potential obstacles stand in my way?

4. What are the specific things I will do to enhance my self-awareness? (For examples, see the Reinforcement Exercises.)

5. When will I do them?

6. How and when will I measure my success?

Endnotes

1. Adapted from S. C. de Janasz, K. O. Dowd, and B. Z. Schneider, *Interpersonal Skills in Organizations* (New York: McGraw-Hill, 2002), pp. 12–13.

2. Peter F. Drucker, "Managing Oneself," *Harvard Business Review* (March–April, 1999), p. 65.

3. Jennifer Robison, "The Essence of Real Leadership," Interview of Bill George, author of *Authentic Leadership* and *True North* in the *Gallup Management Journal Online*, http://gmj.gallup.com (May 10, 2007).

4. Thomas Mannarelli, "Charismatic, Transformation Leadership through Reflection and Self-Awareness," *Accountancy Ireland*, Vol. 38, No. 6 (December 2006), pp. 46–48.

5. Jennifer Robison, "The Essence of Real Leadership," Interview of Bill George, author of *Authentic Leadership* and *True North* in the *Gallup Management Journal Online*, http://gmj.gallup.com (May 10, 2007).

6. Thomas Mannarelli, "Charismatic, Transformation Leadership through Reflection and Self-Awareness," *Accountancy Ireland*, Vol. 38, No. 6 (December 2006), pp. 46–48.

7. Ibid.

8. Hugh McIntosh, "Solitude Provides an Emotional Tune-up," *APA Monitor*, Vol. 27, No. 3 (March 1996), pp. 9–10.

9. Ideas about how to keep and apply a journal for optimal results can be found in M. Csikszentmihalyi, *Flow: The Psychology of Optimal Experience* (New York: Harper & Row, 1990).

10. Reyhan Harmanci, "Time to Get a Life—Pioneer Blogger Justin Hall Bows Out at 31," *San Francisco Chronicle* (February 20, 2005). Retrieved on June 9, 2006.

11. Mallory Jensen, "A Brief History of Weblogs," *Columbia Journalism Review*, No. 5 (September/October 2003), http://cjrarchives.org/issues/2003/5/blog-jensen.asp?

12. Ibid., p. 66.

13. Ibid., pp. 66–67.

14. It should be noted that these assessment instruments have all been validated in North American cultures and that the implications drawn are predominantly oriented for North American business organizations. Different implications may be drawn for managers in countries outside of North America.

15. This assessment is adapted from W. Bloisi, C. W. Cook, and P. L. Hunsaker, *Management and Organisational Behaviour*, Second European ed. (New York: McGraw-Hill/Irwin, 2007), pp. 161–163. It is based on the abilities identified in David Kolb's model of experiential learning described in Joyce S. Osland, David A. Kolb, Irwin M. Rubin, and Marlene E. Turner, *Organizational Behavior: An Experiential Approach*, 8th ed. (Upper Saddle River, NJ: Prentice Hall, 2007), pp. 52–61.

16. See Joyce S. Osland, David A. Kolb, Irwin M. Rubin, and Marlene E. Turner, *Organizational Behavior: An Experiential Approach*, 8th ed. (Upper Saddle River, NJ: Prentice Hall, 2007), pp. 52–61, for a more comprehensive description of learning styles and their development by David Kolb.

17. Ann C. Baker, Patricia J. Jensen, and David A. Kolb, "Conversational Learning: An Experiential Approach to Knowledge Creation," in A. Baker, P. Jensen, and D. Kolb, *Conversational Learning: An Experiential*

Approach to Knowledge Creation (Westport, CT: Quorum Books, 2002).

18. A total of 1,876 entries appear in the 2005 *Experiential Learning Theory Bibliography* by Alice Kolb and David A. Kolb (Cleveland, OH: Experience Based Learning Systems, 2005). See www.learningfromexperience.com.

19. David A. Kolb, "Management and the Learning Process," *California Management Review*, Vol. 18 (Spring 1976), pp. 21–31.

20. Charalampos Mainemelis, Richard Boyatzis, and David A. Kolb, "Learning Styles and Adaptive Flexibility: Testing Experiential Learning Theory," *Management Learning*, Vol. 33 (2002), pp. 5–33.

21. William C. Schutz, *FIRO: A Three Dimensional Theory of Interpersonal Behavior* (New York: Rinehart & Co., 1958). Permission granted from the author for historical purposes only. FIRO-B has been recently revised and updated. Its replacement, ELEMENT B, is described in Will Schutz, *The Truth Option* (Tenspeed, 1984), and is available from WSA, Box 259, Muir Beach, CA 94965. Items in this instrument are not to be reproduced.

22. William C. Schultz, *FIRO: A Three Dimensional Theory of Interpersonal Behavior* (New York: Rinehart & Co., 1958).

23. D. A. Whetten and K. S. Cameron, *Developing Management Skills*, 5th ed. (Upper Saddle River, NJ: Prentice Hall, 2002), pp. 78–79.

24. R. E. Hill, "Interpersonal Needs and Functional Areas of Management," *Journal of Vocational Behavior*, Vol. 4 (1974), pp. 15–24.

25. N. J. Dimarco, "Supervisor–Subordinate Life Style and Interpersonal Need Compatibilities as Determinants of Subordinate's Attitudes Toward the Supervisor," *Academy of Management Journal*, Vol. 17 (1974), pp. 575–578; W. W. Liddell and J. W. Slocum, Jr., "The Effects of Individual-Role Compatibility Upon Group Performance: An Extension of Schutz's FIRO Theory," *Academy of Management Journal*, Vol. 19 (1976), pp. 413–426.

26. Douglas T. Hall, Donald D. Bowen, Roy J. Lewicki, and Francine S. Hall, *Experiences in Management and Organizational Behavior*, 2nd ed. (New York: John Wiley & Sons, 1982), p. 101. With permission.

27. Donald D. Bowen, "Toward a Viable Concept of Assertiveness," in D. T. Hall, D. D. Bowen, R. J. Lewicki, and F. S. Hall (eds.), *Experiences in Management and Organizational Behavior*, 2nd ed. (New York: John Wiley & Sons, 1982), pp. 414–417.

28. Ibid.

29. Joni Rose, "Communication Styles: Aggressive, Passive, Passive-Aggressive or Assertive Communication." http://trainingpd.suite101.com/article.cfm/communication_styles#ixzz0kjpZTuos (January 21, 2007).

30. The questionnaire and norms used in this section are from Gosling, S. D., Rentfrow, P. J., and W. B., Jr., Swann. "A Very Brief Measure of the Big Five Personality Domains," *Journal of Research in Personality, 37* (2003), pp. 504–528. There are used with the authors' permission.

31. If you are looking for a quick way to compute and display your Big Five scores, Daniel DeNeui has created an excel spreadsheet that computes your scores and plots them alongside the norms in the Big Five Interpretation Sheet. To obtain this spreadsheet, go to http://homepage.psy.utexas.edu/homepage/faculty/gosling/scales_we.htm#TenItemPersonalityMeasureTIPI.

32. This definition is adapted from S. F. Maddi, *Personality Theories: A Comparative Analysis* (Homewood, IL: Richard D. Irwin, 1980), p. 10.

33. S. D. Gosling, P. J. Rentfrow, and W. B., Jr., Swann (2003). "A Very Brief Measure of the Big Five Personality Domains," *Journal of Research in Personality, 37,* p. 526.

34. Dorothy Marcic, *Organizational Behavior: Experiences and Cases*, 3rd ed. (New York: West Publishing Company, 1992), pp. 9–12.

35. Adapted from Charles Margerison and Ralph Lewis, "Mapping Managerial Style," *International Journal of Manpower, Special Issue*, Vol. 2, No. 1, 1981, pp. 2–20; Stephen P. Robbins, *Self-Assessment Library*, 2nd ed. (Upper Saddle River, NJ: Prentice Hall, 2004), pp. 3–7; Dorothy Marcic, *Organizational Behavior: Experiences and Cases*, 3rd ed. (New York: West Publishing Company, 1992), pp. 9–12.

36. Carl Jung, *Psychological Types* (Princeton, NJ: Princeton University Press, 1971).

37. I. B. Myers, *The Myers-Briggs Type Indicator Manual* (Princeton, NJ: Education Testing Service, 1962).

38. Carl Jung, *Psychological Types* (Princeton, NJ: Princeton University Press, 1971).

39. Derived from J. B. Rotter (1966) "Generalized Expectancies for Internal versus External Control

of Reinforcement," *Psychological Monographs*, 80 (1, Whole No. 609), pp. 1–28.

40. P. E. Spector, "Behavior in Organizations as a Function of Employee's Locus of Control," *Psychological Bulletin* (May 1982), pp. 482–497; H. M. Lefcourt, "Durability and Impact of the Locus of Control Construct" *Psychological Bulletin,* 112 (1992), pp. 411–414.

41. Created from concepts in Meyer Friedman and Ray Rosenman, *Type A Behavior and Your Heart* (New York: Knopf, 1974).

42. A. P. Brief, R. S. Schuler, and M. Van Sell, Managing Job Stress (Boston: Little, Brown and Co., 1981), p. 138.

43. C. Lee, S. J. Ashford, and P. Bobko, "Interactive Effects of Type A Behavior and Perceived Control of Worker Performance, Job Satisfaction, and Somatic Complaints," *Academy of Management Journal*, 33 (December 1990), pp. 870–882.

44. R. B. Williams, Jr., "Type A Behavior and Coronary Heart Disease: Something Old, Something New," *Behavior Medicine Update,* Vol. 6 (1984), pp. 29–33.

45. "Type-A Managers Stuck in the Middle," *The Wall Street Journal* (June 17, 1988), p. 17.

46. Murray Barrick and Michael Mont,"The Big Five Personality Dimensions and Job Performance: A Meta-Analysis," Personnel Psychology (Spring 1991), p. 11.

3

■ ■ ■

Self-Management: Clarifying Values, Setting Goals, and Planning

SELF-ASSESSMENT EXERCISE: HOW WELL DO I PLAN AND SET GOALS?

This is a two-part assessment. The first part explores how well you plan. The second part helps you assess your goal-setting skills.

Part I: Am I a Good Planner?[1]

The following assessment is designed to help you understand your planning skills. Answer either Yes or No to each of the following questions.

	Yes	No
1. My personal objectives are clearly spelled out in writing.	_____	_____
2. Most of my days are hectic and disorderly.	_____	_____
3. I seldom make any snap decisions and usually study a problem carefully before acting.	_____	_____
4. I keep a desk calendar or appointment book as an aid.	_____	_____
5. I use "action" and "deferred action" files.	_____	_____
6. I generally establish starting dates and deadlines for all my projects.	_____	_____
7. I often ask others for advice.	_____	_____
8. I believe that all problems have to be solved immediately.	_____	_____

Part II: How Well Do I Set Goals?[2]

For each of the following questions, select the answer that best describes how you set goals for yourself. Respond as you have behaved or *would* behave, not as you think you *should* behave. Indicate how much you agree or disagree with each statement. When you finish, review the items that received the lowest scores.

Scale	Strongly Disagree	Disagree	Neutral	Agree	Strongly Agree
	1	2	3	4	5

_____ **1.** I am proactive rather than reactive.
_____ **2.** I set aside enough time and resources to study and complete projects.
_____ **3.** I am able to budget money to buy the things I really want without going broke.
_____ **4.** I have thought through what I want to accomplish in my education.
_____ **5.** I have a plan for completing my education.
_____ **6.** My goals for the future are realistic.

Scoring and Interpretation

Part I: Am I a Good Planner?

According to the author of this first questionnaire, the perfect planner would have answered as indicated below. If you answered differently, look for reasons that the alternative is more desirable as you read the following Skills Concepts.

(1) Yes   (2) No   (3) Yes   (4) Yes   (5) Yes   (6) Yes   (7) Yes   (8) No

Part II: How Well Do I Set Goals?

This assessment helps you focus on basic aspects of the goal-setting processes in your personal life. Several keys to making *any* goal-setting process effective are discussed in the Skills Concepts section that follows. Our intent with this brief assessment is to get you thinking about goal setting as it relates to your personal, interpersonal, school, and work settings.

In the first part of the assessment, we focus on whether your personal goal setting is *passive* or *active*. Question 1 assesses your general tendency around "action" and questions 4 and 5 select a specific example of proaction versus reaction (e.g., having a plan for completing your education). Allocating "resources" for the completion of goals is queried in questions 2 and 3. Question 6 focuses on a cornerstone of effective goal setting: creating goals that are attainable, yet challenging. If your score on any of these questions is 3 or less, you should pay particular attention to the corresponding material that follows.

SKILL CONCEPTS

> *"Cheshire Puss," she [Alice] began, "would you tell me, please, which way I ought to walk from here?" "That depends a good deal on where you want to get to," said the Cat. "I don't much care where," said Alice. "Then it doesn't matter which way you walk," said the Cat.[3]*

Unlike Alice, most of us have places we want to go and other goals that we want to achieve. Otherwise, you probably wouldn't be reading this book. We also have organizational goals assigned to us in school or at work that we are charged to accomplish. Consequently, we need to have a clear idea of who we are, what we want to become, where we are going, and how we are going to get there. To do this, we need to know how to clarify our values and goals and how to develop strategic plans to achieve them.

One reason for increasing your self-awareness is to "look into the mirror" and determine what you are doing that helps and hinders progress toward your goals. If you don't know what your goals are it really doesn't matter what you do because you have no desired outcomes in mind. To behave in a purposeful manner it is important to clarify what you want to achieve, know why it is important, and define a plan for appropriate actions. Finally, you need to influence yourself to implement and follow through on your plans in the most effective ways.

What Is Self-Management?

Self-management, sometimes called self-leadership, is the process of influencing yourself.[4] It is based on the premise that we choose what we are and what we become. Management has been defined as the process of planning, organizing, directing, and controlling others.[5] Self-management is the process of planning, organizing, directing, and controlling ourselves. Leadership is the process of influencing others to achieve a common goal.[6] Self-leadership is the process of influencing ourselves to achieve our own goals. To practice self-management and self-leadership, we first need to be aware of what we want out of life and what desirable means for attaining our goals are. We need to clarify our values, develop a personal mission statement, set our goals, and make plans for achieving our goals. Then we need to implement our plans using many of the skills in this book that have been proven to help us become more personally effective.[7]

What Are Your Values?

Naomi Fujioka was faced with a dilemma. She was about to receive her MBA from a prestigious business school and had two job offers. One offer was to be an investment banker at a very high salary; the other was at a low salary in a nonprofit organization that helps poor children in developing countries. Naomi's choice was heavily influenced by her values. Both jobs were attractive. Naomi valued earning a good income from a challenging position, but she valued even more using her talents to help people in need. She joined the nonprofit organization.

Values are stable, enduring beliefs about what is worthwhile in life (*ends*) and what behaviors are desirable for achieving them (*means*).[8] Since your values determine what you believe is good or bad, important or unimportant, and desirable or undesirable, you need to clarify your values before you can determine what your goals are and how you want to behave to achieve them.

Values influence our decisions and behavior. For example, if an individual values being on time, he or she will be motivated to behave so as to be on time. The thought of being late may stimulate feelings of stress and a subsequent adrenaline rush to hurry to the appointment.

According to the definition, values can be classified into two different types. *Terminal values* refer to desirable ends, or goals. Examples include a comfortable, prosperous life, world peace, wisdom, and salvation. *Instrumental values* are beliefs about what behaviors are appropriate in striving for desired goals and ends. Examples include being loving, honest, and ambitious. You can determine your own terminal and instrumental values in the first group exercise. The modeling exercise and the second group exercise will help you further refine your values and provide feedback on the congruency between your terminal and instrumental values.

Personal Mission Statements

One of the most effective techniques to ensure that you are always behaving in worthwhile ways is to develop a *personal mission statement* that defines your purpose in life and focuses on what you want to become and how you want to achieve this state.[9] Your personal mission statement is your life philosophy or creed. It defines the kind of person you want to be (character), what you want to accomplish (contributions), and what principles guide your behavior (values). A personal mission statement is the basis for proactivity: It provides your vision and the values that direct your life, it is the basis for determining long- and short-term goals, and it serves as the criteria for deciding on the most effective use of your time. Here is an example of one person's mission statement:[10]

> My career goals are to achieve a position of respect and knowledge, to utilize that position to help others, and to play an active role in a public service organization.
>
> I want to go through life with a smile on my face and a twinkle in my eye. For myself, I want to develop self-knowledge, self-love, and self-allowing. I want to use my healing talents to keep hope alive and express my vision courageously in word and action.
>
> In my family, I want to build healthy, loving relationships, in which we let each other become our best selves.
>
> At work, I want to establish a fault-free, self-perpetuating, learning environment. In the world, I want to nurture the development of all life forms, in harmony with the laws of nature.

Personal Goal Setting

It is important to set operational goals that will insure that you are true to your purpose in life. A goal defines a destination point that you want to achieve. Clear objectives and regular evaluations facilitate self-management because they clarify what needs to be done and reveal whether you are being successful.[11] The results of goal setting are long-term vision and motivation to lead your life in a chosen direction, as opposed to simply reacting randomly to forces that develop.

Goal setting also provides a way to measure your success and criteria for making decisions about how to spend your time and energy. With commitment to specific goals, you can focus your behavior toward achieving desired visions that provide motivation and purpose in life. Planning, which we discuss next, provides the map to get you there.

Strategies for Effective Goal Setting

There are several things you can do to ensure that you set the right goals for yourself and that you will be motivated to achieve your objectives. Some of the most important ones are discussed in this section.

Personalize.   You will be less committed and motivated to achieve goals that someone else expects of you. If you are majoring in accounting because your father was an accountant and expects you to follow in his footsteps, this may not be right for you if your heart isn't in it. Your goals should be yours: a direct result of your own mission statement, values, and desires.

Be SMART.   The SMART acronym refers to goals that are specific, measurable, attainable, realistic, and time-bound. Goals with these characteristics are clear, quantifiable, believable, within your control, and have a specific time frame for completion.

Visualize.   If you visualize what it will be like to have achieved your goal, you will be more motivated to stay focused and work hard. Developing a vision is a part of most organizations' mission statements. It should be part of yours also.

Develop a Support Group.   Associate with people who can and will support you in achieving your goals. These can be friends, family, coworkers, or anyone with the resources that you need to be successful.

Reward Small Wins.   When you achieve incremental progress toward your goals, reward yourself. This will help maintain your commitment and motivation.

Continually Evaluate and Make Adjustments.   You need to adapt to changing circumstances and setbacks in a realistic fashion. When things do not work out as planned, be honest with yourself about why. You may encounter unforeseen obstacles, lack of resources, or even changes in your own desires. Goal setting is an ongoing process and changing direction is desirable when appropriate.

Planning for Implementation

Planning involves defining a strategy for achieving goals. It is concerned with what, how, and when things need to be done. The eight-step planning process is illustrated in Figure 3.1. It consists of the following activities: identifying your mission and vision, analyzing the environment for opportunities and threats, assessing your strengths and weaknesses, formulating specific operational objectives, deciding on strategies to implement the plan, and determining how to evaluate results.

Planning begins by identifying your overall purpose, or mission statement. This is the foundation of all operational goals, planning activities, and criteria against which actual accomplishments are measured. Once you know your overall purpose in life, you can perform a SWOT analysis: examine the fit between your personal **S**trengths and **W**eaknesses and environmental **O**pportunities and **T**hreats. This analysis will reveal the operational objectives, or short-term accomplishments, that you need to achieve to arrive at your vision. Next, you should formulate specific strategies for achieving your goals by capitalizing on your strengths and identifying niches that you can excel in because you have distinctive competencies. No matter how effective your strategies are, they cannot succeed if they aren't implemented properly.

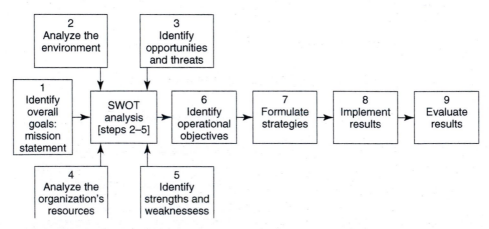

FIGURE 3.1 The Planning Process.

Consequently, you need to establish timelines and checkpoints. Finally, you need to constantly evaluate your progress toward your goals, changing strategies when necessary.

CONCEPT QUIZ

Answer the 10 questions in the following true–false quiz. The correct answers are listed at the end of the quiz. If you get any answers wrong, reread the chapter to find the correct answer.
Circle the right answer.

True False 1. If you don't have goals, it really doesn't matter what you do because you don't have any desired outcomes.

True False 2. Your values determine what you believe is desirable or undesirable.

True False 3. Honesty and ambition are "instrumental" values.

True False 4. Your personal mission statement is your life philosophy or creed.

True False 5. A vision should be a part of your mission statement.

True False 6. Goal setting is an ongoing process and sometimes requires changing direction.

True False 7. Planning is concerned with what, how, and when things need to be done.

True False 8. A SWOT analysis examines the fit between your personal **S**ituation **W**ith appropriate **O**rganizational **T**heories.

True False 9. Once you have found a niche, you can stop scanning the environment and concentrate on producing.

True False 10. No matter how effective your strategies are, they cannot succeed if they aren't implemented properly.

Answers: (1) True; (2) True; (3) True; (4) True; (5) True; (6) True; (7) True; (8) False; (9) False; (10) True

BEHAVIORAL CHECKLIST

The following behaviors are important for effective self-management. Use them when evaluating your own self-management skills and when giving feedback to others.

Self-management Requires:

- Clarifying and sharing your values
- Acting congruently with your personal mission statement
- Sharing your vision of the future
- Committing to specific objectives that will contribute to your vision
- Assessing personal strengths and weaknesses of all parties involved
- Discussing environmental threats and opportunities
- Setting SMART goals that are specific, measurable, attainable, realistic, and time-bound
- Developing plans and implementing strategies to accomplish them
- Continually evaluating progress and making adjustments when necessary
- Rewarding small wins
- Evaluating progress and making changes when necessary

MODELING EXERCISE

The Alligator River[12]

Objectives

To assess terminal and instrumental values and demonstrate how they affect behavior and interpersonal relations.

Procedure.

1. **Group Formation.**   Form groups of five or six members.
2. **Reading.**   Read *The Alligator River Story* that follows.
3. **Individual Ranking.**   After reading the story, *individually* rank the five characters in the story beginning with the one whom you consider the most offensive and ending with the one whom you consider the least objectionable. Briefly note your reasons.

The Alligator River Story

There once lived a woman named **Abigail** who was in love with a man named **Gregory**. Gregory lived on the shore of a river. Abigail lived on the opposite shore of the same river. The river that separated the two lovers was teeming with hungry alligators. Abigail wanted to cross the river to be with Gregory. Unfortunately, the bridge had been washed out by a heavy flood the previous week. So she went to ask **Sinbad**, a riverboat captain, to take her across. He said he would be glad to if she would consent to go to bed with him prior to the voyage. She promptly refused and went to a friend named **Ivan** to explain her plight. Ivan did not want to get involved at all in the situation. Abigail felt her only alternative was to accept Sinbad's terms. Sinbad fulfilled his promise to Abigail and delivered her into the arms of Gregory. When Abigail told Gregory about her amorous escapade in order to cross the river, Gregory cast her aside with disdain. Heartsick and rejected, Abigail turned to **Slug** with her tale of woe. Slug, feeling compassion for Abigail, sought out Gregory and beat him brutally. Abigail was overjoyed at the sight of Gregory getting his due. As the sun set on the horizon, people heard Abigail laughing at Gregory.

INDIVIDUAL RANKING FORM (Abigail, Gregory, Sinbad, Ivan, Slug)

Rank	Name	Reasons
First (Worst)		
Second		
Third		
Fourth		
Fifth		

4. **Sharing.**   After all have finished, group members share their rankings and reasons.
5. **Group Decision.**   Groups agree on a *consensus* decision for a final set of rankings. In reaching your decision, listen to other points of view and share all of yours until everyone is satisfied that the group's agreed-upon ranking is the best that can be achieved in your group. Do not just add up and average individual rankings, assign rankings randomly, or take a quick vote. These quick methods don't allow for learning about yourself and from others. Instead, talk things through and explain all positions until all agree on a common set of rankings.

GROUP CONSENSUS RANKING (Abigail, Gregory, Sinbad, Ivan, Slug)

Rank	Name	Reasons
First (Worst)		
Second		
Third		
Fourth		
Fifth		

6. **Debriefing.** One at a time, group members should give each other feedback on the termi-nal and end values they exhibited through their ranking and behavior during the group ranking exercise. Feedback can also be given about the behaviors members demonstrated when explaining their own ranking preferences and their reactions to others' preferences.

Total Time. 50 minutes (setup, 5 minutes; exercise, 30 minutes; debrief, 15 minutes)

GROUP EXERCISES

Group Exercise 1: What Are Your Values?[13]

Rank the first column, *terminal values*, 1 (most important) through 17 (least important). Rank the second column, *instrumental values*, 1 (most important) through 23 (least important).

Rank	Terminal (End) Values	Rank	Instrumental (Means) Values
_____	Achievement	_____	Action-oriented
_____	Aesthetics	_____	Ambitious
_____	Contentment	_____	Athletic/physical
_____	Equality	_____	Brave
_____	Excitement	_____	Compassionate
_____	Harmony	_____	Competent
_____	Health	_____	Considerate
_____	Liberty	_____	Creative
_____	Love	_____	Decisive
_____	Peace	_____	Dependable
_____	Pleasure	_____	Disciplined
_____	Prosperity	_____	Energetic
_____	Security	_____	Friendly
_____	Self-esteem	_____	Good-natured
_____	Social status	_____	Honest
_____	Spirituality	_____	Intelligent
_____	Wisdom	_____	Open
		_____	Orderly
		_____	Outgoing
		_____	Rational
		_____	Reserved
		_____	Spontaneous
		_____	Tough-minded

Debriefing

Share and compare your rankings with those of someone who knows you well. Discuss what your own past behavior tells about your values. Discuss the difference, if any, between what you say you value (terminal end values) and what you do value (instrumental means values).

Total Time. 25 minutes (ranking, 10 minutes; dyad discussion, 15 minutes)

Group Exercise 2: Write Your Eulogy[14]

Imagine going to the funeral of a loved one. Picture yourself driving to the funeral, parking the car, and getting out. As you walk inside the building, you notice the flowers, the soft organ music. You see the faces of friends and family. You feel the shared sorrow of losing, the joy of having known, that radiates from the hearts of the people there. As you walk down to the front of the room and look inside the casket, you suddenly come face to face with yourself. This is your funeral, 3 years from today. All these people have come to honor you and to express their feelings of love and appreciation for your life.

As you take a seat and wait for the services to begin, you look at the program in your hand. There are to be four speakers. The first speaker represents your family, immediate and also extended—children, brothers, sisters, nephews, nieces, aunts, uncles, cousins, and grandparents who have come from all over the country to attend. The second speaker is one of your friends, someone who can give a sense of who you were as a person. The third speaker is from your work or profession, and the fourth is from your church or some community organization where you've been involved in service.

Think about what you would like each of these speakers to say about you and your life. What kind of husband, wife, father, or mother would you like their words to reflect? What kind of son or daughter or cousin? What kind of friend? What kind of working associate?

What character would you like them to have seen in you? What contributions and achievements would you want them to remember? Look carefully at the people around you. What difference would you like to have made in their lives? Take a few minutes to jot down your impressions.

1. Family
2. Friends
3. Work
4. Community

If you participated seriously in this exercise, your responses touched on some of your most fundamental values for living a desirable life. The idea of beginning with the end in mind is to behave each day in ways that contribute to the criteria you have established for living a worthwhile life. If your values are clear, you can be proactive and make decisions about how to act instead of reacting to emotions and circumstances. You can act with integrity, which means practicing what you preach regardless of emotional or social pressure, and not allowing any irrational consideration to overwhelm your convictions.[15]

Total Time. 15 minutes for writing personal eulogy

Group Exercise 3: Determine Your Personal Mission Statement

One of the most effective techniques to ensure that you always behave in worthwhile ways is to develop a personal mission statement that focuses on what you want to become (your life goals) and how you want to achieve this state (your instrumental values).[16]

Preparation

Take a few minutes to review your values, rankings, and the eulogy that you wrote in the previous exercises. Next, review the examples of mission statements in the text.

Write Your Personal Mission Statement

Your personal mission statement is your life philosophy or creed. As you write it down, include sections on (1) the kind of person you want to be (*character*), (2) what you want to accomplish in your life (*contributions*), and (3) the principles you want to guide your behavior (*values*).

Debriefing

When you are finished writing your personal mission statement, pick a partner you know well and share the statement with him or her. Your partner will ask clarifying questions and provide feedback. Then share your eulogy and values rankings. Your partner will provide feedback about the congruency between the three. When you are finished, switch roles and provide your partner with feedback.

Total Time. 45 minutes (writing personal mission statement, 15 minutes; dyad sharing, 30 minutes)

Summary Checklist

Take a few minutes to reflect on your performance in the exercises you just completed and on the feedback you have received from other team members about clarifying your values, personal goal setting, and planning. Make a check (✓) next to those behaviors in which you want to improve to increase your self-management skills.

_____ Clarifying and sharing your values

_____ Acting congruently with your personal mission statement

_____ Sharing your vision of the future

_____ Committing to specific objectives that will contribute to your vision

_____ Assessing personal strengths and weaknesses of all parties involved

_____ Discussing environmental threats and opportunities

_____ Setting SMART goals that are specific, measurable, attainable, realistic, and time-bound

_____ Developing plans and implementing strategies to accomplish them

_____ Continually evaluating progress and making adjustments when necessary

_____ Rewarding small wins

APPLICATION QUESTIONS

1. What are your operational goals in important life areas that when achieved will contribute to your personal mission?
   - Career
   - Family

- Education
- Finances
- Religion
- Community
- Others

2. What opportunities and threats does the future hold with respect to achieving your goals described in question 1? How can you keep abreast of developments that may affect your goal achievements?

3. What are your strengths and weaknesses with respect to achieving your goals described in question 1? What can you do to increase your ability to achieve your goals?

4. What were the differences in missions, visions, values, and plans of the last two presidential candidates?

5. How can you ensure that you continually assess your progress toward your goals? What can you do if you discover that you are off course?

REINFORCEMENT EXERCISES

1. On a sheet of paper, draw a large pyramid with five levels. In the bottom level, write out your terminal or end values. They are your foundation for decisions about what goals to pursue. Write your mission statement in the fourth level. In level three, fill in the instrumental values that will guide your behavior in achieving your goals. In level four, write your long-term goals (determined in application question 1). In level five, write your operational goals for the coming year. Carry your pyramid with you and refer to it for guidance whenever you are in doubt about making short-term or daily decisions. Remember that any action you take should be congruent with your values and goals.

2. Apply the SMART formula to goals you wrote down for the first application question. Make sure each goal is specific, measurable, attainable, realistic, and time-bound.

3. Watch an episode of a current TV series. Determine the differences between characters in their goals, values, and planning processes.

4. Watch a movie in which the story is about achieving an important goal. Try to discern the main character's mission, values, and plan. Look for how the main character applied the planning process and reacted to environmental threats and opportunities.

5. Determine a strategic plan for achieving your mission and vision in life. Use Figure 3.1—The Planning Process, as a guide. Your plan should start with (1) a clear mission statement, followed with your (2) vision of what it will be like five years from now if you are successful, (3) a personal SWOT analysis, (4) a gap analysis, (5) a statement of your operational goals, and finally (6) an action plan for achieving your operational goals.

ACTION PLAN

1. In what areas of value clarification, goal setting, and planning do I most need to improve?

2. Why? What will be my payoff?

3. What potential obstacles stand in my way?

4. What are the specific things I will do to enhance my self-awareness? (For examples, see the Reinforcement Exercises.)

5. When will I do them?

6. How and when will I measure my success?

Endnotes

1. Copyright 1994 by National Research Bureau, P.O. Box 1, Burlington, IA 52601-0001. Reprinted by permission.

2. Adapted from R. E. Quinn, S. R. Faerman, M. P. Thompson, and M. R. McGrath, *Becoming a Master Manager* (New York: John Wiley & Sons, 1990), pp. 33–34.

3. Lewis Carroll, *Alice's Adventures in Wonderland* (New York: The Platt & Peck Co., 1900), pp. 62–63.

4. Christopher P. Neck & Charles C. Manz, *Mastering Self-Leadership*, 4th ed. (Upper Saddle River, NJ: Prentice Hall, 2007), p. 5.

5. Phillip L. Hunsaker, *Management: A Skills Approach*, 2nd ed. (Upper Saddle River, NJ: Prentice Hall, 2005), p. 4.

6. Peter G. Northouse, *Leadership Theory and Practice*, 4th ed. (Thousand Oaks, CA: Sage Publications, 2007), p. 3.

7. Bill Brooks, "Self-Management and Character," *The American Salesman*, February 2006, pp. 19–21.

8. Milton Rokeach, *The Nature of Human Values* (New York: Free Press, 1973).

9. Adapted from Stephen R. Covey, *The Seven Habits of Highly Effective People* (New York: Simon & Schuster, 1990), pp. 106–109.

10. Adapted from Stephen R. Covey, *First Things First* (New York: Simon & Schuster, 1995), pp. 318–319.

11. Judith Sills, "How to Become Your Own Boss," *Psychology Today* (September/October 2006), pp. 65–66.

12. Adapted from Sidney B. Simon, Howard Kirschenbaum, and Leland Howe, *Values Clarification, The Handbook*, revised ed. (Sunderland, MA: Values Press, 1991).

13. Adapted from Milton Rokeach, *The Nature of Human Values* (New York: Free Press, 1973).

14. Adapted from Stephen R. Covey, *The Seven Habits of Highly Effective People* (New York: Simon & Schuster, 1990), pp. 96–97.

15. Becker, Thomas E., "Integrity in Organizations: Beyond Honesty and Conscientiousness," *Academy of Management Review*, 23 (January 1998), pp. 154–161; quote, p. 157.

16. Stephen R. Covey, *The Seven Habits of Highly Effective People* (New York: Simon & Schuster, 1990), pp. 106–109.

4

■ ■ ■

Applying Emotional Intelligence

SELF-ASSESSMENT EXERCISE: WHAT'S YOUR EMOTIONAL INTELLIGENCE?[1]

For each of the following items, rate how well you are able to display the ability described. Before responding, try to think of actual situations in which you have had the opportunity to use the ability.

	Low Ability		Moderate Ability		High Ability
1. Associate different internal physiological cues with different emotions.	1	2	3	4	5
2. Relax when under pressure in situations.	1	2	3	4	5
3. Know the impact that your behavior has on others.	1	2	3	4	5
4. Initiate successful resolution of conflict with others.	1	2	3	4	5
5. Calm yourself quickly when angry.	1	2	3	4	5
6. Know when you are becoming angry.	1	2	3	4	5
7. Recognize when others are distressed.	1	2	3	4	5
8. Build consensus with others.	1	2	3	4	5
9. Know what senses you are currently using.	1	2	3	4	5
10. Produce motivation when doing uninteresting work.	1	2	3	4	5
11. Help others manage their emotions.	1	2	3	4	5
12. Make others feel good.	1	2	3	4	5
13. Identify when you experience mood shifts.	1	2	3	4	5
14. Stay calm when you are the target of anger from others.	1	2	3	4	5
15. Show empathy to others.	1	2	3	4	5
16. Provide advice and emotional support to others as needed.	1	2	3	4	5
17. Know when you become defensive.	1	2	3	4	5
18. Follow your words with actions.	1	2	3	4	5
19. Engage in intimate conversations with others.	1	2	3	4	5
20. Accurately reflect people's feelings back to them.	1	2	3	4	5

Scoring

Sum your responses to the 20 questions to obtain your overall emotional intelligence (EI) score. Your score for *self-awareness* is the total of questions 1, 6, 9, 13, and 17. Your score for *self-management* is the total of questions 2, 5, 10, 14, and 18. Your score for *social awareness* is the sum of questions 3, 7, 11, 15, and 19. Your score for *relationship management* is the sum of questions 4, 8, 12, 16, and 20.

Scores and Norms

Component	Your Questions Sum	Score	High	Medium	Low
Overall EI	All	_____	80+	50–80	below 50
Self-awareness	1, 6, 9, 13, 17	_____	20+	10–20	below 10
Self-management	2, 5, 10, 14, 18	_____	20+	10–20	below 10
Social awareness	3, 7, 11, 15, 19	_____	20+	10–20	below 10
Relationship management	4, 8, 12, 16, 20	_____	20+	10–20	below 10

Interpretation

This questionnaire provides an indication of your EI. If you received a total score of 80 or more, you have a high level of EI. A score from 50 to 80 means you have a good platform of EI from which to develop your leadership capability. A score below 50 indicates that you realize that you are probably below average in EI. For each of the four components of EI—self-awareness, self-management, social awareness, and relationship management—a score above 20 is considered high, while a score below 10 would be considered low.

Review the following discussion about the four components of EI and think about what you might do to develop those areas where you scored low. Compare your scores to those of other students. What will you do to improve your scores?

Keep in mind that EI can be learned, so you can strengthen your abilities in any of these four categories with practice. Review your scores in the self-assessment exercise and as you read the following concepts, determine a plan for improving in those areas in which you scored low.

SKILL CONCEPTS

EI is very different from the common intelligence measure intelligence quotient (IQ), which does not have an emotional component. While IQ measures intellectual ability, EI focuses on awareness of self and others, emotional management, and interpersonal skills—which is the focus of this book.

What Is Emotional Intelligence?

EI is "the ability to monitor one's own and others' feelings and emotions, to discriminate among them, and to use this information to guide one's thinking and action."[2] The more people you interact with, the more important high EI becomes. While appropriate technical skills are prerequisites for success in all organizational positions, applying EI skills, such as articulating ideas so others can understand them, developing rapport, building trust, and obtaining consensus, becomes increasingly necessary in higher leadership positions. For example, a leader who leads a project team of diverse people most likely will possess technical knowledge sufficient to complete the tasks. However, it is also very important that the leader is able to understand others, form trust bonds, inspire and motivate, and facilitate others to cope with difficult situations.[3] So, what exactly does EI consist of?

Emotional Competence

EI is scientifically anchored by four cognitive components: (1) the capacity to perceive emotion, (2) to integrate emotion in thought, (3) to understand emotions, and (4) to manage emotions effectively.[4] When these cognitive components are effectively exhibited in interactions with others, a person has ***emotional competence***, which includes self-awareness, impulse control, persistence, confidence, self-motivation, empathy, social deftness, trustworthiness, adaptability, and the ability to work collaboratively.[5]

Self and Other Dimensions of EI

Daniel Goleman and others have categorized the components of EI into two areas of concern, each with an awareness and application dimension. The first concern is yourself: your degree of emotional self-awareness and your degree of self-management of your emotions. The second concern is others: your degree of empathy or awareness of others' emotions, and your ability to productively manage relationships with others.[6] The competencies and abilities making up each of these four fundamental skills of EI are summarized in Exhibit 4.1.

SELF-AWARENESS   Self-awareness is the ability to recognize and understand your own emotions and how they affect your life and work. It is considered the basis of all the other competencies. If you are self-aware, you are conscious of the feelings and emotions within yourself. People who are in touch with their emotions are better able to guide their own lives. We need to be in touch with our emotions in order to interact effectively and appreciate emotions in others.

Self-Awareness	**Social Awareness**
• Emotional self-awareness • Accurate self-assessment • Self-confidence	• Empathy • Organizational awareness • Service orientation
Self-Management	**Relationship Management**
• Emotional self-control • Trustworthiness • Conscientiousness • Adaptability • Optimism • Achievement-orientation • Initiative	• Development of others • Inspirational leadership • Influence • Communication • Change catalyst • Conflict management • Bond building • Teamwork and collaboration

EXHIBIT 4.1   The Four Components of Emotional Intelligence.

People with high levels of self-awareness recognize their "gut feelings" and realize that these feelings can provide useful information about difficult decisions. Self-awareness allows us to assess our own strengths and limitations with a healthy sense of self-confidence.

SELF-MANAGEMENT   Self-management is the ability to understand your feelings and to use this understanding to effectively deal with emotional situations. This does not mean suppressing or denying emotions, but using them to deal with situations productively, for example, controlling your moods so that worry, anxiety, fear, or anger do not get in the way of thinking clearly about what needs to be done.[7] To do this, you need to recognize a mood or feeling, think about what it means and how it affects you, and then decide the most effective way to act.

SOCIAL AWARENESS   Social awareness is the ability to understand and empathize with others. Socially aware people are empathic: they have the ability to put themselves in someone else's shoes, sense their emotions, and understand their perspective. People with high social awareness are capable of understanding divergent points of view and interacting effectively with many different types of people and emotions. This characteristic makes it easier for them to get along in organizational life, build networks, and use political behavior to accomplish positive results.

RELATIONSHIP MANAGEMENT   Relationship management is the ability to connect with others in ways that build positive relationships. Good relationship managers treat others with compassion, sensitivity, and kindness. They use their understanding of emotions to inspire change and lead people toward something better, to build teamwork and collaboration, and to resolve conflicts as they arise.

What Research Tells Us about EI

Research on EI is ongoing and has had an unusually important impact on managerial practice.[8] Some studies have found that in today's business world, EI may override sheer intellectual ability as the primary component of success for many leaders.[9] Leaders who are attuned to their own feelings and the feelings of others use this understanding to enhance personal, team, and organizational performance.[10] Based on these findings, several organizations have incorporated EI into their employee development programs,[11] and some business schools have added the training of emotional competencies to their curriculums.[12]

Research on EI and job performance—defined as the degree to which an individual helps the organization reach its goals[13]—is mixed. Some studies suggest that EI and job performance are positively related. EI makes a positive difference in sales performance and supervisory ratings of job performance, for example.[14] Other studies have found inconsistent relationships between EI and performance on particular tasks, such as academic performance and supervisory ratings of job performance and team performance.[15] These variations across studies have led some researchers to suggest that moderating variables exist between EI and workplace performance.[16] For example, an individual who is low on an ability that is related to performance can compensate for that weakness by being high on a different ability that is also related to performance[17] and some individual difference characteristics may compensate for low cognitive intelligence.[18]

A United States Department of Labor study of the characteristics corporations are seeking in MBA candidates revealed that the three most desirable traits are components of EI: communication skills, interpersonal skills, and initiative.[19] Research has found that although standard measures of cognitive IQ and technical competence are important entry-level requirements for executive positions, individuals who distinguish themselves as leaders tend to be substantially higher in EI than lower level managers.[20] The most effective leaders are more aware of their own emotions, exhibit self-confidence, regulate emotional impulses, empathize emotionally with others, and apply a wider range of social influence tactics than nonleaders.[21]

So what's the bottom line? It is commonly believed that organizations that attract and retain the smartest people will have a competitive advantage because cognitive intelligence helps workers to process large amounts of increasingly technical information.[22] Current research, however, suggests that EI compensates for low cognitive intelligence. Consequently, organizations can also be successful if they attract and retain people who have high EI.[23]

What Can You Do To Apply EI?

EI has been validated with about 25 major skill areas, many of which are covered in this book, that can improve your worth at work and enhance your career. These EI skills can count for far more than regular IQ when it comes to being a "star performer" at just about any job and for reaching the top of any career ladder. Successful people use their EI to manage feelings both appropriately and effectively to achieve the common good and goals of the work group. The key EI skills that affect all aspects of work include accurate self-assessment, self-confidence, self-control, conscientiousness, adaptability, innovation, commitment, initiative, political awareness, optimism, understanding others, conflict management skills, team capabilities, communication, and the ability to initiate or manage change (Exhibit 4.2).[24]

In general, coworkers seem to appreciate managers' abilities to control their impulses and anger, to withstand adverse events and stressful situations, to be happy with life, and to be a cooperative member of the group. Leaders who possess these characteristics are more likely to be seen as participative, self-aware, composed, and balanced. The Center for Creative Leadership has determined that the key behavioral skills leaders need to apply EI effectively include the following:[25]

BE SELF-AWARE AND ACT CONGRUENTLY   The most respected leaders are those who accurately understand their strengths and weaknesses, are aware of their feelings, and have control of their impulses. If you get anxious in difficult and challenging situations or explode into anger easily, but deny feeling these ways, it is likely that others will interpret this as a lack of self-awareness.

- Participative management
- Putting people at ease
- Self-awareness
- Balance between personal life and work
- Straightforwardness and composure
- Building and mending relationships
- Doing whatever it takes
- Decisiveness
- Confronting problem people
- Change management

EXHIBIT 4.2   Areas Where Higher Emotional Intelligence Causes Better Performance.

Source: Ruderman, M.N., Hannum, K., Leslie, J.B., & Steed, J.L. (2001). *Leadership Skills and Emotional Intelligence,* Research Synopsis Number 1, Unpublished manuscript (Greensboro, NC: Center for Creative Leadership, 2001).

SHARE YOUR FEELINGS IN A STRAIGHTFORWARD AND COMPOSED MANNER   Remaining calm in a crisis and recovering from mistakes is related to high degrees of perceived impulse control, stress tolerance, optimism, and social responsibility. Straightforwardness and composure have to do with controlling your impulses during difficult times, being responsible toward others, and maintaining an optimistic disposition.

TREAT OTHERS WITH COMPASSION, SENSITIVITY, AND KINDNESS   If you enable people you interact with to be relaxed and comfortable in your presence, they will probably perceive you as being able to control your own impulses and having empathy toward others. This will generate more trust and openness in your relationships.

ALTERING YOUR ACTIONS BASED ON THE POTENTIAL REACTIONS OF OTHERS   Emotionally intelligent people make conscious choices on how and when to say or do something because of the reaction that it may cause.[26] This first step of this EI skill is being sensitive to and assessing how your actions cause emotional reactions in others. Those reactions may be different for each person involved. It is important to be able to predict reactions so that you can alter your forthcoming actions if you think it is appropriate before getting an undesirable reaction.

BE OPEN TO THE OPINIONS AND IDEAS OF OTHERS   Getting buy-in at the beginning of an initiative is an extremely important relationship-building skill in today's management climate in which organizations value interdependency within and between groups. Managers who are seen as good at listening to others and gaining their input before implementing change are likely to be assessed as cooperative, caring, in control of their impulses, and understanding their own and others' emotions. So practice participative management.

BUILD AND MEND RELATIONSHIPS   If you practice the four skills just described, you probably have the ability to develop and maintain productive working relationships with most other people. On the other hand, difficulties handling stress or inability to control hostility and explosive behavior obviously will not translate into strong relationships.

DO WHAT IT TAKES TO BRING ABOUT NECESSARY CHANGES   Doing whatever it takes to bring about necessary change requires the assertiveness to go after what you want, standing alone when necessary, persevering in the face of obstacles, and being optimistic about future outcomes. Assertiveness has to do with letting others know what you want and expressing your feelings, thoughts, and beliefs in a nondestructive manner. Success depends to a large degree on the effectiveness of the strategies used to facilitate change initiatives in socially responsible ways. The ability to establish satisfying relationships with those who must implement the change through the application of the EI skills discussed above establishes a perception that you are a cooperative member of the team and is associated with effectiveness in introducing change. Optimism helps the change targets look at the brighter side of the change.

DECISIVELY CONFRONT PROBLEM EMPLOYEES   High EI managers act decisively, but fairly, when dealing with problem employees. They are assertive when expressing their beliefs and feelings, but do so in a nondestructive manner. Decisiveness is manifest in quick and specific actions when problems arise, versus putting off dealing with problem employees for as long as possible and then tiptoeing around the problems with ambiguous and nondirect solutions.

MAINTAINING A BALANCE BETWEEN PERSONAL LIFE AND WORK   The degree to which work and personal life activities are prioritized so that neither is neglected is associated with the EI measures of social responsibility, impulse control, and empathy. Giving others the impression that you are balanced is also connected with perceptions of being able to contribute to a group, controlling your impulses, and understanding the emotions of others.

CONCEPT QUIZ

Answer the 10 questions in the following true–false quiz. The correct answers are listed at the end of the quiz. If you get any answers wrong, reread the chapter to find the correct answer.

Circle the right answer.

True	**False**	1.	EI can be learned.
True	**False**	2.	Intelligence quotient (IQ) has an emotional component.
True	**False**	3.	Leaders tend to be higher in EI than lower level managers.
True	**False**	4.	Self-awareness is recognizing and understanding your own emotions.
True	**False**	5.	"Gut feelings" can provide useful information about difficult decisions.
True	**False**	6.	Self-management is the ability to suppress or deny your emotions.
True	**False**	7.	Socially aware people are empathic.
True	**False**	8.	People with high social awareness are more capable of understanding divergent points of view.
True	**False**	9.	Relationship management is the ability to connect with others in ways that build positive relationships.
True	**False**	10.	Emotional intelligence can compensate for low cognitive intelligence.

Answers: (1) True; (2) False; (3) True; (4) True; (5) True; (6) False; (7) True; (8) True; (9) True; (10) True.

BEHAVIORAL CHECKLIST

The following behaviors are important for applying EI at work. Some of these are skills covered in more detail in other chapters of this book. Use them when evaluating your own application of EI and when giving feedback to others.

Applying Emotional Intelligence at Work Requires:

- Sharing your feelings in a straightforward and composed manner
- Being true to yourself—acting congruently with your needs
- Treating others with compassion, sensitivity, and kindness
- Altering your actions based on the reactions of others
- Being open to the opinions and ideas of others
- Building and mending relationships
- Doing what it takes to bring about necessary changes
- Constructively confronting problem people

MODELING EXERCISE

Changes in Company Travel Policy[27]

Assign six students to play one of the roles from the following roster. Role-players should read the description of the situation and their assigned role. They should not read the roles for the other actors.

The rest of the class members will be observers. They should read the description of the situation and all of the roles. They should also review the Observer's Rating Sheet at the end of this exercise to rate the EI skills of the actor playing Fran Meltzer.

Actors.   Fran Meltzer, section head of the design engineering group. Lee Clark, senior design engineer, 21 years with the company, has two technicians. Chris Manos, senior design engineer, 16 years with the company, has one technician. B. J. Pelter, senior design engineer, 15 years with the company, has two technicians. Pat Rosen, design engineer, 8 years with the company, has one technician. Sandy Solas, design engineer, 3 years with the company, has one technician.

Situation.   Five electronics engineers design new products for the Alta Electronics Company, a medium-sized firm that manufactures a variety of electronics products. The engineers work individually on projects, aided by technicians and, when needed, drafters. The engineers in the design group are all proud of the products they have designed because of the technical developments they incorporate and their reliable performance. Fran Meltzer is in charge of the group and has called a meeting to discuss some changes in the company travel policy.

For the last several years, the company has been experiencing financial difficulties. These problems have not resulted in layoffs, but wage increases have been severely restricted and an absolute freeze has been placed on building alterations, travel to professional meetings, magazine subscriptions, and similar expenditures. Most of these have been of a minor nature, but some (such as not attending professional meetings) have made it difficult for you and other engineers to keep abreast of technical developments and to maintain your professional contacts. Recently, you have heard that the company has begun to see a modest economic upturn.

Company policy dictates that engineers are responsible for a project not only through the design phase but also through production startup to the point where acceptable products are being produced regularly. On many projects the amount of time spent on handling problems in production is minor. On others, especially those with particularly difficult standards, the time spent in handling production problems can be considerable.

Fran Meltzer's Role.   You are the section head of the design engineering group and have reporting to you a competent group of engineers who individually handle design products. Because of financial difficulties, the company has not allocated funds to send engineers to professional meetings for the last several years. You have just heard from your superior that enough money has been appropriated to send one engineer from each group to the national meetings of your professional society next month. He also stated that the vice president of engineering thought it would be best if the limited travel funds were allocated to engineers rather than to managerial personnel, which includes section heads such as yourself.

You are sure that all of your engineers will want to go and know that hurt feelings and resentment could develop over this matter unless it is handled properly. Therefore, you have decided that rather than make the decision yourself, you will call a meeting of your group, turn the matter over to them, and let them make the decision. You will tell them of the funds available for travel and that you want them to make the decision of who will go in the way they believe is most fair. Your superior also has reminded you that these funds can be used only to send someone to the professional meetings. Do not take a position yourself as to who should be selected to go to the meetings. Use your EI skills to obtain the most satisfactory outcome for all involved.

Sandy Solas's Role.   You feel like the low person on the totem pole in this group. A lot of your equipment is old and frequently breaks down. You don't think Fran has been particularly concerned about the inconvenience this has caused you. Furthermore, ever since you graduated from college, you have not been able to attend a professional meeting because of the freeze the company has had on travel of this sort. You feel that this has kept you from making the contacts you need to develop professionally. You hope that the recent upturn in the company's business will finally make some money available to go to professional meetings.

Chris Manos's Role.   You have been feeling a strong need to get to some professional meetings. Through no fault of your own, you missed attending meetings for several years before the freeze on travel was imposed. For 2 years, crash projects kept you tied to the plant. The year before that, your daughter had gotten married. This has been an unplanned chain of events, but one that has kept you from building new professional contacts or even maintaining old ones. As a result, you feel you are losing your professional edge and contacts.

Pat Rosen's Role.   Lately, you have been overwhelmed with making numerous lengthy tests on some new equipment you have designed. The work has completely swamped your technician, and you have had to work along with him to keep the job moving. Even with your effort, however, it looks as if you might be on this for a long time. You would like very much to get to the professional meetings next month to see the new testing equipment that will be on display in the hope that some manufacturer might have come out with an item that would ease your testing problem. You are thinking seriously of making a strong pitch for this to Fran even though you know that no money has been available for such trips for the last several years. Additional technician help would be an alternative, but you doubt there is any possibility of hiring a new technician.

B. J. Pelter's Role.   The line of work you are now in is taking you in exciting new directions, not only for yourself and the company, but also for your professional area. You feel a real need to talk to other engineers who are doing similar work to confirm what you have been doing and also to get ideas on some problems you have been facing. You know that several will be giving papers on topics in the new area at the professional meeting next month. Fortunately, you recently finished debugging the production problems on the last product you designed and now have more time to travel.

Lee Clark's Role.   If funds become available for sending people to professional meetings but not enough to send everyone, you feel that you should be the person to go because you have the most seniority. You feel strongly that in professional work, seniority should count. In addition, you have a wide array of contacts developed over the years through which you can pick up much information that would be useful to the company.

Total Time. 25 minutes (preparation, 5 minutes; role-play, 10 minutes; debriefing, 10 minutes)

OBSERVER'S RATING SHEET

Evaluate the EI skills of Fran Meltzer on a 1 to 5 scale (5 being the highest). Use the spaces between checklist behaviors to make comments to explain your ratings when providing feedback.

Acted congruently with own needs   _____

Shared personal feelings in a straightforward and composed manner   _____

Treated others with compassion, sensitivity, and kindness   _____

Altered actions based on reactions of others   _____

Was open to the opinions and ideas of others   _____

Built and mended relationships   _____

Did what was necessary to bring about change   _____

Constructively confronted problem people   _____

GROUP EXERCISES

The first group exercise is designed to stretch your sensitivity to others' reactions to your actions. The second is a comparison of your EI strengths and weaknesses as perceived by yourself and others. The third is a case discussion that demonstrated the consequences of low EI.

Group Exercise 1: Action/Reaction[28]

Every action you take or don't take sends a message. The purpose of this exercise is to stretch your sensitivity to others' reactions to your actions. It is important to be able to predict reactions because you can alter your actions if you think it is appropriate before getting an undesirable reaction. This exercise will sensitize you to the wide range of reactions that one simple action can cause. The intent isn't to determine if the action is appropriate or inappropriate but to realize that many interpretations of the same action may exist depending on who is interpreting.

Objectives

- To realize the impact of actions on others
- To recognize the need for assessing the emotional impact of actions before taking them
- To understand how actions can create an emotionally positive environment

Directions

Complete the following worksheet by reflecting on recent memos, e-mails, or verbal communications that you have initiated. For each of your actions, imagine the many possible reactions that others might have to them. Try to be very creative in your answers. Have fun and stretch your imagination with this exercise.

Individually. Recall the last 10 memos, e-mails, phone calls, or verbal instructions that you have sent to your employees, teammates, or friends. In the left-hand column write the intent of each message. In the right-hand column write down some possible interpretations the receivers could have made that would be different from your intention. Be empathetic and think about how the messages might have made the receivers feel. Several examples to a safety reminder message are provided in the first row below.

Form Groups of Three. One at a time, share your messages, intentions, and possible interpretations. After a person has shared an entry, other group members add their ideas for possible misinterpretations and resulting feelings. Then another person shares an entry and group members again share their ideas for how the receiver might react. Continue around the group until all members have shared and heard other group members' interpretations of their messages.

Debrief

As a class, answer and discuss the following questions:

a. Why is it important to give forethought to reactions to your actions?
b. What impact could this practice have on creating a desired work culture?
c. What responsibility do you have to anticipate reactions?

Time: 45 minutes total. (Instructions, 5 minutes; individual answers, 10 minutes; group sharing, 20 minutes; debriefing, 10 minutes.)

Action/Reaction Worksheet	
Message and Intent	*Possible Misinterpretations and Feelings*
I sent an e-mail to remind John, copied to all of his work team, about wearing goggles for safety compliance. My intent was to make it easier for John to protect himself from danger when his work group thinks safety precautions are for weaklings.	I don't think John is strong enough to resist the group norm on his own. Feelings—anger, gratitude, etc.
	I don't think John is smart enough to take care of himself. Feelings—anger, resentment, etc.
	I think safety is important for everyone and all need to comply. Feelings—trust, gratitude, hostility, etc.
	I think John is in the early stages of Alzheimer's and can't remember. Feelings—anger, resentment, etc.
	I'm being helpful and care about others. Feelings—trust

Group Exercise 2: Thinking It Through and Talking It Over[29]

Daniel Goleman offers 12 questions to ask yourself to see if you work with EI. If you answer "yes" to half or more, and if other people who know you agree with your self-rating, then you are doing okay with your EI. Answer the following questions to see where you score on EI.

1. Do you understand both your strengths and weaknesses?
2. Can you be depended on to take care of every detail? Do you hate to let things slide?
3. Are you comfortable with change and open to novel ideas?
4. Are you motivated by the satisfaction of meeting your own standards of excellence?
5. Do you stay optimistic when things go wrong?
6. Do you see things from another person's point of view and sense what matters most to that person?
7. Do you let customers' needs determine how you serve them?
8. Do you enjoy helping coworkers develop their skills?
9. Do you read office politics accurately?
10. Are you able to find "win–win" solutions in negotiations and conflicts?
11. Are you the kind of person other people want on a team? Do you enjoy collaborating with others?
12. Are you usually persuasive?

Scoring and Interpretation

Add up the number of questions to which you could answer yes. How did you score? Answering yes to six or more of the EI skill items indicates that you are working well and with maturity in the workplace. Do you have more than five questions to which you answered no?

Form groups of three or four people who know you well. One at a time share your answers and receive feedback whether the others agree with your high number of negative scores. If so, what suggestions do they have to help you change and improve your EI scores?

Total Time. 30 minutes. (Ten minutes for answering the 12 EI questions; 20 minutes for group members to share feedback and suggestions about your areas needing improvement.)

Group Exercise 3: Head versus Heart[30]

Read the following case. Then form groups and answer the questions following the case.

Head versus Heart Case

Stuart is a senior manager at a well-known pharmaceutical company. He is brilliant, and everyone who knows him believes he has the potential to achieve great things. His primary strength is strategic thinking; colleagues say he has an uncanny ability to predict and plan for the future.

As Stuart has advanced in the organization, however, his dark side has become increasingly apparent: He often lashes out at people, and he is unable to build relationships based on trust. Stuart knows he is intelligent and tends to use that knowledge to belittle or demean his coworkers. Realizing that Stuart has extraordinary skills and much to offer the company in terms of vision and strategy, some of his colleagues have tried to help him work past his flaws. But they're beginning to conclude that it's a hopeless cause; Stuart stubbornly refuses to change his style, and his arrogant modus operandi has offended so many people that Stuart's career may no longer be salvageable.

Every company probably has someone like Stuart—a senior manager whose IQ approaches the genius level but who seems clueless when it comes to dealing with other people. These types of managers may be prone to getting angry easily and verbally attacking coworkers, often come across as lacking compassion and empathy, and usually find it difficult to get others to cooperate with them and their agendas. The Stuarts of the world make you wonder how people so smart can be so incapable of understanding themselves and others.

Questions for Group Discussion

1. Using the Behavioral Checklist, what is Stuart lacking in EI?
2. Is there any hope of salvaging Stuart's career? What are the alternatives?
3. Can his EI be developed and enhanced?

Time: 20 minutes total. (Five minutes to read the case; 15 minutes for groups to answer and discuss the questions.)

Summary Checklist

Take a few minutes to reflect on your performance in the exercises you just completed and on the feedback you have received from other team members about your EI skills. Make a check (✓) next to those behaviors you want to improve.

_____ Acting congruently with your needs

_____ Sharing your feelings in a straightforward and composed manner

_____ Treating others with compassion, sensitivity, and kindness

_____ Altering your actions based on the reactions of others

_____ Being open to the opinions and ideas of others

_____ Building and mending relationships

_____ Doing what it takes to bring about necessary changes

_____ Constructively confronting problem people

APPLICATION QUESTIONS

1. Given that EI starts with self-awareness, how likely is someone with a low EI to be able to judge the level of their own EI or someone else's?
2. If men test (on average) significantly lower than women in Social Responsibility, but significantly higher than women in Stress Tolerance, how can you motivate a team consisting of both men and women to accept a volunteer project to help the community?
3. If the first rule of cross-cultural communication is to assume you've been misunderstood (see Chapter 7), what's a good way to give instructions to a subordinate?
4. If maintaining self-control is a developmental area for you, what can you do to improve in the EI area?
5. If having empathy for others is a developmental area for you, what can you do to improve in the EI area?

REINFORCEMENT EXERCISES

1. Self-awareness can be developed through the practice of seeking ongoing feedback. Ask supervisors, coworkers, and friends who know you well for honest feedback on how your behavior is impacting them. Use opportunities to self-reflect upon adversity, such as relationship failures, unchallenging jobs, and personal traumas.
2. The ability to demonstrate yourself as a cooperative, contributing, and constructive member of the group is critical for long-term career success. Involve yourself in a new and inexperienced work or class team that is resisting an assignment. Think about what you can do to contribute positively to group and organizational goals. Then act on your thoughts to see if you can make a contribution.
3. If you become aware of something that you are doing that produces negative consequences, such as an annoying bad habit, start self-monitoring yourself for this behavior. Determine a better alternative behavior that will help you perform positively. Writing down on a piece of paper each time you misbehave or misspeak can make you focus on changing behavior to a more positive alternative.
4. Another powerful aid to developing those EI skill areas that you want to reinforce is to make a commitment to another person, who in turn will put pressure on you when you don't comply with the area in need of improvement.

ACTION PLAN

1. In what areas of applying EI do I most need to improve?

2. Why? What will be my payoff?

3. What potential obstacles stand in my way?

4. What are the specific things I will do to enhance my EI? (For examples, see the Reinforcement Exercises.)

5. When will I do them?

6. How and when will I measure my success?

Endnotes

1. Adapted from Hendrie Weisinger, *Emotional Intelligence at Work* (San Francisco, CA: Jossey-Bass, 1998), pp. 214–215.
2. P. Salovey and J. D. Mayer, "Emotional Intelligence," *Imagination, Cognition, and Personality*, Vol. 9 (1990), p. 189.
3. This discussion is based on B. Murray, "Does Emotional Intelligence Matter in the Workplace?" *APA Monitor* (July 1998), p. 21; A. Fisher, "Success Secret: A High Emotional IQ," *Fortune* (October 26, 1998), pp. 293–298; D. Coleman, *Working with Emotional Intelligence* (New York: Bantam Books, 1998); R. E. Boyatzis and D. Goleman, *The Emotional Competence Inventory—University Edition* (Boston, MA: The Hay Group, 2001); and D. Goleman, "Leadership That Gets Results," *Harvard Business Review* (March–April 2000), pp. 79–90.
4. P. Salovey and J. D. Mayer, "Emotional Intelligence," *Imagination, Cognition, and Personality*, Vol. 9 (1990), pp. 185–211.
5. Anne Fisher, "Success Secret: A High Emotional IQ," *Fortune* (October 26, 1998), pp. 293–298.
6. See, for example, R. E. Boyatzis and D. Goleman, *The Emotional Competence Inventory—University Edition* (Boston, MA: The Hay Group, 2001); D. Goleman, *Emotional Intelligence* (New York: Bantam Books, 1995); and D. Goleman, "Leadership That Gets Results," *Harvard Business Review* (March–April 2000), pp. 79–90.
7. H. Weisinger, *Emotional Intelligence at Work* (San Francisco, CA: Jossey-Bass, 1998), pp. 214–215.
8. N. Ashkanasy and C. S. Daus, "Emotion in the Workplace: The New Challenge for Managers," *Academy of Management Executive*, Vol. 16, No. 1 (2002), pp. 76–86.
9. J. D. Mayer, P. Salovey, and D. R. Caruso, "Emotional Intelligence as Zeitgeist, as Personality, and as a Mental Ability," in R. Bar-On and J. D. A. Parker (eds.), *The Handbook of Emotional Intelligence* (San Francisco, CA: Jossey-Bass, 2000), pp. 92–117.

10. D. Goleman, R. Boyatzis, and A. McKee, *Primal Leadership: Realizing the Power of Emotional Intelligence* (Boston, MA: Harvard Business School, 2002), pp. 12–18.

11. "How Do You Feel?" *Fast Company*, Vol. 35 (2000), p. 296.

12. R. E. Boyatzis, E. C. Stubbs, and S. N. Taylor, "Learning Cognitive and Emotional Intelligence Competencies through Graduate Management Education," *Academy of Management Learning and Education,* Vol. 1 (2002), pp. 150–162.

13. S. J. Motowidlo, W. C. Borman, and M. J. Schmit, "A Theory of Individual Differences in Task and Contextual Performance," *Human Performance*, Vol. 10 (1997), pp. 71–83.

14. See, for example, L. T. Lam and S. L. Kirby, "Is Emotional Intelligence an Advantage?: An Exploration of the Impact of Emotional and General Intelligence on Individual Performance," *Journal of Social Psychology*, Vol. 142 (2002), pp. 133–143; C. Sue-Chan and G. P. Latham, "The Situational Interview as a Predictor of Academic and Team Performance: A Study of the Mediating Effects of Cognitive Ability and Emotional Intelligence," *International Journal of Selection and Assessment,* Vol. 12 (2004), pp. 312–320; J. Bachman, S. Stein, K. Campbell, and G. Sitarenios, "Emotional Intelligence in the Collection of Debt," *International Journal of Selection and Assessment,*" Vol. 8 (2000), pp. 176–182; M. Slaski and S. Cartwright, "Health, Performance and Emotional Intelligence: An Exploratory Study of Retail Managers," *Stress and Health*, Vol. 16 (2002), pp. 63–68.

15. E. J. Austin, "An Investigation of the Relationship between Trait Emotional Intelligence and Emotional Task Performance," *Personality and Individual Differences*, Vol. 36 (2004), pp. 1855–1864; A. L. Day and S. A. Carroll, "Using an Ability-Based Measure of Emotional Intelligence to Predict Individual Performance, Group Performance, and Group Citizenship Behaviors," *Personality and Individual Differences,* Vol. 36 (2004), pp. 1443–1458; K. V. Petrides, N. Frederickson, and A. Furnham, "The Role of Trait Emotional Intelligence in Academic Performance and Deviant Behavior at School," *Personality and Individual Differences,* Vol. 36 (2004), pp. 277–293; A. E. Feyerherm and C. L. Rice, "Emotional Intelligence and Team Performance: The Good, the Bad, and the Ugly," *International*

Journal of Organizational Analysis, Vol. 10 (2002), pp. 343–362.

16. D. L. Van Rooy and C. Viswesvaran, "Emotional Intelligence: A Meta-Analytic Investigation of Predictive Validity and Nomological Net," *Journal of Vocational Behavior*, Vol. 65 (2004), pp. 71–95.

17. J. B. Carroll, *Human Cognitive Abilities: A Survey of Factor-Analytic Studies* (New York: Cambridge University Press, 1993).

18. C. Viswesvaran and D. S. Ones, "Agreements and Disagreements on the Role of General Mental Ability (GMA) in Industrial, Work, and Organizational Psychology," *Human Performance*, Vol. 15 (2002), pp. 212–231.

19. Edward Chan, "Cultivating Emotional Intelligence," *The New Straits Times Press* (January 30, 1999).

20. Donald E. Gibson, "Emotional Episodes At Work: An Experiential Exercise in Feeling and Expressing Emotions," *Journal of Management Education*, Vol. 30, No. 3 (June 2006), pp. 477–500.

21. The following researchers and others have provided compelling evidence for the notion that EI is important for organizational leaders and managers: Mayer and Salovey, 1995; D. Goleman, *Working with Emotional Intelligence* (New York: Bantam, 1998); D. Goleman, "Leadership That Gets Results," *Harvard Business Review*, Vol. 78, No. 2 (2000), pp. 78–90; D. Goleman, R. Boyatzis, and A. McKee, *Primal Leadership: Realizing the Power of Emotional Intelligence* (Boston, MA: Harvard Business School, 2002), pp. 12–18.

22. E. Michaels, H. Handfield-Jones, and B. Axelrod, *The War for Talent* (Boston, MA: Harvard Business School Press, 2001).

23. Stéphane Côté and Christopher T. H. Miners, "Emotional Intelligence, Cognitive Intelligence, and Job Performance," *Administrative Science Quarterly*, Vol. 51, Issue 1 (March 2006), pp. 1–28.

24. Daniel Goleman, "Working Smart," *USA Weekend* (October 2–4, 1998), pp. 4–5.

25. M. N. Ruderman, K. Hannum, J. B. Leslie, and J. L. Steed, (2001). *Leadership Skills and Emotional Intelligence,* Research Synopsis Number 1, Unpublished manuscript (Greensboro, NC: Center for Creative Leadership, 2001).

26. Adele B. Lynn, "Emotional Intelligence Quotient 23: Action/Reaction," *The Emotional Intelligence Activity Book: 50 Activities for Promoting EQ at Work* (New York: AMACOM/HRD Press, 2002).

27. Adapted from Roy J. Lewicki and Joseph A. Litterer, *Negotiation: Readings, Exercises, and Cases* (Homewood, IL: Richard D. Irwin, 1985), pp. 423–425, 565, 568, 572, 606, 627.

28. This exercise is adapted from Adele B. Lynn, "Emotional Intelligence Quotient 23: Action/Reaction," *The Emotional Intelligence Activity Book: 50 Activities for Promoting EQ at Work* (New York: AMACOM/HRD Press, 2002).

29. This exercise is adapted from Daniel Goleman, "Working Smart," *USA Weekend* (October 2–4, 1998), pp. 4–5.

30. Marian N. Ruderman, Kelly Hannum, Jean Brittain Leslie, and Judith L. Steed, "Making the Connection: Leadership Skills and Emotional Intelligence," *Leadership in Action*, Vol. 21, No. 5 (Hoboken, NJ: Wiley, November/December 2001), p. 3. Accessed October 1, 2007, via media.wiley.com/assets/51/46/jrnls_jb_lia_21_5_ruderman.pdf.

5

■ ■ ■

Sending Interpersonal Messages

SELF-ASSESSMENT EXERCISE: WHAT ARE MY MESSAGE-SENDING HABITS?

For each of the following questions, select the answer that best describes your message-sending habits:

> When sending messages to other people, I:

	Usually	Sometimes	Seldom
1. Use technical language or lingo for efficiency.	_____	_____	_____
2. Make sure my messages are congruent with my actions.	_____	_____	_____
3. Don't waste time providing background information and details.	_____	_____	_____
4. Use personal pronouns such as *I* and *my* when expressing feelings.	_____	_____	_____
5. Own up to my motives at the very beginning of a conversation.	_____	_____	_____
6. Avoid being warm and friendly so that people take me seriously.	_____	_____	_____
7. Don't use multiple channels of communication to avoid confusion.	_____	_____	_____
8. Ask the receivers to restate their understanding of my message.	_____	_____	_____
9. Am honest despite how complicated or personal a situation is.	_____	_____	_____
10. Avoid looking dumb by pretending to know what I am talking about even when I don't.	_____	_____	_____

Scoring and Interpretation

For questions 2, 4, 5, 8, and 9, give yourself 3 points for Usually, 2 points for Sometimes, and 1 point for Seldom. For questions 1, 3, 6, 7, and 10, reverse the scale.

Sum up your total points. Scores of 26 or higher demonstrate a strong understanding of message-sending techniques. A score of 21–25 indicates that you can improve your message-sending skills. Scores of 20 or less suggest that you have significant room for improvement.

SKILL CONCEPTS

Communication is the basis for all human interaction, and interpersonal relationships cannot exist without it. It is through communication that members in relationships interact to exchange information and transmit meaning. All cooperative action is contingent upon effective communication. Managers and subordinates, team members, and friends depend on communication to understand each other, build trust, coordinate their actions, plan strategies for goal accomplishment, agree on a division of labor, and conduct group activities.[1]

How Do People Communicate?

Interpersonal communication includes much more than just exchanging words. All behavior conveys some message and is a form of communication when it is perceived by others. Because two people who are interacting with each other have a continuous effect on each other's perceptions and expectations of what the other is going to do, interpersonal communication can be defined broadly as any verbal or nonverbal behavior that is perceived by another person.[2] Figure 5.1 depicts the interpersonal communication process.[3]

The main components of this model are the sender, the receiver, the message, and the channel. First, the message is encoded by the sender into a format that will get the idea across to the receiver. Then it is transmitted through various channels orally (e.g., speeches, meetings, phone calls, or informal discussions), nonverbally (e.g., touch, facial expression, and tone of voice), in writing (e.g., letters or memoranda), or electronically (e.g., e-mail, voicemail, or fax). These are the sending functions and the skills required to send messages effectively, which are described in this chapter.

No matter how effectively a message is encoded and transmitted, communication will not be effective if the receivers fail to perceive and understand the sender's message. Decoding is the receiver function of perceiving the communication and interpreting its meaning. Listening, the topic of Chapter 6, is often more than half the equation.

Noise is anything that interferes, at any stage, with the communications process. The success of the communications process depends to a large degree on overcoming various sources of noise. Feedback is the primary tool for determining how clearly a message was understood and what effect it had on the receiver. This chapter contains ideas for providing effective feedback to others.

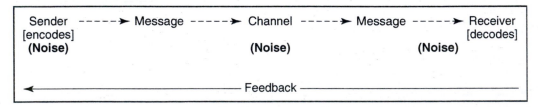

FIGURE 5.1 The Communication Process.

Effective communication occurs only when noise is avoided, the sender transmits ideas and feelings completely and accurately, and the receiver interprets the message exactly as the sender intended. In this chapter, we are concerned with senders transmitting messages to receivers with the conscious intent of affecting the receivers' behavior. This includes all sender behaviors, verbal or nonverbal, that are consciously evoked to obtain responses from others. For example, a person sends the message "How are you?" to evoke the response "Fine," or a teacher shakes her head to get two students to stop talking.

What Skills Are Required to Send Messages Effectively?

Consistently effective communication requires considerable skill in sending and receiving information. Research has determined that better transmission of messages can be achieved by increasing the clarity of messages, developing credibility, and soliciting feedback.[4]

SKILLS FOR INCREASING CLARITY OF MESSAGES   A sender should take the initiative in eliminating communication barriers by making sure a message is clear and understandable to the receiver. A number of things can be done to accomplish this goal.[5]

1. *Use multiple channels.*   The probability of a message being understood accurately can be increased by transmitting it in several different ways. Examples include matching a verbal message with facial and body gestures or diagramming it on a piece of paper. This kind of multiple-mode communication of the same message ensures that the receiver has the opportunity to receive the message through more than one sense. A manager speaking about the need to increase quality of production, for example, could convey the urgency of the message through the multiple channels of words, voice tones, facial expressions, gestures, pictures, postures, and audiovisual presentations.

2. *Be complete and specific.*   When the subject matter of a message is new or unfamiliar to the receiver, the sender can make the message complete and specific by providing sufficient background information and details. Once receivers understand the sender's frame of reference, they are more likely to interpret the message accurately. By referring to concrete deadlines and examples, a sender can decrease the probability of misinterpretation.

3. *Take responsibility.*   Senders should take responsibility for the feelings and evaluations in their messages by using personal pronouns such as *I* and *mine*. General statements such as "Everyone feels this way" leave room for doubt, since someone might not feel that way. "You" messages, as in "you are so self-centered," most often make the receiver defensive. But an "I" message, such as "I feel angry when I have to wait because you are late," is not ambiguous, and it describes the sender's feelings.

4. *Be congruent.*   Make sure your messages are congruent with your actions. Being incongruent by saying one thing and doing another confuses receivers. If, for example, managers tell subordinates that they are "always available" to help them but then act condescending and preoccupied when those people come to them with problems, they are communicating something quite different from the verbal message.

5. *Simplify your language.*   Complex rhetoric and technical jargon confuse individuals who do not use such language. Most organizations develop a lingo, or language that is distinctly the company's own, made up of words and phrases for people, situations, events, and things. At Walt Disney, for example, all employees are called cast members. They're "on stage" when they're working and "off stage" when at lunch or taking a break. Any positive situation or event is a "good Mickey." Anything less is a "bad Mickey."

Jargon and lingo are efficient ways to communicate inside the organization. However, when used with associates outside the company who don't know the jargon, lingo can hinder communication. Effective communicators avoid jargon, slang, clichés, and colorful metaphors when communicating with people outside the industry or those who do not speak the language fluently. By being empathetic and envisioning themselves in the receiver's situation, managers can encode messages in terms that are meaningful to the specific receivers.[6]

SKILLS FOR DEVELOPING AND MAINTAINING CREDIBILITY   The credibility of a sender is probably the single most important element in effective interpersonal communications.[7] Sender credibility is reflected in the receiver's belief that the sender is trustworthy. Factors that increase the clarity of communication, such as congruence of verbal and nonverbal messages, contribute to the sender's credibility,[8] as do the additional dimensions discussed next.[9]

1. *Know what you are talking about.*   Receivers will be more attentive when they perceive that senders have expertise in the area about which they are communicating, as when instructions are given by someone authorized to dispense that information. You will lose credibility if people think that you don't know what you are talking about. If you don't know an answer, say so and then develop the expertise to provide a correct answer later.

2. *Establish mutual trust.*   Receivers prefer to have a sender's motives clarified: Are they selfish or altruistic? Owning up to your motives at the beginning of a conversation can eliminate the receiver's anxiety about your real intentions and do much to establish common trust. The following suggestions about being honest, reliable, and self-disclosing all appropriate information also contribute to establishing a trust bond.

3. *Share all relevant information.*   Interpersonal communications are ethical when they facilitate a person's freedom of choice by presenting all relevant information accurately. They are unethical when they prevent another person from securing information relevant to a choice or force other people to make a choice they would not normally make or decline to make choices they would normally make.[10]

4. *Be honest.*   In every national poll, the most important thing people want in a leader, friend, partner, or coworker is honesty.[11] Therefore, you want to avoid any form of deception, which is the conscious alteration of information to influence another's perceptions significantly.[12] Deception includes lying—concealing or distorting truthful information—and other behaviors that do not reflect our true feelings or beliefs.

5. *Be reliable.*   A sender's perceived dependability, predictability, and consistency in providing all relevant information (being consistent in applying performance criteria when evaluating subordinates and treating subordinates fairly and equally, for example) reinforce the sender's perceived trustworthiness.

6. *Be warm and friendly.*   A warm, friendly, supportive attitude is more conducive to personal credibility than is a posture of hostility, arrogance, or abruptness. People are more trusting of those who are friendly than those who appear to be trying to impress or control them.

7. *Be dynamic.*   If you are dynamic, confident, and positive in your delivery of information, you will be more credible than someone who is passive, withdrawn, and unsure. Receivers tend to be more attentive to messages when the senders are enthusiastic and confident.

8. *Appropriate self-disclosure.*   Self-disclosure is the process of revealing our feelings, reactions, needs, and desires to others. Most of us have encountered "overdisclosures" who talk too much and too intimately about themselves in situations in which that kind of intimacy is

not relevant. Other people are "underdisclosures" who are unwilling to let others know anything about them, even when it is desirable to enhance relationships or productivity. Self-disclosure can be visualized on a continuum, with appropriate self-disclosure in accordance with the goal.

Responsible self-disclosure is essential to the establishment of supportive relationships in which people understand each other's needs, values, goals, strengths, and weaknesses. This is crucial to personal and team development: People need to know each other's needs and receive feedback about the impact of their behavior on each other. Finally, appropriate self-disclosure is a component of effective message sending because it facilitates congruency, builds trust and credibility, and helps receivers develop empathy and understanding.[13]

Self-disclosures that have the most payoffs are ones that relate to the "here and now," that is, what a person is experiencing right now. Unfortunately, most of us withhold our feelings about other people because we are afraid of hurting their feelings, making them angry, or being rejected; or we do not know how to self-disclose in a constructive way. Regardless of the reason, the result is that other people continue to be totally unaware of our reactions to their behaviors and vice versa. Consequently, many relations that could be productive and enjoyable gradually deteriorate under the accumulated load of tiny annoyances, hurt feelings, and misunderstandings that were never talked about openly.

SKILLS FOR OBTAINING FEEDBACK   Feedback is the receiver's response to your message. You need to obtain feedback to determine exactly what the receiver heard and what the receiver thinks the meaning of the message is. If the receiver's response indicates a lack of understanding, you can modify the original message to make sure your intentions are understood accurately.

Statements that carry a number of potential meanings are highly susceptible to misunderstanding on the part of their receivers. If, for example, someone says "Call me later and we'll discuss it" while walking out the door, does the person mean 15 minutes from now, 2 hours from now, tomorrow, or next week? Without clarification, such ambiguous directions are unlikely to be followed according to the sender's intentions, thus the relationship between the parties will be strained.[14] By soliciting and listening to feedback, you can transform such highly ambiguous statements into specific, effective communications. Some skills you can practice to obtain honest and reliable feedback include the following:

1. *Take the initiative to ask receivers for feedback.*   This is necessary to help you ascertain whether your message came across the way you intended it. If you are unable to obtain feedback on how your messages are being received, inaccurate perceptions on the part of a receiver might never be corrected.
2. *Don't be defensive.*   Challenging the validity of feedback, rationalizing your actions, and arguing with receivers' perceptions will extinguish receivers' willingness to provide you with the information you need. Seek only to understand how you have come across to the receiver, and then clarify misunderstandings if any exist.
3. *Check your understanding by summarizing what you have heard.*   What you are doing is providing feedback to the receiver to make sure you understand the feedback the receiver gave you. Clarifying feedback typically begins with a statement such as "Let me be sure I understand what you have said," or "Let me see if I have your understanding correct." Often it ends with a question: "Did I understand you properly?" or "Were those your major concerns?"
4. *Check out underlying assumptions.*   If the feedback you receive does not seem to be in sync with what you intended to communicate, it might be because of the assumptions the

receiver is making about your intentions, expectations, or motivation. You can check the receiver's assumptions by asking clarifying questions directly or by summarizing what you perceive the receiver's assumptions to be and then seeing if you are correct.

5. *Be sensitive to the provider's nonverbal messages.*   Through the use of their bodies, eyes, faces, postures, and senses, receivers communicate a variety of positive or negative attitudes, feelings, and opinions that serve as feedback about how they are reacting to your message. Examples are eye contact, gestures, facial expressions, and vocal intonations. Read nonverbal feedback and use it to structure the content and direction of the conversation by changing the pace of your words, the tone of your voice, or your physical position to regain other people's attention and interest.

6. *Ask questions to clarify.*   Questions should be asked to clarify feedback; check understanding; check assumptions; determine which issues need further discussion; and confirm all uncertain verbal, vocal, and visual cues. When in doubt, check it out with a clarifying question.

CONCEPT QUIZ

Take the following 10-question, true–false quiz. The answers are at the end of the quiz. If you miss any answers, go back and check your understanding of the concepts to determine why you got them wrong.

Circle the right answer.

True	**False**	1.	Effective communication occurs when the sender sends all information.
True	**False**	2.	Successful communications depend on overcoming sources of noise.
True	**False**	3.	It is more important to be efficient than effective when communicating.
True	**False**	4.	You should obtain feedback to check how accurately the receiver decoded your message.
True	**False**	5.	Human interaction and interpersonal relationships cannot exist without communication.
True	**False**	6.	Communications are unethical when they prevent another person from securing information relevant to a choice.
True	**False**	7.	Nonverbal messages can provide effective feedback.
True	**False**	8.	A warm, friendly, supportive attitude is conducive to personal credibility.
True	**False**	9.	Senders should use the phrase "everyone feels this way" to avoid personal conflict with receivers.
True	**False**	10.	When in doubt, check it out with a clarifying question.

Answers: (1) False; (2) True; (3) False; (4) True; (5) True; (6) True; (7) True; (8) True; (9) False; (10) True

BEHAVIORAL CHECKLIST

Be aware of these specific behaviors when evaluating your own message-sending skills. Also use them as criteria for providing feedback to others about their message-sending skills.

Sending Effective Messages Requires That You:

- Provide all relevant information
- Are honest

- Use multiple channels
- Are complete and specific
- Use "I" statements to claim your message as your own.
- Are congruent in your verbal and nonverbal messages.
- Use language the receiver can understand.
- Maintain credibility by knowing what you are talking about and being reliable.
- Communicate in a style that is warm, friendly, and dynamic.
- Obtain feedback to ensure that you have been understood accurately.

ATTENTION!

Do not read the following until assigned to do so by your instructor.

MODELING EXERCISE

Sending Messages With and Without Feedback[15]

The purpose of this exercise is to demonstrate to senders the importance of obtaining feedback to determine exactly what receivers think the meaning of their message is. If the receiver's response indicates a lack of understanding, the sender can clarify the message to make sure intentions are understood accurately. Without feedback, the sender must rely on personal judgment that may not be accurate. There are three parts to this exercise: a one-way communication demonstration, a two-way communication demonstration, and a debriefing session.

Instructor Note. Make copies and transparencies of the diagrams to be used in this exercise and debriefing from the *Instructor's Manual* previous to the class session. Do the same for the summary sheet that can be used for recording and presenting times, confidence, and accuracy data.

Instructions

One-Way Communication: No Feedback

Pick a sender who will stand in the front of the room facing away from the class. The sender's job is to describe a diagram to the class as accurately as possible so that they can make duplicate drawings. The diagram will be provided by the instructor. The rest of the class should not look at the diagram. The class members are to draw what is being described to them as accurately as possible. Class members work alone and make no audible responses. When the sender begins, the instructor times how long it takes for the sender to describe the diagram.

When the sender indicates that he or she is finished, the instructor records how long it took to describe the diagram. Then class members write down how many objects in the diagram they think they have drawn correctly. The sender writes down an estimate of the average number of objects the class members have drawn correctly. When finished, move on to the two-way communication exercise.

Two-Way Communication: With Feedback

The sender now faces the group and describes a second diagram to the class. The second diagram is also provided by the instructor. The rest of the class should not look at the diagram. Class members are to draw what is being described to them as accurately as possible from the sender's descriptions. This time, participants are allowed to ask questions and discuss the objects with the sender. However, drawings cannot be shown and hand gestures are not allowed. When the sender indicates that the second task is complete, the instructor notes the length of time it took. Then class members write down how many objects they think they have drawn correctly. The sender writes down an estimate of the average number of objects the class members have drawn correctly.

Debriefing

1. *Communication confidence.*   The instructor asks for a show of hands for how many objects the class members believe they drew correctly for the one-way exercise and estimates the average that is written on the board or summary transparency. The sender's estimate of the average number of correct drawings is placed on the board next to the actual class average. The same is done for the number of correct drawings in the two-way exercise. The class then discusses which estimates are higher and what the implications are for communications with and without feedback.

2. *Communication accuracy.*   The instructor shows the class a transparency of the first diagram. Students compare their drawings in the one-way communication part of the exercise and write down how many squares they drew in the correct positions. Then the instructor asks for a show of hands for how many objects the class members drew correctly in the one-way exercise and writes an estimate of the average on the board or transparency summary sheet. The same is done for the number of correct drawings in the two-way exercise. The class then discusses which communication process resulted in greater accuracy and what the implications are for communications with and without feedback.

Discussion Questions

1. What happened during the drawing of the first object? How did you respond? How did you feel while doing the task?
2. What happened during the drawing of the second object? How did you respond? Did you ask for any clarifications? How did you feel while doing the task?
3. From the class results, what can you conclude from comparing one-way versus two-way communication? Does it take more time to communicate effectively?
4. Referring back to the Behavioral Checklist for sending messages effectively, how well did the sender do in the one-way exercise? Why?
5. Referring back to the Behavioral Checklist for sending messages effectively, how well did the sender do in the two-way exercise? Why?

Total Time. 35 minutes (setup, 5 minutes; one-way exercise, 10 minutes; two-way exercise, 10 minutes; debrief, 10 minutes)

GROUP EXERCISES

There are three different types of exercises in this section. The first exercise is a role-play in which the class provides feedback on the message-sending skills of the student assigned to the supervisor role. The second exercise focuses on stating feelings in appropriate ways. The third exercise compares self-perceptions of message-sending behavior to the perceptions of others.

As an option to any of the group exercises in the skill chapters, students can create their own scenario and scripts for a 5-minute role-play demonstrating the application of relevant chapter skills.

Group Exercise 1: "A Difference of Opinion"[16]

The entire class should read the following situation. Next, the class should split up into trios and decide who will be actors and who will be an observer. The two people who volunteer to play the roles of Dana and Blair should read only their own role, not the other person's role, and prepare for the role-play. The observer can read both roles and then study the Observer's Rating Sheet for evaluating the role-play.

Actors.   Dana (head of personnel) and Blair (employee-relations manager)

Situation.   Dana, head of personnel, is preparing for a performance appraisal with Blair, the employee-relations manager. A difference of opinion has arisen about Blair's job performance and promotional timetable.

Dana's Role.   You are head of personnel for a manufacturing firm. You are well thought of in the firm and have an excellent rapport with your boss, the vice president for administration. Blair is your employee-relations manager. You know that Blair is reasonably good at her job. But you also know that Blair believes herself to be "outstanding," which isn't true. Blair is scheduled have a meeting with you in 5 minutes, and you would like to establish clearer communication well as convince Blair to adopt a less grandiose self-image.

You believe that Blair is on the right track, but it will take her about 2 years to re stage at which she can be promoted. As for Blair's performance, you have received so reports as well as three letters of complaint. Blair prepared four research reports that y ered to be above average, but to keep her motivated and happy, you exaggerated ar were "excellent." Maybe that was a mistake.

You are worried about the impact on other employees, whose performanc good as Blair's, if Blair is promoted. So, you plan to set meaningful targets for evaluate her performance a year or two from now, and then give her the promc she deserves it.

Blair's Role.   You are the employee-relations manager in a manufacturin boss, and his title is head of personnel. You know that you are one of the be department, and might even be the best. However, you were not promoted you expected to be, so you would like to be promoted this year.

You expect your boss to raise some obstacles to your promotion. three letters of complaint against you, for instance. Dana seems to poi front, you plan to remind Dana that you wrote four research reports excellent. If Dana tries to delay your promotion unnecessarily, yor necessary, take the issue to Dana's boss, the vice president for a have been many instances in which you were rated better on perf the department. You have decided that you will press your point in a professional manner.

Total Time. 30 minutes (setup, 5 minutes; role-play, 15 mir

OBSERVER'S RATING SHEET

Rate your assigned role-player's message-sending skills on a 1 to 5 scale (5 being the highest). Provide comments for specific feedback in the space under each skill criterion.

Rating	Behavioral Skills	Role-Player Observed: _____
_____	Provided all relevant information	
_____	Was honest	
_____	Used multiple channels	
_____	Was complete and specific	
_____	Used "I" statements to claim message as own	
_____	Was congruent in verbal and nonverbal messages	
_____	Used language the receiver can understand	
_____	Maintained credibility	
	Communicated in a style that was warm, friendly, and dynamic	
	Obtained feedback to ensure accurate understanding	

Group Exercise 2: Communicating Feelings[17]

One of the most frequent sources of difficulty in relationships is communicating feelings. We all have feelings about the people we interact with, but many times we do not communicate these feelings effectively. Instead we repress, deny, distort, or disguise our feelings, or we communicate them in an ineffective way, which can cause relationship problems.[18] This exercise is designed to allow you to become more aware of the problems associated with not stating your feelings clearly and directly and to give you a chance to experiment with better ways of communicating.

Instructions

1. Divide into groups of three.
2. For each of the following situations, write individual descriptions of two different feelings that might have given rise to the expression of feelings in the statement.
3. Compare your answers with the answers of the other members of your trio. Discuss them until you understand each other's answers.
4. In the class as a whole, discuss the results of ambiguity in expressing feelings in interpersonal relationships.
   a. What skills are required to send messages containing feelings effectively?
   b. What happens when people make ambiguous statements of feeling? How do other people respond? How do they feel?
   c. Why would you state feelings ambiguously? In what circumstances would you prefer to be ambiguous rather than direct and concrete? What would be the probable consequence?

Feeling Statements in Interpersonal Situations

1. One person asks another, "Why can't you ever be anyplace on time?" What might the first person have said that would have described his or her feelings better?
2. You notice that a person in the group who was talking a lot has suddenly become silent. What might the person have said to describe his or her feelings openly?
3. During a group meeting, you hear John tell Bill, "Bill, you're talking too much." What might John have said to describe his feelings more accurately?
4. Sally abruptly changed the subject after Ann made a comment. What might Sally have said to describe her feelings more openly?
5. You hear a passenger say to a taxi driver, "Do we have to drive this fast?" What might the passenger have said to describe his or her feelings openly?
6. Sam says to Jane after she has agreed to substitute for him by giving a presentation to a client, "You're really wonderful." What might Sam have said to describe his feelings more accurately?

Total Time. 33 minutes (setup, 3 minutes; individual questions, 10 minutes; trio discussions, 10 minutes; debrief, 10 minutes)

Group Exercise 3: Your Message-Sending Behavior

Instructions.   Individually answer the following questions.

1. How would you now describe your message-sending behavior in a problem-solving group?

2. What are your strengths when sending messages?
3. What message-sending skills do you still wish to improve?

After answering these questions, meet with two people who know you well.

1. One person volunteers to be the sender. The sender shares and explains his or her answers.
2. The other two people are receivers. When the sender is finished, they provide feedback about the accuracy of the sender's perceptions compared to how they perceive the sender in general, and just now when sending this information. If they can, the two receivers provide additional feedback by adding new strengths and suggestions that the sender should work on to improve message sending.

Total Time. 28 minutes (setup, 3 minutes; individual questions, 5 minutes; triad sharing and listening, 10 minutes; debrief, 10 minutes)

Summary Checklist

Take a few minutes to reflect on your performance and look over others' ratings of your message-sending skills. Now assess yourself on each of the key sending behaviors. Make a check (✓) next to those behaviors on which you need improvement.

I provide all relevant information.   _____

I am honest.   _____

I use multiple channels.   _____

I am complete and specific.   _____

I use "I" statements to claim your message as my own.   _____

I am congruent in my verbal and nonverbal messages.   _____

I use language the receiver can understand.   _____

I maintain credibility, and I am reliable and know what I'm talking about.   _____

I am warm, friendly, and dynamic.   _____

I obtain feedback to ensure understanding.   _____

APPLICATION QUESTIONS

1. Think of one of the most effective professors you have had. What does the professor do to send messages to the class successfully?
2. Remember a time when you were unable to communicate a message effectively. What was the root of your problem? What can you do to prevent a recurrence?
3. Have you ever held back information that you should have disclosed? What was the result? Have you ever disclosed things you wish you hadn't? What happened?
4. Pick someone in the class whom you feel is a good speaker and is easy to listen to. What communication behaviors does this person exhibit? Are all of them positive?
5. Have you ever communicated unethically to anyone? Why did this happen? What were the circumstances? What were the consequences?

REINFORCEMENT EXERCISES

1. Watch five television commercials. How do they attempt to send messages to keep the viewers' attention and effectively convince them of the value of the product or service being advertised?

2. Ask some of your friends if they can think of times when others communicated unethically to them. What were the circumstances? Why did this happen? What were the consequences?

3. The next time you make a formal oral presentation in class or at a meeting, ask someone to observe what you do well when sending messages and what you can improve on.

4. Ask some of your friends if your verbal messages are usually congruent with your body language. Ask them if they can give examples.

5. You have just joined a large firm as a manager. How can you apply your communication skills to increase the probability of succeeding in this job?

ACTION PLAN

1. Which message-sending behavior do I want to improve the most?

2. Why? What will be my payoff?

3. What potential obstacles stand in my way?

4. What specific things will I do to improve? (For examples, see the Reinforcement Exercises.)

5. When will I do them?

6. How and when will I measure my success?

Endnotes

1. David W. Johnson and Frank P. Johnson, *Joining Together: Group Theory and Group Skills*, 5th ed. (Boston, MA: Allyn & Bacon, 1994), pp. 130–131.

2. David W. Johnson, *Reaching Out*, 5th ed. (Boston, MA: Allyn & Bacon, 1993), p. 97.

3. D. K. Berlo, *The Process of Communication* (New York: Holt, Rinehart & Winston, 1960), pp. 30–32.

4. David W. Johnson, "Communication and the Inducement of Cooperative Behavior in Conflicts," *Speech Monographs*, Vol. 41 (1974), pp. 64–78.

5. L. L. Tobias, "Twenty-Three Ways to Improve Communication," *Training and Development Journal* (1989), pp. 75–77.

6. Michael W. Miller, "At Many Firms, Employees Speak a Language That's All Their Own," *Wall Street Journal* (December 29, 1987), p. 15.

7. David W. Johnson, *Reaching Out*, 5th ed. (Boston, MA: Allyn & Bacon, 1993), pp. 65–66.

8. Sandra G. Garside, and Brian H. Kleiner, "Effective One-to-One Communication Skills," *Industrial & Commercial Training*, Vol. 23, No. 7 (1991), pp. 24–28.

9. David W. Johnson, *Reaching Out*, 5th ed. (Boston, MA: Allyn & Bacon, 1993).

10. J. A. DeVito, *The Interpersonal Communication Book*, 6th ed. (New York: HarperCollins Publishers, 1992), p. 77.

11. Roger C. Mayer, and James H. Davis, "An Integrative Model of Organizational Trust," *Academy of Management Review* (July 1995), pp. 143–157.

12. M. Knapp, and M. Comadena, "Telling It Like It Isn't: A Review of Theory and Research on Deceptive Communication," *Human Communication Research* (1979), pp. 270–285.

13. Gerard Egan, *Face-to-Face: The Small-Group Experience and Interpersonal Growth* (Monterey, CA: Brooks/Cole, 1973), pp. 40–41.

14. Phillip L. Hunsaker and Anthony J. Alessandra, *The Art of Managing People* (New York: Free Press, 2008), pp. 155–156.

15. This exercise is adapted from Harold I. Leavitt, *Managerial Psychology* (Chicago, IL: University of Chicago Press, 1958), pp. 118–128.

16. Based on Srinivasan Umapathy, "Teaching Behavioral Aspects of Performance Evaluation: An Experiential Approach," *Accounting Review* (January 1985), pp. 107–108. With permission.

17. Adapted from David W. Johnson, *Reaching Out*, 5th ed. (Boston, MA: Allyn & Bacon, 1993), pp. 150–151.

18. David W. Johnson, *Reaching Out*, 5th ed. (Boston, MA: Allyn & Bacon, 1993), p. 141.

6

■ ■ ■

Listening and Reading Nonverbal Messages

SELF-ASSESSMENT EXERCISE: MY LISTENING HABITS

For each of the following questions, select the answer that best describes your listening habits.

	Usually	Sometimes	Seldom
1. I maintain eye contact with the speaker.	_____	_____	_____
2. I determine whether or not speakers' ideas are worthwhile solely by their appearance and delivery.	_____	_____	_____
3. I try to understand the message from the speaker's point of view.	_____	_____	_____
4. I listen for specific facts rather than for the big picture.	_____	_____	_____
5. I listen for factual content and the emotion behind the literal words.	_____	_____	_____
6. I ask questions for clarification and understanding.	_____	_____	_____
7. I withhold judgment of what speakers are saying until they are finished.	_____	_____	_____
8. I make a conscious effort to evaluate the logic and consistency of what is being said.	_____	_____	_____
9. While listening, I think about what I'm going to say as soon as I have my chance.	_____	_____	_____
10. I try to have the last word.	_____	_____	_____

Scoring and Interpretation

For questions 1, 3, 5, 6, 7, and 8, give yourself 3 points for Usually; 2 points for Sometimes; and 1 point for Seldom.

For questions 2, 4, 9, and 10, give yourself 3 points for Seldom; 2 points for Sometimes; and 1 point for Usually.

Sum up your total points. A score of 27 or higher means you're a good listener. A score of 22–26 suggests that you have some listening deficiencies. A score below 22 indicates that you have developed a number of bad listening habits.

SKILL CONCEPTS

Many communication problems develop because listening skills are ignored, forgotten, or just taken for granted.[1] We confuse hearing with listening. Hearing is merely picking up sound vibrations. Listening is making sense out of what we hear. Listening requires paying attention, interpreting, and remembering sound and visual stimuli. As we show in this chapter, listening is a skill that can be learned. Although it's something we've done all our lives, few of us do it well.

If we want to consider interpersonal skills in order of importance, listening tops the list. For instance, a survey of personnel directors in 300 organizations found that effective listening was ranked highest among the skills defined as most important in becoming a manager.[2] Listening is also a vital ingredient for learning most interpersonal skills. Throughout this book, you'll be asked to participate in and observe interpersonal exercises. You'll need effective listening skills to do this. Another reason to begin with listening is that if you aren't an effective listener, you're going to have consistent trouble developing all the other interpersonal skills.

ACTIVE VERSUS PASSIVE LISTENING

Effective listening is active rather than passive. In passive listening, you are like a tape recorder, but not nearly as accurate. You try to absorb as much of the information presented as possible. Even if speakers provide you with a clear message and make their delivery interesting enough to keep your attention, your comprehension of a presentation two or more days later will always be incomplete and usually inaccurate.[3]

Active listening requires you to empathize with speakers so that you can understand the communication from their point of view. As you'll see, active listening is hard work. You have to concentrate and you have to want to understand fully what a speaker is saying. Students who use active listening techniques for an entire 50-minute lecture are almost as tired as their instructor when that lecture is over because they have put as much energy into listening as the instructor put into speaking.

Active listening has four essential requirements. You need to listen with (1) intensity, (2) empathy, (3) acceptance, and (4) a willingness to take responsibility for completeness.[4]

Our brain is capable of handling a speaking rate of about four times the speed of the average speaker.[5] That leaves a lot of time for your mind to wander while listening. The active listener concentrates intensely on what the speaker is saying and tunes out the thousands of miscellaneous thoughts (about work deadlines, money, sex, parties, friends, getting the car fixed, and the like) that create distractions. What do active listeners do with their idle brain time? They summarize and integrate what has been said. They put each new bit of information into the context of what has preceded it.

Empathy requires you to put yourself in the speaker's shoes. You try to understand what the speaker wants to communicate rather than what you want to understand. Empathy demands knowledge of the speaker and flexibility on your part. You need to suspend your own thoughts and feelings and adjust what you see and feel to your speaker's world. In that way, you increase the likelihood that you will interpret the message being spoken in the way the speaker intended.

Active listeners demonstrate acceptance. They listen objectively without judging content. This is no easy task. It is natural to be distracted by the content of what a speaker says, especially when we disagree with it. When we hear something we disagree with, we begin formulating our mental arguments to counter what is being said. In doing so, we miss the rest of the message. The challenge for the active listener is to absorb what is being said and to withhold judgment on content until the speaker is finished.

The final ingredient of active listening is taking responsibility for completeness. That is, the listener does whatever is necessary to get the full, intended meaning from the speaker's communication. Two widely used active listening techniques to achieve this end are listening for feelings as well as for content and asking questions to ensure understanding.

Active listeners listen with their ears, their eyes, and their minds. They take in the objective information by listening to the literal words that are spoken. But every spoken message contains more than words. Speakers also communicate subjective information—their feelings and emotions—through other vocal sounds and nonverbal signals. These include verbal intonations such as loudness, emphasis, hesitations, voice inflections, and the rate of speaking. Nonverbal signals include the speaker's eye movements, facial expressions, body posture, and hand gestures. By listening for feelings and emotions as well as for literal words, you can grasp the total meaning behind the speaker's message. Yet, no matter how good you become at listening for total meaning, the potential for misunderstanding still remains. That's why the active listener verifies completeness by asking questions. The use of questions can uncover distortions and clarify misunderstandings. Again, notice that questioning is consistent with taking a positive and responsible role in the communication process. The success of a verbal communication does not rest solely with the speaker. By seeking clarification, active listeners ensure that they are receiving and understanding the message as the speaker intended.

WHAT WE KNOW ABOUT EFFECTIVE LISTENING

The active listening model forms the foundation for making you an effective listener. In this section, we summarize 14 specific characteristics or techniques used by effective listeners. Some of these characteristics are explicit behaviors that can be observed directly. For instance, asking questions is a directly observable behavior. Others, such as listening without judging content, are cognitive processes that can only be evaluated indirectly. As we review these 14 characteristics, ask yourself whether each represents an observable behavior. For those that don't, try to determine what you might look for that could tell you indirectly if someone is using the technique.

1. *Be motivated.* If a listener is unwilling to exert the effort to hear and understand, no amount of additional advice is going to improve listening effectiveness. As we previously noted, active listening is hard work. Your first step toward becoming an effective listener is a willingness to make the effort.

2. *Make eye contact.* How do you feel when somebody doesn't look at you when you're speaking? If you're like most people, you're likely to interpret this as aloofness or disinterest. It's ironic that while "you listen with your ears, people judge whether you are listening by

looking at your eyes.[6] Making eye contact with the speaker focuses your attention, reduces the likelihood that you will become distracted, and encourages the speaker.

3. *Show interest.*   The effective listener shows interest in what is being said.[7] How? The answer is through nonverbal signals. Affirmative head nods and appropriate facial expressions, when added to steady eye contact, convey to the speaker that you're listening.

4. *Avoid distracting actions.*   The other side of showing interest is avoiding actions that suggest your mind is somewhere else. When listening, don't look at your watch, shuffle papers, play with your pencil, or engage in similar distractions. They make the speaker feel that you're bored or uninterested. More importantly, they indicate that you aren't fully attentive and might be missing part of the message that the speaker wants to convey.

5. *Empathy.*   We said that active listeners try to understand what the speaker sees and feels by putting themselves in the speaker's shoes. Don't project your own needs and intentions onto the speaker. When you do so, you're likely to hear what you want to hear. So ask yourself: Who is this speaker and where is he or she coming from? What are his or her attitudes, interests, experiences, needs, and expectations?

6. *Take in the whole picture.*   The effective listener interprets feelings and emotions as well as factual content.[8] If you listen to words alone and ignore other vocal cues and nonverbal signals, you will miss a wealth of subtle messages. To test this point, read the script of a play. Then go and see that play live in a theater. The characters and the message take on a much richer meaning when you see the play acted out on stage.

7. *Ask questions.*   Critical listeners analyze what they hear and ask questions. This behavior provides clarification, ensures understanding, and assures the speaker that you're listening.

8. *Paraphrase.*   Paraphrasing means restating what the speaker has said in your own words. The effective listener uses phrases such as "What I hear you saying is . . ." or "Do you mean . . .?" Why rephrase what has already been said? Two reasons. First, it's an excellent control device to check on whether you're listening carefully. You can't paraphrase accurately if your mind is wandering or if you're thinking about what you're going to say next. Second, it's a control for accuracy. By rephrasing what the speaker has said in your own words and feeding it back to the speaker, you verify the accuracy of your understanding.

9. *Don't interrupt.*   Let speakers complete their thoughts before you try to respond. Don't try to second-guess where the speaker's thoughts are going. When the speaker is finished, you'll know it.

10. *Integrate what's being said.*   Use your spare time while listening to better understand the speaker's ideas. Instead of treating each new piece of information as an independent entity, put the pieces together. Treat each part of the message as if it were an additional piece of a puzzle. By the time the speaker has finished, instead of having 10 unrelated bits of information, you'll have 10 integrated pieces of information that form a comprehensive message. If you don't, you should ask the questions that will fill in the blanks.

11. *Don't overtalk.*   Most of us would rather speak our own ideas than listen to what someone else says. Too many of us listen only because it's the price we have to pay to get people to let us talk. Talking may be more fun and silence may be uncomfortable, but you can't talk and listen at the same time. The good listener recognizes this fact and doesn't overtalk.[9]

12. *Confront your biases.*   Evaluate the source of the message. Notice things such as the speaker's credibility, appearance, vocabulary, and speech mannerisms. But don't let them distract you. For instance, all of us have red-flag words that spark our attention or cause us to draw premature conclusions. Examples might include terms like racist, gay, chauvinist,

conservative, liberal, feminist, environmentalist, and Religious Right. Use information about speakers to improve your understanding of what they have to say, but don't let your biases distort the message.

13. ***Make smooth transitions between speaker and listener.*** As a student sitting in a lecture hall, you find it relatively easy to get into an effective listening frame of mind. Why? Because communication is essentially one way: The teacher talks and you listen. However, the teacher–student dyad is atypical. In most work situations, you're continually shifting back and forth between the roles of speaker and listener. The effective listener, therefore, makes transitions smoothly from speaker to listener and back to speaker. From a listening perspective, this means concentrating on what a speaker has to say and practicing not thinking about what you're going to say as soon as you get your chance.

14. ***Be natural.*** An effective listener develops a style that is natural and authentic. Don't try to become a compulsive good listener. If you exaggerate eye contact, facial expressions, the asking of questions, a show of interest, and the like, you'll lose credibility. A good listener is not a manipulator. Use moderation and develop listening techniques that are effective and fit well with your interpersonal style.

READING NONVERBAL MESSAGES

Nonverbal communication is made up of visual, tactile, and vocal signals, and the use of time, space, and image.[10] As much as 93 percent of the meaning that is transmitted between two people in a face-to-face conversation can come from nonverbal channels.[11] This means that as little as 7 percent of the meaning we derive from others may come through their words alone.

Very often a person says one thing but communicates something totally different through vocal intonation and body language. These *mixed signals* force the receivers to choose between the verbal and nonverbal aspects of a message. Mixed messages create tension and distrust because the receivers sense that the communicator is hiding something or is being less than candid. Most often, the receiver chooses the nonverbal aspects because they are more reliable than verbal communications when the two contradict each other.[12] Nonverbal signals function as a lie detector to aid a watchful listener in interpreting another's words. Although many people can convincingly misrepresent their emotions in their speech, focused attention on facial and vocal expressions can often detect leakage of the concealed feelings.[13]

Visual Communication

The visual component of nonverbal communication has been called *body language*, or *kinesics*. It includes facial expressions, eye movements, posture, and gestures.

The face is the best communicator of nonverbal messages. By "reading" a person's facial expressions, we can often detect unexpressed feelings like happiness, sadness, surprise, fear, anger, and disgust. Caution is advised, however, because different cultures impose emotional restraints to hold back true feelings, and the same facial expression can mean different things in different cultures. For example, agreement is indicated by up-and-down head nods in American culture, but it is expressed by side-to-side head movements in India.[14]

We've all heard the phrases "One glance is worth a thousand words" and "The eyes are the windows to the soul." How do you feel when you are talking to someone wearing mirrored sunglasses? Most of us are uncomfortable because we are cut off from the most significant body expression of that person's mood.

Eye contact allows us to read and communicate a number of things. Direct eye contact, for example, is generally perceived as a sign of honesty, interest, openness, and confidence. If eye contact is avoided, we feel that the other is embarrassed, nervous, or hiding something. As with all body language, eye contact varies by culture. In some Latin American cultures, for example, people with lower status are not supposed to look directly in the face of higher status individuals. In the United States, on the other hand, lack of eye contact could be interpreted as a sign of deceit.[15]

Posture provides clues about the attitude of the bearer. How we carry ourselves signals such feelings as self-confidence, aggressiveness, fear, guilt, or anxiety. Self-confidence could be portrayed by a relaxed posture, such as sitting back in a chair with legs stretched out and hands behind the head. Contrast this image to that of someone hunched down, looking away, and biting his or her fingernails. A shift in posture means that something is changing, but it is up to the receiver to figure out what.[16]

Gestures combine facial expressions and posture movements to indicate meaning, control conversation, or complement words. Some gestures have universal symbolism. Raising both hands above the head indicates surrender and submission. A salute, a tip of the hat, a handshake, a wave of farewell, a *V* for victory, and a wink of the eye are just a few of the familiar symbols that transcend most language and cultural barriers.

Many gestures are culturally bound and susceptible to misinterpretation, however. It is very easy for Americans to misread Japanese body language, for example. The Japanese try to avoid personal confrontation; they usually exhibit a noncontroversial demeanor and use excessive politeness and tact to smooth over any differences that arise. When negotiating among themselves, this presents no difficulties. But for Americans, serious misinterpretations can arise.[17]

Each isolated gesture is like a word in a sentence and should be considered in light of the other simultaneous forms of communication. When individual gestures are put together in clusters, they paint a more precise picture of what the other person is feeling and thinking.

To the sender of a message, a receiver's gestures serve as feedback; by observing the emotions and attitudes that are expressed nonverbally, he or she can tell how acceptable the message is.[18] For example, disagreement will be evident when someone shakes his or her head or raises his or her eyebrows in amazement or doubt. A smile and a nod, on the other hand, will signal agreement.

Tactile Communication

Tactile communication is the use of touch to impart meaning, as in a handshake, a pat on the back, an arm around the shoulder, or a push or slap. Gentle touching such as a hand on an arm, a kiss, or a hug indicates support, liking, or intimacy. Rough touching such as squeezing someone's hand too hard, kicking people under the table, and bumping into them in the hallway is hostile behavior indicating negative sentiment.

Vocal Communication

Vocal intonations are how things are said, as exemplified by the common phrase, "It's not what you say but how you say it." Simply changing the intonation of your voice can alter the meaning of words. Try changing your vocal qualities while you say the word "no." You can express mild doubt, amazement, terror, and anger; you can give a command, decline an invitation, or answer a simple question. Each vocal intonation conveys a separate and unique feeling. Changes in loudness, pitch, rate, rhythm, and clarity all produce different meanings.

Vocal meanings also vary across cultures. For example, if an American raises his or her voice, we assume that the person is excited or angry, and we usually have a difficult time concentrating on what is being said once the volume has risen beyond what we consider a comfortable level. We focus instead on the projected emotions. In Latin American cultures, however, the noise level is generally higher than in the United States. The normal American vocal level would be considered too subdued to indicate genuine involvement and appropriate concern for what the Latin American is communicating.[19]

The most important aspect of vocal intonation is a change in vocal quality. When people change their normal vocal qualities, it's a sign that they are communicating something extra.[20] For example, in statements tinged with sarcasm the vocally transmitted message has a meaning quite different from that of its actual verbal content.

Communicating through Time

Time is a scarce, continuous, and irreversible resource. Consequently, whom we spend it with and how much of it we give to someone communicates our feelings about who and what are important to us.[21] Most people are probably ready a little early for a first date with an attractive person. If either party is very late, a suitable explanation is in order to ease the assumption of indifference. Similarly, it is not uncommon for teams to assume that a member who is frequently late to meetings does not care about them, whether this is accurate or not.

Proxemics

Proxemics refers to the use of physical space to communicate. The three main dimensions of proxemics that are used for communication are territory, things, and personal space zones.[22]

TERRITORY   How do you feel when you return from a class break and find someone sitting in your seat? Or when someone is standing so close to you that you feel uncomfortable? Although how space is used to communicate differs by culture, people seek to extend their territory in many ways to attain power and intimacy. We silently say things by manipulating space, as when we intrude on another person's space or guard our own. When you walk into a meeting, you establish a *semi-private territory* by fixing movable objects: laying out notebooks and folders, placing a coffee cup on a table, or hanging a jacket on a chair. Being assigned *private territory*, such as an office, is a sign of increased status, because a rare resource has been assigned for your exclusive use and you can communicate how important you or others are by shutting people out or holding private meetings. The larger your private space, the more status and importance are communicated.

THINGS   The things within your space also communicate to others. A clean desk or palm pilot communicates efficiency. Expensive things communicate higher status than do cheap ones. Personal things in your space, such as trophies, photographs, pictures, plants, and other decorations, also convey messages about you to others.

PERSONAL SPACE ZONES   We all carry an invisible personal territory, much like a private air bubble. We feel a proprietary right to this space and resent others entering it unless they are invited. The exact dimensions of these private bubbles vary from culture to culture and person to person, but adult Americans usually become anxious when others intrude on their *intimate zone*, from actual physical contact to about 2 feet away. During meetings with established teams, members are usually comfortable interacting within their *personal zones*, approximately 2–4 feet apart. How other people react if you enter into their personal space can be a nonverbal signal about how comfortable they are with you.

People can generally be classified into two major proxemic categories. Although space preferences are based on personal and experience factors, Americans and northern Europeans, for example, typify the *noncontact* group because of the small amount of touching and relatively large space between them during their transactions. Arabs and Latinos are examples from the *contact* group, who normally stand very close to each other and use a lot of touching when they communicate. When people do not appreciate differences in personal zones, discomfort, distrust, and misunderstanding can occur. Contact people can unknowingly get too close to or touch non-contact people, which makes the latter uncomfortable.

Image Communication[23]

People do judge a book by its cover. Through clothing, hairstyle, body adornments, and other dimensions of physical appearance, we communicate our values and expectations. People react favorably to an expected image. But it is unusual to overcome a bad initial impression and reveal genuine assets hidden underneath.

First impressions made by the initial impact of your clothing, voice, grooming, hand-shake, eye contact, and body posture are lasting images. Projecting both a depth and breadth of knowledge builds your credibility, commands respect from others, and helps develop rapport. Flexibility, enthusiasm, and sincerity create a positive image that can enhance your communication effectiveness. In terms of dress, colors have meanings (e.g., brown for trusting, white for purity, dark colors for power), as do style (e.g., formal vs. casual for more or less status, respectively) and material (e.g., synthetic fibers such as polyester convey lower class, while pure fibers such as wool convey higher class).[24]

CONCEPT QUIZ

Take the following 10-question, true–false quiz. The answers are at the end of the quiz. If you read the previous material carefully, you should get them all correct. If you miss any, go back and find out why you got them wrong.

    Circle the right answer.

True	**False**	1. Active listening is hard work.
True	**False**	2. One of the essential requirements for being an active listener is to anticipate what the speaker is going to say.
True	**False**	3. Empathy means reading nonverbal as well as verbal messages.
True	**False**	4. The first step toward effective listening is the motivation to make the effort.
True	**False**	5. The effective listener maintains constant, penetrating eye contact with the speaker.

True	**False**	6. Efficient listeners listen to what is being said and, at the same time, develop a response.
True	**False**	7. If you can't paraphrase a speaker's message, something was missing from the speaker's explanation.
True	**False**	8. You should let speakers complete their thoughts before you try to respond.
True	**False**	9. The effective listener uses idle brain time to get the big picture from the speaker's message.
True	**False**	10. A speaker's looks or accent can enhance the content and your understanding of the message.

Answers: (1) True; (2) False; (3) False; (4) True; (5) False; (6) False; (7) False; (8) True; (9) True; (10) True

BEHAVIORAL CHECKLIST

The following represents important behaviors related to effective listening. These are the specific behaviors you should look for when evaluating your listening skills and those of others.

The Effective Listener:

- Makes eye contact.
- Exhibits affirmative head nods and appropriate facial expressions.
- Avoids distracting actions or gestures that suggest boredom.
- Asks appropriate questions.
- Paraphrases using his or her own words.
- Avoids interrupting the speaker.
- Doesn't talk too much.
- Deciphers nonverbal messages.

ATTENTION!

Do not read the following exercises until assigned to do so by your instructor.

MODELING EXERCISE

Job Interview Role-Play

Actors. Lee Wilson—college recruiter for Procter & Gamble (P&G). M.B.A. from a prestigious business school; 2 years' experience. Chris Bates—Job candidate. Graduating M.B.A.

Situation. Preliminary interview (in a college placement center) for a marketing management trainee position with P&G. A brief job description and Chris's resumé follow.

Lee Wilson's Role. You will be interviewing approximately 150 students over the next 6 weeks to fill four trainee positions. You're looking for candidates who are bright, articulate, ambitious, and have management potential. The P&G training program is 2 years in length. Trainees will be sales representatives calling on retail stores and will spend the first 15 weeks taking formal P&G classes at the head office. The compensation to start is $32,000 a year plus a car. You are to improvise other information as needed.

Questions you might ask include the following: Where do you expect to be in 5 years? What's important to you in a job? What courses did you like best in your M.B.A. program? Least? What makes you think you would do well in this job? Is there anything else you think is relevant?

Chris Bates's Role.   Review your resumé. You are a top student whose previous work experience has been limited to selling in retail stores in the summer months during your undergraduate collegiate days. This is your first interview with P&G, but you're very interested in their training program. Fill in any voids in information as you see fit.

Total Time. 45 minutes (preparation, 15 minutes; role-play, 15 minutes; debriefing, 15 minutes)

Abbreviated Job Description

Title: Marketing Management Trainee—Consumer Products Group
Reports to: District Marketing Manager
Duties and Responsibilities: Completes formal training program at headquarters in Cincinnati. Thereupon:

- Calls on retail stores.
- Introduces new products to store personnel.
- Distributes sales promotion materials.
- Stocks and arranges shelves in stores.
- Takes sales orders.
- Follows up on complaints or problems.
- Completes all necessary sales reports.

Abbreviated Resumé

Name: Chris Bates
Age: 24
Education: B.A. in Economics; G.P.A.: 3.8 (out of 4.0); M.B.A., with specialization in marketing; G.P.A.: 3.95.
Work Experience: Worked summers, during undergraduate days, at The Gap and Walden Books.

Honors: Top graduating M.B.A. student in marketing; graduate assistantship; Dean's Honor Roll.
Extracurricular activities: Intercollegiate tennis team (undergraduate); Vice President, Graduate Business Students Association; College Marketing Club.

OBSERVER'S RATING SHEET

During the exercise, observers rate the listening behaviors of the people playing the roles of Lee and Chris. Use the following scale to rate each player between 1 and 5. Write in concrete examples in the space for comments to use in explaining your feedback.

	Lee		Chris	
Listening Behaviors	**Rating**	**Comments**	**Rating**	**Comments**
Makes eye contact	_____		_____	
Gives affirmative responses	_____		_____	
Avoids distractions	_____		_____	
Asks questions	_____		_____	
Paraphrases	_____		_____	
Avoids interrupting	_____		_____	
Doesn't overtalk	_____		_____	
Makes smooth transitions	_____		_____	
Deciphers nonverbal messages	_____		_____	

GROUP EXERCISES

The class will be divided into groups of three. (Some groups of four may be necessary to ensure that everyone participates.) Each of the following exercises will have two role-players and an observer. Rotate actors and observers so that everyone in your trio gets a chance to be the actor being observed in one of the three role-plays that follow. The actor and observer guidelines are the same as previously described in the introduction to modeling exercises.

Group Exercise 1: Promotion Decision

Actors.   Pat Driver is the manufacturing manager. Sandy Babson is a supervisor.

Situation.   To accommodate 10 percent growth, a new assistant to the manufacturing manager position has been created. Dave and Sandy, two supervisors who report to Pat, have applied for the job. A meeting has been scheduled in Pat's office with Sandy to discuss Pat's decision on filling the position.

Pat Driver's Role.   You've decided to appoint Dave to the assistant's position. Both Dave and Sandy have bachelor's degrees in engineering and have been with the company for 4 years. Both have approximately 2 years' experience as production supervisors. Dave's and Sandy's job performance evaluations have been consistently excellent. You've chosen Dave over Sandy essentially because he has completed about one-third of the requirements for an M.B.A. by taking courses at night. You know Sandy has wanted this promotion badly, both for the added responsibility and the extra money. Sandy, a single parent with two small children whose spouse died in a car accident last year, could probably really use the additional pay. You expect Sandy to be quite disappointed with your decision.

Sandy Babson's Role.   You have a B.S. degree in industrial engineering. You've been with this company for 4 years, spending more than half that time as a production supervisor. You have consistently received outstanding performance evaluations. You figure that the only other supervisor with similar qualifications is Dave, a workaholic bachelor who even attends night school to work toward an M.B.A. degree. You're ambitious and want to move ahead in the company. Part of your motivation is to earn more money to help with the expenses of raising two children alone since the death of your spouse a year ago in a car accident. You have told Pat that you think you're the best candidate for the recently created position of Pat's assistant. You hope this meeting is going to bring good news.

Observers' Role.   Turn to page 102 and use this rating sheet to evaluate *both* actors.

Total Time. 25 minutes (preparation, 5 minutes; role-play, 10 minutes; debriefing, 10 minutes)

Group Exercise 2: A Debate

Situation.   A debate. Actor A can choose any contemporary issue (e.g., business ethics, value of unions, prayer in schools, stiffer college grading policies, gun control, money as a motivator). Actor B then selects a position on that issue. Actor A must automatically take the counterposition. The debate is to proceed with only one catch. Before the speakers speak, they must first summarize, in their own words and without notes, what the other has said. If the summary doesn't satisfy the speaker, it must be corrected until it does.

Observers' Role.   In addition to rating both debaters on the rating sheet, the observer should remind each debater to paraphrase the other's statements until acknowledged as correct, before stating their own points.

Total Time. 25 minutes (preparation, 5 minutes; debate, 10 minutes; debriefing, 10 minutes)

Group Exercise 3: Computer Breakdown Emergency

Actors.   Alex Jacobs and Dale Traynor

Situation.   Alex Jacobs (Actor A) is the corporate controller for a restaurant chain, responsible for financial and information control. Over the past weekend, the computer system at one of the restaurants went down. The restaurant's manager called Dale Traynor, who reports to Alex and oversees the chain's computer operations. Dale authorized an emergency service call. Because it was a weekend, local people were not available, and the computer firm had to fly in a repairper-son from 600 miles away. Alex has just learned about the emergency call in a casual conversation with the restaurant manager.

Alex Jacobs's Role.   You have phoned the computer firm and found out that the cost of the serv-ice call is $1,400. You're fuming. Not only is $1,400 a large, unexpected expenditure, but also Dale's authority limit is only $500. You can't figure out why you were neither advised of the problem nor asked to approve the expenditure. You have called Dale to your office.

Dale Traynor's Role.   You have been called into your boss's office. You suspect it has to do with the weekend computer breakdown. The restaurant manager had called you, as she is sup-posed to do when a computer problem occurs. Because it was Sunday morning and you expected Sunday to be a busy day at the restaurant, you decided against going to the backup manual sys-tem until a local repairperson could go out on Monday. Instead, you authorized an overtime emergency call. You expected the cost to be within your $500 authority, although you did not ask for an estimate.

Observers' Role.   Use the rating sheet at the end of this exercise set to provide feedback on the listening effectiveness of both role-players.

Total Time. 25 minutes (preparation, 5 minutes; role-play, 10 minutes; debriefing, 10 minutes)

Group Exercise 4: Interpreting Body Language

One person in the group uses just his or her face, keeping all other parts of the body still, to con-vey a feeling or message to others in the group. Other group members try to guess the meaning the sender is trying to convey. After 3 minutes, or when the receivers correctly determine the message, discuss the experience from both the sender's and receiver's viewpoints.

Another person in the group uses just hand gestures, keeping all other parts of the body still, to convey a feeling or message to others in the group. Other group members try to guess the meaning the sender is trying to convey. After 3 minutes, or when the receivers cor-rectly determine the message, discuss the experience from both the sender's and receiver's viewpoints.

The third person in the group uses just different vocal intonations, keeping all other parts of the body still and saying no words, to convey a feeling or message to others in the group. Other group members try to guess the meaning the sender is trying to convey. After 3 minutes, or when the receivers correctly determine the message, discuss the experience from both the sender's and receiver's viewpoints.

Total Time. 24 minutes (preparation, 6 minutes; nonverbal acting, 3 minutes each for a total of 9 minutes; debriefing, 3 minutes each for a total of 9 minutes)

OBSERVER'S RATING SHEET

For the exercise in which you are an observer, evaluate both participants on a 1 to 5 scale (5 being the highest). Enter examples for feedback in the Comments columns.

Exercise: 1 2 3 (Circle one)

Actor A		Behavior	Actor B	
Comments	Rating		Rating	Comments
	_____	Makes eye contact	_____	
	_____	Paraphrases	_____	
	_____	Gives affirmative responses	_____	
	_____	Avoids interrupting	_____	
	_____	Avoids distractions	_____	
	_____	Doesn't overtalk	_____	
	_____	Makes smooth transitions	_____	
	_____	Asks questions	_____	
	_____	Reads nonverbal cues	_____	

Summary Checklist

Take a few minutes to reflect on your performance and look over others' ratings of your skill. Now assess yourself on each of the key learning behaviors. Make a check (✓) next to those behaviors on which you need improvement.

I make effective eye contact.   _____

I exhibit affirmative head nods and appropriate expressions.   _____

I avoid distracting actions or gestures that suggest boredom.   _____

I ask questions.   _____

I paraphrase using my own words.   _____

I avoid interrupting the speaker.   _____

I don't talk too much.   _____

I decipher nonverbal messages.   _____

APPLICATION QUESTIONS

1. "Symbols, not meanings, are transferred from sender to receiver." Discuss this statement and its ramifications for effective listening.
2. How do your personal values distort your interpretation of meaning? What are some examples?
3. Does everyone you work with and everything they have to say deserve your effective listening skills? Explain.
4. Have you taken a formal speech course? If so, did it include listening skills? Is there a bias in our society toward speaking over listening?
5. Who do you find it easiest to listen to? Why? Is this person a good listener also? What behaviors make you think so?
6. Are you a contact or a noncontact person? How does your preference for closeness affect your interpersonal communications with others?

REINFORCEMENT EXERCISES

The following suggestions are activities you can do to practice and reinforce the listening techniques you learned in this chapter. You may want to adapt them to the Action Plan you will develop next, or try them independently.

1. In another class—preferably one with a lecture format—practice active listening. Ask questions, paraphrase, and exhibit affirming nonverbal behaviors. Then ask yourself: Was this harder for me than a normal lecture? Did it affect my note taking? Did I ask more questions? Did it improve my understanding of the lecture's content? What was the instructor's response?
2. During your next telephone conversation, close your eyes and concentrate on being an effective listener; for example, ask questions and paraphrase. Then ask yourself: Did I get more out of the conversation?
3. Spend an entire day fighting your urge to talk. Listen as carefully as you can to everyone you talk to and respond as appropriately as possible to understand, but not to make your own point.
4. Watch one of your favorite TV shows without the volume on. How much of the show did you understand? Why?

ACTION PLAN

1. Which listening behavior do I want to improve the most?

2. Why? What will be my payoff?

3. What potential obstacles stand in my way?

4. What specific things will I do to improve? (For examples, see the Reinforcement Exercises.)

5. When will I do them?

6. How and when will I measure my success?

Endnotes

1. Om P. Kharbanda and Ernest A. Stallworthy, "Listening—A Vital Negotiating Skill," *Journal of Managerial Psychology*, Vol. 6, No. 4 (1991), pp. 6–9, 49–52.
2. J. Crocker, Paper presented at the Speech Communication Association meeting (Minneapolis, MN, 1978). Reported in D. A. Whetten and K. S. Cameron, *Developing Management Skills* (Glenview, IL: Scott-Foresman, 1984), p. 218.
3. Gerald M. Goldhaber, *Organizational Communication,* 4th ed. (Dubuque, IA: William C. Brown, 1980), p. 189.
4. Carl R. Rogers and Richard E. Farson, *Active Listening* (Chicago, IL: Industrial Relations Center of the University of Chicago, 1976).
5. Ralph G. Nichols and Leonard A. Stevens, *Are You Listening?* (New York: McGraw-Hill, 1957).
6. Phillip L. Hunsaker and Anthony J. Alessandra, *The Art of Managing People* (New York: Simon & Schuster, 1986).
7. Kevin J. Murphy, *Effective Listening* (New York: Bantam Books, 1987).
8. Ibid.
9. Ibid.
10. F. Williams, *The New Communications* (Belmont, CA: Wadsworth, 1989), p. 45.
11. Ibid.
12. A. Mehrabian, "Communication Without Words," *Psychology Today* (September 1968), pp. 53–55.
13. Paul Ekman, "Facial Expression and Emotion," *American Psychologist* (April 1993), pp. 384–392.
14. J. W. Gibson and R. M. Hodgetts, *Organizational Communication: A Managerial Perspective* (Orlando, FL: Academic Press, 1986), p. 95.

15. Ibid.

16. Albert Mehrabian, *Nonverbal Communication* (Chicago, IL: Aldine/Atherton, 1972), pp. 25–30.

17. Om P. Kharbanda and Ernest A. Stallworthy, "Verbal and Non-Verbal Communication," *Journal of Managerial Psychology*, Vol. 6, No. 4 (1991), pp. 10–13, 49–52.

18. G. I. Nierenberg and H. H. Calero, *How To Read a Person Like a Book* (New York: Pocket Books, 1973).

19. J. W. Gibson and R. M. Hodgetts, *Organizational Communication: A Managerial Perspective* (Orlando, FL: Academic Press, 1986), pp. 103–105.

20. R. Rosenthal et al., "Body Talk and Tone of Voice: The Language without Words," *Psychology Today* (September 1974), pp. 64–68.

21. Phillip L. Hunsaker and Anthony J. Alessandra, *The New Art of Managing People* (New York: Free Press, 2008), Chapter 12.

22. P. L. Hunsaker, "The Space Case," *Registered Representative* (April 1984), pp. 67–72.

23. Phillip L. Hunsaker and Anthony J. Alessandra, *The Art of Managing People* (New York: Free Press, 2008), pp. 180–186.

24. Anat Rafaeli and Michael G. Pratt, "Tailored Meanings: On the Meaning and Impact of Organizational Dress," *Academy of Management Review*, Vol. 18, No. 1 (1993), pp. 32–55.

7

■■■

Providing Feedback

SELF-ASSESSMENT EXERCISE: MY FEEDBACK STYLE

For each of the following questions, select the answer that best describes you. Remember to respond as you have behaved or would behave, not as you think you should behave.

When giving feedback to another person, I:

	Usually	Sometimes	Seldom
1. Focus my comments on specific, job-related behaviors.	_____	_____	_____
2. Keep my comments descriptive rather than evaluative.	_____	_____	_____
3. Prefer to save up my comments so that they can be presented and discussed in detail during the person's annual performance review.	_____	_____	_____
4. Ensure that my feedback is clearly understood.	_____	_____	_____
5. Supplement criticism with suggestions for what the person can do to improve.	_____	_____	_____
6. Tailor the type of feedback to reflect the person's past performance and future potential.	_____	_____	_____

Scoring and Interpretation

For questions 1, 2, 4, 5, and 6, give yourself 3 points for Usually; 2 points for Sometimes; and 1 point for Seldom. For question 3, give yourself 3 points for Seldom; 2 points for Sometimes; and 1 point for Usually. Sum up your total points. A score of 16 points or higher indicates excellent skills at providing feedback. Scores in the 13–15 range suggest some deficiencies in providing feedback. Scores below 13 indicate considerable room for improvement.

SKILL CONCEPTS

Ask managers how much feedback they give subordinates and you're likely to get a qualified answer. If the feedback is positive, it's likely to be given promptly and enthusiastically. Negative feedback, however, often is treated differently. Managers, like most of us, don't particularly enjoy being the bearers of bad news. They fear offending the recipient or having to deal with defensiveness. The result is that negative feedback often is avoided, delayed, or substantially distorted.[1] The purposes of this chapter are to show you the importance of providing positive and negative feedback and to identify specific techniques to make your feedback more effective.

What do we mean by the term "feedback"? Feedback is any communication that gives people information about some aspect of their behavior and its effect on you.[2] Although our concern in this chapter is predominantly with performance feedback, the skill techniques presented here can be generalized to most types of interpersonal feedback. When you tell people sitting at an adjacent table in a restaurant that their cigarette smoking is bothering you, you're providing them with feedback.

The Value of Feedback

An important reason to be skilled at giving feedback is that it can increase employee performance.[3] This is true for a number of reasons.

First, feedback can induce a person who previously had no goals to set some. As we demonstrated in the previous chapter, goals act as motivators to higher performance. Second, when goals exist, feedback tells people how well they're progressing toward those goals. To the degree that the feedback is favorable, it acts as positive reinforcement. Third, if the feedback indicates inadequate performance, this knowledge can result in increased effort, and the content of the feedback can suggest ways—other than exerting more effort—to improve performance. Fourth, feedback often induces people to raise their goal sights after attaining a previous goal. Finally, providing feedback to employees conveys that others care how they're doing. Therefore, feedback is an indirect form of recognition that can motivate people to higher levels of performance.[4]

Positive versus Negative Feedback

We said earlier that managers treat positive and negative feedback differently. So, too, do recipients. You need to understand this fact and adjust your style accordingly.

Positive feedback is perceived more readily and accurately than negative feedback is. Positive feedback is almost always accepted, but the negative variety often meets resistance.[5] Why? The logical answer seems to be that people want to hear good news and block out the bad. Positive feedback fits what most people want to hear and already believe about themselves.

Does this mean you should avoid giving negative feedback? No. What it means is that you need to be aware of potential resistance and learn to use negative feedback in situations in which it is most likely to be accepted.[6] What are those situations? Research indicates that negative feedback is most likely to be accepted when it comes from a credible source or if it is objective in form. Subjective impressions carry weight only when they come from a person with high status and credibility.[7] This suggests that negative feedback that is supported by hard data—numbers, specific examples, and the like—has a good chance of being accepted. Negative feedback that is subjective can be a meaningful tool for experienced managers, particularly those high in the organization who have earned the respect of their employees. From less experienced managers—those in the lower ranks of the organization and those whose reputations have not yet been established—negative feedback is not likely to be well received.

What We Know about Providing Feedback

Now it's time to look at basic feedback techniques. The following should guide you in determining how and when to provide feedback.

1. ***Focus on specific behaviors.***   Feedback should be specific rather than general.[8] Avoid statements such as "You have a bad attitude" or "I'm really impressed with the good job you did." Those comments are vague, and although they provide information, they don't tell the recipient enough to correct the bad attitude or on what basis you concluded that a good job had been done. Suppose you said something such as, "Bob, I'm concerned with your attitude toward your work. You were a half hour late to yesterday's staff meeting and then told me you hadn't read the preliminary report we were discussing. Today you tell me you're taking off 3 hours early for a dental appointment." Or "Jan, I was really pleased with the job you did on the Phillips account. They increased their purchases from us by 22 percent last month, and I got a call a few days ago from Dan Phillips complimenting me on how quickly you responded to those specification changes for the MJ-7 microchip." These statements focus on specific behaviors. They tell the recipient why you are being critical or complimentary.

2. ***Keep feedback impersonal.***   Feedback, particularly the negative kind, should be descriptive rather than judgmental or evaluative.[9] No matter how upset you are, keep the feedback job-related and never criticize someone personally because of an inappropriate action. Telling people they're stupid, incompetent, or the like is almost always counterproductive. It provokes such an emotional reaction that the performance deviation itself is apt to be overlooked. When you're criticizing, remember that you're censuring a job-related behavior, not the person. You might be tempted to tell someone they are rude and insensitive (which might well be true); however, that's hardly impersonal. It would be better to say something such as "You interrupted me three times with questions that were not urgent when you knew I was talking long-distance to a customer in Scotland."

3. ***Keep feedback goal-oriented.***   Feedback should not be given primarily to dump or unload on someone.[10] If you have to say something negative, make sure it's directed toward the recipient's goals. Ask yourself who the feedback is supposed to help. If the answer is essentially you—"I've got something I just want to get off my chest"—bite your tongue. Such feedback undermines your credibility and weakens the meaning and influence of future feedback.

4. ***Make your feedback well timed.***   Feedback is most meaningful to recipients when only a short interval of time has passed between the behavior and the receipt of feedback about that behavior.[11] To illustrate, a football player who makes a mistake during a game is more likely to respond to his coach's suggestions for improvement right after the mistake, immediately following the game, or during the review of that game's films a few days later rather than to feedback provided by the coach several months later. If you have to spend time re-creating a situation and refreshing someone's memory of it, the feedback you're providing is likely to be ineffective.[12] Moreover, if you are particularly concerned with changing behavior, delays providing feedback on the undesirable actions lessen the likelihood that the feedback will be effective in bringing about the desired change.[13] However, making feedback prompt merely for the sake of promptness can backfire if you have insufficient information, if you're angry, or if you're otherwise emotionally upset. In such instances, well timed might mean "somewhat delayed."

5. ***Ensure understanding.*** Is your feedback concise and complete enough that the recipient clearly and fully understands your communication? Every successful communication requires transference and understanding of meaning. If feedback is to be effective, you need to ensure that the recipient understands it.[14] Consistent with our discussion of listening techniques, you should have the recipient rephrase the content of your feedback to see whether it fully captures the meaning you intended.

6. ***If negative, make sure the behavior is controllable by the recipient.*** There's little value in reminding people of shortcomings over which they have no control. Therefore, negative feedback should be directed toward behavior that the recipient can do something about.[15] For example, to criticize an employee who is late because he forgot to set his alarm is valid. To criticize him for being late when the subway he takes to work every day had a power failure, trapping him underground for half an hour, is pointless. He could do nothing to correct what happened.

   Additionally, when negative feedback is given concerning something that is controllable by the recipient, it might be a good idea to indicate specifically what can be done to improve the situation. This takes some of the sting out of the criticism and offers guidance to recipients who understand the problem but don't know how to resolve it.

7. ***Tailor the feedback to fit the person.*** Our final piece of advice regarding feedback is to take into consideration the person to whom the feedback is directed. You should consider recipients' past performance and your estimate of their future potential in designing the frequency, amount, and content of performance feedback.[16] For high performers with potential for growth, feedback should be frequent enough to prod them into taking corrective action, but not so frequent that it is experienced as controlling and saps their initiative. For adequate performers who have settled into their jobs and have limited potential for advancement, little feedback is needed because they have displayed reliable and steady behavior in the past, know their tasks, and realize what needs to be done. For poor performers—that is, people who will need to be removed from their jobs if their performance doesn't improve—feedback should be frequent and specific, and the connection between acting on the feedback and negative sanctions such as being laid off or fired should be made explicit.

CONCEPT QUIZ

Take the following 10-question, true–false quiz. The answers are at the end of the quiz. If you read the previous material carefully, you should get them all correct. If you miss any, go back and find out why you got them wrong.

Circle the right answer.

True	**False**	1.	The givers and the receivers of feedback tend to treat negative and positive feedback differently.
True	**False**	2.	Managers should refrain from giving an employee negative feedback.
True	**False**	3.	Feedback, by definition, is concerned only with an employee's performance and its effect on you.
True	**False**	4.	Feedback tells people how well they're progressing toward their goals.

True	**False**	5. Negative feedback is more likely to be accepted when combined with positive feedback.
True	**False**	6. Objective negative feedback is more likely to be accepted than the subjective variety.
True	**False**	7. Specific feedback is more effective than general feedback.
True	**False**	8. Effective feedback avoids criticism of a person's personality or personal style.
True	**False**	9. Delays between a recipient's undesirable behavior and providing feedback on that behavior should be avoided.
True	**False**	10. Don't give criticism unless it is desired by the recipient.

Answers: (1) True; (2) False; (3) False; (4) True; (5) True; (6) True; (7) True; (8) True; (9) True; (10) False

BEHAVIORAL CHECKLIST

Look for these specific behaviors when evaluating your feedback skills and those of others.

Providing Effective Feedback Requires:

- Supporting negative feedback with hard data.
- Focusing on specific rather than general behaviors.
- Keeping comments impersonal and job-related.
- Ensuring that the recipient has a clear and full understanding of the feedback.
- Directing negative feedback toward behavior that is controllable by the recipient.
- Adjusting the frequency, amount, and content of feedback to meet the needs of the recipient.

ATTENTION!

Do not read the following until assigned to do so by your instructor.

MODELING EXERCISE

How Is Your Instructor Doing?

This exercise is a chance for the students to provide real feedback to their instructor early in the semester. Thus, it is not only an opportunity to learn important skills but also a chance to improve the class process in general.

Instructions

A class leader is selected (either a volunteer or someone chosen by the instructor) to provide feedback to the instructor. The class leader will preside over a discussion of the instructor's classroom performance and then will provide feedback to the instructor about the class's consensus ratings.

After explaining the exercise, the instructor leaves the room for about 20 minutes. During that time, the student chosen as leader conducts a class discussion based on agreed-upon performance criteria and prepares feedback for the instructor on each dimension of his or her performance.

The class can utilize the following performance dimensions that have been identified to be critical to a college instructor's job performance:[17] instructor knowledge, testing procedures, student–teacher relations, organizational skills, communication skills, subject relevance, and utility of assignments. The class may also want to add other rating dimensions relevant to their particular class.

The leader has 15 minutes to get input from the class and to prepare the ratings. (The leader should take notes for personal use but will not be required to give the instructor any written documentation.) After the 15-minute period is up, the leader takes 5 more minutes to prepare for the feedback session, and another student invites the instructor back into the class-room. The feedback session begins as soon as the instructor knocks on the door. The class leader applies the appropriate skills and provides the feedback to the instructor.

Important Note. Your instructor understands that this is only an exercise and is prepared to accept criticism (and any praise you might want to convey). Your instructor also recognizes that the leader's feedback is a composite of many students' input. Be open and honest in your feedback and have confidence that your instructor will not be vindictive.

Debriefing

After the leader has delivered the feedback to the instructor, the rest of the class then provides feedback to the leader based on their observations from the Observer's Rating Sheet. Then the instructor can provide the leader feedback about the feelings and reactions experienced. The instructor should also take a couple of minutes to share with the class the value of the feedback received and how it will be applied.

Total Time. 50 minutes (not to exceed 15 minutes for class discussion; 5 minutes for preparation of feedback; 15 minutes for instructor feedback session; 10 minutes for debriefing the leader's effectiveness in providing feedback; 5 minutes for instructor to share reactions to the feedback).

OBSERVER'S RATING SHEET

Evaluate the feedback skills of your classmate who is playing the role of the leader using a 1 to 5 scale (5 being the highest). Provide examples for specific feedback in the space under each skill criterion.

Provides support for negative feedback.   _____

Focuses on specific behaviors.   _____

Keeps comments impersonal and job-related.   _____

Makes sure recipient understands feedback.   _____

Criticizes only controllable behaviors.   _____

Adjusts feedback to needs and situation of recipient.   _____

GROUP EXERCISES

The following group exercises consist of three role-plays that allow you to practice your feedback skills in a variety of situations. Form trios and rotate roles for observer and actors so that all people receive feedback.

Group Exercise 1: Reviewing the Resident Manager

Actors.   Dr. Fargo and Robin Munson

Situation.   Robin Munson is a graduate student at State College and supplements her income by acting as resident manager of one of the college dormitories. Robin is responsible for overseeing the dorm's four wing residents (undergraduates who receive a small monthly stipend) and 250 students. This essentially means ensuring that dorm rules are obeyed (visiting hours in rooms, quiet hours, etc.) and notifying the appropriate maintenance personnel when problems arise. Robin is provided with a free residential suite in the dorm and a salary of $350 a month. Robin reports to the college's dean of students, Dr. Fargo.

This is Robin's first semester as a resident manager. Though only on the job for 3 months, Robin is aware that several complaints have been registered against her by students in the dorm. Robin knows this because Dr. Fargo called yesterday and said so. Dr. Fargo has asked Robin to come over to discuss the complaints.

Robin Munson's Role.   You graduated from college 3 years ago and decided to return for a graduate degree. Money is a problem, though, so you applied for and received a resident manager position. You were told the job would take little of your time. That was important because you were taking a full load of graduate courses and would have to spend almost all of your time studying. Dr. Fargo called yesterday and told you some students were displeased with the way you were running the dorm. You had no idea to what Dr. Fargo was alluding. You thought everything was going OK because none of the students had said anything to you. So far, you have liked the resident manager's job—mostly because you don't have to spend more than an hour or two a week on it.

Dr. Fargo's Role.   Within the past 2 weeks, you've received visits from several groups of students living in Robin's dorm. On the positive side, the students complimented Robin for keeping the common areas clean and for making sure that maintenance problems are attended to quickly. However, their main concern was that the noise level at night made studying impossible. The students said that attempts to talk to Robin had been unsuccessful—the consensus was that Robin was never available. You called two of the four wing residents and they confirmed that they were having trouble keeping the noise level down and that Robin's studies clearly had priority over problems in the dorm.

You believe that problems should be addressed as they arise. Therefore, you have decided to have a discussion with Robin. Your position on resident managers is basically that they need to spend as much time as necessary to keep things running smoothly. If they can do the job in a few hours a week, that's great, but if it takes 20 hours a week, so be it. You hired Robin because she seemed responsible and came highly recommended by several faculty members in her graduate department. You were impressed with Robin during the job interview and thought she would be a good addition to the staff. In retrospect, you might not have been as honest as you should have been about the demands of the job, but you've had trouble in past years getting and keeping good dorm resident managers.

Observers' Role.   Provide feedback to the student playing Dr. Fargo using the Observer's Rating Sheet. Make sure that you use the same behaviors listed on the rating sheet when you give your own feedback to the observer.

Total Time. 30 minutes (preparation, 5 minutes; role-play, 15 minutes; debriefing, 10 minutes)

Group Exercise 2: McDonald's on Probation

Actors.   Kelly King and Fran Thomas

Situation.   Kelly King is a shift manager at a McDonald's restaurant. Kelly has been in this position for 18 months and supervises 20 people (counter clerks and cooks) on the day shift. One of these people is Fran Thomas.

   Fran is a 19-year-old high school graduate. Fran's prior work experience includes being an attendant at a laundromat and selling jewelry in a small department store. Kelly hired Fran 3 months ago from among half a dozen job applicants. What impressed Kelly about Fran was (1) her high school diploma; (2) her prior work experience; and (3) references that reported that Fran was dependable, honest, good with numbers, and followed directions well.

   McDonald's employees are on probation for their first 3 months, after which they are considered permanent. Fran has completed the 3-month probationary period, and Kelly is now required to give a performance review. It's 10:00 AM, the restaurant is quiet, and Kelly has asked Fran to sit down in a booth and talk.

Kelly King's Role.   Your job is hectic. Supervising 20 people in a busy fast-food restaurant allows little time for planning. You often feel that all you do each day is run around putting out "fires." Because of the hectic pace, you haven't had time to point out to Fran a few of her problems. As with other employees, you plan to use the 3-month review as an opportunity to tell Fran that her job performance has been satisfactory on the whole, but two things concern you. First, Fran has long hair and is required by health regulations to wear a hair net at all times. You've had to remind her three or four times to wear the hair net. Second, you're aware that Fran has been dating Terry—another employee in the restaurant. You don't consider the fact that they are dating to be your business, but what does concern you is that the two show demonstrative affection (touching and caressing) toward each other while working behind the counter. You've decided to extend Fran's probation for one more month and then give her a 25-cent-per-hour raise. (Fran is currently making $4.75 an hour, and the standard 3-month raise is 50 cents per hour.)

Fran Thomas's Role.   You've been on the job for 3 months. You find it strange that your boss—Kelly King—hasn't said one word to you about how well you've been performing. This lack of communication has been bothering you for a number of weeks, but you haven't brought it up because you think it is King's job to initiate such a discussion. This lack of communication got so bad last week that you thought about quitting. The only reason you didn't is that Terry—a coworker you've been dating—convinced you not to. Terry agreed with you that Kelly King is curt, thoughtless, and a lousy communicator. However, you think you've been doing a good job, you like your coworkers, and the promotion opportunities at McDonald's are good. As you sit down to talk with Kelly King, you expect King to tell you you're one of the best employees and that you can expect a pay raise. (You're currently making $4.75 an hour.) After all, you're conscientious and energetic, and the only comments that Kelly has ever made to you that could even possibly be construed as negative were on the few occasions you forgot to wear a hair net to control your long hair. You remember that during your initial job interview, King said you could count on a pay raise at the end of 3 months if your work proved satisfactory. No figure was mentioned, but you know that Terry got a 50-cent-an-hour increase after 3 months.

Total Time. 30 minutes (preparation, 5 minutes; role-play, 15 minutes; debriefing, 10 minutes)

Group Exercise 3: Reining in Barry

Actors. Barry Irwin and Dana Douglas

Situation.   Barry Irwin is a sales representative for Atlas Metals, a distributor of aluminum sheet and tubing. Atlas sells predominantly to large aerospace-, automobile-, and truck-manufacturing firms. Barry has worked for Atlas for several years. Last year, Atlas's sales reached $12 million. Barry's sales manager is Dana Douglas.

Barry Irwin's Role.   You've been trying for 8 months to get Boeing Aerospace as a customer. Last month you saw a real opportunity. They were taking bids for a specific size of aluminum tubing that your firm carries. The order wouldn't be very big, but you thought it could get you in the door at Boeing. You submitted a bid of $19,300 for the order. You did so without checking with your boss, but you didn't think it necessary because you have authorization to make bids up to $40,000 without approval from above. The catch, however, is that the company sales policy (which is stated specifically in the sales manual) is never to sell below cost. You knew that your bid would result in a small loss for the company, but you saw the potential for annual sales to Boeing of $2 or $3 million. Atlas had never been able to get Boeing's business before. You knew you were wrong in breaking company policy, but you also knew that Atlas has wanted Boeing as a customer for years. To avoid a debate with your boss, you decided to act on your own and go for the Boeing order even though it would generate a loss. You got the order. In your view, the potential long-term benefits from the order far exceed the short-term costs.

Dana Douglas has just called you into his office. The reason? Dana just received the monthly sales analysis and wants to talk to you about the Boeing order.

Dana Douglas's Role.   Barry Irwin is one of your best salespeople. You admire Barry's drive and determination. You particularly value Barry's success in developing new accounts and expanding sales with established customers. Barry has, at times, bent the rules at Atlas but has never broken them.

Today you received the monthly sales analysis, broken down by salesperson and customer. You noticed that Barry got a small order—less than $20,000—from Boeing. It's the first you've heard of it. You have mixed feelings. On the one hand, it's the first time Atlas has gotten a Boeing order. Though Atlas has wanted their business for years, it has never gotten an order before. It might be the beginning of a profitable relationship. On the other hand, the order generates a loss of $2,600. Company policy (which Barry knows perfectly well) allows salespeople to approve, on their own, sales of up to $40,000; however, taking orders that produce a loss are strictly prohibited. You know you have to talk to Barry about this. You don't want to stifle Barry's initiative, but company policy needs to be followed. You're a reasonable person, and salespeople like Barry are hard to find. Yet you know Atlas's president will be on your back if salespeople begin taking it upon themselves to break company policies whenever they see fit. You have called Barry into your office to discuss the problem.

Total Time. 25 minutes (preparation, 5 minutes; role-play, 10 minutes; debriefing, 10 minutes)

OBSERVER'S RATING SHEET

For the exercise for which you are an observer, evaluate key feedback behaviors of the actor you were observing on a 1 to 5 scale (5 being the highest). Insert examples for feedback in the space between behavioral criteria.

Provides support for negative feedback.   _____

Focuses on specific behaviors.   _____

Keeps comments impersonal and job-related.   _____

Makes sure recipient understands feedback.   _____

Criticizes only controllable behaviors.   _____

Adjusts feedback to needs and situation of recipient.   _____

Summary Checklist

Review your performance and look over others' ratings of your skills. Now assess yourself on each of the key learning behaviors. Make a check (✓) next to those behaviors in which you need improvement.

I provide hard data to support negative feedback.   _____

I focus on specific behaviors.   _____

I keep my comments impersonal and job-related.   _____

I make sure the recipient understands my feedback.   _____

I direct negative feedback to behaviors that are controllable
by the recipient.   _____

I adjust my feedback to the needs and situation of the recipient.   _____

APPLICATION QUESTIONS

1. Contrast the effects from positive and negative feedback.
2. Relate the feedback concepts in this chapter to your knowledge of how parents are supposed to raise children properly.
3. Some jobs provide their incumbents with internal feedback, thus lessening the need for the manager to provide feedback. Give some examples of jobs that provide a lot of internal feedback. Now give some examples of jobs for which the feedback responsibility falls heavily on the manager.
4. Would you criticize a good friend who has a mannerism (speech, body movement, style of dress, or the like) that you think is inappropriate and detracts from the overall impression that he or she makes? If not, why wouldn't you? If so, how would you do it?

REINFORCEMENT EXERCISES

The following suggestions are activities you can do to practice and reinforce the feedback techniques you learned in this chapter.

1. The next time a friend or relative does something well, give him or her positive feedback. See what the reaction is.
2. Provide constructive feedback to a person you know who has distracting mannerisms such as cracking knuckles, chewing gum too loudly, talking too loudly on the phone, or not using deodorant. After you are finished, ask for feedback about the person's reactions.
3. During your instructor's office hours, stop by and provide feedback about how this course is going so far.

ACTION PLAN

1. Which behavior do I want to improve the most?

2. Why? What will be my payoff?

3. What potential obstacles stand in my way?

4. What specific things will I do to improve? (For examples, see the Reinforcement Exercises.)

5. When will I do them?

6. How and when will I measure my success?

Endnotes

1. Cynthia Fisher, "Transmission of Positive and Negative Feedback to Subordinates: A Laboratory Investigation," *Journal of Applied Psychology* (October 1979), pp. 533–540.
2. Cyril R. Mill, "Feedback: The Art of Giving and Receiving Help," in Larry Porter and Cyril R. Mill (eds.), *The Reading Book for Human Relations Training* (Bethel, ME: NTL Institute for Applied Behavioral Science, 1976), pp. 18–19.
3. Judith L. Komaki, Robert L. Collins, and Pat Penn, "The Role of Performance Antecedents and Consequences in Work Motivation,"*Journal of Applied Psychology* (June 1982), pp. 334–340; Edwin A. Locke and Gary P. Latham, *Goal-Setting: A Motivational Technique That Works!* (Englewood Cliffs, NJ: Prentice Hall, 1984).
4. Robert E. Coffey, Curtis W. Cook, and Phillip L. Hunsaker, *Management and Organizational Behavior* (Burr Ridge, IL: Austin Press/Irwin, 1994).
5. Daniel Ilgen, Cynthia D. Fisher, and M. Susan Taylor, "Consequences of Individual Feedback on Behavior in Organizations,"*Journal of Applied Psychology* (August 1979), pp. 349–371.
6. Fernando Bartolome, "Teaching About Whether to Give Negative Feedback," *Organizational Behavior Teaching Review,* Vol. 11, Issue 2 (1986–87), pp. 95–104.
7. Keith Halperin, C. R. Snyder, Randee J. Shenkel, and B. Kent Houston, "Effect of Source Status and Message Favorability on Acceptance of Personality Feedback," *Journal of Applied Psychology* (February 1976), pp. 85–88.

8. Robert E. Coffey, Curtis W. Cook, and Phillip L. Hunsaker, *Management and Organizational Behavior* (Burr Ridge, IL: Austin Press/Irwin, 1994).

9. Tony Alessandra and Phillip Hunsaker, *Communicating at Work* (New York: Simon & Schuster, 1993), pp. 86–90.

10. Cyril R. Mill, "Feedback: The Art of Giving and Receiving Help," in Larry Porter and Cyril R. Mill (eds.), *The Reading Book for Human Relations Training* (Bethel, ME: NTL Institute for Applied Behavioral Science, 1976), pp. 18–19.

11. Ibid.

12. Kathleen S. Verderber and Rudolph F. Verderber, *Inter-Act: Using Interpersonal Communication Skills,* 4th ed. (Belmont, CA: Wadsworth, 1986).

13. Lyle E. Bourne, Jr., and C. Victor Bunderson, "Effects of Delay of Information Feedback and Length of Post-Feedback Interval on Concept Identification," *Journal of Experimental Psychology* (January 1963), pp. 1–5.

14. Cyril R. Mill, "Feedback: The Art of Giving and Receiving Help," in Larry Porter and Cyril R. Mill (eds.), *The Reading Book for Human Relations Training* (Bethel, Maine: NTL Institute for Applied Behavioral Science, 1976), pp. 18–19.

15. Kathleen S. Verderber and Rudolph F. Verderber, *Inter-Act: Using Interpersonal Communication Skills,* 4th ed. (Belmont, CA: Wadsworth, 1986).

16. Larry L. Cummings, "Appraisal Purpose and the Nature, Amount, and Frequency of Feedback." Paper presented at the American Psychological Association meeting, Washington, DC (September 1976).

17. H. John Bernardin and C. S. Walter, "Effects of Rater Training and Diary-Keeping on Psychometric Error in Ratings," *Journal of Applied Psychology* (February 1977), pp. 64–69.

8

■ ■ ■

Communicating Across Cultures

SELF-ASSESSMENT EXERCISE: HOW WELL DO I COMMUNICATE WITH PEOPLE FROM DIFFERENT CULTURES?

For each of the following questions, select the answer that best describes your behavior when you are communicating with someone from a different culture.

	Usually	Sometimes	Seldom
1. I assume differences until similarity is proven.	_____	_____	_____
2. I emphasize evaluation rather than description.	_____	_____	_____
3. I interpret the person's action from the perspective of his or her culture rather than my own.	_____	_____	_____
4. I treat my first interpretations as working hypotheses rather than facts.	_____	_____	_____
5. I pay careful attention to feedback.	_____	_____	_____
6. If we are speaking the same language I assume the same words and phrases mean the same thing.	_____	_____	_____
7. I don't assume that facial expressions mean the same things in both cultures.	_____	_____	_____
8. I interpret direct eye contact as a sign of honesty, interest, openness, and confidence.	_____	_____	_____
9. I back off if the person raises his or her voice and talks louder than I do because he or she is becoming excited or angry.	_____	_____	_____
10. I use stereotypes to make sense of their behavior.	_____	_____	_____

Scoring and Interpretation

For questions 1, 3, 4, 5, and 7 give yourself 3 points for Usually; 2 points for Sometimes; and 1 point for Seldom. For questions 2, 6, 8, 9, and 10, give yourself 3 points for Seldom; 2 points for Sometimes; and 1 point for Usually. Sum up your total points. A score of 27 or higher means you're skilled at communicating with someone from a different culture. A score of 22–26 suggests that you have some deficiencies that should be corrected. A score below 22 indicates that you have developed a number of bad habits when communicating with someone from a different culture. You should learn and practice the skills in this chapter.

SKILL CONCEPTS

Achieving effective communication is a challenge even when the workforce is culturally homogeneous, but when one company includes a variety of languages and cultural backgrounds, it becomes even more difficult. The greater the differences in backgrounds between senders and receivers, the greater the differences in meanings attached to particular words and behaviors. This is equally true for communicators from different countries, different sexes, or different subcultures in the same country.

GLOBAL CULTURAL DIFFERENCES

While most European businesspeople speak several languages, the average American businessperson speaks only English. The same year that 20 million Japanese were studying English, only 23,000 Americans were studying Japanese.[1] Nevertheless, the vast majority of people in the world do not understand English, making foreign language training a necessity in today's international business environment.

When working in a global environment, it is important to recognize the difficulties of cross-cultural communication. Cross-cultural misinterpretation is influenced by many different factors. Some of the important ones are discussed below.

Different Cultures Interpret, Behave, and Interact Differently

People working in a global environment should acknowledge and understand how different cultures interpret, behave, and interact. It is inappropriate to assume a particular working style or mode of communication that works in the United States is transferable across cultures. An American manager might be shocked if not a single person shows up to a 7:30 AM meeting in Italy. Additionally, the manager might not understand why some Italians do not leave work at 6:00 PM for dinner, preferring to eat at 10:00 or 11:00 PM.

The Same Words Mean Different Things to People from Different Cultures

Even if two communicators are speaking the same language, the same words and phrases may mean different things to people from different cultures. For example, the phrase "That would be very hard to do" means to Americans that some adjustments or extra contributions may be necessary, but the deal is still possible. To Japanese, the phrase clearly means, "No, it won't be possible." For a nonverbal example, Americans think that maintaining eye contact is important and others who don't are dishonest or rude. Japanese, on the other hand, lower their eyes as a gesture of respect when speaking with a superior.[2]

The Same Nonverbal Behavior Means Different Things to People from Different Cultures

Many gestures are culturally bound and susceptible to misinterpretation. It is very easy for Americans to misread Japanese body language, for example. The Japanese try to avoid personal confrontation; they usually exhibit a noncontroversial demeanor and use excessive politeness and tact to smooth over any differences that arise. When negotiating among themselves, this presents no difficulties. But for Americans, serious misinterpretations can arise.[3]

The same facial expression can mean different things in different cultures. For example, agreement is indicated by up-and-down head nods in American culture, but it is expressed by side-to-side head movements in India.[4]

Eye contact also varies by culture. Direct eye contact is generally perceived as a sign of honesty, interest, openness, and confidence in the United States. If eye contact is avoided, most North Americans feel that the other is embarrassed, nervous, or hiding something. In some Latin American and Asian cultures, however, people with lower status are not supposed to look directly in the face of higher status individuals. In the United States, this lack of eye contact could be interpreted as a sign of deceit.[5]

Vocal meanings also vary across cultures. For example, if an American raises his or her voice, we assume that the person is excited or angry and we focus on the projected emotions. In Latin American cultures normal, vocal volume is generally higher than in the United States. The normal American vocal level would be considered too subdued to indicate genuine involvement and appropriate concern for what the Latin American is communicating.[6]

Stereotypes Can Cause Misunderstanding

The use of categories and stereotypes, either conscientiously or subconscientiously, allows people to make order or sense of different situations. However, in a multicultural environment, the use of categories and stereotypes can cause significant misunderstanding.[7] The American manager could stereotype the Italian colleagues who did not show up to the 7:30 AM meeting as "lazy" or "not serious about the project." However, the American manager is not recognizing the fact that his Italian colleagues worked until 11:00 PM the night before. The rush to categorize or stereotype, rather than attempting to objectively understand, permitted the American manager to quickly explain to himself why the Italian colleagues did not show up to the early meeting, but it will no doubt cause significant misunderstanding and additional problems later on.

GENDER DIFFERENCES

Gender can create subculture communication barriers within the same country. In the United States, for example, men frequently use talk to emphasize status differences because of their need for independence, while women more often use it to create interpersonal connections based on common ground because of their greater need for intimacy. Men frequently complain that women talk a lot about their problems, and women criticize men for not listening. Men tend to present factual information in attempts to establish power positions. However, women tend to focus on relationships and gain a consensus to a larger extent than men.[8] What men are doing is asserting their independence and desire for control by providing solutions that women do not necessarily want in their quest for support, understanding, and connection.[9]

Male leaders' communication behaviors are often characterized by task orientation, dominance, challenges to others, and attempts to control the conversation. For example, males talk more and interrupt more often than do females. Females are usually more informative, receptive to ideas, focused on interpersonal relations, and concerned for others. They are more reactive and show more emotional support.[10]

Women are more precise in their pronunciation than men, who, for example, tend to shorten the ends of words (using -*in* instead of -*ing*).[11] Males and females also differ in word choice. Females tend to select more intense adverbs, such as "awfully friendly," whereas males use words that are more descriptive and defining.

Women more often use *qualifying terms*, which are phrases that soften or qualify the intent of our communication. They make language less absolute and less powerful. Examples include "maybe," "you know what I mean," "it's only my opinion," and so on.[12]

Women also frequently use *tag questions*, which are qualifying words at the end of a sentence that ask the other for confirmation of the statement presented. When using these, they automatically defer to others: "It's really time for a break now, right?" or "We did the job right, didn't we?" By adding the tag question, the speaker gives the impression of being unsure and surrenders decision-making power.[13]

A clear difference has even been found in the language used by males and females online. Language styles online may be different because they reflect the different goals of the users.[14] Aggressive expressions in messages written by men far outnumber those written by women. Men utilize more openly aggressive language, including personal attacks and put-downs. Women, on the other hand, use more expressions offering support and a deepening of their relationship with the readers. Women used much more open expressions of appreciation and thanks, while men used "tighter" and less direct expressions. Men are more interested in presenting their personal point of view in order to present an authoritative contribution to the discussion, while women were more interested in the essence of the contribution itself. Men apparently use email as a chance to further their own influence, by gaining valuable information and by extending their own authority, while women use this technology to nurture existing relationships and develop new ones.

GUIDELINES FOR IMPROVING CROSS-CULTURAL COMMUNICATION

Thousands of successful cross-cultural business communications take place every day. Familiarizing yourself with cultural differences and being aware of your own cultural frame of reference can help you communicate more effectively when working with people from different cultures or subcultures. The following more specific guidelines can facilitate cross-cultural communication.[15]

Assume Differences until Similarity Is Proven

Effective cross-cultural communicators know that they don't know how people with different backgrounds perceive a situation or interpret certain forms of communication. They do not assume that a person from another culture interprets a word or behavior the same way that they do. Therefore, to avoid embarrassing misinterpretations, first assume that individuals from different cultures will interpret communication or behaviors differently until some similarities are proven.

Emphasize Description Rather Than Interpretation or Evaluation

Effective cross-cultural communicators delay judgment until they have observed and interpreted the situation from the perspectives of all cultures involved. Description emphasizes observation of what has occurred rather than interpretation or evaluation, which are based more on the observer's culture and background than on the actual facts.

Empathize with the Person from Another Culture

When trying to understand the words, motives, and actions of a person from another culture, try to interpret them from the perspective of that culture rather than your own. When you view behaviors from your own perspective, you can completely misinterpret the other's actions if he or she has different values, experiences, and objectives. Therefore, to reduce cross-cultural misinterpretations, it is important to reflect and view behaviors from the other person's culture.

Treat Your Interpretations as Guesses until You Can Confirm Them

Check with others from other cultures to make sure that your evaluation of a behavior is accurate if you are in doubt. Treat your first interpretations as working hypotheses rather than facts, and pay careful attention to feedback in order to avoid serious miscommunications and resulting problems.

CONCEPT QUIZ

When communicating with a person from a different culture, indicate whether the response given is true or false. After answering the following 10 questions, grade your quiz with the key that follows the questions. Then check your understanding of any questions you missed by rereading that section in the text.

Circle the right answer.

True   False   1. You should assume differences until similarity is proven.

True   False   2. It is better to emphasize evaluation rather than description.

True   False   3. The person's actions should be interpreted from his or her cultural perspective rather than your own.

True   False   4. You should treat first interpretations as working hypotheses rather than facts.

True   False   5. You should pay careful attention to feedback.

True   False   6. The same words and phrases in the same language mean the same things regardless of what culture a person is from.

True   False   7. Facial expressions mean the same things in most cultures.

True   False   8. Lack of direct eye contact is a sign of dishonesty in most cultures.

True   False   9. If the other person talks louder than you are used to it is because he or she is becoming angry.

True   False   10. Stereotypes explain the behavior of people from different cultures.

Answers: (1) True; (2) False; (3) True; (4) True; (5) True; (6) False; (7) False; (8) False; (9) False; (10) False

BEHAVIORAL CHECKLIST

Look for these specific behaviors when evaluating your skills and the skills of others when communicating cross-culturally.

Communicating Effectively Across Cultures Requires That You:

- Assume differences until similarity is proven.
- Emphasize description rather than interpretation or evaluation.

- Interpret words, motives, and actions from the perspective of the other culture.
- Treat your interpretations as guesses until you can confirm them.
- Ask for and pay attention to feedback to make sure that your evaluation of words and behavior is accurate.
- Avoid the use of stereotypes to explain the behavior of people from different cultures.

ATTENTION!

Do not read the following until assigned to do so by your instructor.

MODELING EXERCISE

The Jimmy Lincoln Case[16]

Instructions.   Six people need to volunteer to conduct the Jimmy Lincoln role-play. One should be designated as the chairperson who has 25 minutes to lead the group members who are playing the other five roles in a decision-making meeting. The rest of the class will serve as observers and provide the role-players with feedback based on the Observer's Rating Sheet that evaluates how well the role-players communicate cross-culturally. An equal number of observers should be assigned to observe each specific role-player.

Before conducting the meeting, the entire class should read the situation describing Jimmy in the following case. Each role-player should then read their assigned role (but not the other roles) and rank-order their *personal preference* solution on the Worksheet. The observers should also rank-order their *personal preference* solution on the Worksheet. Then a member should individually fill out the personal preference part of the Worksheet that follows from the perspective of his or her assigned role.

Actors.   The roles in this exercise are supervisor, crew chief, seasoned manager, union representative, member of the human resources department, and member of the company's affirmative action office.

Situation.   Jimmy Lincoln has a grim personal background. He is the third child in an inner-city, minority family. He has not seen his parents for several years. He recalls that his father used to come home drunk and beat up family members; everyone ran when he came staggering home.

His mother, according to Jimmy, wasn't much better. She was irritable and unhappy, and she always predicted that Jimmy would come to no good end. Yet she worked, when her health allowed, to provide the family with food and clothing. She frequently decried the fact that she was not able to be the kind of mother she would like to be.

Jimmy quit school in the seventh grade. He had great difficulty conforming to the school routine—misbehaving often, being truant frequently, and getting into fights with schoolmates. On several occasions, he was picked up by the police and, along with other members of his group, questioned during investigations into cases of both petty and grand larceny. The police regarded him as a high-potential troublemaker.

The juvenile officer of the court saw in Jimmy some good qualities that no one else seemed to sense. This man, Mr. O'Brien, took it upon himself to act as a father figure to Jimmy. He had several long conversations with Jimmy, during which he managed to penetrate Jimmy's defensive shell to some degree. He represented to Jimmy the first semblance of a personal, caring influence in his life. Through Mr. O'Brien's efforts, Jimmy returned to school and obtained a high school diploma. Afterward, Mr. O'Brien helped him obtain his first job.

Now, at age 22, Jimmy is a stockroom clerk at Costello Pharmaceutical Laboratory. On the whole, his performance has been acceptable, but with some glaring exceptions. One involved a clear act of insubordination, though the issue was fairly unimportant. On another occasion, Jimmy was accused by a coworker, on circumstantial grounds, of destroying some expensive equipment. Though the investigation is still open, it appears that the destruction was accidental. He also appears to have lost an extremely important requisition (although he claims he never saw it). In addition, his laid-back attitude and wisecracking ways tend to irritate his coworkers.

It is also important to note that Jimmy's appearance is disheveled. Researchers in the lab have commented that his appearance doesn't fit in with the company's image. Others have half jokingly wondered aloud whether he is counting or *taking* the drugs in the stockroom.

ATTENTION!

Read Your Assigned Role Only!

ROLES

Jimmy's Supervisor's Role.   You are fairly new to management and are not sure how to handle this situation. You see merit in giving Jimmy the benefit of the doubt and helping him out, but you frankly wonder if it's worth the hassle. Seeking advice, you organize a committee of individuals close to the situation. These include the crew chief (who has expressed frustration about the effects of Jimmy's performance and reputation on the morale of the work group), a seasoned manager (who has a reputation for being evenhanded), a union representative (who tends to view most acts of employee discipline as an infringement on employee rights), a member of the human resources department (who is concerned about following proper company procedures), and a member of the company's affirmative action office (who is concerned that managers at Costello do not fully understand the handicap that workers like Jimmy bring with them to the workplace).

Crew Chief's Role.   You are frustrated about the effects of Jimmy's performance and reputation on the morale of the work group. Something has to be done to stop these problems. You want Jimmy fired or moved.

Seasoned Manager's Role.   You understand the situation from all points of view. Your main concern is that the problem is solved in an evenhanded way. You take offense to any heavy-handed, myopic suggestions.

Union Representative's Role.   You tend to view most acts of employee discipline as an infringement on employee rights, so you are concerned about the possibility of unfair discipline of an individual who is probably doing the best he can under the circumstances. You are here to support Jimmy's rights and protect him from unfair treatment.

Member of the Human Resources Department's Role.   You have just lost a case regarding a firing for insufficient cause. You are concerned primarily about following proper company procedures. As long as it is done right, you don't particularly care what the outcome is. You want to know the exact procedures that will be followed for any suggested action.

Member of the Company's Affirmative Action Office's Role. You are concerned that managers at Costello do not fully understand the handicap that workers like Jimmy bring with them to the workplace. Consequently, you plan to give them an education, special assistance, and direction in helping Jimmy grow and achieve his potential.

Instructions. When individuals have completed their personal preferences on the worksheet, the supervisor should act as chair of the committee and begin the discussion. The group's assignment is to reach consensus on the rank-ordered options (from this list). Group members should stay in role during the meeting. They should not use any statistical process to reach a rank order or show their worksheets to anyone else.

Total Time. 45 minutes (preparation, 10 minutes; reach a decision, 25 minutes; debriefing, 10 minutes)

Worksheet: Jimmy Lincoln Decision

Group members should rank in order their preferred solutions from the perspective of the role character being played after reading the case and before the group meeting in the Personal Preference column. Do not show anyone else your rankings.

After the meeting, list the group's consensus rank ordering in the Group Decision column.

Personal Preference	Group Decision	
_____	_____	1. Give Jimmy a warning that, at the next sign of trouble, a formal reprimand will be placed in his file.
_____	_____	2. Do nothing, as it is unclear that Jimmy has done anything seriously wrong. Back off and give him a chance to prove himself.
_____	_____	3. Create strict controls (do's and don'ts) for Jimmy with immediate discipline for any misbehavior.
_____	_____	4. Give Jimmy a great deal of warmth and personal attention (overlooking his annoying mannerisms) so that he will feel accepted.
_____	_____	5. Fire Jimmy. It's not worth the time and effort spent for such a low-level position.
_____	_____	6. Treat Jimmy the same as everyone else, but provide an orderly routine so that he can develop proper work habits.
_____	_____	7. Call Jimmy in and logically discuss the problem with him and ask what you can do to help.
_____	_____	8. Do nothing now, but watch Jimmy so that you can reward him the next time he does something good.

OBSERVER'S RATING SHEET

Rate your assigned role-player's cross-cultural communicating skills on a 1 to 5 scale (5 being the highest). Provide comments for specific feedback in the space under each skill criterion.

Rating	Behavioral Skills	Role-Player Observed: _____
_____	Assumed differences until similarity was proven	
_____	Emphasized description rather than interpretation or evaluation	
_____	Interpreted words, motives, and actions from the perspective of Jimmy's culture	
_____	Treated interpretations as guesses until they could be confirmed	
_____	Asked for feedback to make sure evaluations of words and behavior were accurate	
_____	Avoided the use of stereotypes to explain Jimmy's behavior	

GROUP EXERCISES

The first group exercise is a role-play designed to demonstrate how cultural and language differences can cause conflict. The second exercise is an opportunity for direct communicators, such as most North Americans, to practice indirect communication techniques that can help them understand and be understood better by more indirect communicating cultures. The third exercise explores American and Japanese cultural intersections.

Group Exercise 1: What Just Happened?[17]

Objectives

- To increase your awareness of how many cross-cultural interactions happen in your daily life
- To strengthen your observation skills
- To see where judgments and assumptions can distort your observations

Instructions

Form groups of three or four. Three people will play one of the three characters and if there is a fourth, he or she will serve as an observer. Actors should read the situation and their own role—do not read the other actors' roles. Observers will observe the exercise and provide feedback to the role-players using the Observer's Rating Sheet that follows the exercise. Observers should read the situation and all of the roles.

Actors.   *Chip*, a sophomore from Connecticut. *Yoshio*, a Japanese exchange student. *Rick*, a sophomore from New England.

Situation.   Yoshio is an exchange student who is attending an East Coast college his sophomore year. He was assigned a dorm room with Chip, who has been a member of the college debate team since the beginning of his freshman year. Rick lives in the dorm room next to Chip and Yoshio. Rick has been friends with Chip since they moved into the dorm their freshman year. Yoshio mostly hangs out with other students from Asia and is in the room much more often than Chip.

It is around 11:00 PM. Chip and Rick have been talking in Chip and Yoshio's dorm room for about a half hour when Yoshio comes in. He says hello and then starts to study. A few minutes later the phone rings. Chip doesn't answer it and says to Yoshio, "It is probably for you."

Yoshio answers the phone and begins talking in Japanese. His voice was much more animated than before. After about 5 minutes, Chip waves his arms and says, "Hey, could you take the phone in the hall? Rick and I are having a conversation here!"

Yoshio stops talking right away and hangs up. He says, "I'm very, very sorry, I'll try to be a better roommate." Then he went back to reading his textbook. Chip says, "Would you quit apologizing all the time? Just take the phone out in the hall next time."

Rick feels that the atmosphere between the two roommates is very tense. He explains his uncomfortable feelings to Chip and Yoshio and starts a dialogue to get to the bottom of the problem and hopefully find a way to help the two roommates understand each other and get along better.

Chip's Role.   You find Yoshio's quiet manner boring and sometimes irritating. What really bugs you is his constant apologizing, but then Yoshio goes and does whatever he wants to anyway. You also think that speaking a foreign language in front of you is rude. You are a debater, and you expect people to stand up for themselves. Your background is white working class and you have learned to deal with conflicts directly, immediately, and verbally. You think Yoshio should lighten up or at least to make a joke of your differences.

Yoshio's Role.   It is important in Japan for people to get along, or at least look like they're getting along. When Chip makes a blunt request, you think it is very rude and perhaps the tip of a serious conflict. You also think that Chip is insensitive and doesn't take hints. A polite person would have left the room because it is easier for Rick and Chip to go next door to Rick's room than for you to take the phone out in the hall where the reception is bad. Also, it is difficult to speak in a foreign language all day. Talking in Japanese is restful and much easier for you when you are talking to other Japanese students.

Rick's Role.   You feel that the atmosphere between the two roommates is very tense. It seems like Yoshio was an odd combination of noisy and quiet. Sometimes he's very polite, sometimes he's rude. You know it isn't true (because he's Japanese) but your gut reaction is that he makes apologies because he's afraid of Chip, but he isn't really sorry, because he turns around and does the same things again the next day. Also, you suppose you and Chip could have gone to your room to talk, but you figured you were there first, and anyway it is inconsiderate to speak a foreign language when others in the room don't understand.

Total Time. 25 minutes (preparation, 5 minutes; role-play, 10 minutes; debriefing, 10 minutes)

OBSERVER'S RATING SHEET

Rate the role-players' cross-cultural communicating skills on a 1 to 5 scale (5 being the highest). Provide comments for specific feedback in the column under each actor.

Behavioral Skills	Actor 1 _____	Actor 2 _____	Actor 3 _____
Assumed differences until similarity was proven			
Emphasized description rather than interpretation or evaluation			
Interpreted words and actions from other person's perspective			
Treated interpretations as guesses until they could be confirmed			
Asked for feedback to make sure evaluations of words and behavior was accurate			
Avoided the use of stereotypes to explain the other's behavior			

Group Exercise 2: Being Less Direct[18]

Sometimes in cross-cultural communications its how things are said and not what is being said that is giving you the true message. If you are a direct person, like most North Americans, operating in a country that uses indirect communications may seem as if you speaking two different languages even if you are speaking the same one. The Peace Corps has isolated the following indirect communication techniques to help direct communicators understand and be understood better.

1. Using a qualified yes can be a way to really say no.
2. Telling a story can be a way of saying no delicately.
3. Changing the subject is often done to avoid saying no.
4. Asking a question is sometimes a way to give a negative answer.
5. Returning to a previous point of discussion can signal disagreement.

Instructions

In this exercise developed by the Peace Corps, you are to try to rephrase the direct statement in a more indirect manner. For example, instead of saying, "I don't think that's such a good idea," you can say/ask, "Do you think that's a good idea? Are there any other ideas? I like most parts of that idea."

Form groups of three to five people and take turns rephrasing the following direct statements in a more indirect manner. When you are finished, check the Appendix for some suggested answers. Compare your own answers to see if you have mastered the technique of being less direct.

1. "That's not the point."
2. "I think we should…"
3. "What do you think, Mr. Cato?" (What can you do to find out what he thinks without calling on him directly? It may embarrass him for you to do so.)
4. "Those figures are not accurate."
5. "You're doing that wrong."
6. "I don't agree."

Time: 10–15 minutes total

Group Exercise 3: The Good Worker

As a homogeneous island people, Japanese culture is more cohesive and developed than most other peoples'. They share a language, a history, racial similarity, and cultural patterns that make it difficult for foreigners to understand or be part of the society. In yet other situations, Japanese and Americans are creating new cultural and social forms, cutting and pasting pieces to suit their own local contexts. In this case, the differences, similarities, contradictions, and intermixings provide fertile ground for anyone studying American and Japan intersections.

Instructions: Form groups of three to five students and answer the questions following the Cleaning the Van Case below. When you are finished, share your answers with the entire class. Then go to Appendix A and discuss your answers relative to those suggested there.

Cleaning the Van Case[19]

American and Japanese college students were on a summer volunteer mission in Indonesia helping villagers replant foliage on mountainsides after a forest fire. After spending long, hot days replanting, they were also responsible for cleaning the camp van every evening. Their Japanese supervisors were senior students who insisted that the van be washed, vacuumed, and polished until it shone inside and out. It was tedious work, especially after a rough day laboring on the mountain.

One day because of the intense heat, all students were allowed to stay at the camp and didn't work with the villagers on the mountainsides. At 6:00 PM, the senior male Japanese students broke out beer and cards and told the Japanese women to go cook and all of the groups to go do their chores. The Americans in the group grinned and said, "Lucky us, no chores! We didn't use the van today."

Then the head senior male Japanese student got up in a fury and shouted at them not to be irresponsible, to go do their job. The angry Americans begrudgingly finished their beverages and went outside where they found the lone Japanese woman student in their group silently cleaning the van all by herself.

Questions for Discussion

What is going on here?

How do the Americans probably interpret the situation?

How do the Japanese senior male students probably interpret the situation?

How did the Japanese woman student probably interpret the situation?

What can be done to bring about a common perception of what to do in these situations?

Time: 30 minutes total: 15 minutes for reading and team discussion; 15 minutes for class discussion and comparison with the suggested answers

Summary Checklist

Take a few minutes to reflect on your performance in the above exercises and look over others' ratings of your skill. Now assess yourself on each of the key learning behaviors. Make a check (✓) next to those behaviors on which you need improvement.

_____ Assume differences until similarity is proven

_____ Emphasize description rather than interpretation or evaluation

_____ Interpret words and actions from another persons' perspective

_____ Treat interpretations as guesses until they could be confirmed

_____ Ask for feedback to make sure evaluations of words and behavior are accurate

_____ Avoid the use of stereotypes to explain the other's behavior

_____ Assume differences until similarity is proven

_____ Emphasize description rather than interpretation or evaluation

APPLICATION QUESTIONS

1. In cross-cultural interactions, why are your customary evaluations and interpretations more likely to be off base?
2. How can you become more aware of cross-cultural situations that you may respond emotionally to? What are some of the ones you are presently aware of?
3. When you are experiencing a cross-cultural situation, how can you effectively evaluate what is going on through description, checking your own cultural interpretation, and thinking about the other culture's interpretation?
4. How can you test the accuracy of your observations and conclusions of your interactions with someone from another culture with the persons involved or with some other source who has relevant cultural knowledge?

REINFORCEMENT EXERCISES

You don't need to live in a multinational setting to experience cross-cultural interactions. Here are a few everyday activities you can do to practice and reinforce cross-cultural communication techniques you learned in this chapter. You may want to adapt them to the Action Plan you will develop next, or try them independently.

1. Observe a political argument between students or coworkers from different backgrounds or who are strongly affiliated with particular political groups.
2. Watch the interactions between a parent/teacher/supervisor with someone of a different generation.
3. Have a conversation about the different reactions that you and a friend who comes from a different background have to a TV show or political event.
4. Attend a public meeting that involves several constituencies.
5. Watch a conversation between a man and woman, where gender-based differences in life experience or upbringing seem to influence their interaction.
6. Visit a place that isn't part of your culture—such as an immigrant grocery, a church that's not your religion, or a laundromat in another neighborhood—and record a few minutes of the interaction (verbal or not) that you had with people there.

ACTION PLAN

1. Which communicating across cultures behavior do I want to improve the most?

2. Why? What will be my payoff?

3. What potential obstacles stand in my way?

4. What specific things will I do to improve? (For examples, see the Reinforcement Exercises.)

5. When will I do them?

6. How and when will I measure my success?

Endnotes

1. Phillip Harris and Robert Moran, *Managing Cultural Differences*, 3rd ed. (Houston, TX: Gulf Publishing, 1991), p.13.
2. Jeswald Salacuse, *Making Global Deals* (Boston, MA: Houghton Mifflin, 1991), pp. 14–15.
3. Om P. Kharbanda and Ernest A. Stallworthy, "Verbal and Non-Verbal Communication," *Journal of Managerial Psychology*, Vol. 6, No. 4 (1991), pp. 10–13, 49–52.
4. J. W. Gibson and R. M. Hodgetts, *Organizational Communication: A Managerial Perspective* (Orlando, FL: Academic Press, 1986), p. 95.
5. Ibid.
6. Ibid., pp. 103–105.
7. N. J. Adler, *International Dimensions of Organizational Behavior*, 3rd ed. (Cincinnati, OH: South-Western College Publishing, 1997), pp. 74–75.
8. Herminia Ibarra and Kristin M. Daly, *Gender Differences in Managerial Behavior: The Ongoing Debate* (Boston, MA: Harvard Business Press, March 12, 1995), pp. 1–5.
9. Deborah Tannen, *You Just Don't Understand: Women and Men in Conversation* (New York: Ballantine Books, 1991), pp. 24–25.
10. J. Bard and P. Bradley, "Styles of Management and Communication: A Comparative Study of Men and Women," *Communication Monographs* 46 (1979), pp. 101–111.
11. J. Hunsaker and P. Hunsaker, *Strategies and Skills for Managerial Women* (Cincinnati, OH: South-Western Publishing, 1991), pp. 252–253.
12. B. Eakins and R. Eakins, *Sex Differences in Human Communication* (Boston, MA: Houghton Mifflin, 1977), pp. 117–119.
13. J. Hunsaker and P. Hunsaker, *Strategies and Skills for Managerial Women* (Cincinnati, OH: South-Western Publishing, 1991), p. 139.
14. Paolo Rossetti, "Gender Differences in E-mail Communication," *The Internet TESL Journal*, http://iteslj.org/Articles/Rossetti-GenderDif.html. Retrieved April 28, 2010.
15. N. J. Adler, *International Dimensions of Organizational Behavior*, 5th ed. (Cincinnati, OH: South-Western College Publishing, 2008), pp. 88–93.
16. Adapted from David A. Whetten and Kim S. Cameron, *Developing Management Skills: Applied Communication Skills* (New York: HarperCollins, 1993), pp. 45–47, 111.
17. http://www.culture-at-work.com/xcexercises.html. Accessed September 16, 2007.
18. T. Bowens, *Cross-Cultural Training*, Lesson 4: Global Communications, http://www.suite101.com/lesson.cfm/16618/112/7. Accessed September 16, 2007.
19. Adapted from J. E. Beer, "The Competent Employee," *Culture at Work* (Lansdowne, PA, JB International Consulting, 2003). Accessed September 16, 2007, from Culture at Work Website: http://www.culture-at-work.com/goodworker.html.

9

■ ■ ■

Setting Goals for Others

SELF-ASSESSMENT EXERCISE: SETTING GOALS FOR OTHERS

For each of the following questions, select the answer that best describes how you would treat people who work for you. Remember to respond as you have behaved or would behave, not as you think you should behave. If you have no managerial experience, answer the questions as if you were a manager.

The people who work for me have:

	Usually	Sometimes	Seldom
1. Complete autonomy to set their own goals.	____	____	____
2. Goals for all key areas relating to job performance.	____	____	____
3. Challenging goals that are beyond their current abilities, to make them stretch.	____	____	____
4. The opportunity to participate in setting their goals.	____	____	____
5. A say in deciding how to implement their goals.	____	____	____
6. To determine when they would like to accomplish the goals assigned to them on their own.	____	____	____
7. Sufficient skills and training to achieve their goals.	____	____	____
8. Sufficient resources (time, money, equipment) to achieve their goals.	____	____	____
9. Feedback on how well they are progressing toward their goals.	____	____	____
10. Rewards (i.e., pay, promotions, time off) allocated to them according to how hard they try to reach their goals.	____	____	____

Scoring and Interpretation

For questions 2, 4, 5, 7, 8, and 9, give yourself 3 points for Usually; 2 points for Sometimes; and 1 point for Seldom. For questions 1, 3, 6, and 10, reverse the scale.

Sum up your total points. Scores of 26 or higher demonstrate a strong understanding of goal-setting techniques. A score of 21–25 indicates that you can improve your goal-setting skills. Scores of 20 or less suggest that you have significant room for improvement.

SKILL CONCEPTS

People should have a clear idea of what they're trying to accomplish in their jobs. Furthermore, managers have the responsibility for making sure that this is achieved by helping others set work goals. These two statements seem obvious. People need to know what they're supposed to do, and it's the manager's job to provide this guidance. Simple? Hardly.

Goal setting is frequently dismissed by managers as self-evident.[1] It's not. Setting goals is a sophisticated skill that many managers perform poorly. But when managers follow the goal-setting sequence that we'll describe in this chapter, they can expect improved employee perform-ance.[2] They're also likely to hear comments such as "Finally, I know what you expect from me on this job."

The Basics of Effective Goals

Five basic rules should guide you in defining and setting goals. The goals should be (1) specific, (2) challenging, (3) set with a time limit for accomplishment, (4) mutually determined, and (5) designed to provide feedback about progress.

1. *Specific.*   Goals are meaningful only when they're specific enough to be verified and measured. This is best achieved by stating them in quantitative terms: "Drill three new wells" rather than "Drill wells," "Limit spending to $10 million" rather than "Be frugal," "Increase sales in my territory by 10 percent" rather than "Try to improve sales," or "I'm going to get at least three A's and two B's this term" rather than "I'm going to do my best."[3] When no confusion exists over the desired result, the likelihood of a goal being achieved is increased.

2. *Challenging.*   Goals should be set that require the employee to stretch to reach them. If goals are too easy to achieve, they offer no challenge. If set unrealistically high, they create frustration and are likely to be abandoned. The employee should view goals as challenging yet reachable. Keep in mind, however, that one person's "challenging" is another person's "impossible." It's a question of perception. "Hard goals are more likely to be perceived as challenging rather than impossible if the person has a high degree of self-assurance and has previously had more success in goal attainment than failures."[4]

3. *Set a time limit for accomplishment.*   Open-ended goals are likely to be neglected be-cause no sense of urgency is associated with them. Therefore, whenever possible, goals should include a specific time limit for accomplishment.[5] Instead of stating "I'm going to complete the bank management training program with at least a score of 85," a time-specific goal would be "I'm going to complete the bank management training program, with at least a score of 85, by February 1 of next year."

4. *Mutually determined.*   Goals typically can be set in two ways: They can be assigned to people by the manager, or they can be determined in collaboration between the manager and the employee. The research comparing the effects of participatively set and assigned goals on employee performance has not resulted in strong or consistent relationships.[6] When goal difficulty is held constant, assigned goals as well as participatively determined

ones are frequently achieved.[7] However, participation does seem to increase a person's goal-aspiration level and leads to the setting of more difficult goals.[8] Also, participatively set goals are often more readily accepted, and accepted goals are more likely to be achieved.[9] Therefore, although assigned goals might be achieved as effectively as participative ones, collaboration is likely to result in more ambitious goals and more commitment to those goals by those who must implement them. Participation makes the whole goal-setting process more acceptable. Employees are less likely to question or resist a process in which they actively participate than one that is imposed on them from above.

5. ***Designed to provide feedback.***   Feedback lets people know if their level of effort is sufficient or needs to be increased. It can also induce them to raise their goal level after attaining a previous goal and inform them of ways in which to improve performance. Ideally, feedback on goal progress should be self-generated rather than provided externally.[10] When employees are able to monitor their own progress, the feedback is less threatening and less likely to be perceived as part of a management control system.

How to Set Goals

Seven steps need to be followed to obtain the optimum results from goal setting.[11]

1. ***Specify the general objective and tasks to be done.***   Goal setting begins when you define what you want your employees to accomplish. The best source for this information is each employee's job description, if one is available. It details information such as what tasks an employee is expected to perform, how these tasks are to be done, and what outcomes the employee is responsible for achieving.

2. ***Specify how performance will be measured.***   After an employee's tasks are defined, you can determine how the outcomes from these tasks are to be measured. Typically, work outcomes are measured in physical units (e.g., quantity of production, number of errors), time (e.g., meeting deadlines, coming to work each day), or money (e.g., profits, sales, costs). For many jobs, developing valid individual measures of performance is difficult or even impossible. For example, upper-level management jobs are complex and often defy clear measurement. Similarly, when employees are part of a work team, it is often difficult to single out their individual contributions. In such cases, the available outcome measures can be combined with inputs (behaviors) that are controllable by the employee and that are assumed to lead to successful outcomes. A senior executive might be evaluated on criteria such as "listens to employees' concerns" or "explains how changes will affect employees" in addition to "completes monthly forecast by the 25th of the preceding month."

3. ***Specify the standard or target to be reached.***   The next step requires identifying the level of performance expected. In step 2, you might determine that one of the criteria by which a salesperson will be judged is customer returns. In this step, you need to specify a target; for example, monthly returns will not represent more than 1 percent of that month's sales. If properly selected, the target will meet the requirements of being specific and challenging for the employee.

4. ***Specify the time span involved.***   After the targets are set, deadlines for each goal need to be put in place. Typically, the time span increases at upper levels of management. The goals of operative employees tend to be in the range of 1 day to several months; middle managers' goals are more likely to fall into the 3-months-to-a-year range; and top-level managers' goals often will extend to 2, 3, or 5 years.

Putting a time target on each goal is important because it reduces ambiguity, but keep in mind that deadlines should not be chosen arbitrarily. The reason is that people tend to stress whatever time span is attached to any given goal. If daily goals are assigned, the time focus will be 1 day. If quarterly goals are set, actions will be directed accordingly. The message here is twofold. First, to rephrase Parkinson's law, effort toward a goal will be expended to fill the time available for its completion. Give people a month to complete a task that requires a week, and they'll typically take the full month. Second, overemphasis on short-term goals can undermine long-term performance. Short-range time targets encourage people to do whatever is necessary to get immediate results, even if it's at the expense of achieving long-term goals.

5. *Prioritize goals.*   When someone is given more than one goal, it is important to rank the goals in order of importance. The purpose of this step is to encourage the employee to take action and expend effort on each goal in proportion to its importance.

6. *Rate goals according to their difficulty and importance.*   Goal setting should not encourage people to choose easy goals in order to ensure success. This is an extreme illustration, but no employee should be able to say, "My goal was to do nothing and I'm pleased to say I achieved it." Goal setting needs to take into account the difficulty of the goals selected and whether individuals are emphasizing the right goals.

In this step, each goal should be rated for its difficulty and importance. When these ratings are combined with the actual level of goal achievement, you will have a more comprehensive assessment of overall goal performance. This procedure gives credit to individuals for trying difficult goals even if they don't fully achieve them. An employee who sets easy goals and exceeds them might get a lower overall evaluation than one who sets hard goals and only partially attains them. Similarly, an employee who reaches only low-priority goals and neglects those with high priorities could be evaluated lower than one who tries for important goals and only partially achieves them.

7. *Determine coordination requirements.*   Is the achievement of any person's goals dependent on the cooperation and contribution of other people? If so, a potential for conflict exists. It is important in such cases to ensure that these goals are coordinated. Failure to coordinate interdependent goals can lead to territorial fights, abdication of responsibility, and overlapping of effort.

Obtaining Goal Commitment

The mere existence of goals is no assurance that employees accept and are committed to them. However, certain actions by managers can increase acceptance of and commitment to goals.[12]

1. *Managerial support.*   Managers need to create a supportive climate in which goals are seen as a device for clarifying employee expectations rather than as a manipulative tool for threatening and intimidating subordinates. Managers exhibit support by helping employees select challenging goals and by reducing barriers that stand between employees and the attainment of their goals. This means, for example, making sure employees have the necessary equipment, supplies, time, and other resources to complete their tasks. Managers are supportive when subordinates view them as goal facilitators.

2. *Use participation.*   Employee participation in goal setting is a key to getting goals accepted. To be effective, however, the participation must be authentic. That is, employees must perceive that managers are truly seeking their input. If a manager merely goes

through the motions of soliciting employee input, participation will not succeed. Employees are not stupid. If managers attempt to co-opt them—pretending to want their participation when, in fact, they already have specific goals, levels of performance, and target dates firmly in mind—the employees will be quick to label the process for what it is: assigned goals from above.

3. ***Know your subordinates' capabilities.***   Individuals differ in terms of their skills and abilities. If these differences are taken into consideration, each person's goals will realistically reflect that employee's capabilities. Furthermore, matching goal difficulty and an individual's capabilities increases the likelihood that the employee will see the goals as fair, realistic, attainable, and acceptable. If a person's abilities aren't adequate to meet the minimally satisfactory goals, this matching effort might signal the need for additional skill training for that employee.

4. ***Use rewards.***   There's an old saying: What's worth doing is worth doing for money. Offering money, promotions, recognition, time off, or similar rewards to employees contingent on goal achievement is a powerful means of increasing goal commitment. When the going gets tough on the road toward meeting a goal, people are prone to ask themselves, "What's in it for me?" Linking rewards to the achievement of goals helps employees answer that question.

5. ***Clarify expectations.***   For people to achieve mutually acceptable goals, they need to hold commonly agreed-upon expectations.[13] When the expectations of either side are not fulfilled, anger and resentment can undermine trust and good faith in the relationship. A company staffed by individuals who feel cheated because they expected more stock options will not get maximum performance from employees. The free rider that refuses to meet a group's work expectations becomes a stumbling block to team productivity and morale.[14] Expectations about the five factors summarized in Figure 9.1 need to be explicitly clarified to effectively manage performance agreements between people involved in any interdependent endeavor.

A clear, mutual understanding up front in these areas provides a common vision of desired results and creates standards against which people can measure their own success. Consequently, managers do not have to worry about controlling people. Instead, because of the up-front agreement, people know exactly what is expected, so your role as a manager is to be a facilitator. People will take personal responsibility and judge their own performances. In many cases, people know in their hearts how things are going much better than the records show. Personal discernment by responsible people is often far more accurate than managers' observation or measurement.[15]

---

1. *Desired results* (not methods) identify what is to be done and when.
2. *Guidelines* specify the parameters (principles, policies, etc.) within which results are to be accomplished.
3. *Resources* identify the human, financial, technical, or organizational support available to help accomplish the results.
4. *Accountability* sets up the standards of performance and the time of evaluation.
5. *Consequences* specify what will happen as a result of the evaluation.

FIGURE 9.1   Five Factors for Mutual Agreement in Performance Contracts.

Source: Stephen R. Covey, *The 7 Habits of Highly Effective People* (New York: Simon & Schuster, 1990), pp. 194–195.

CONCEPT QUIZ

After answering the following quiz, remember to go back and check your understanding of any questions you missed.

     Circle the right answer.

True   **False**   1.   Specific goals reduce ambiguity about what an employee is expected to do.

True   **False**   2.   Goals should be set just a little beyond what a person can realistically achieve to maximize motivation.

True   **False**   3.   Hard goals are more likely to be perceived as challenging rather than impossible if the person has a college degree.

True   **False**   4.   Participation reduces employee commitment to goals.

True   **False**   5.   Feedback on goal progress is best if self-generated.

True   **False**   6.   Everything an employee does on the job can and should be quantified and have a goal set for it.

True   **False**   7.   In goal setting, short-term goals take priority over long-term goals.

True   **False**   8.   Coming up short in trying to achieve a difficult goal should always be evaluated more positively than fully achieving an easy goal.

True   **False**   9.   Managers are able to facilitate employee goal attainment.

True   **False**   10.   People accept goals more readily when the goals are tied to rewards they desire.

Answers: (1) True; (2) False; (3) False; (4) False; (5) True; (6) False; (7) False; (8) False; (9) True; (10) True

BEHAVIORAL CHECKLIST

Look for these specific behaviors when evaluating your goal-setting skills and those of others.

The Effective Goal Setter:

- Identifies an employee's key job tasks.
- Establishes specific and challenging goals for each key task.
- Specifies deadlines for each goal.
- Allows the subordinate to actively participate.
- Prioritizes goals.
- Rates goals for difficulty and importance.
- Builds in feedback mechanisms to assess goal progress.
- Commits rewards contingent on goal attainment.

ATTENTION!

Do not read the following until assigned to do so by your instructor.

MODELING EXERCISE

Setting Goals at State Bank of Vermont

Actors.   Robin Gordon and Lou Millan

Objectives.   To challenge the role-players and class to identify tangible, verifiable, and measurable goals through applying the behavioral skills described in this chapter.

Situation.   Kelly Frum has recently been promoted to the position of operations officer at one of the largest branches of State Bank of Vermont. Her staff includes three supervisors who report directly to her, and another 35 or so operatives who answer to the supervisors. One of these supervisors is responsible for directing the 15 tellers, and the others direct customer relations and computer functions. Kelly reports to the bank manager, who, in turn, works under the State Bank of Vermont's president.

Kelly has suggested to all three supervisors that they establish goals for themselves and their employees. One supervisor, Robin Gordon, who is responsible for the tellers, has set up a meeting with her most senior teller—Lou Millan—to begin the goal-setting process.

Robin Gordon's Role.   Your job is to establish goals for Lou Millan. These goals should address issues such as prompt attention to customer needs, showing courtesy to customers, selling bank services such as Christmas Club accounts, keeping the cash drawer balanced, and taking bank-sponsored courses to improve skills. Examples of goals identified in the past exercises include (1) smile, greet customers with eye contact, and call them by name; (2) cross-sell the product of the month through verbal suggestions; (3) complete all regular transactions within 90 seconds; and (4) thank all customers for their business. You are a strong believer in joint decision making and want to encourage participation from Lou, who has more experience as a teller than anyone else in the bank.

Lou Millan's Role.   You are the lead teller. You are meeting with your supervisor, Robin, today to review the behavioral goals for your job description. You want to make sure you understand exactly what is expected of you, since the less-experienced employees use you as their role model. Make sure that you are clear about the specifics of all goals and expectations. Since you have more experience than anyone else in the bank, including Robin, in the teller's job, you want to be sure to get your own ideas considered. If fact, you should probably act more as an expert adviser to Robin for setting the goals for tellers.

Observers' Role.   During the 5 minutes in which the role-players plan and organize, the class observers should review the behavioral criteria and think about how to perform the exercise if they were in Robin's role. During the role-play, they evaluate Robin Gordon's goal-setting skills using the following Observer's Rating Sheet. Remember to make notes of examples of particularly good behaviors and those that need improvement.

Total Time. 25 minutes (preparation, 5 minutes; role-play, 15 minutes; debriefing, 5 minutes)

OBSERVER'S RATING SHEET

Evaluate Robin Gordon's goal-setting skills on a 1 to 5 scale (5 being the highest). Insert examples for feedback in the spaces between behavioral criteria.

Identifies key tasks _____

Sets specific and challenging goals _____

Sets deadlines _____

Provides for subordinate participation _____

Prioritizes goals _____

Rates for difficulty and importance _____

Builds in feedback _____

Commits rewards _____

GROUP EXERCISES

Break into groups of three and perform the three role-plays that follow. Remember that observers are to evaluate goal-setting skills using the behaviors on the Observer's Rating Sheet later in the chapter.

Group Exercise 1: Goals for Probation[16]

Actors.   Terry Donahue and Chris Espo

Situation.   Terry Donahue is a probation supervisor. Chris Espo is a newly hired juvenile probation officer. Following is a description of the job of juvenile probation officer and Chris's qualifications. Both are currently in Terry's office to establish Chris's goals for the coming year.

Juvenile Probation Officer

Juvenile probation officers have a caseload of up to 60 probationers. Appointments for weekly meetings with probationers are scheduled by a receptionist.

Tasks
- Meets with probationers weekly to assess their current behavior.
  - a. Procedures stated in rules and regulations must be adhered to.
  - b. The officer's supervisor can be called in to help with difficult cases.
- Prepares pre-sentence reports on clients.
  - a. Average five reports per week.
  - b. Prepared per instructions issued by judge.
  - c. Supervisor will review and approve.

Standards

- All probationers must be seen weekly; those showing evidence of continued criminal activity or lack of a job will be reported to supervisor.
- Reports must be complete and accurate as determined by judges.
- Judges must accept 75 percent of pre-sentence recommendations.

Skills, Knowledge, and Abilities Required

- Knowledge of the factors contributing to criminal behavior.
- Ability to counsel probationers.
- Ability to write clear and concise probation reports.
- Knowledge of judge's sentencing habits for particular types of offenders and offenses.
- Knowledge of law concerning probation.

Chris Espo's Qualifications

- B.S. in Business Administration from state university
- Four years' part-time experience running recreation programs for juvenile offenders in halfway homes
- 3.5 G.P.A in all college work
- Golf team captain and Amateur State Golf Champion 2 years in a row

Terry Donahue's Role.   You are happy to have been allocated a new juvenile probation officer because your department is understaffed and has a heavy caseload. Chris Espo seems like a bright and capable addition to your staff who wants to learn the job quickly. You are concerned that his recent business degree has not provided some of the essential knowledge and skills desired for the job, but with some extra classes and training, that can be upgraded. Everyone in your agency has read about Chris's golf championships and he is quite a hero in your small town. You want to set goals for Chris's job that will challenge his professional development.

Chris Espo's Role.   You are happy to have the juvenile probation officer job because, next to golf, you really like working with kids. It was a tough decision to stay off of the pro golf tour, but you married your high school sweetheart 2 years ago and just had a new baby. Both of your families still live in the small town you've grown up in, and you feel OK about your trade-offs as long as you can use your spare time to practice and compete in amateur golf tournaments—your first love, which you do not want to compromise.

Observers' Role.   Review the Observer's Rating Sheet and determine how you would conduct the goal-setting session yourself. After the student playing Terry Donahue has assessed his or her own performance, provide feedback on the strengths and weaknesses you observed.

Total Time. 35 minutes (breaking the job into key tasks and making a prioritized goal sheet, 10 minutes; role-play, 20 minutes; debriefing, 5 minutes)

Group Exercise 2: New Faculty Goals

Actors.   Lee Davis and Jan Reeves

Situation.   It's the first week of the fall semester at your college. Lee Davis recently received a doctorate from a prestigious eastern university and has been hired as a new faculty member by the psychology department. Lee's major area is social psychology, and his dissertation was on how norms impact decision making in groups. Lee's department head, Jan Reeves, has invited Lee to sit down and discuss Lee's future plans.

The following advertisement appeared in psychology journals for the position that Lee accepted. It provides the faculty responsibilities for which specific goals need to be set.

Position Available

Entry-level assistant professor of psychology. Completed Ph.D. required. Teach in areas of introductory psychology, social psychology, and industrial psychology. Teaching load: three courses per term. Strong research and publication interests. University service and active involvement in professional associations expected. Contact Dr. Jan Reeves.

Jan Reeve's Role.   As department head, you strongly believe that every faculty member should have goals for all areas of responsibility. This is especially true of junior staff, who are often so concerned about new class preparations that they forget about their service and publication responsibilities. You believe new faculty must be particularly concerned with excellence in the classroom and publishing research articles that will reinforce the prestigious reputation of the department and university.

Lee Davis's Role.   You are looking forward to a productive academic career as a teacher and scholar. Like most new faculty members, you are concerned about preparing well for your new courses and getting started publishing some research. You have a good start with your dissertation data for writing some journal articles, but you know you must start some new experiments to generate new data. This is a prestigious "publish or perish" university with a reputation for teaching excellence. You hope you can avoid serving on make-work committees until you get your teaching and research established. You only have 6 years before an up-or-out decision will be made.

Total Time. 25 minutes (preparation, 5 minutes; role-play, 15 minutes; debriefing, 5 minutes)

Group Exercise 3: Coaching Goals

Actors.　R. J. Simpson (athletic director at State College) and Pat Bell (new women's basketball coach at State College)

Situation.　R. J. Simpson made a recent offer to Pat Bell to join State College as the college's new women's basketball coach at a salary of $85,000 per year. Pat has accepted. Pat will replace the previous coach, who held the job for 3 years and had a combined record of 20 wins and 42 losses. Pat previously was head women's basketball coach at a junior college (JC) where she won 92 percent of her games and two national JC championships.

State College has 12,000 students and is a member of the 10-school Northwest Athletic Conference. During the past 3 years, State College has finished no higher than sixth in the conference and has not been in any postseason tournaments. The team averages 1,500 fans for its home games in the college's arena, which has a capacity of 9,000. The women's basketball program, which last year had a budget of $250,000, was responsible for a loss of $60,000 to the college's overall athletic program.

This meeting is to set goals for the women's basketball program's coming season. These goals will be used to judge Pat's performance and as a basis for allocating performance-based bonuses, provided by alumni and athletic boosters, of up to $20,000 annually.

R. J. Simpson's Role.　You are delighted to have hired Pat Bell, who has such an excellent record from a competitive JC league. State College is at a crucial juncture with its women's basketball program this year, after losing $60,000 last year. If you can't get at least a breakeven this year, the Board of Governors is insisting that the program be dropped, which means you will face women's rights protests, possible discrimination lawsuits, and problems in meeting NCAA requirements that universities spend equally (excluding football) on men's and women's intercollegiate sports programs. You want to make sure that Pat has extremely clear-cut goals, is motivated to achieve them, and that the two of you have mutual expectations about what is involved.

Pat Bell's Role.　You feel that you are at the right place at the right time. You were fortunate over the last 2 years at JC to have some extraordinary talent playing for you. Nevertheless, you have to pat yourself on the back because you were able to capitalize on your team's skills by implementing some creative strategies during the national championship playoffs. You have enjoyed the complete independence and freedom to do as you choose as a coach. If you can get the right recruits and do things your way, you feel that you can turn State's record around, improve the school's prestige, and boost your career. You feel confident in your experience and abilities to make good things happen for your team and the university. All you need is the go-ahead to do it.

Total Time. 30 minutes (determine key tasks and prioritize goals, 5 minutes; role-play, 20 minutes; debriefing, 5 minutes)

OBSERVER'S RATING SHEET

For the exercise in which you are an observer, evaluate key goal-setting behaviors on a 1 to 5 scale (5 being the highest). Insert comments for feedback in the spaces between behavioral criteria.

Rating	Behavior
_____	Identifies key tasks
_____	Prioritizes goals
_____	Sets specific and challenging goals
_____	Rates for difficulty and importance
_____	Sets deadlines
_____	Builds in feedback
_____	Provides for subordinate participation
_____	Commits rewards

Summary Checklist

Review your performance and look over others' ratings of your skill. Now assess yourself on each of the key learning behaviors. Put a check (✓) next to those behaviors in which you need improvement.

I identify key tasks in employees' jobs.   _____

I establish specific and challenging goals for each key task.   _____

I specify deadlines for each goal.   _____

I allow subordinates to participate actively.   _____

I prioritize goals.   _____

I rate goals for difficulty and importance.   _____

I build in feedback mechanisms to assess goal progress.   _____

I commit rewards contingent on goal attainment.   _____

APPLICATION QUESTIONS

1. Does goal setting emphasize short-term results at the expense of long-term effectiveness?
2. How does goal setting deal with employees who have multiple goals, some of which are conflicting?
3. What barriers in an organization can you identify that might limit the effectiveness of a goal-setting program? How can these barriers be overcome?
4. Explain what an instructor can do to use goal setting with students in a classroom.

REINFORCEMENT EXERCISES

The following suggestions are activities you can do to practice and reinforce the goal-setting techniques you learned in this chapter.

1. Where do you want to be in 5 years? Write out three specific goals you want to achieve in 5 years. Make sure they are specific, challenging, and verifiable. Share your goals with a classmate and get feedback.
2. Set specific and challenging goals for yourself in this class. Do the same for your other classes.
3. Set 10 personal and academic goals that you want to achieve by the end of this year. Prioritize and rate them for difficulty.

ACTION PLAN

1. Which behavior do I want to improve the most?

2. Why? What will be my payoff?

3. What potential obstacles stand in my way?

4. What specific things will I do to improve? (For examples, see the Reinforcement Exercises.)

5. When will I do them?

6. How and when will I measure my success?

Endnotes

1. Gary P. Latham and Edwin A. Locke, "Goal Setting—A Motivational Technique That Works," *Organizational Dynamics* (Autumn 1979), pp. 68–80.
2. Edwin A. Locke, Karyll N. Shaw, Lise M. Saari, and Gary P. Latham, "Goal Setting and Task Performance: 1969–1980," *Psychological Bulletin* (July 1981), pp. 125–152.
3. Edwin A. Locke and Gary P. Latham, *Goal-Setting: A Motivational Technique That Works!* (Englewood Cliffs, NJ: Prentice Hall, 1984).
4. Gary P. Latham and Gary A. Yukl, "A Review of Research on the Application of Goal Setting in Organizations," *Academy of Management Journal* (December 1975), pp. 824–845.
5. Gary P. Latham and Edwin A. Locke, "Goal Setting—A Motivational Technique That Works," *Organizational Dynamics* (Autumn 1979), pp. 68–80.
6. Gary P. Latham and Lise M. Saari, "The Effects of Holding Goal Difficulty Constant on Assigned and Participatively Set Goals," *Academy of Management Journal* (March 1979), pp. 163–168.
7. Gary P. Latham and Gary A. Yukl, "A Review of Research on the Application of Goal Setting in Organizations," *Academy of Management Journal* (December 1975), pp. 824–845.
8. Gary P. Latham, Terence R. Mitchell, and Dennis L. Dossett, "Importance of Participative Goal Setting and Anticipated Rewards on Goal Difficulty and Job Performance," *Journal of Applied Psychology* (April 1978), pp. 163–171.
9. Edwin A. Locke and David M. Schweiger, "Participation in Decision Making: One More Look," in B. M. Staw (ed.), *Research in Organizational Behavior*, Vol. 1 (Greenwich, CT: JAI Press, 1979), pp. 265–339.
10. John M. Ivancevich and J. T. McMahon, "The Effects of Goal Setting, External Feedback, and Self-Generated Feedback on Outcome Variables: A Field Experiment," *Academy of Management Journal* (June 1982), pp. 359–372.
11. Edwin A. Locke and Gary P. Latham, *Goal-Setting: A Motivational Technique That Works!* (Englewood Cliffs, NJ: Prentice Hall, 1984).
12. Gary P. Latham and Edwin A. Locke, "Goal Setting—A Motivational Technique That Works," *Organizational Dynamics* (Autumn 1979), pp. 68–80.
13. D. M. Rousseau, *Psychological Contracts in Organizations: Understanding Written and Unwritten Agreements* (Newbury Park, CA: Sage, 1995).
14. Joyce S. Osland, David A. Kolb, and Irwin M. Rubin, *Organizational Behavior: An Experiential Approach*, 7th ed. (Upper Saddle River, NJ: Prentice Hall, 2001), pp. 11–26.
15. Stephen R. Covey, *The 7 Habits of Highly Effective People* (New York: Simon & Schuster, 1990), pp. 194–195.
16. Adapted from Donald E. Klingner, "When the Traditional Job Description Is Not Enough." Reprinted with the permission of *Personnel Journal*, Inc., Costa Mesa, CA, all rights reserved, 1979.

10

■ ■ ■

Coaching, Counseling, and Mentoring

SELF-ASSESSMENT EXERCISE: DEVELOPING PEOPLE

For each of the following actions, indicate whether you believe it is effective for developing people by circling either True (T) or False (F).

_____	1. Tell people the right way to do their job.	T	F
_____	2. Suspend judgment and evaluation.	T	F
_____	3. Act as a role model.	T	F
_____	4. Provide long-term career planning.	T	F
_____	5. Use a collaborative style.	T	F
_____	6. Apply active listening.	T	F
_____	7. Respect peoples' individuality.	T	F
_____	8. Focus on getting each person's performance up to a minimum standard.	T	F
_____	9. Dismiss mistakes.	T	F
_____	10. Delegate responsibility for performance outcomes to the person responsible.	T	F
_____	11. If possible, assist rather than educate others because assistance is much faster.	T	F
_____	12. Save feedback for yearly performance evaluations where it can all be given at once.	T	F
_____	13. Be flexible in your helping approach based on the specific problem.	T	F
_____	14. Exhibit warm regard for the employee as a person of unconditional self-worth and value no matter what the problem is.	T	F
_____	15. Approach mistakes as opportunities to learn.	T	F

Scoring and Interpretation

Check the following scoring key and add up the number of answers you had correct:
(1) F; (2) T; (3) T; (4) F; (5) T; (6) T; (7) T; (8) F; (9) F; (10) F; (11) F; (12) F; (13) T; (14) T; (15) T
Number of correct answers = _____

Scores of 12 or above indicate that you possess a valid working knowledge about developing subordinates. Scores of 8–11 indicate that you may be good as some aspects of helping but not at others. Scores of 7 or below indicate that you need to improve on most aspects of your helping behavior.

SKILL CONCEPTS

Helping people become more competent is an important part of any manager's job. It results in a three-way win for the organization, yourself, and the employees. First of all, more skilled and competent people make your job as a manager a lot easier because you can delegate more responsibilities without worrying so much. Second, by helping others resolve their personal problems and develop their skill competencies, you will motivate them to better results.

Before discussing specific procedures and skills, it should be pointed out that not all helping is done—or should be done—by managers. In most work groups, buddy systems develop in which more experienced people informally help new members develop necessary skills and offer them guidance when they have problems. Organizations sometimes formalize buddy systems into *mentoring* programs in which senior people are assigned junior protégées to whom they lend the benefit of their experience. Mentors perform as both coaches and counselors as they guide their less-experienced associates toward improved performance.

Helping Others

This chapter is designed to help you develop others by helping them to resolve personal problems and enhance job competencies. It covers how you can coach others about performance problems, counsel them about personal problems, and mentor them for long-term career development.

Coaching is similar to but not synonymous with counseling. They both have the same objective: to improve people's performance. *Coaching*, however, deals with ability issues; *counseling* deals with personal problems. When people need help mastering skills and figuring out how to apply instructions, coaching is required. For example, when someone doesn't know how to run team meetings, you can teach them how to do it and give them practice and feedback. When someone has a problem, however—attitude, emotional, alcohol or substance abuse, or family—counseling is called for.

Both coaching and counseling apply essentially the same problem-solving process: listening and understanding, identifying the problem, clarifying alternatives, deciding on an action plan, and implementing the action plan. Both also require the same behavioral skills: establishing a supportive climate, active listening, being nonjudgmental and understanding, solving problems jointly, and educating employees to solve their own problems rather than assisting by doing it yourself. The following actions help you apply these skills more effectively.

Determine the Source of the Problem

What is the correct helping approach to take when others are not performing well? It depends on what causes the problem. Unsatisfactory performance often has multiple causes, some that are within the control of the person experiencing difficulties and some that are not. Here are some questions you can ask to determine what type of help would be most appropriate.[1]

1. Is the person aware that performance is unsatisfactory? If the answer is no, you can start by providing feedback.
2. Does poor performance occur because others are not really sure what is expected of them? If so, you can provide clear expectations. (For more on this, see Chapter 7 on goal setting.)
3. Is performance hampered by obstacles beyond the person's control? If this is the case, determine how to remove the obstacles.
4. Does the person know how to do a task? If not, provide coaching or training.

5. Is good performance followed by negative consequences? If yes, determine how to eliminate the negative consequences.

6. Is poor performance being rewarded by positive consequences? If it is, determine how to eliminate the positive reinforcement.

If all of these steps have been taken to ensure good performance, and employees are still not able or willing to perform well enough, it is time to try counseling to see if it is a personal problem. Although there are differences in coaching, counseling, and mentoring, common steps should be followed before, during, and after these helping sessions. These are summarized in Exhibit 10.1.

Demonstrate Positive Regard

When you coach, counsel, and mentor others, you are engaging in a helping relationship. For a helping relationship to be successful, it is important to hold the person being helped in "unconditional positive regard." This means that you accept and exhibit warm regard for the person needing help as a person of unconditional self-worth—a person of value no matter what the conditions, problems, or feelings. If you can communicate this regard, it provides a climate of warmth and safety because the person feels liked and prized as a person. This is a necessary condition for developing the trust that is crucial in a helping relationship.[2]

Provide Meaningful Feedback for Learning

You learned about the importance of feedback in any type of communication in Chapter 6. Feedback about the consequences of their actions is necessary for people to learn what is working

---

Prior to the helping session:

- Acquire all the facts about the situation.
- Decide what type of coaching the situation requires.
- Consider how the person might react and feel about the discussion.
- Think about the best way to present what you want to say to the person seeking help.

During the helping session:

- Discuss the purpose of the session.
- Try to make the person comfortable.
- Establish a nondefensive climate characterized by open communication and trust.
- Praise positive aspects of performance.
- Mutually define the problem (performance or attitude).
- Mutually determine the causes. Do not interpret or psychoanalyze behavior; instead, ask questions such as, "What's causing the lack of motivation you describe?"
- Help the other person establish an action plan that includes specific goals and dates.
- Make sure expectations are clearly understood.
- Summarize what has been agreed upon.
- Affirm your confidence in the person's ability to make needed changes based on his or her strengths or past history.

After the session:

- Follow up to see how the employee is progressing.
- Modify the action plan if necessary.

EXHIBIT 10.1   Guidelines for Conducting Effective Helping Sessions.[3]

1. Make sure your comments are intended to help the recipient.
2. Speak directly and with feeling.
3. Describe what the person is doing and the effect the person is having.
4. Don't be threatening or judgmental.
5. Be specific, not general (use clear and recent examples).
6. Give feedback when the recipient is open to accepting it.
7. Check to ensure the validity of your statements.
8. Include only things the receiver can do something about.
9. Don't overwhelm the person with more than can be handled.

EXHIBIT 10.2   Guidelines for Giving Effective Feedback.[4]

or not working and then change those actions to become more effective.[5] Effective feedback alone can increase performance and positive personal development.[6] There are a number of reasons why.

First, feedback can induce a person who previously had no goals to set some, and goals act as motivators to higher performance. Second, where goals exist, feedback tells people how well they're progressing toward those goals. Third, favorable feedback is a positive reinforcement. Fourth, if feedback indicates inadequate performance, this knowledge may result in increased effort or suggest ways to improve performance. Fifth, feedback often induces people to raise their goal sights after attaining a previous goal. Finally, providing feedback conveys that you care how they're doing.[7]

The application of feedback in the coaching, counseling, and mentoring processes involves four actions in the following sequence:[8]

Describing observed behaviors and the results. *Assessing* the impact of the observed behaviors in terms of organizational vision and goals. *Predicting* the personal consequences for the person involved if no changes take place. *Recommending* changes for improving behavior. The characteristics of effective feedback are summarized in Exhibit 10.2.

Coaching to Improve Performance

Coaching is the ongoing process of helping people improve their performance. A coach analyzes performance, provides insight into how to improve, and offers the leadership, motivation, and supportive climate to help achieve that improvement. As a coach, your job is to provide instruction, guidance, advice, and encouragement. There are three general skills that you can apply to help others generate breakthroughs in performance.[9]

1. *Seek ways to improve performance.*   A coach continuously looks for opportunities to expand peoples' performance capabilities. How? By *ongoing observations* of the other person's behavior, by *asking questions* ("Why do you do a task this way?"), by *listening* to understand the other person's perspective, and by *respecting* the other person's individuality and crafting unique improvement strategies.
2. *Create a supportive climate.*   Effective coaches reduce barriers to development and facilitate climates that encourage performance improvement. How? Through *active listening* to promote free and open exchange of ideas. By *empowering* others to implement appropriate ideas that they suggest. By being available for assistance, guidance, or advice if asked. By being *positive and upbeat* to provide encouragement. By *never using threats* of punishment for poor performance. Threats only create fear and inhibition. By focusing on *mistakes as learning opportunities.* By *validating peoples' efforts* with rewards when they succeed.

3. *Influence others to change their behavior.* The criterion for coaching effectiveness is whether an employee's performance improves. This is not a static concept—it applies to ongoing development. How can you motivate others to continually improve? One way is by *recognizing and rewarding even small improvements.* Another is by using a *collaborative decision style* that encourages others to be responsive to change as they participate in identifying and choosing among improvement ideas. Also, *breaking complex projects into a series of simpler tasks* can boost confidence for small wins when confronting seemingly large, complex projects. Finally, *modeling* the qualities that you expect from others, such as openness, dedication, commitment, and responsibility, will demonstrate your own commitment to these qualities. Others will look to you as a role model, so make sure your deeds match your words. The steps in coaching to develop new skills are summarized in Exhibit 10.3.

Counseling to Resolve Personal Problems

Counseling is the discussion of an emotional problem to resolve it or to help the person better cope with it. Examples of problems that might require counseling include divorce, serious illness, financial problems, interpersonal conflicts, drug and alcohol abuse, or frustration over a lack of career progress. Although most of us are not qualified as psychologists, there are several things we can do in a counseling role before referring someone to a professional therapist.

Facilitate Problem Recognition and Solutions

People don't always feel comfortable asking for assistance with personal problems. Consequently, getting them to recognize the problem is often the first step. Then you can follow up by helping them gain insights into their feelings, behaviors, and alternatives.

Maintain Confidentiality

When dealing with emotional and personal problems, it is important to maintain *confidentiality.* To open up and share the reasons for many personal problems, people must feel that they can trust you and that there is no threat to their self-esteem or their reputation with others. As soon as it is determined that counseling is called for, emphasize that everything said regarding personal matters will be treated in confidence.

Clarify Feelings and Thoughts

Sometimes people just need a sounding board for *releasing tension* that can become a prelude to clarifying the problem, identifying possible solutions, and taking corrective action. Emotions

---

The coaching process for teaching new skills consists of the following steps.

1. Explain the purpose and importance of what you are trying to teach.
2. Explain the process to be used.
3. Demonstrate how it is done.
4. Observe while the person practices the process.
5. Provide immediate and specific feedback (coach again or reinforce success).
6. Express confidence in the person's ability to be successful.
7. Agree on follow-up actions.

EXHIBIT 10.3 Behavioral Steps for Teaching New Skills.[10]

typically cloud rational thinking; counseling can help people sort out their feelings into more logical and coherent thoughts.

Be Supportive and Provide Reassurance

People need to know that their problems have solutions and that they have the ability to improve. If problems are beyond a person's capability to solve, you can explain how professional treatment can be obtained through Employee Assistance Programs or employee benefit health plans. Situations in which severe depression, debilitating phobias, family disorders, and substance abuse are discovered are all examples of problems that require professional help.

Mentor for Long-Term Development

The role of a mentor is to help another person achieve his or her career goals. More experienced people formally pair up with less-experienced ones to help show them "the ropes" and provide emotional support and encouragement on an ongoing basis. In essence, being a mentor means serving as someone's permanent coach and counselor. Some companies, such as IBM, have formal mentoring programs in which pair assignments are made. Others, such as AT&T, rely on informal mentoring because they think it is more flexible and effective.[11] Mentors help others reduce the stress caused by uncertainty about how to do things and deal with challenging assignments. They are also a source of comfort when newer, less-experienced people just need to let off steam or discuss career dilemmas.[12]

For new organization members, mentoring sessions can help them gain a better understanding of the organization, its goals, and advancement criteria. They may also become more politically savvy and avoid potential career traps and dead ends. In general, mentors strive to help others live up to their full potential and encourage them to be more proactive in managing their careers.

CONCEPT QUIZ

Do you understand the basic principles for helping others? Answer the following 10-question, true–false quiz. The answers are at the end of the quiz. If you miss any, go back and find out the correct answer.

Circle the right answer.

True	**False**	1.	Coaching is synonymous with counseling.
True	**False**	2.	You have to be judgmental about people's problems for them to improve.
True	**False**	3.	You should always be looking for opportunities for others to improve.
True	**False**	4.	You should focus on mistakes as learning opportunities.
True	**False**	5.	The test of helping effectiveness is whether an employee's performance improves.
True	**False**	6.	Threats are a potent development tool.
True	**False**	7.	Sometimes it is more beneficial for others' development just to solve their problems for them.
True	**False**	8.	Once another has mastered a task satisfactorily, your coaching job is finished.

True   False   9. If you want others to behave in a certain way, model the behavior yourself.

True   False   10. It's preferable to let others come up with their own ways to improve rather than to provide solutions for them.

Answers: (1) False; (2) False; (3) True; (4) True; (5) True; (6) False; (7) False; (8) False; (9) True; (10) True

BEHAVIORAL CHECKLIST

The following skills are important for helping others. Use them when evaluating your own helping skills and those of others.

To Help Others Improve:

- Ask questions to help discover sources of problems.
- Actively listen to employees and show genuine interest.
- Demonstrate unconditional positive regard by suspending judgment and evaluation.
- Seek to educate rather than to assist.
- Accept mistakes and use them as learning opportunities.
- Provide meaningful feedback for learning.
- Encourage continual improvement.
- Recognize and reward even small improvements.
- Model the behaviors desired.
- Help develop action plans for improvement.

ATTENTION!
Don't read the following exercises until assigned to do so by your instructor.

MODELING EXERCISE

Building Problems in Napa Valley

Actors.   Lorin Wilcox (manager) and T. J. Corsetti (broker)

Situation.   Lorin Wilcox is the supervisor of the Napa Valley office of a large mortgage brokering company that has 30 offices in California. Lorin supervises seven mortgage brokers, an assistant, and a secretary. The business entails helping home buyers find mortgages and acting as a link between lenders and borrowers in getting loans approved and processed.

T. J. Corsetti is one of the brokers. T. J. has been in the Napa Valley office for 2½ years. Before that, he sold commercial real estate. Lorin Wilcox has been in the Napa Valley job for 14 months. Before that Loren supervised a smaller office for the same company.

Lorin Wilcox's Role.   You have not been pleased with T. J.'s job performance, so you've decided to review his personnel file. T. J.'s first 6-month review stated: "Enthusiastic. A bit disorganized but willing to learn. Seems to have good potential." After a year, T. J.'s previous supervisor had written, "T. J. seems to be losing interest. Seems frequently disorganized. Often rude to clients. Did not mention these problems to him previously. Hope T. J. will improve. Long-term potential now much more in question."

You have not spent much time with T. J.; your offices are far apart. But probably the real reason is that T. J. is not easy to talk to and you have little in common. When you took the Napa Valley job, you decided that you'd wait some time before attacking any problems to make sure you had a good grasp of the people and the situation.

But T. J.'s problems have gotten too visible to ignore. He is consistently missing quarterly sales projections. Based on mortgages processed, T. J. is your lowest performer. In addition, T. J.'s reports are constantly late. After reviewing last month's performance reports, you made an appointment yesterday to meet him today at 9:00 AM. But T. J. wasn't in his office when you arrived for that appointment. You waited 15 minutes and gave up. Your secretary tells you that T. J. regularly comes in late for work in the morning and takes extra-long coffee breaks.

Last week, Valerie Oletta, who has the office next to T. J.'s, complained to you that T. J.'s behavior was demoralizing to her and to some of the other brokers.

You don't want to fire T. J. It wouldn't be easy to find a replacement. Moreover, T. J. has a lot of contacts with new-home builders, which bring in a number of borrowers to your office. In fact, maybe 60 percent of the business generated by your entire office comes from builders who have personal ties to T. J. If T. J. were to leave your company and go to a competitor, he would probably be able to convince the builders to take their business somewhere else.

T. J. Corsetti's Role. The mortgage brokering business has been pretty good for you. From your previous job in commercial real estate you developed a lot of contacts with new-home builders, which bring in a number of borrowers to your office. In fact, maybe 60 percent of the business generated by your entire office comes from builders who have personal ties with you.

Although your old builder buddies supply you with plenty of business, you realized early in your first year that the brokering business required some word-processing, mathematical, and computer skills that you never acquired 10 years ago when you graduated from high school. Most of the other brokers have college degrees in business administration and one even has a M.B.A. You have been embarrassed to ask for help because you are older than most of the other brokers. Consequently, it takes you quite a bit longer than other brokers to process the mortgages; your reports are often late because you have to type one key at a time.

To try to get up to speed, you have enrolled in an 8:00 AM extension course in typing and word-processing at the community college, which makes you about an hour late for work 3 days a week, but you think it certainly is going to be worth it in the long run. You're hoping that the correspondence course in business mathematics you signed up for will have an equal payoff. You are working on it in the evenings and during your breaks at work.

All this is a bit overwhelming at the moment, and you have fallen a little behind in your work. You overheard some of the other brokers discussing your lack of involvement with them a couple of weeks ago, but you're too busy to worry about that until you complete your courses. Then you will be right up with the best of them. Besides, you're still making a contribution in a way. Your contacts with the builders bring in a majority of the business for your office. In fact, you are also taking a broker course on weekends so that you can take these contacts with you and start your own company next year.

The broker in the next office mentioned that your boss, Lorin Wilcox, was at your office for an appointment that Lorin had scheduled for 9:00 AM yesterday. You went to your usual class and completely forgot about it. You decide to go up to Lorin's office to see what the appointment was about.

Total Time. 25 minutes (setup, 5 minutes; exercise, 10 minutes; debrief, 10 minutes)

OBSERVER'S RATING SHEET

On completion of the exercise, evaluate the development skills of Lorin Wilcox from 1 to 5 (5 being the highest) using the following scale. Write concrete examples in the space for comments below each criterion skill to use in explaining your feedback.

1	2	3	4	5
Unsatisfactory	**Weak**	**Adequate**	**Good**	**Outstanding**

_____   Asked questions to help discover sources of problems and how to best help employees improve

_____   Actively listened to employees and showed genuine interest

_____   Demonstrated unconditional positive regard by suspending judgment and evaluation

_____   Tried to educate versus assist

_____   Delegated increased responsibilities and authority

_____   Accepted mistakes and used them as learning opportunities

_____   Provided meaningful feedback for learning

_____   Encouraged continual improvement

_____   Recognized and rewarded even small improvements

_____   Modeled qualities expected from employees

_____   Helped develop action plans for improvement

GROUP EXERCISES

There are three exercises in this section. The first is a case discussion that can be completed by the whole class or in small groups. Next is a helping session in which one person helps another with a problem. A third serves as an observer/commenter on the application of helping skills. The trios can rotate roles: helper, client, observer for three rounds—or shift to the role-play that follows if all do not have personal problems they want to share and work on. Each trio member should have a chance to be the helper in one exercise.

Group Exercise 1: Confessions of a Sales Manager[13]

Read the following case; then form groups of five or six and answer the questions for discussion.

Writing Mike Off

During the managers' meeting, when we were discussing difficult subordinates, I realized that I had completely written Mike off and had stopped any effective communication with him. Mike was a 53-year-old sales representative who had been with the company for more than 12 years. He was well liked by the central office staff but had not met his sales plan for 5 of the last 6 years. Furthermore, I was starting to hear complaints about him from some of our clients.

I first tried to put myself in Mike's shoes. What must it be like to be near the end of one's career and starting to go downhill? If I were Mike, how receptive would I be to criticism? I might then be able to understand one of his habitual behaviors that had been particularly annoying to me: his tendency to look only to external factors for his failures, to blame "bad luck," the market, competitors who used unfair tactics, and the like.

Still, before meeting with Mike, I did two things. I considered what would be a reasonable goal for him in 6 months: What exactly did I expect of him in terms of sales level, generating new business, and the like. Then I thought, "What is it in Mike's behavior that would cause him trouble in making sales? Is it something in his style or is some knowledge lacking?"

I then sat down with Mike and began by acknowledging that our relationship had deteriorated, that I had been dissatisfied with him but hadn't confronted him before, and also that I probably hadn't helped him as much as I could have. Mike immediately blamed me for everything that had gone wrong. It was fortunate that I had thought this out before, because my first response was defensive—to attack back. What helped was that I had already thought about why Mike must be hurting—clearly his pain was greater than anything I was now feeling about his comments.

After Mike had vented his feelings, I repeated that I wanted to change our relationship so that I could be more helpful. In return we needed to get agreement on some specific goals for Mike. Although I would help him, it would be his responsibility to meet certain objectives. He was to be accountable for them and if he failed to meet or substantially reach them in 6 months he would be placed on probation. We mutually negotiated these goals. When I felt he was setting them too low, I pointed out what other sales personnel would do. We ended up with my original list modified, but in a way that both of us could live with.

I then asked Mike what he thought might cause him difficulty in going about reaching his goals. In what areas did he need more training? Were there ways he behaved that caused problems? (I also asked him to discuss what he thought was easy for him—what his especially strong areas were.) As he shared his self-perception, I also shared my perception. I tried to point to specific behaviors at specific times that illustrated the problem areas I saw. At one point he got very defensive and offered external reasons why the problems I identified were not his fault. I used his response as an illustration of what I was pointing out in his behavior.

In this discussion, we agreed to specific areas in which he could benefit from training. I sent him to a training program to work on his time-management problem. Also, we set up regular meetings (every 2 weeks) for progress reviews. I said that I was always available if he had a question but that the initiative was up to him.

Mike did not meet the goals at the end of 6 months. I placed him on probation, with notice of termination in 3 months. I again met with him on a regular basis to offer assistance and coaching. Seven days before the end of his probation, Mike came in and said that the fit between him and the job was not right and quit.

As a result of this process, there was minimal reaction by the office staff (who had very much liked Mike). There was neither a decrease in morale nor a rise in paranoia among the others. Mike found another job in an area both of us had discussed as being more in line with his skills. Perhaps most gratifying to me, he expressly thanked me for my concern. He is doing well in his new position and is much happier.

Questions

1. Is this manager acting as a coach or a counselor? What did he do that causes you to say this?
2. Compare the sales manager's behaviors to those for developing subordinates on the Behavioral Checklist. How well did the manager do in helping Mike? What could he have done better?

Total Time. 20 minutes (case discussion, 15 minutes; debriefing, 5 minutes)

Group Exercise 2: Helping with a Peer Problem

Instructions.   Divide the class into groups of three. Each trio will conduct three coaching/counseling sessions, allowing every student the opportunity to share a school-related performance problem to get help with, and to play the role of coach to help and counsel a peer.

The person receiving help should think of a school-related problem you are currently experiencing or have had in the past. Briefly share the nature of the problem and its consequences with your coach. If you do not have a school-related problem you want to share, you can role-play someone else's problem from exercises 3 or 4 instead.

Now the coach takes over and conducts the most appropriate type of coaching or counseling session. At the conclusion of the session the observer will provide the coach with feedback based on the following observer's rating sheet.

Total Time. 60 minutes (each helping session, 20 minutes)

OBSERVER'S RATING SHEET

On completion of the exercise, evaluate the development skills of the person acting as the helper from 1 to 5 (5 being the highest) using the following scale. Write concrete examples in the space for comments below each criterion skill to use in explaining your feedback.

1	2	3	4	5
Unsatisfactory	Weak	Adequate	Good	Outstanding

_____ Asked questions to help discover sources of problems

_____ Actively listened and showed genuine interest

_____ Demonstrated unconditional positive regard by suspending judgment and evaluation

_____ Tried to educate versus assist

_____ Accepted mistakes and used them as learning opportunities

_____ Provided meaningful feedback for learning

_____ Encouraged continual improvement

_____ Recognized and rewarded even small improvements

_____ Modeled desired behaviors

_____ Helped develop action plans for improvement

Group Exercise 3: Why Is the Camera Out of Focus?

Actors.   Fran Delano (a camera operator) and Alex Maher (Fran's supervisor)

Situation.   Alex has supervised the 11 camera operators at KSLC for more than 5 years. Fran has worked for Alex for more than 4 of those years. Two years ago, Fran Delano was the number-one-rated camera operator at KSLC-TV in Salt Lake City. Of the 11 operators that the station employed, Fran was every producer's first choice. Fran had a choice of hours and shows. Fran was extremely competent, creative, and dependable. Fran's supervisor, Alex Maher, had even been a bit protective. As Alex said 18 months ago, "Everyone knows Fran's the best we've got. Everyone wants Fran for their shows. I've got to make sure we don't burn out our best camera operator."

Alex Maher's Role.   You have become far less enthusiastic about Fran over the past 4 months. The problems began with Fran coming in late for assigned shifts. First she was just 10 or 15 minutes late. Then it was 30 minutes. Last week, Fran was more than an hour late for shifts twice, and 15–20 minutes late each of the other 3 days. Yesterday, Fran called in sick just 10 minutes before the show was to go on the air. This morning, Fran came in 40 minutes late.

In addition to the lateness, you have noticed two other disturbing signs. Fran is not nearly as talkative and outgoing as usual. And, several times last week, you are certain that you smelled alcohol on Fran's breath. Nick Randolph, another camera operator, told you 2 weeks ago that he was certain Fran had been drinking before coming to work, and again during the lunch break. Nick was particularly upset about the quality of Fran's work. You knew, of course, what he was talking about. Fran's mind seemed to be wandering during shows: missing director's instructions and slow in getting the camera into new positions.

You don't know much about Fran's personal life. You've heard Fran lives with or is married to a graphic artist but that's about all you know.

Up to this point, you haven't said anything to Fran about this behavior. But now something has to be done. After today's work shift, you called Fran into your office. As Fran walks in, you can't help noticing the smell of alcohol.

Fran Delano's Role.   Becoming the number-one-rated camera operator at KSLC-TV paid off in giving you your choice of hours and shows. The problem is that you take every show you can possibly do. You feel that your place on the top rung is precarious because of the multitude of other talented camera operators jockeying to get some of your shows. It's very lucrative for you right now and you feel that you had better get all you can while the getting is good. Actually, you don't have much choice if you are to maintain your house payments because your spouse has been unemployed as a graphic artist for the past 2 years and the prospects don't look good; hundreds of others are in the same situation. In fact, your spouse has quit looking recently and is quite depressed.

This is not an easy business and it requires all you've got to handle it: the intense concentration when everything depends on you during the show, the relentless hours from the early-morning news broadcasts to late-night variety shows, and the constant worry that someone else will show their stuff if you miss a show for any reason. As if this wasn't enough, you constantly worry about your spouse's deteriorating state of mind.

You are so exhausted when you get off work, often close to midnight, that you just go home and have a few drinks. That's what your spouse is doing anyway. You are usually happy when your spouse is already in bed because your relative success seems to cause hostile attacks or the silent treatment. You can't decide which is worse, but your relationship is definitely floundering.

Lately you've noticed that it takes a whole bottle of wine or more than a six-pack of beer to calm you down enough to get to sleep. You've discovered that a shot of brandy in your morning coffee seems to help the dull headaches you wake up with. Also, a couple of glasses of wine at lunch can make the stress seem much less severe, and a short nip from the flask of Wild Turkey you keep in your coat pocket helps you relax between shows.

You know you are probably drinking a little too much, but that seems to be the only way you can avoid worrying about your problems enough to focus on your work or even get a little sleep. You are sure that as soon as your spouse finds a job and you can cut back a little, you will be just fine.

Observer's Role.   Use the previous observer's rating sheet.

Total Time. 30 minutes (setup, 5 minutes; role-play, 15 minutes; debriefing, 10 minutes)

Summary Checklist

Review your performance and look over others' ratings of your development skills. Now assess yourself on each of the following key helping behaviors. Make a check (✓) next to those behaviors in which you need improvement.

_____ I determine the *best approach* for helping others improve.

_____ I provide meaningful *feedback* for learning.

_____ I *coach* others about performance problems caused by ability issues.

_____ I *counsel* others about personal problems.

_____ I mentor others for long-term development.

_____ I help others develop action plans for improvement.

APPLICATION QUESTIONS

1. Think of a particularly effective mentor or coach you had in high school, college, or any other situation (e.g., sports, debate, music). Describe why he or she was so effective. How do this helper's qualities match up with those in the Behavioral Checklist?
2. How have your parents served as helpers for your development? What did they do that was particularly helpful? What could they have done better?
3. How is coaching similar to counseling? How are the two different?
4. Which of the earlier skills in this book contribute to coaching and counseling? How do they relate?
5. How can you tell if are being effective in helping others? When is a coaching or counseling job completed? When is a mentoring job completed?
6. What are three things you should never do when developing others and why?
7. What are three things you should always do when developing others and why?

REINFORCEMENT EXERCISES

1. Ask a coach of a local sports team (high school, college, club, or professional) for permission to observe him or her at work. Spend a few hours watching the coach do his or her job. How do this coach's behaviors match up with those in the Behavioral Checklist?

2. Watch several episodes of a TV series. Determine incidences of people trying to develop others. Do they assist or educate, coach or counsel? How effectively do they use the skills described in this chapter?

3. Help someone develop. For example, help a less-able student with a class-related problem, coach someone to develop an athletic skill, counsel a friend who wants to improve a difficult relationship, or mentor a younger or less-experienced sibling or friend.

4. Visit the counseling department at your university. Talk to a counselor about what procedures are used when helping students solve problems and which are most effective.

ACTION PLAN

1. Which helping behaviors do I want to improve the most?

2. Why? What will be my payoff?

3. What potential obstacles stand in my way?

4. What are the specific things I will do to improve? (For examples, see the Reinforcement Exercises.)

5. When will I do them?

6. How and when will I measure my success?

Endnotes

1. Ferdinand Fournies, *Coaching for Improved Work Performance* (New York: Van Nostrand Reinhold, 1978).

2. John C. Kunich and Richard I. Lester, "Leadership and the Act of Feedback: Feeding the Hands that Back Us," *Journal of Leadership Studies*, Vol. 3 (1996), pp. 3–22.

3. Cyril R. Mill, "Feedback: The Art of Giving and Receiving Help," in Larry Porter and Cyril R. Mill (eds.), *The Reading Book for Human Relations Training* (Bethel, Maine: NTL Institute for Applied Behavioral Science, 1976), pp. 18–19.

4. Phillip L. Hunsaker, *Management: A Skills Approach, Second Edition* (Upper Saddle River, NJ: Prentice Hall, 2005), p. 65.

5. Curtis W. Cook, Phillip L. Hunsaker, and Robert E. Coffey, *Management and Organizational Behavior*, 2nd ed. (Burr Ridge, IL: Irwin, 1997), pp. 271–273.

6. Mary Mavis, "Painless Performance Evaluations," *Training and Development* (October 1994), pp. 40–44.

7. Charles D. Orth, Harry E. Wilkinson, and Robert C. Benfari, "The Manager's Role as Coach and Mentor," *Organizational Dynamics* (Spring 1987), p. 67.

8. K. E. Kram and D. T. Hall, "Mentoring as an Antidote to Stress During Corporate Trauma," *Human Resource Management* (Winter 1989), pp. 493–511.

9. Based on David A. Kolb, Irwin M. Rubin, and Joyce S. Osland, *Organizational Behavior: An Experiential Approach* (Englewood Cliffs, NJ:

Prentice Hall, 1991), pp. 448–450, who provide an extended discussion of each of these guidelines.

10. Summarized from William C. Byham with Jeff Cox, *Zapp! The Lightning of Empowerment* (Pittsburgh, Penn.: DDI Press, 1989), p. 129.

11. Carl Rogers, *On Becoming a Person* (Boston, MA: Houghton Mifflin, 1961), p. 34.

12. "Labor Letter," *Wall Street Journal* (March 24, 1992), p. A1.

13. Excerpted from David Bradford and Allen R. Cohen, *Managing for Excellence* (New York: John Wiley, 1984), pp. 157–158.

11

■ ■ ■

Empowering People Through Delegation

SELF-ASSESSMENT EXERCISE: HOW DO I DELEGATE TO OTHERS?

For each of the following questions, select the answer that best describes your approach to delegating tasks to subordinates. Remember to respond as you have behaved or would behave, not as you think you should behave. If you have no managerial experience, answer the questions assuming you are a manager.

When delegating to a subordinate, I:

	Usually	Sometimes	Seldom
1. Explain exactly how the task should be accomplished.	_____	_____	_____
2. Specify the end results I expect.	_____	_____	_____
3. Feel that I lose control.	_____	_____	_____
4. Expect that I'll end up doing the task over again myself.	_____	_____	_____
5. Only delegate routine or simple tasks.	_____	_____	_____
6. Clarify to subordinates the limits of their authority.	_____	_____	_____
7. Establish progress report dates with the subordinate.	_____	_____	_____
8. Inform all who will be affected that delegation has occurred.	_____	_____	_____

Scoring and Interpretation

For questions 2, 6, 7, and 8, give yourself 3 points for Usually; 2 points for Sometimes; and 1 point for Seldom. For questions 1, 3, 4, and 5, give yourself 3 points for Seldom; 2 points for Sometimes; and 1 point for Usually.

Sum up your total points. A score of 20 or higher suggests superior delegation skills. A score of 15–19 indicates that you have room for improvement. A score below 15 suggests that your approach to delegation needs substantial improvement.

SKILL CONCEPTS

Managers are responsible for getting things done through other people. This description recognizes that limits apply to any manager's time and knowledge and that employees need to be motivated to achieve assigned tasks. Effective managers empower subordinates to accomplish assigned goals by delegating responsibility and authority to them. Empowerment means increasing your employees' involvement in their work through greater participation in decisions that control their work and by expanding responsibility for work outcomes.[1] Empowering others through delegation is one of the most powerful managerial tools for increasing productivity.[2]

What Is Delegation?

Delegation is assigning the authority and responsibility for work to others. It allows a subordinate to make decisions by transferring authority from one organizational level to another, lower level.[3] Delegation should not be confused with participation, which is a sharing of authority when making decisions. With delegation, subordinates make decisions on their own.

Delegation frequently is depicted as a four-step process: (1) allocation of duties, (2) delegation of authority, (3) assignment of responsibility, and (4) creation of accountability.

ALLOCATION OF DUTIES   Duties are the tasks and activities that a manager wants to have someone else do. Before you can delegate authority, you must allocate to a subordinate the duties over which the authority extends.

DELEGATION OF AUTHORITY   The essence of the delegation process is empowering the subordinate to act for you. It is passing to the subordinate the formal right to act on your behalf.

ASSIGNMENT OF RESPONSIBILITY   When authority is delegated, you must assign responsibility; that is, when you give someone rights, you also must assign to that person a corresponding obligation to perform. Ask yourself: Did I give my subordinate enough authority to get the materials, the use of equipment, and the support from others necessary to get the job done? Imbalances either way can cause problems. Authority in excess of responsibility creates opportunities for abuse; however, people should not be held responsible for what they have no authority over.

CREATION OF ACCOUNTABILITY   To complete the delegation process, you must create accountability; that is, you must hold your subordinates responsible for properly carrying out their duties. Although responsibility means a subordinate is obliged to carry out assigned duties, accountability means the subordinate has to perform the assignment in a satisfactory manner. Subordinates are responsible for the completion of tasks assigned to them and are accountable to you for the satisfactory performance of that work.

Delegation Is Not Abdication

If you dump tasks on a subordinate without clarifying exactly what is to be done, the range of the subordinate's discretion, the expected level of performance, when the tasks are to be completed, and similar concerns, you are abdicating responsibility and inviting trouble.[4] However, don't fall into the trap of assuming that to avoid the appearance of abdicating, you should minimize delegation. Unfortunately, this is the approach taken by many new and inexperienced managers. Lacking confidence in their subordinates, or fearful that they will be criticized for their subordinates' mistakes, they try to do everything themselves.

It might well be true that you're capable of doing the tasks that you delegate to your subordinates better, faster, or with fewer mistakes. The catch is that your time and energy are scarce resources. It's not possible for you to do everything yourself. You need to learn to delegate if you're going to be effective in your job.[5] This suggests two important points. First, you should expect and accept some mistakes by your subordinates. It's part of delegation. Mistakes are often good learning experiences for your subordinates, as long as the costs are not excessive. Second, to ensure that the costs of mistakes don't exceed the value of the learning, you need to put adequate controls in place. As we'll discuss later in this chapter, delegating without feedback controls that let you know when serious problems arise is abdication.

Why Delegate?

Perhaps the primary reason managers delegate is that they can't do everything themselves. However, some other benefits can also accrue from delegating.

1. *Delegation frees up a manager's time.* Every manager gets the same time resource with which to work: 24 hours a day, 7 days a week, 52 weeks a year. The fact that managers differ so greatly in what they accomplish with this common time allocation attests to the value of time management. Delegation is one means by which managers can use their time more efficiently and effectively. Many decisions can be delegated with little or no loss in quality, thus allowing managers—especially those in the middle and upper ranks—to focus on overall direction and coordination.

2. *Delegation can improve decision making.* In many cases, decisions can improve as a result of delegation. Why? Delegation pushes decisions down in the organization. Therefore, the decision maker is closer to the problem and often has better and more complete information about it. This increases the likelihood that the final solution will be of higher quality. Also, because subordinates are closer to the problem, they are able to respond more quickly. Therefore, delegation can improve the quality and the speed of decisions.

3. *Delegation helps develop subordinates.* Delegation is an excellent device for stimulating subordinate growth and development. It encourages subordinates to expand their job capabilities and knowledge. Moreover, it helps them develop their decision-making skills and prepares them for future promotion opportunities.

4. *Delegation enhances subordinate commitment.* No matter how good a decision is, it is likely to be less than fully successful if implemented improperly. One means to improve implementation is to increase the commitment of those who are going to do the implementing. Delegation positively influences commitment; that is, subordinates are much more likely to enthusiastically embrace a decision that they personally made than one imposed from above.

5. *Delegation improves manager–subordinate relations.* The act of delegation shows that a manager has trust and confidence in the delegatee. This explicit demonstration of support for a subordinate often leads to better interpersonal relations between the manager and the subordinate.

Determinants of Delegation

In spite of all of these benefits of empowering employees through delegation, some managers still have a hard time doing it. Why? They often are afraid to give up control. "I like to do things myself," says Cheryl Munro Sharp of London Life, "because then I know it's done and

I know it's done right." Lisa Flaherty of the Della Femina McNamee advertising agency says, "I have to learn to trust others. Sometimes I'm afraid to delegate the more important projects because I like to stay hands-on." Although delegation increases a manager's effectiveness, and when done properly still provides control, several other factors determine whether a manager delegates.

The organizational culture tends to be a powerful influence on managers.[6] If the organization is characterized by tolerance of risk, support for employees, and a high degree of autonomy for subordinates, managers will feel a great deal more comfortable delegating than they would in a risk-averse, nonsupportive, and high-control culture.

Even within a supportive culture, however, managers vary in their propensity to delegate. Research has identified three factors that influence managers in this decision.[7] The most important is the manager's perception of a subordinate's competence. Managers consistently appear reluctant to delegate if they question their subordinates' capability, trustworthiness, or motivation to assume greater responsibility. The second factor is the importance of the decision. Managers tend to delegate the less important decisions. The third factor is the manager's workload. Heavy workloads put stress and time pressures on managers, which lead to more delegation of authority. This research also found that the manager's personality plays a relatively minor part in influencing the delegation decision. That is, an individual's personal predisposition toward subordinates is not a key factor. The important implication of these findings for developing your delegation skills is that effective managers put delegation into context. For example, even if the organizational culture supports delegation and a manager strongly believes in its value, managers are not likely to delegate if they don't feel that subordinates have the necessary ability and motivation.

Delegation Skills

A number of actions differentiate the effective from the ineffective delegator. The following sections summarize these actions.[8]

1. *Clarify the assignment.*   The place to begin is to determine what is to be delegated and to whom. You need to identify the person most capable of doing the task and then determine whether that person has the time and motivation to do the job.

     Assuming you have a willing and able subordinate, it is your responsibility to provide clear information on what is being delegated, the results you expect, and any time or performance expectations you hold. Unless there is an overriding need to adhere to specific methods, you should delegate only the end results; that is, find agreement on what is to be done and the end results expected, but let the subordinate decide on the means. By focusing on goals and allowing employees the freedom to use their own judgment about how those goals are to be achieved, you increase the trust between you and the employee, improve that employee's motivation, and enhance accountability for the results.

2. *Specify the subordinate's range of discretion.*   Every act of delegation comes with constraints. You're delegating authority to act, but not unlimited authority. What you're delegating is authority to act on certain issues and within certain parameters pertaining to those issues. You need to specify what those parameters are so that subordinates know, in no uncertain terms, the range of their discretion. When this has been communicated successfully, you and the subordinate will have the same idea of the limits to the latter's authority and how far that person can go without checking further with you.

How much authority do you give a subordinate? In other words, how tight do you draw the parameters? The best answer is that you should allocate enough authority to allow the subordinate to complete the task successfully.

3. ***Allow the subordinate to participate.***   One of the best sources for determining how much authority will be necessary to accomplish a task is the subordinate who will be held accountable for that task. If you allow employees to participate in determining what is delegated, how much authority is needed to get the job done, and the standards by which they'll be judged, you increase employee motivation, satisfaction, and accountability for performance.

Be alert, however, that participation can present its own set of potential problems as a result of subordinates' self-interest and biases in evaluating their own abilities. Some subordinates, for example, are personally motivated to expand their authority beyond what they need and beyond what they are capable of handling. Allowing such people too much participation in deciding what tasks they should take on and how much authority they must have to complete those tasks can undermine the effectiveness of the delegation process.

4. ***Inform others that delegation has occurred.***   Delegation should not take place in a vacuum. Not only do the manager and the subordinate need to know specifically what has been delegated and how much authority has been granted, but anyone else who might be affected by the delegation act also needs to be informed. This includes people outside the organization as well as inside it. Essentially, you need to convey what has been delegated (the task and amount of authority) and to whom. If you fail to follow through on this step, the legitimacy of your subordinate's authority probably will be called into question. Failure to inform others makes conflicts likely and decreases the chances that your subordinate will be able to accomplish the delegated task efficiently.

5. ***Establish feedback controls.***   To delegate without instituting feedback controls is to invite problems. The possibility always exists that subordinates will misuse the discretion that they have been delegated. The establishment of controls to monitor the subordinate's progress increases the likelihood that important problems will be identified early and that the task will be completed on time and to the desired specifications.

Ideally, controls should be determined at the time of the initial assignment. Agree on a specific time for completion of the task, and then set progress dates when subordinates will report back on how well they are doing and any major problems that have surfaced. This can be supplemented with periodic spot checks to ensure that authority guidelines are not being abused, organization policies are being followed, proper procedures are being met, and the like. Too much of a good thing can be dysfunctional. If the controls are too constraining, the subordinate will be deprived of the opportunity to build self-confidence, and much of the motivational property of delegation will be lost. A well-designed control system permits your subordinate to make small mistakes but quickly alerts you when big mistakes are imminent.

6. ***When problems surface, insist on recommendations from the subordinate.***   Many managers fall into the trap of letting subordinates reverse the delegation process: The subordinate runs into a problem and then comes back to the manager for advice or a solution. Avoid being sucked into reverse delegation by insisting from the beginning that when subordinates want to discuss a problem with you, they come prepared with a recommendation. When you delegate downward, the subordinate's job includes making necessary decisions. Don't allow the subordinate to push decisions back upward to you.

CONCEPT QUIZ

The following 10-question, true–false quiz is based on the previous material. If you miss any of these questions, be sure to go back and find out why you got them wrong.

Circle the right answer.

True	False	1. Delegation requires shifting decision-making authority to a lower-level employee in the organization.
True	False	2. Delegation is the sharing of authority between a manager and a subordinate.
True	False	3. Responsibility is the passing of formal rights to a subordinate so that person can act on a manager's behalf.
True	False	4. Authority should be equal to responsibility.
True	False	5. Accountability adds a performance requirement to responsibility.
True	False	6. Managers who delegate can never be accused of abdicating responsibility.
True	False	7. Delegation works because most subordinates can perform tasks better than their managers can.
True	False	8. The most important determinant of whether or not a manager delegates is how heavy the manager's workload is.
True	False	9. Reverse delegation is synonymous with participation.
True	False	10. Delegation still can be effective if subordinates make occasional mistakes.

Answers: (1) True; (2) False; (3) False; (4) True; (5) True; (6) False; (7) False; (8) False; (9) False; (10) True

BEHAVIORAL CHECKLIST

Look for these specific behaviors when evaluating your delegating skills and those of others.

The Effective Delegator:

- Clarifies the assignment.
- Explains the benefits of doing the job.
- Specifies the range of discretion.
- Allows participation.
- Informs others who might be affected that delegation has occurred.
- Establishes feedback controls.
- Asks questions to test for understanding.
- Insists on recommendations if problems occur.

ATTENTION!

Do not read the following until assigned to do so by your instructor.

MODELING EXERCISE

The Annual Budget

Actors.   Chris Hall and Dale Morgan

Situation.   Chris Hall is director of research and development for a large pharmaceutical manufacturer. Chris has six direct subordinates: Sue Traynor (Chris's secretary), Dale Morgan (the laboratory manager), Todd Connor (quality standards manager), Linda Peters (patent coordination manager), Ruben Gomez (market coordination manager), and Marjorie England (senior project manager). Dale is the most senior of the five managers and is generally acknowledged as the chief candidate to replace Chris when Chris is promoted.

Chris Hall's Role.   You have received your annual instructions from the CEO to develop next year's budget for your area. The task is relatively routine but takes quite a bit of time. In the past, you've always done the annual budget yourself. However, this year, because your workload is exceptionally heavy, you've decided to try something different. You're going to assign budget preparation to one of your subordinate managers. The obvious choice is Dale Morgan. Dale has been with the company longest, is highly dependable and, as your probable successor, is most likely to gain from the experience. The budget is due on your boss's desk in 8 weeks. Last year, it took you about 30–35 hours to complete. However, you had done a budget many times before. For a novice, it might take double that amount of time.

The budget process is generally straightforward. You start with last year's budget and modify it to reflect inflation and changes in departmental objectives. All the data that Dale will need are in your files or can be obtained from your other managers.

You have decided to walk over to Dale's office and inform him of your decision.

Dale Morgan's Role.   You like Chris Hall. You think Chris is a first-rate boss and you've learned a lot from her. You also consider yourself Chris's heir apparent. To better prepare yourself to take Chris's job, you'd like to take on more of Chris's responsibilities.

Running the lab is a demanding job. You regularly come in around 7:00 AM and it's unusual for you to leave before 7:00 PM. For four of the last five weekends, you've even come in on Saturday mornings to get your work done. However, within reasonable limits, you'd try to find the time to take on some of Chris's responsibilities.

As you sit behind your desk reviewing a lab report, Chris walks into your office.

Total Time. 20 minutes (read and prepare, 5 minutes; role-play, 10 minutes; debriefing, 5 minutes)

OBSERVER'S RATING SHEET

Evaluate the delegation skills of Chris Hall on a 1 to 5 scale (5 being the highest). Insert examples for feedback between behavioral criteria.

Clarifies the assignment.   _____

Explains the benefits of the job.   _____

Specifies the subordinate's range of discretion.   _____

Allows subordinate participation.   _____

Informs others who might be affected that delegation has occurred.   _____

Establishes feedback controls.   _____

Asks questions to test understanding.   _____

Insists on recommendations if problems occur.   _____

GROUP EXERCISES

Group Exercise 1: Park City Toyota

Actors.   Dana Porter and C. J. Stone

Situation.   Dana Porter is the sales manager for Park City Toyota. Dana oversees a 15-member sales force at the dealership. In a typical week, Park City Toyota sells 45 new cars and 20 used cars. Dana is responsible for supervising the sales force, approving all car sales, and handling customer relations.

Dana Porter's Role.   You received a notice yesterday that you have been called for jury duty. You will have to appear in court next week and could be gone from work for as long as 3 weeks. Someone will have to take your place during your absence. No one is fully qualified to handle your job. In past years, when you went on vacation or were called away from the dealership, the owner would cover for you. However, he recently had a heart attack and can't work. You've decided that C. J. Stone, one of your salespeople, is the best person to cover for you. C. J. is young and has only been with the company for about 8 months but is bright and assertive.

You have the authority to approve any and all sales. In fact, all new and used car sales require your approval. For instance, you decide on trade-in allowances and any discounts from the suggested list price. You're uncomfortable delegating such broad authority to C. J., so you've decided on a rather cumbersome arrangement. You propose to give C. J. total authority to sell any car at sticker (suggested retail) price, to allow price discounts of up to 3 percent on new cars and up to 5 percent on used cars, and to accept trade-ins at prices not to exceed high wholesale blue book values. Whenever these limits are exceeded by one of the salespeople, C. J. will be allowed to make only a tentative commitment to the customer. You will come in every night after court lets out, review the exceptions, and either approve or reject them. If you have to reject a sale, you will leave a note for C. J. on how far to go to get the sale.

You've called C. J. into your office to discuss your plan.

C. J. Stone's Role.   You are a young and bright salesperson at Park City Toyota. You work for Dana Porter. You've been with the company for 8 months and have been the number-one salesperson in 6 of those 8 months. You've heard through the grapevine that Dana has been called for jury duty. It has crossed your mind that you might be selected to cover for Dana in his absence. You've decided that if asked, you will accept, but you want full authority to approve all sales and resolve any customer complaints. You feel you understand the business and are capable of using good judgment. From your standpoint, any limits placed on a sales manager's discretion hinder the sales staff's ability to close a sale quickly. Moreover, you think it will be fun to call all the shots on the sales floor for a few weeks.

Observer's Role.   Use the observer's rating sheet to provide feedback to the student playing Dana Porter regarding his delegation skills.

Total Time. 25 minutes (read and prepare, 10 minutes; role-play, 10 minutes; debriefing, 5 minutes)

Group Exercise 2: The Meeting Substitute

Actors.   W. L. Lawrence and Alex Drexel

Situation.   W. L. Lawrence is president and CEO of Lawrence Electronics, a San Francisco firm with 5,000 employees and sales in excess of $800 million per year. Reporting directly to W. L. Lawrence are seven vice presidents. The vice president for finance is Alex Drexel.

W. L. Lawrence's Role.   The quarterly meeting of the American Electronics Manufacturers Association is scheduled for the early part of next week. The meeting will be held in Chicago and will last 2 days. Because of prior commitments, you realized a few days ago that you can't attend. However, someone from Lawrence Electronics should be there to represent you. This person's duties would include attending two sessions of committees you belong to, entertaining several important customers, and presenting a short speech at one of the sessions. The speech already has been prepared by someone in the company's public relations department. Although any of your vice presidents could handle the assignment, you think Alex Drexel is best qualified. Alex has been to several of these meetings before and knows the ropes. You sent a memo yesterday asking Alex to attend in your absence. Alex has asked to see you to discuss the matter. Alex has just entered your office.

Alex Drexel's Role.   You're one of seven vice presidents at Lawrence Electronics. You've been with the firm for a dozen years and were promoted to vice president 5 years ago. Yesterday you got a note from your boss, W. L. Lawrence, asking you to take his place at next week's American Electronics Manufacturing Association meeting in Chicago. You've been to two or three of these meetings before with W. L. They're incredibly boring. More important, though, you don't have the extra time to devote 2 days to the meeting. If pushed to the wall, you'll do it, but you don't want to. You've called W. L.'s secretary and set up a meeting to discuss this with W. L. You are walking into W. L.'s office now.

Total Time. 25 minutes (read and prepare, 10 minutes; role-play, 10 minutes; debriefing, 5 minutes)

Group Exercise 3: The Deadline Has Come and Gone

Actors.   Adrian Jackson and Pat Brennan

Situation.   Adrian Jackson is director of the Sonoma County Hospital. Adrian's assistant is Pat Brennan. About 6 weeks ago, Adrian assigned Pat the job of developing a reorganization plan for the hospital, and Pat accepted. It was agreed that Pat would complete the project in 5 weeks. The project is now a week past that deadline, and Adrian has heard nothing from Pat regarding the project or when it will be completed.

Adrian Jackson's Role.   The hospital has grown a great deal in recent years. New departments have been added and others have expanded considerably. To facilitate efficiency and coordination, you decided that a reorganization was necessary. You delegated the reorganization plan to Pat 6 weeks ago. A memo was sent to all hospital personnel advising them of Pat's assignment and requesting their cooperation.

You're new in your job—you were hired only 3 months ago. Pat, a legacy from the previous director, has held the assistant to the director position at the hospital for 6 years. Because of Pat's experience, you assumed that he could do the reorganization plan with minimal supervision and that it would be completed by the agreed-upon deadline. However, that deadline has come and gone. Moreover, you've heard nothing from Pat about how the project is going or when it will be completed. In retrospect, you realize you probably should have kept closer tabs on Pat, but because Pat had so much experience in the position, you were afraid that he would interpret almost any monitoring negatively.

You've decided to confront Pat. The monthly staff meeting has just ended, and Pat was among the dozen or so in attendance. As everyone else is getting up to leave the conference room, you ask Pat to stay for a few minutes. Your intention is to find out the status of the reorganization plan.

Pat Brennan's Role.   You are the assistant to the director. You have held your position for 6 years under three different directors. Your current boss, Adrian, is new to the hospital. Adrian has been in the director's job for only 3 months.

You're used to being left on your own. You have a number of routine tasks that you've been doing for years. For instance, you do the weekly bed-utilization report and the monthly departmental efficiency report. Occasionally, directors have given you special assignments. About 6 weeks ago, Adrian asked you to develop a reorganization plan in response to the rapid growth the hospital has experienced. You agreed to have it completed in 5 weeks. A memo was sent out by Adrian to all hospital personnel advising them of your assignment and requesting their cooperation. You accepted the assignment with some reservations, although you didn't say anything to Adrian at the time. You had some ideas on how to reorganize the hospital, but it wasn't a project that especially interested you. Because you never heard anything from Adrian after receiving the initial assignment, you just let the plan sit in your basket.

The monthly staff meeting, which Adrian leads, has just concluded. As you are gathering your papers and preparing to leave, Adrian has asked you to stay for a few minutes. You don't know the purpose of this request. However, if it's to discuss the reorganization plan, you've decided to take a two-pronged approach. First, you will put Adrian on the defensive. If the reorganization plan was important, why hasn't he followed up on it with you? Second, you intend to throw the decision back at Adrian by asking him for possible suggestions.

Total Time. 25 minutes (read and prepare, 10 minutes; role-play, 10 minutes; debriefing, 5 minutes)

OBSERVER'S RATING SHEET

For the exercise in which you were the observer, evaluate the delegator on the following behaviors. Rate the delegator's effectiveness on each behavior from 1 to 5 (5 being the highest). Use the space between behaviors to jot down notes to use for feedback.

Clarifies the assignment.   _____

Explains the benefits of the job.   _____

Specifies the subordinate's range of discretion.   _____

Allows subordinate participation.   _____

Informs others who might be affected.   _____

Establishes feedback controls.   _____

Asks questions to test for understanding.   _____

Insists on recommendations if problems occur.   _____

Summary Checklist

Take a few minutes to reflect on your performance and look over others' ratings of your skill. Now assess yourself on each of the key learning behaviors. Make a check (✓) next to those behaviors in which you need improvement.

I clarify assignments to my subordinates.   _____

I explain the benefits of the job.   _____

I specify the subordinate's range of discretion.   _____

I allow subordinates to participate.   _____

I inform others who might be affected that delegation has occurred.   _____

I establish feedback controls.   _____

I ask questions to ensure understanding.   _____

I insist on recommendations if problems occur.   _____

APPLICATION QUESTIONS

1. Why do many managers who want to empower their subordinates find it difficult to delegate authority?
2. What can top management do to encourage managers to delegate to their subordinates?
3. When should a manager purposely avoid delegation?
4. If the students on a project team needed to delegate the typing of a term paper to a fellow student, what specific directions should be given?

REINFORCEMENT EXERCISES

1. When watching a video of a movie that has examples of "managers" delegating assignments, pay explicit attention to the incidence of delegation. Was delegating done effectively? What was good about the practice? How might it have been improved? Examples of movies with delegation examples are *The Godfather, The Firm, Star Trek, Nine to Five*, and *Working Girl*.
2. The next time you have to do a group project for a class, pay explicit attention to how tasks are delegated. Does someone assume a leadership role? If so, note how closely the delegation process is followed. Is delegation different in project or study groups than in typical work groups?
3. Do you delegate in your personal life? What do you delegate? To whom do you delegate? The next time you need to delegate, think through the delegation skills and use them to guide your behavior.

ACTION PLAN

1. Which behavior do I want to improve the most?

2. Why? What will be my payoff?

3. What potential obstacles stand in my way?

4. What specific things will I do to improve? (For examples, see the Reinforcement Exercises.)

5. When will I do them?

6. How and when will I measure my success?

Endnotes

1. Stephen P. Robbins, *Supervision Today* (Englewood Cliffs, NJ: Prentice Hall, 1994).
2. Carl Holmes, "Fighting the Urge to Fight Fires," *Harvard Business Review* (November–December 1999), p. 30.
3. Carrie R. Leana, "Predictors and Consequences of Delegation," *Academy of Management Journal* (December 1986), pp. 754–774.
4. Lawrence L. Steinmetz, *The Art and Skill of Delegation* (Reading, MA: Addison-Wesley, 1976), p. 248.
5. Charles D. Pringle, "Seven Reasons Why Managers Don't Delegate," *Management Solutions* (November 1986), pp. 26–30.
6. Alice M. Sapienza, "Believing Is Seeing: How Culture Influences the Decisions Top Managers Make," in R. H. Kilmann, M. J. Saxton, and R. Serpa (eds.), *Gaining Control of the Corporate Culture* (San Francisco, CA: Jossey-Bass, 1985), pp. 66–83.
7. Carrie R. Leana, "Predictors and Consequences of Delegation," *Academy of Management Journal* (December 1986), pp. 754–774.
8. Dale D. McConkey, *No-Nonsense Delegation* (New York: AMACOM, 1974); Lawrence L. Steinmetz, *The Art and Skill of Delegation* (Reading, MA: Addison-Wesley, 1976), p. 248.

12

■ ■ ■

Politicking

SELF-ASSESSMENT EXERCISE: MY ATTITUDE TOWARD POLITICKING[1]

For each of the following statements, circle the number that most closely resembles your attitude.

Statement	Disagree			Agree	
	A lot	A little	Neutral	A little	A lot
1. The best way to handle people is to tell them what they want to hear.	1	2	3	4	5
2. When you ask someone to do something for you, it is best to give the real reason for wanting it rather than reasons that might carry more weight.	1	2	3	4	5
3. Anyone who completely trusts someone else is asking for trouble.	1	2	3	4	5
4. It is hard to get ahead without cutting corners here and there.	1	2	3	4	5
5. It is safest to assume that all people have a vicious streak, and it will come out when they are given a chance.	1	2	3	4	5
6. One should take action only when it is morally right.	1	2	3	4	5
7. Most people are basically good and kind.	1	2	3	4	5
8. There is no excuse for lying to someone else.	1	2	3	4	5
9. Most people forget more easily the death of their father than the loss of their property.	1	2	3	4	5
10. Generally speaking, people won't work hard unless forced to do so.	1	2	3	4	5

Scoring and Interpretation

This exercise is designed to compute your Machiavellianism (Mach) score. Mach is a personality characteristic that taps people's power orientation. The high-Mach personality is pragmatic, maintains emotional distance from others, and believes that ends can justify means. To obtain your Mach score, add up the numbers you checked for questions 1, 3, 4, 5, 9, and 10. For the other four questions, reverse the numbers you have checked, so that 5 becomes 1, 4 is 2, 2 is 4, and 1 is 5. Then total both sets of numbers to find your score. A random sample of adults found the national average to be 25. Students in business and management typically score higher.

The results of research using the Mach test have found that (1) men are generally more Machiavellian than women; (2) older adults tend to have lower Mach scores than younger adults; (3) there is no significant difference between high Machs and low Machs on measures of intelligence or ability; (4) Machiavellianism is not significantly related to demographic characteristics such as educational level or marital status; and (5) high Machs tend to be in professions that emphasize the control and manipulation of people—for example, managers, lawyers, psychiatrists, and behavioral scientists.

SKILL CONCEPTS

In the real world of organizations, the good guys don't always win. Demonstrating openness, trust, objectivity, support, and similar humane qualities in relationships with others doesn't always lead to improved managerial effectiveness. At times, to get things done that you want done or to protect your interests against the maneuvering of others, you'll have to play "hard ball"; that is, you'll have to engage in politicking. How and when should you go about politicking? Those are the questions this chapter addresses.

What Is Politicking?

Politics relates to who gets what, when, and how. Politicking is the actions you can take to influence, or attempt to influence, the distribution of advantages and disadvantages within your organization.[2]

Unlike such issues as goal setting and delegation, you don't learn much about politicking in the typical college program in business management. Why? One reason might be the prescriptive nature of business programs. They emphasize what managers should do rather than what they actually do.[3] Another reason might be the underground nature of politics.[4] Much of it is subtle, disguised, or veiled in secrecy, and successful politicians in organizations are often highly adept at framing their political actions in nonpolitical terms. As a result, it is difficult to get meaningful insights into the political process in organizations. This is unfortunate because political incompetence, political naiveté, and the inability or unwillingness to perform required political tasks effectively are all sources of management failure.[5]

Why Is There Politics in Organizations?

Can you conceive of an organization that is free of politics? It's possible but most unlikely.

Organizations are made up of individuals and groups with different values, goals, and interests.[6] This sets up the potential for conflict over resources. Departmental budgets, space allocations, project responsibilities, and salary adjustments are just a few examples of the resources that must be allocated, resulting in disagreements among organization members.

Resources in organizations are also limited, which often turns potential conflict into real conflict. If resources were abundant, all the various internal constituencies within the organization could satisfy their goals. However, because they're limited, not everyone's interests can be provided for. Furthermore, whether true or not, gains by one individual or group are often perceived as being at the expense of others within the organization. These forces create competition among members for the organization's limited resources.

Maybe the most important factor leading to politics within organizations is the realization that most of the "facts" that are used to allocate the limited resources are open to interpretation. What, for instance, is a good performance? What is a good job? What is an adequate improvement? The manager of any major league baseball team knows a .400 hitter is a high performer and a .125 hitter is a poor performer. You don't need to be a baseball genius to know you should play your .400 hitter and send the .125 hitter back to the minors. But what if you have to choose between players who hit .280 and .290? Then other factors—less objective ones—come into play: fielding, attitude, potential, ability to perform in the clutch, and so on. Most managerial decisions in organizations more closely resemble choosing between a .280 and a .290 hitter than deciding between a .125 hitter and a .400 hitter. It is in this large and ambiguous middle ground of organizational life—where the facts don't speak for themselves—that politics takes place.

Finally, because most decisions have to be made in a climate of ambiguity—where facts are rarely fully objective and thus are open to interpretation—people within the organization will use whatever influence they can to taint the facts to support their goals and interests. That creates the activities we call politicking.

Political Diagnostic Analysis

Before you consider your political options in any situation, you need to evaluate that situation. Political diagnostic analysis is a three-step process designed to make you a better evaluator.

1. *Assess your organization's culture.*   The place to begin is with an assessment of your organization's culture to ascertain which behaviors are desirable and which aren't. Every organization has a system of shared meaning called its *culture*.[7] This culture is a set of unwritten norms that members of the organization accept and understand and that guide their actions. For example, some organizations' cultures encourage risk taking, accept conflicts and disagreements, allow employees a great deal of autonomy, and reward members according to performance criteria. Other cultures differ by 180 degrees: They punish risk taking; seek harmony and cooperation at any price; minimize opportunities for employees to show initiative; and allocate rewards to people according to such criteria as seniority, effort, or loyalty. The point is that every organization's culture is somewhat different, and if a political strategy is to succeed, it must be compatible with the culture.

   One of the fastest and most effective means for tapping an organization's culture is to learn as much as you can about the organization's performance-appraisal system and the criteria used for determining salary increases, promotions, and other rewards. Take a look at the organization's performance-appraisal form. What does it look like? What does it evaluate: traits, behaviors, goal accomplishments? How much emphasis is placed on factors such as getting along with others, teamwork, and loyalty to the organization? Does style count as much as substance? Are people rated against absolute standards or against each other? How are people ranked? How often are appraisals required? How does top management view performance appraisal: to identify deficiencies, as a basis for reward allocations, or to facilitate employee growth and development? Then turn your attention to the reward system.

Who gets the raises and promotions? Maybe more important, who doesn't? These reward-allocation decisions should tell you what behaviors pay off in your organization.

2. *Assess the power of others.*   At first glance, it seems that either people are powerful or they're not. However, power is differential. On some issues, a person might be very powerful, yet that same person might be relatively powerless on other issues. Therefore, you need to determine which individuals or groups will be powerful in a given situation.

   Some people have influence as a result of their formal position in the organization. Therefore, that is probably the best place to begin your power assessment. What decision or issue do you want to influence? Who has formal authority to affect that issue? These questions are, however, only the beginning. After that, you need to consider others—individuals, coalitions, formal departments—that might have a vested interest in the decision's outcome. Who might gain or lose as a result of one choice being selected over another? This helps you identify the power players—those motivated to engage in politicking. It also pinpoints your likely adversaries.

   Now you need to assess the power of each player or group of players specifically. In addition to each one's formal authority, you should evaluate the resources each controls[8] and the person's centrality in the organization.[9] Research confirms that the control of scarce and important resources is a source of power in organizations. Control and access to key information or expert knowledge and possession of special skills are examples of resources that might be scarce and important to the organization—and hence potential means of influencing organizational decisions. It also has been found that centrality, meaning being in the right place in the organization, can be a source of power. People or groups with network centrality gain power because their position allows them to integrate other functions or to reduce organization dependence. This explains, for instance, the frequent power of secretaries or the influence of the accounting department when a firm is experiencing a major financial crisis.

   On a more micro level, you should not overlook assessing your boss's influence in any power analysis. What is your boss's position on the issue at hand—for, against, or neutral? If his or her position is for or against, how intense is your boss's stand? What is your boss's power status in the organization? Is it strong or weak? Answers to these questions can help you assess whether the support or opposition of your boss will be relevant. The support of a powerful boss can be a plus. On the other hand, the support of a weak boss is likely to mean little and can even be harmful to your cause. If your boss is an up-and-comer with an expanding power base, you'll want to tread carefully. As an adversary, such a person can be a major hindrance to your future in the organization. However, as an ally, such a boss can open doors previously closed to you and possibly provide the vehicle to accelerate your rise in the organization. If your power assessment uncovers that your boss is widely perceived throughout the organization as dead wood, your political strategy might need to include distancing yourself to avoid guilt by association.

3. *Assess your power.*   After looking at others' power, you need to assess your own power base. What's your personal power level? What power, if any, does your position in the organization provide? Where do you stand relative to others who hold power? Figure 12.1 summarizes peoples' main sources of power in organizations.

Some people project a personal charisma or magnetic personality that draws others to them. They have those hard-to-define leadership qualities and often are perceived as socially adept, popular, outgoing, self-confident, aggressive, and intelligent.[10] If you happen to be seen in your organization as a charismatic leader, you'll find that others will want to know your position

Power originates from an individual's *personal characteristics* and *position* in an organization. Additional power can be acquired by creating dependency, impression management, and politicking. Each of these sources is summarized here.

POSITION POWER BASES

- **Authority.**   The right to give orders because of one's position in the organization.
- **Reward.**   The ability to give people things they value.
- **Coercive.**   Based on the ability to punish people by taking away or withholding things they value.

PERSONAL POWER BASES

- **Expertise.**   Possession of special skills others depend on to achieve goals.
- **Information.**   Possession of information others depend on to achieve goals.
- **Charisma.**   Charisma exists when others identify with and are attracted to someone they look up to. If others like, admire, and want to be accepted by you, you have what is known as *referent* power.
- **Association.**   Close associations with people who have position and/or personal power. "It's not *what* you know, but *who* you know."
- **Dependency.**   The control of a resource that others need to meet their needs.
- **Favorable Impression.**   Shaping the image you project to favorably influence how others perceive you.
- **Politicking Skills.**   The use of influencing strategies to gain power and influence decision outcomes in your favor.

FIGURE 12.1   Power Bases.

Source: Based on French, J.R.P. Jr. and B. Raven, "The Bases of Social Power," in D. Cartwright, ed., *Studies in Social Power* (Ann Arbor: University of Michigan Institute for Social Research, 1959), pp. 150–67; Littlepage, G. E., J. L. Van Hein, K. M. Cohen, and L. L. Janiec, "Evaluation and Comparison of Three Instruments Designed to Measure Organizational Power and Influence Tactics," *Journal of Applied Social Psychology* (January 16–31,1993), pp. 107–125; Drory, A. and T. Romm, "The Definition of Organizational Politics: A Review," *Human Relations* (November 1990), pp. 1133–1154.

on issues, that your arguments often will be perceived as persuasive, and that your position is likely to carry considerable weight in others' decisions.

Few of us are charismatic leaders. We're more likely to develop a personal power base through our expertise. By controlling specialized information that others need, we increase others' dependence on us. If lots of people in the organization can do what you can do, or if your talent could be replaced easily by hiring an outsider, your expert power is low.

If you have neither charismatic nor expert power, possibly your position in the organization can be a source of power. If you're a manager, you'll have some reward and coercive powers derived solely from the authority of your position. For instance, you might be able to reassign people, approve time off, hand out salary increases, initiate suspensions, or even fire employees. In addition to formal authority, your position also might provide centrality, high visibility, access to important or guarded information, and the like. Depending on the issue, your position might prove to be an asset.

Finally, don't ignore the dynamics inherent in the relationships between you and other power holders.[11] Determine the degree to which players support or oppose you. Assess their power to influence the ultimate outcome and then determine the priority they assign to your objective. In this way, you can identify who your allies are; who your opponents are likely to be; the intensity of support or opposition each can be expected to exert; and the personal, positional, and coalitional power you and your supporters can bring to bear to counter the resistance of opponents.

General Guidelines for Political Action

Now we turn from analysis to action. This section offers some general guidelines for successful political behavior. The next section describes specific strategies.

1. *Frame arguments in terms of organizational goals.* Effective politicking requires covering up self-interest. No matter that your objective is self-serving; all the arguments you marshal in support of your objective must be framed in terms of the benefits that will accrue to the organization. People whose actions appear to blatantly further their own interests at the expense of the organization's are almost universally denounced, are likely to lose influence, and often suffer the ultimate penalty of being expelled from the organization.

2. *Practice Impression Management.* Impression management—that is, attempting to behave in ways that will create and maintain desired impressions in the minds of others[12]—is an important part of political success. If you have assessed your organization's culture, you are aware of appropriate dress codes, which associates to cultivate and which to avoid, whether to appear to be a risk taker or to be risk aversive, the preferred leadership style, the importance placed on getting along well with others, and so forth. Then you are equipped to project the appropriate image. Because effectiveness in an organization is not a fully objective outcome, style as well as substance must be attended to. Social networking can facilitate this process.

3. *Utilize Social Networking.* A social network is a communication structure made up of individuals, groups, or organizations that are connected by common interests or interdependencies such as friendship, financial goals, career paths, or political agenda. Examples of internet networks often used for impression management and career advancement are Linkedin, Twitter, and MySpace. Figure 12.2 summarizes some networking skills you can use for impression management.

Impressions are being formed about you as soon as you enter into new relationships. Start building social networks immediately to help influence how others perceive you by doing the following things.

1. *Map out your ideal network.*
   - Determine who knows what's going on.
   - Figure out who is critical in the workflow.
   - Assess who knows how to get around roadblocks.
   - Determine who can help you the most.

2. *Take action to build the network.*
   - Don't be shy; most other people will be receptive and want to help.
   - Start conversations with: "I'm new here. Can you help me get to know people who...?"

3. *Reciprocate and invest in your network.*
   - Share information useful to others.
   - Take the time to stay in touch with network members.
   - Update your network as people and situations change.

FIGURE 12.2 Networking Skills for Impression Management.

Source: Adapted from William C. Byham, "Start Networking Right Away (Even If You Hate It)," Vol. 87, No. 1, *Harvard Business Review* (January 2009), p. 22.

Social network analysis graphs the relationships between parties in a communication network. It is a useful tool to identify the informal groups and networks of relationships that are active in an organization. The resulting map shows how much work really gets done in organizations.[13]

A social network map can give you insights into political coalitions, common interest groups, and who the leaders, facilitators, most active members, and isolates are. Social net working is a useful tool for facilitating the implementation of many of the politicking skills described in this chapter, such as political diagnostic analysis, image management, making yourself visible, appearing indispensable, finding a mentor, building a coalition, and avoiding tainted members.

4. ***Gain control of organizational resources.***   The control of organizational resources that are scarce and important is a source of power. Knowledge and expertise are particularly effective resources to control. They make you more valuable to the organization and therefore more likely to gain security, advancement, and a receptive audience for your ideas.

5. ***Make yourself appear indispensable.***   Because we're dealing with appearances rather than objective facts, you can enhance your power by appearing to be indispensable. You don't have to be indispensable as long as key people in the organization believe that you are. If the prime decision makers believe no ready substitute is available for what you are giving to the organization, they are likely to go to great lengths to ensure that your desires are satisfied. How do you make yourself appear indispensable? The most effective means is to develop expertise through experience, contacts, secret techniques, natural talents, and the like. It must be perceived as critical to the organization's operations, and key decision makers must believe that no one else possesses this expertise to the extent that you do.

It also helps if others in your organization perceive you as mobile and believe you have employment options available at other organizations. Combining perceived mobility with perceived indispensability lessens the likelihood that your rise in your present organization will be stalled by the excuse that "we can't promote you right now because your current unit can't afford to lose your expertise."

6. ***Be visible.***   The evaluation of managerial effectiveness has a substantial subjective component, so it is important that your boss and those in power in the organization be made aware of your contributions. If you are fortunate enough to have a job that brings your accomplishments to the attention of others, it might not be necessary to take direct measures to increase your visibility. However, your job might require you to handle activities that are low in visibility, or your specific contribution might be indistinguishable because you're part of a group endeavor. In such cases—without creating the image of a braggart—you'll want to call attention to yourself by giving progress reports to your boss and others, being seen at social functions, being active in your professional associations, developing powerful allies who speak positively about your accomplishments, and using similar tactics. Skilled politicians actively and successfully lobby to get projects that will increase their visibility.

7. ***Get a mentor.***   A mentor is someone, typically higher up in the organization, from whom you can learn and who can encourage and help you. When you have a mentor, that person can be expected to stand up for you at meetings and relay inside information that you otherwise wouldn't have access to. Additionally, just the fact that you have a mentor provides a signal to others in the organization that you have the resources of a powerful higher-up behind you.

How do you get a mentor? Typically, mentors do the choosing. They spot someone lower in the organization with whom they identify and take that person on as a protégé. The more contacts you make with higher-ups, formally and informally, the greater chance you have of being singled out as someone's protégé. Participating in company golf tournaments, going out for drinks with colleagues after work, and taking on visible projects are examples of activities that are likely to bring you to the attention of a potential mentor.

8. *Develop powerful allies.*   It helps to have powerful people in your camp. In addition to a mentor, you can cultivate contacts with potentially influential people above you, at your level, and in the lower ranks. They can provide you with important information that might not be available through normal channels. In addition, decisions will at times be made by those with the greatest support. Sometimes, though not always, there is strength in numbers. Having powerful allies can provide you with a coalition of support if and when you need it.

9. *Avoid tainted members.*   Almost every organization has some fringe members whose status is questionable. Their performance or loyalty is under close scrutiny. Such individuals, while they are under the microscope, are tainted. Carefully keep your distance from them. We all tend to judge others by the company they keep. Given the reality that effectiveness has a large subjective component, your own effectiveness might be called into question if you are perceived as being too closely associated with tainted people.

10. *Support your boss.*   Your immediate future is in the hands of your current boss. Because your boss evaluates your performance, you typically will want to do whatever is necessary to have your boss on your side. You should make every effort to help your boss succeed and look good. Provide support if your boss is under siege, and spend the time to find out what criteria will be used to assess your effectiveness. Don't undermine your boss. Don't speak negatively of this person to others. If your boss is competent, visible, and in possession of a power base, he or she is likely to be moving up in the organization. By being perceived as supportive, you increase the likelihood of being pulled along too. At the worst, you'll have established an ally higher up in the organization.

What should you do, though, if your boss's performance is poor and his or her power is low? Politically, it's better to switch than to fight. Your credibility will be challenged if your boss is perceived as weak. Your performance evaluations, even if highly positive, are not likely to carry much weight. You'll suffer from guilt by association. It is extremely difficult to distance yourself from your immediate boss without your boss perceiving you as a traitor. The most effective solution in such a situation, and the one that carries the least risk, is to lobby quietly for a transfer. If you have a mentor, use that person to lobby for you. Consistent with what we said earlier, couch your request for a transfer in terms of the organization's best interests (i.e., a transfer will increase your experience, prepare you to assume greater responsibilities, and allow you to make bigger contributions to the organization).

Specific Political Strategies

What specific strategies can you use to influence others and get them to support your objectives? When is one strategy preferable to another? Research has identified seven widely used options.[14]

1. **Reasoning** is the use of facts and data to make a logical or rational presentation of ideas. This strategy is most likely to be effective in a culture characterized by trust, openness, and logic and where the vested interests of other parties in your request are low.

2. **Friendliness** is using flattery, creating goodwill, acting humble, and being friendly prior to making a request. It is more effective for obtaining favors than for selling ideas. It also requires that you be well liked and that your interpersonal relations with the target of influence are good.
3. **Coalitions** get the support of other people in the organization to back up their request. Because this strategy is complex and requires coordination, it tends to be used for important outcomes and when the final decision relies more on the quantity than on the quality of support (as in committees that make their decisions by majority rule).
4. **Bargaining** is the use of negotiation through the exchange of benefits or favors. This strategy is applicable when you and the person you want to influence are interdependent and when the culture promotes give and take.
5. **Higher authority** relies on gaining the support of higher-ups in the organization to back your requests. This is an effective strategy only if the higher-ups are liked or feared. Although appropriate in bureaucratic cultures that have great respect for authority, this strategy is inappropriate in less-structured cultures.
6. **Assertiveness** is a direct and forceful approach, such as demanding compliance with requests, issuing reminders, ordering individuals to do what you need done, and pointing out that rules require compliance. This strategy is effective when the balance of power is clearly in your favor: You have considerable ability to reward and punish others, and their power over you is low. The drawback is that the target is likely to feel resentful and look for opportunities to retaliate later.
7. **Sanctions** refer to the use of organizationally derived rewards and punishments, such as preventing or promising a salary increase, threatening to give an unsatisfactory performance appraisal, or withholding a promotion. This strategy is similar to assertiveness, except the influence here depends solely on your position. This is not an approach for influencing superiors, and even when used with subordinates, it might be perceived as manipulative or illegitimate.

Considering the Cost–Benefit Equation

Before you select a political strategy, be sure to assess any potential costs of using it against its potential benefits. The inexperienced politician needs to be reminded that all forms of power are not alike. Some are accepted more readily than others, and in many instances, the costs of applying influence exceed the benefits derived from such action. Although the benefits of power are obvious, the costs are often overlooked. As Lawless[15] has noted, "Power is effective when held in balance. As soon as power is used, it gets out of balance and the person against whom the power is used automatically resorts to some activities designed to correct the power imbalance."

In physics, we know that for every action there is a reaction. In the study of management, we know that for every use of power there is a corollary use of power. Therefore, your choice of a strategy should depend only partly on whether it will allow you to achieve your short-term goal. You should also try to minimize resentment and use up the least possible amount of future credit. This suggests a preference for reason, friendliness, and rewards to obtain compliance, and avoidance of coercive approaches whenever possible.[16] Remember, whenever you use the do-this-or-else approach, you run the risk that your bluff will be called. The result might not be desirable in cost–benefit terms; you might win the battle but lose the war.

CONCEPT QUIZ

Do you understand the basic concepts in politicking? The following 10-question, true–false quiz will help answer that question. Remember, if you miss any, go back and find out why you got them wrong.

Circle the right answers.

True **False**	1.	Organizations are made up of individuals and groups with different values, goals, and interests.
True **False**	2.	Politics exists in organizations because decisions are made in a climate of ambiguity.
True **False**	3.	The existence of a formal performance appraisal system in an organization reduces the likelihood that politics will surface.
True **False**	4.	Because power tends to accrue to positions, all you need to know about a person's power in an organization is the position that person holds.
True **False**	5.	For the control of a resource to convey power, the resource must be scarce and important.
True **False**	6.	Your boss's support can be a negative as well as a positive.
True **False**	7.	Most middle- and upper-level managers are charismatic leaders.
True **False**	8.	All managerial positions come with some rewards and coercive powers.
True **False**	9.	All other things being equal, you should try to avoid the use of coercive power.
True **False**	10.	"I did that for you, now you do this for me" is an example of a coalition strategy.

Answers: (1) True; (2) True; (3) False; (4) False; (5) True; (6) True; (7) False; (8) True; (9) True; (10) False

BEHAVIORAL CHECKLIST

Look for these specific behaviors when evaluating your politicking skills and those of others.

An Effective Politicker:

- Assesses the power bases of all players (self included).
- Frames arguments in terms of organizational goals.
- Practices impression management to develop a desirable image.
- Gains control of scarce resources (e.g., knowledge, expertise) to appear indispensable.
- Uses networking skills to develop powerful coalitions.
- Is assertive and visible.
- Avoids "tainted" members.
- Is friendly, reasonable, and willing to bargain.

ATTENTION!

Read all the cases in the Group Exercises section before coming to class. Do not read anything else.

MODELING EXERCISE

The Truck-Trading Problem[17]

All class members should read the following situation.

Situation.   A large electric appliance company has six repair technicians. It is necessary for them to drive to various locations in the city to complete their work. Each repair technician drives a small truck and takes pride in keeping it looking good. The technicians have a possessive feeling about their trucks and like to keep them in good running order. Naturally, the technicians would prefer to have new trucks, which give them a feeling of pride.

A new truck has just been allocated to the crew. The new truck is a Chevrolet. The supervisor has just called a meeting to determine who will get the new truck.

Here are some facts about the trucks and the repair technicians in the crew who report to Sean Marshall, the supervisor of appliance repairs. Most technicians do all of their driving in the city, but Jo and Charlie cover the jobs in the suburbs.

- Jo: 7 years with the company; has a 9-year-old Ford truck
- Bo: 11 years with the company; has a 5-year-old Dodge truck
- Jean: 21 years with the company; has a 4-year-old Ford truck
- Charlie: 5 years with the company; has a 3-year-old Ford truck
- Fran: 3 years with the company; has a 5-year-old Chevrolet truck

Instructions.   After the class reads the previous situation, pick one role-player to be the foreman, Sean Marshall, and five more role-players to be crew members. The role-players should read the reminders for role-playing and for their own roles, but not for the other roles, and prepare for the role-play.

The remainder of the class will be observers and provide feedback on the power dynamics in the role-play. They should be divided into five equal groups, each of which is assigned to observe one of the specific role-players. Observers should *not* read any of the roles. The observers' job is to see if they can determine which power bases and political tactics the various role-players are applying. They also provide specific feedback to their assigned role-player on his or her effectiveness in applying power in the exercise. Observers should review the observer's rating sheet to prepare for providing meaningful feedback at the end of the exercise.

Sean Marshall's Role.   You are the foreman of a crew of repair technicians, each of whom drives a small service truck to and from various jobs. Every so often you get a new truck to exchange for an old one, and you have to decide which of your crew will receive the new truck. Even though you always try to be fair, the decision often generates hard feelings because each crew member feels entitled to the new truck. No matter what you decide, most of the crew is unsatisfied. You now have to face the issue again because a new Chevrolet truck has just been allocated to you for distribution.

Most of the crew drive in the city and make fairly short trips. The exceptions are Jo and Charlie, who cover the suburbs. To solve the problem this time you have decided to allow the crew themselves to decide who gets the new truck. You will tell them about the new truck and will put the problem in terms of what they think would be the most fair way to distribute the truck. You will avoid taking a position yourself because you want to do what the crew thinks is fair.

If the crew is unable to reach a consensus themselves, you can always exercise your supervisor's authority to make the final decision. You know that it is your responsibility as supervisor to guide and direct the meeting.

Jo's Role.   You have to do more driving than most of the other technicians because you work in the suburbs. You have a fairly old truck and feel your large amount of driving makes you the best candidate for a reliable new truck. You were an automobile mechanic prior to becoming an appliance technician and you know that several trucks have problems that can be easily fixed to make them perfectly satisfactory for their current drivers. If any of these drivers argue for the new truck, you will explain how to make easy repairs rather than discarding the vehicles. You plan to assertively use your expertise in favor of winning the new truck for yourself.

Jean's Role.   When a new Chevrolet truck becomes available, you think you should get it because you have the most seniority and don't like your present truck. Your personal car is a Chevrolet, and you prefer the Chevy truck you drove before you were allocated the current Ford truck. You have known Sean Marshall's boss since you both were hired on as technicians more than 20 years ago. If your seniority won't get you the new truck, maybe a tactful bit of name-dropping will do the job.

Fran's Role.   You have the least desirable truck in the company. It is 5 years old, and before you got it, it was in a bad wreck. It never has driven very well and feels unsafe, but you've put up with it for 3 long years. It's about time you got a good truck to drive, and you feel the next one should be yours. You have an admirable accident record. In fact, the only accident you ever had occurred when you sprang the door of Charlie's truck when he opened it as you backed out of the garage. You hope the new truck is a Ford since you prefer driving them to other brands. You are well liked by the rest of the crew because of your charismatic personality. You plan to use friendliness, flattery, and humility to really sweet-talk the crew during the meeting in hopes of securing the new truck for yourself.

Charlie's Role.   The heater in your present truck is inadequate. The door lets in too much cold air, and you attribute your frequent colds to this problem. You want a warm truck since you have a good deal of driving to do. As long as it has good tires, brakes, and is comfortable, you don't care about its make. Although Fran never admitted it was his fault, you know that it was Fran who backed into the open door of your truck. The door has never been repaired to fit right. You also know that Dodge trucks have better maintenance records than other makes and that there is currently an allocation pending for another new truck next month. You plan to use this information to bargain for the new truck for yourself.

Bo's Role.   You feel you deserve a new truck. Your present truck is old, and since the senior man has a fairly new truck, you should get the next one. You have taken excellent care of your present Dodge and have kept it looking like new. A person deserves to be rewarded for treating a company truck like a personal vehicle. You plan to use this logic to reason with the others that those who conscientiously maintain their vehicles should get their just deserts.

Total Time. 55 minutes (preparation, 20 minutes; role-play, 20 minutes; debriefing, 15 minutes)

OBSERVER'S RATING SHEET

On completion of the exercise, observers rate how well the role-players applied the politicking skills. Use the following rating scale: (1) Unsatisfactory, (2) Weak, (3) Adequate, (4) Good, (5) Outstanding. Write concrete examples in the space below for each skill component to use when explaining your feedback. Also note examples of behaviors that demonstrate applications of *power tactics* and *political strategies* and indicate how effective they were.

1	2	3	4	5
Unsatisfactory	Weak	Adequate	Good	Outstanding

Name of Person Observed _____

SKILL COMPONENT	RATING
Assessed the power bases of all players (self included).	_____
Framed arguments in terms of organizational goals.	_____
Practiced impression management.	_____
Used control of scarce resources to appear indispensable.	_____
Used networking skills to develop powerful coalitions	_____
Was assertive and visible.	_____
Avoided "tainted" members.	_____
Was friendly, reasonable, and willing to bargain.	_____

GROUP EXERCISES

One way to demonstrate that you can use the political skills described in this chapter is to apply them to a set of cases. The following cases can be discussed in groups or by the class as a whole.

Three different types of group exercises are presented. First is a case for you to practice your awareness, analysis, and action planning skills. Second is an exercise for you to apply and get feedback about your personal power strategies. Third is an opportunity to solicit the help of others to analyze and plan how to better build your power base.

Group Exercise 1: The Bill and Mary Show: Bendix to Morrison Knudsen[18]

Instructions.   The following case can be discussed in small groups or by the class as a whole.

Case.   Mary Cunningham was a hot topic at Bendix Corporation long before September 1980, when Bill Agee stood before more than 600 employees and denied that her rapid advancement had anything to do with "a personal relationship that we have." Cunningham joined the company right after obtaining her M.B.A. from Harvard in June the previous year. She was hired as executive assistant to the CEO, Bill Agee, after a 3-hour interview in New York at the Waldorf-Astoria. "A meeting of kindred spirits," she said. Exactly 1 year later, Agee gave her a promotion—vice president for corporate and public affairs. Three months after that came another promotion to vice president for strategic planning. Agee tried to confront the uproar that immediately followed by announcing to employees that his new vice president and he were "very, very good friends" but not romantically involved. The comment backfired, creating a national media furor so intense and so focused on Cunningham's youth, blond hair, and shapely figure that in the fall of 1980 the Bendix board of directors forced her resignation.

Inside Bendix, gossip about the relationship between Cunningham and Agee escalated after her June promotion, and all sorts of additional events kept the noise level up. A TV camera focusing on former President Gerald Ford at the Republican National Convention happened to find Agee and Cunningham sitting next to him. Some Bendix people suggested that Agee was less accessible than he had once been, and Cunningham's growing influence with him did not help allay suspicions. She had called herself his "alter ego" and "most trusted confidante"; he said she was his "best friend."

Top corporate executives in the United States had been accused of almost everything imaginable except having romances with one another. But what was one to think? Here were two attractive people working together, traveling together, even staying in the same two-bedroom suite at the Waldorf Towers. They had to be having an affair, which would explain Cunningham's sprint up the ranks. On the other hand, was Cunningham, as Gail Sheehy portrayed her in a four-part newspaper series, a brilliant, idealistic corporate missionary destroyed by jealous cynics? Barbara Seaners interviewed Cunningham; feminist leaders such as Gloria Steinem rallied to her defense, asking if this meant that young, talented, attractive, ambitious, and personable female executives were permitted only slow climbs upward, lest they invite gossip?

Insisting that their relationship had been platonic until after she left Bendix, Agee and Cunningham married in June 1982. By then, Agee had converted to Catholicism and divorced his wife of 25 years. Cunningham's 6-year marriage to Howard Gray, an executive with American Express, was annulled. The same year, after resurfacing as a vice president at Seagram's, Cunningham acted as Agee's unpaid adviser during Bendix's attempted takeover of the Martin Marietta Corporation. But their ambitious plan collapsed when Bendix was swallowed by the

Allied Corporation in a merger that cost hundreds of Bendix employees their jobs. The fiasco was blamed, in part, on the chair's young wife, the strategic planner.

In 1988, Bill Agee was named CEO of the Morrison Knudsen Corporation (MK) in Boise, Idaho. Six years later, in 1994, Morrison Knudsen posted losses of $310 million and lurched toward bankruptcy. In February 1995, Bill Agee was ousted as MK stock fell from $30 a share to $5.50; employees and retirees alike watched their futures evaporate. In February, too, Mary Agee resigned as executive director of the nonprofit Morrison Knudsen Foundation, a position critics say she used to benefit the Nurturing Network, a nonprofit women's organization that she founded in 1983.

The Boise community did not regret the Agees' demise. It wasn't only the shareholders' losses and the hundreds of MK workers Bill Agee fired, but the fact that the Agees rubbed Boise the wrong way almost from the start—so much so that after being excluded from the town's private clubs and most prestigious boards, the couple and their two children abruptly relocated in 1992 to a $3.4 million estate in Pebble Beach, California. From that Pacific Coast setting 600 miles away from their offices, Mary Agee managed her charity and Bill Agee ran Morrison Knudsen by phone, fax, FedEx, and from a $17 million corporate Falcon jet that peeved MKers, dubbed "Mary's taxi."

Now, with more than a dozen lawsuits filed by shareholders charging that Bill Agee and the Morrison Knudsen board wasted assets and managed the company recklessly, Mary Agee's role is under legal as well as public scrutiny regarding the use of MK assets to benefit the Nurturing Network. The lawyers are also eyeing the close relationship linking MK and its foundation with the Nurturing Network—a complex web of friendships, business interests, and moral commitments. In 1992, half the MK board members had wives on the Nurturing Network board, and Bill Agee served on both boards. "Once so many of the directors and their wives had joined with the Agees in a moral crusade," the *New York Times* pointedly asked, "how likely was it that they would challenge Mr. Agee in the boardroom?"

Total Time. 45 minutes (preparation, 15 minutes; discussion, 30 minutes)

READER'S RATING SHEET

When you finish reading the case, evaluate the politicking skills of both Bill Agee and Mary Cunningham on a 1 to 5 scale (5 being the highest). Provide comments to explain your ratings in the spaces between the behavioral checklist skills.

SKILL COMPONENT	Bill	Mary
Assessed the power bases of all players (self included).	_____	_____
Framed arguments in terms of organizational goals.	_____	_____
Practiced impression management.	_____	_____
Used control of scarce resources to appear indispensable.	_____	_____
Used networking skills to develop powerful coalitions.	_____	_____
Was assertive and visible.	_____	_____
Avoided "tainted" members.	_____	_____
Was friendly, reasonable, and willing to bargain.	_____	_____

Questions

1. What are the major political issues in this case?
2. What were Mary Cunningham's original power bases when she first joined Bendix? What other sources of power did she acquire? How?
3. What bases of power did Bill Agee have? Did he acquire any more?
4. How effective were Bill Agee's political strategies? Explain.
5. How effective were Mary Cunningham's political strategies? Explain.
6. What could Bill and Mary have done differently to avoid the negative outcomes?

Group Exercise 2: The Savemore Corporation[19]

Situation. The Savemore Corporation is a chain of 400 retail supermarkets located primarily in the northeastern section of the United States. Store 5116 employs more than 50 persons, all of whom live within suburban Portage, New York, where the store is located.

Wally Shultz served as general manager of store 5116 for 6 years. Last April he was transferred to another store in the chain. At that time the employees were told by the district manager, Mr. Finnie, that Wally Shultz was being promoted to manage a larger store in another township.

Most of the employees seemed unhappy to lose their old manager. Nearly everyone agreed with the opinion that Shultz was a "good guy to work for." As examples of his desirability as a boss, the employees told how Wally had frequently helped the arthritic black porter with his floor mopping, had shut the store 5 minutes early each night so that certain employees might catch their buses, had held a Christmas party each year for employees at his own expense, and had been generally willing to pitch in. All employees had been on a first-name basis with the manager. About half of them had begun work with the Savemore Corporation when the Portage store was opened.

Wally Shultz was replaced by Clark Raymond. Raymond, about 25 years old, was a graduate of an Ivy League college and had been with Savemore a little more than a year. After completion of his 6-month training program, he served as manager of one of the chain's smaller stores before being advanced to store 5116. In introducing Raymond to the employees, Mr. Finnie stressed his rapid advancement and the profit increase that occurred while Raymond had been in charge of his last store.

I began my employment in store 5116 early in June. Mr. Raymond was the first person I met in the store, and he impressed me as being more intelligent and efficient than the managers I had worked for in previous summers at other stores. After a brief conversation concerning our respective colleges, he assigned me to a cash register, and I began my duties as a checker and bagger.

In the course of the next month I began to sense that relationships between Raymond and his employees were somewhat strained. This attitude was particularly evident among the older employees of the store, who had worked in store 5116 since its opening. As we all ate our sandwiches together in the cage (an area about 20 feet square in the cellar, fenced in by chicken wire, to be used during coffee breaks and lunch hours), I began to question some of the older employees as to why they disliked Mr. Raymond. Laura Morgan, a fellow checker about 40 years of age and the mother of two grade-school boys, gave the most specific answers. Her complaints were:

1. Raymond had fired the arthritic black porter on the grounds that a porter who "can't mop is no good to the company."
2. Raymond had not employed new help to make up for normal attrition. Because of this, everybody's workload was much heavier than it ever had been before.
3. The new manager made everyone call him "mister." He's unfriendly.

4. Raymond didn't pitch in. Wally Schultz had, according to Laura, helped people when they were behind in their work. She said that Shultz had helped her bag on rushed Friday nights when a long line waited at her checkout booth, but "Raymond wouldn't lift a finger if you were dying."

5. Employees were no longer let out early to catch buses. Because of the relative infrequency of this means of transportation, some employees now arrived home up to an hour later.

6. "Young Mr. Know-it-all with his fancy degree takes all the fun out of this place."

Other employees had similar complaints. Gloria, another checker, claimed that "He sends the company nurse to your home every time you call in sick." Margo, a meat wrapper, remarked, "Everyone knows how he's having an affair with that new bookkeeper he hired to replace Carol when she quit." Pops Devery, the head checker, who had been with the chain for more than 10 years, was perhaps the most vehement of the group. He expressed his views in the following manner: "That new guy's a real louse, got a mean streak a mile long. Always trying to cut corners. First it's not enough help, then no overtime, and now, come Saturday mornings, we have to use boxes for the orders 'til the truck arrives. If it wasn't just a year 'til retirement, I'd leave. Things just aren't what they used to be when Wally was around." The last statement was repeated in different forms by many of the other employees. Hearing all this praise of Wally, I was rather surprised when Mr. Finnie dropped the comment to me one morning that Wally had been demoted for inefficiency, and that no one at store 5116 had been told this. It was important that Mr. Schultz save face, Mr. Finnie told me.

A few days later, on Saturday of the busy weekend preceding the July 4 holiday, store 5116 again ran out of paper bags. However, the delivery truck did not arrive at 10:00, and by 10:30 the supply of cardboard cartons was also low. Mr. Raymond put in a hurried call to the warehouse. The men there did not know the whereabouts of the truck but promised to get an emergency supply of bags to us around noon. By 11:00, there were no more containers of any type available, and the truck from the company warehouse bringing merchandise for sale and store supplies normally arrived at 10:00 on Saturday morning. Frequently, the stock of large paper bags would be temporarily depleted. It was then necessary to pack orders in cardboard cartons until the truck was unloaded.

Mr. Raymond reluctantly locked the doors to all further customers. The 20 checkers and packers remained in their respective booths, chatting among themselves. After a few minutes, Mr. Raymond requested that they all retire to the cage because he had a few words for them. As soon as the group was seated on the wooden benches in the chicken-wire-enclosed area, Mr. Raymond began to speak, his back to the cellar stairs. In what appeared to be an angry tone, he began, "I'm out for myself first, Savemore second, the customer third, and you last. The inefficiency in this store has amazed me from the moment I arrived here."

At about this time I noticed Mr. Finnie, the district manager, standing at the head of the cellar stairs. It was not surprising to see him at this time because he usually made three or four unannounced visits to the store each week as part of his regular supervisory procedure. Mr. Raymond, his back turned, had not observed Finnie's entrance.

Mr. Raymond continued, "Contrary to what seems to be the opinion of many of you, the Savemore Corporation is not running a social club here. We're in business for just one thing—to make money. One way that we lose money is by closing the store on Saturday morning at 11:00. Another way that we lose money is by using a 60-pound paper bag to do the job of a 20-pound bag. A 60-pound bag costs us over 20 cents apiece; a 20-pound bag costs less than a penny. So when you sell a couple of quarts of milk or a loaf of bread, don't use the big bags. Why do you think we have four different sizes, anyway? There's no great intelligence or effort required to pick the right size. So do it. This store wouldn't be closed right now if you'd used your common sense. We started out this week with enough bags to last 'til Monday and they would have lasted 'til Monday if you'd only used your brains. This kind of thing doesn't look good for the store, and it doesn't look good for me. Some of you have been bagging for over 5 years. You oughta be able to do it right by now." Mr. Raymond paused and then said, "I trust I've made myself clear on this point."

The cage was silent for a moment, and then Pops Devery, the head checker, spoke up: "Just one thing, Mis-tuh Raymond. Things were running pretty well before you came around. When Wally was here, we never ran outta bags. The customers never complained about over-loaded bags or the bottoms falling out before you got here. What're you gonna tell somebody when they ask for a couple extra bags to use in garbage cans? What're you gonna tell some-body when they want their groceries in a bag, an' not a box? You gonna tell them the manager's too damn cheap to give 'em bags? Is that what you're gonna tell 'em? No sir, things were never like this when Wally Shultz was around. We never had to apologize for a cheap manager who didn't order enough then. Whatta you got to say to that, Mis-tuh Raymond?"

Mr. Raymond, his tone more emphatic, began again. "I've got just one thing to say to that, Mr. Devery, and that's this: Store 5116 never did much better than break even when Shultz was in charge here. I've shown a profit better than the best he ever hit in 6 years every week since I've been here. You can check that fact in the book upstairs any time you want. If you don't like the way I'm running things around here, there's nobody begging you to stay."

At this point, Pops Devery interrupted and, looking up the stairs at the district manager, asked, "What about that, Mr. Finnie? You've been around here as long as I have. You told us how Wally got promoted 'cause he was such a good boss. Supposin' you tell this young feller here what a good manager is really like? How about that, Mr. Finnie?"

A rather surprised Mr. Raymond turned around to look up the stairs at Mr. Finnie. The manager of store 5116 and his checkers and packers waited for Mr. Finnie's answer.

Questions

1. What is happening in this situation? What are the consequences?
2. Referring to the Behavioral Checklist, how do you rate Mr. Raymond's politicking skills? Why?
3. If you were Mr. Finnie, what would you do now?

Total Time. 30 minutes (preparation, 5 minutes; case discussion, 20 minutes; debriefing, 5 minutes)

Group Exercise 3: The New Superintendent[20]

Situation.   When Boyd Denton was appointed superintendent of the Washington County School System in 1987, he was given the charge, by the school board, to improve the quality of student performance. His strategy for achieving this was to implement his philosophy of "competence and delegation." First, he would find very strong and very competent principals for each of the schools. Second, he would give each of them a great deal of autonomy. He allowed principals to make hiring decisions, to evaluate teachers, to make salary decisions, and to decide how to spend the budget allocated to each school.

From 1987 to 1992, the school system made significant gains in student achievement. However, there was one school, Brewton, that was a problem for Denton. The principal at Brewton was David Starr. Starr was one of the first principals that Denton hired, but now Denton believed that he had made a mistake.

At Brewton, the teachers did not seem to care about the students. They were, by any measure, mediocre. However, they were very loyal to Starr. He was well liked by them and they supported him. The reason is that Starr never put any pressure on them for performance and did not really hold them accountable.

When Denton became aware of this, he discussed it with Starr. Starr became angry and threatened to quit. He told Denton that the reason Brewton wasn't a good school was because Denton didn't give them enough resources to do the job right. Denton pointed out the opposite. In fact, by every budget measure, Starr and the Brewton School were treated well.

By 1992, Starr and Denton were on very bad terms. They argued often and all the other principals saw Starr as a prima donna and uncooperative. In one of their arguments, Starr threatened to resign. Denton told him, "Bring me the letter, now." Starr left the office and returned 20 minutes later with a letter of resignation. Denton didn't hesitate. "I'll take it," he said.

Denton searched for a replacement and found Joe Melcan, a bright, young assistant superintendent in a nearby district. When he hired Melcan, Denton told him, "I want you to get Brewton straightened out and I'll help you. The teachers are well paid, and you've got good resources there, but the job does not get done. One of the main problems you will have is that most of the teachers are very loyal to Starr. They won't help you much, but I'll give you whatever help and support you need."

Melcan's approach was a straightforward one. He would let everyone know what was expected of them, make pay as contingent on performance as possible, and hire good new teachers. He thought that in 3 or 4 years, there would be enough turnover that with subsequent replacements, he could make Brewton into a high-performing school.

Denton watched Melcan's progress and he was pleased. Three young teachers were hired. Melcan instituted a different evaluation approach than Starr. He started to give substantial recognition to the good teachers and less to those who weren't so good. This was a major departure from the way Starr had managed and many of the Starr loyalists were angry. Some complained to Denton and some filed grievances. When Denton and the union investigated, they found that the charges were without foundation. It was true that things had changed, but now the school was not managed in the style of Starr, but in a performance-oriented style by Melcan.

This was exactly what Denton thought had to be done. Between 1992 and 1995, student performance improved considerably. However, many of the teachers who were old Starr supporters were dissatisfied. They continued to complain and grumble. Each time they came to Denton, however, he supported Melcan.

In 1995, Denton left Washington County to become an assistant to the State Superintendent of Schools. He was replaced by Mitchell Kraut. Kraut had been an assistant superintendent for Denton for several years. There were two things about Kraut that were of concern to Melcan. First, Kraut had been a teacher at Brewton during the first years of Starr's time as principal. They had, in fact, become close friends. Second, Kraut announced that he was going to centralize many activities that had been performed previously by the principals. No longer would the principals make budgeting decisions, evaluate personnel, or hire faculty. Joe Melcan was very worried.

Questions

1. What is happening in this situation? What are the consequences?
2. What examples of good politicking do you detect? What are the consequences?
3. What examples of ineffective politicking do you detect? What are the consequences?
4. If you were Joe Melcan, what would you do?

Total Time. 30 minutes (preparation, 5 minutes; case discussion, 20 minutes; debriefing, 5 minutes)

Summary Checklist

Take a few minutes to reflect on your performance and look over others' ratings of your skill. Now assess yourself on each of the key learning behaviors. Make a check (✓) next to those behaviors in which you need improvement.

I assess the power bases of all players (self included).	_____
I frame arguments in terms of organizational goals.	_____
I practice impression management to develop a desirable image.	_____
I gain control of scarce resources to appear indispensable.	_____
I use networking skills to develop powerful coalitions.	_____
I am assertive and visible.	_____
I avoid "tainted" members.	_____
I am friendly, reasonable, and willing to bargain.	_____

APPLICATION QUESTIONS

1. Why does politicking have a negative connotation in most organizations?
2. Can you avoid politics in large organizations by being an outstanding performer? Explain.
3. Is politicking dysfunctional to an organization's operations? Explain.
4. You have just joined a large organization as a first-line supervisor. Using your political skills, what can you do to increase the probability of succeeding in this job?

REINFORCEMENT EXERCISES

1. Review half a dozen recent issues of *Business Week* or *Fortune* magazines. Look for articles on reorganizations, promotions, and departures from upper management. Do these articles suggest that political factors were involved in the management changes? Explain.
2. Interview three managers from three different organizations. Ask them to describe the role that they perceive politics plays in decision making in their organization. Ask for examples that they have participated in or been affected by.
3. Identify a politically adept person in an organization you are a member of. What does this person do that makes him or her politically effective? Next, identify a politically inept person in an organization you are a member of. What does this person do that makes him or her politically ineffective?

ACTION PLAN

1. Which political behavior do I want to improve the most?

2. Why? What will be my payoff?

3. What potential obstacles stand in my way?

4. What specific things will I do to improve? (For examples, see the Reinforcement Exercises.)

5. When will I do them?

6. How and when will I measure my success?

Endnotes

1. R. Christie and F. L. Geis, *Studies in Machiavellianism* (New York: Academic Press, 1970). Reprinted by permission.
2. Dan Farrell and James C. Petersen, "Patterns of Political Behavior in Organizations," *Academy of Management Review* (July 1982), pp. 430–442.
3. Stephen P. Robbins, "Reconciling Management Theory with Management Practice," *Business Horizons* (February 1977), pp. 38–47.
4. Douglas Yates, Jr., *The Politics of Management* (San Francisco, CA: Jossey-Bass, 1985).
5. Stanley Young, "Developing Managerial Political Skills: Some Issues and Problems." Paper presented at the National Academy of Management Conference, Chicago, IL (August 1986).
6. Jeffrey Pfeffer, *Power in Organizations* (Marshfield, MA: Pitman Publishing, 1981).
7. Phillip L. Hunsaker, *Training in Management Skills* (Upper Saddle River, NJ: Prentice Hall, 2001), pp. 317–337.
8. Jeffrey Pfeffer and Gerald R. Salancik, The *External Control of Organizations: A Resource Dependence Perspective* (New York: Harper & Row, 1978).
9. Daniel Brass, "Being in the Right Place: A Structural Analysis of Individual Influence in an Organization," *Administrative Science Quarterly* (December 1984), pp. 518–539.
10. Robert W. Allen, Daniel L. Madison, Lyman W. Porter, Patricia A. Renwick, and Bronston T. Mayes, "Organizational Politics: Tactics and Characteristics of Its Actors," *California Management Review* (Fall 1979), pp. 77–83.
11. William D. Coplin, Michael K. O'Leary, and Carole Gould, *Power Persuasion: A Surefire Way to Get Ahead* (Boston, MA: Addison-Wesley, 1985).
12. William L. Gardner and Mark J. Martinko, "Impression Management in Organizations," *Journal of Management* (June 1988), p. 332.
13. B. R. Schlenker and M. F. Weigold, "Interpersonal Processes Involving Impression Regulation and Management," in M. R. Rosenzweig and L. W. Porter (eds.), *Annual Review of Psychology,* vol. 43 (Palo Alto, CA: Annual Reviews Inc., 1992), pp. 133–168.
14. David Kipnis, Stuart M. Schmidt, C. Swaffin-Smith, and Ian Wilkinsin, "Patterns of Managerial

Influence: Shotgun Managers, Tacticians, and Bystanders," *Organizational Dynamics* (Winter 1984), pp. 58–67.

15. David J. Lawless, *Effective Management* (Englewood Cliffs, NJ: Prentice Hall, 1972), p. 243.

16. Adapted from N. R. F. Maier, *Problem Solving and Creativity in Individuals and Groups* (Belmont, Calif.: Brooks/Cole Publishing Company, 1970), pp. 298–302.

17. Based on Laura Berman, "The Gospel According to Mary," *Working Woman* (August 1995), pp. 47–49, 68–72; P.W. Bernstein, "Things the B-School Never Taught," *Fortune* (November 3, 1980), pp. 53–56.

18. Reprinted by permission of John W. Hennessey, Jr., the University of Vermont. At the time of this case, the author, a college student, was employed for the summer as a checker and stockboy in store 5116.

19. Adapted from Henry Tosi, John Rizzo, and Stephen Carroll, *Managing Organizational Behavior* (Boston: Ballinger Publishing Co., 1986). Reprinted with permission from Ballinger Publishing Company.

20. John R. Schermerhorn, James G. Hunt, Richard N. Osborn, and Mary Uhl-Bien, *Organizational Behavior*, 11th ed. (John Wiley & Sons, 2010), p. 159.

13

■ ■ ■

Persuading

SELF-ASSESSMENT EXERCISE: HOW I PERSUADE

For each of the following statements, select the answer that best describes your approach to oral persuasion.

	Usually	Sometimes	Seldom
1. I have a clear objective in mind before I ask someone for something.	_____	_____	_____
2. I tailor my arguments to the personality of the person I'm trying to influence.	_____	_____	_____
3. When I want something from people, I make it clear to them how doing it will further their self-interest.	_____	_____	_____
4. If I were a manager, I'd expect my subordinates to obey my requests because of the authority of my position.	_____	_____	_____
5. If I want something from someone, I assume that person is intelligent and will respond to logic.	_____	_____	_____
6. When I want something from someone, I explain to the person why what I want is important.	_____	_____	_____
7. When I want something from someone, I try to use emotional appeals as well as logic.	_____	_____	_____

Scoring and Interpretation

For questions 1, 2, 3, 5, 6, and 7, give yourself 3 points for Usually; 2 points for Sometimes; and 1 point for Seldom. For question 4, give yourself 3 points for Seldom; 2 points for Sometimes; and 1 point for Usually.

Sum up your total points. A score of 19 or higher indicates that you make effective use of your persuasive resources. A score of 16–18 suggests that you can be more persuasive in your interpersonal relations. A score below 16 indicates that you have room for significant improvement in your oral persuasion techniques.

SKILL CONCEPTS

If one skill differentiates successful politicians from unsuccessful ones, it is the ability to persuade others. Successful politicians are able to make forceful arguments that appear logical and compelling, although they have no monopoly on this skill. We all know people whom we consider persuasive. They seem to know just what to say and when to say it. Were these people born with this skill? No. They were, however, probably exposed to people—parents, other relatives, teachers, friends—who were excellent role models for learning this skill. In this chapter, we review what it is that persuasive people do, and then we provide you with opportunities to practice these behaviors. Our objective is to equip you with techniques that will make you more persuasive in your interpersonal relations.

What Is Persuasion?

Persuasion is the conscious manipulation of face-to-face communication to induce others to take action. How is persuasion different from authority or power? All three are means of influence; that is, they focus on getting other people to do what you want them to do. However, power and authority are means of making others do something they otherwise would not have done. Persuasion preserves others' freedom to do whatever they want after you have tried to convince them to choose a certain course of action. "'Persuadees' feel they are acting of their own accord within the goals and guidelines set for them."[1]

Authority represents the rights that go with a managerial position and, for the most part, it's an effective device for gaining subordinates' compliance with requests. However, it has its limitations. Authority is of little value in dealing with peers, superiors, or those outside your direct command; it's constrained by employees' perception of your legitimate rights; it's not likely to motivate employees; and it's more suitable for autocratic organizations than for democratic ones.

Authority works well with subordinates. Unfortunately, your interpersonal relations in an organization are not confined to dealing with people who work directly for you. You'll need your boss's cooperation, but you can't get that through authority. You'll be in meetings in which you'll need the support of other managers who are at the same level as you. That support can't be obtained through authority. At times, you'll undoubtedly find yourself needing the assistance of others—inside and outside the organization—to get your job done. For example, you might need a report from another department outside your chain of command or a favor from a supplier. Again, authority won't work. What you'll need in these varied situations is the ability to persuade.

Authority also has its limits. Every employee sets up a psychological line that defines the boss's authority. If you want your employees to do something that crosses that line—to work overtime, to assume an additional project, to take on an unpleasant task, or the like—authority isn't likely to be effective. At times when authority won't work, persuasion often can.

Even in situations in which you have authority and know it will work, you might not want to use it because it could have negative repercussions. Authority implies obligation. In contrast, when you persuade someone to do something—even though you have the authority to demand it instead—that person will be more likely to perform the task with commitment and enthusiasm, so persuasion might motivate employees better than authority does. Remember, no matter how good your idea is, its final effectiveness will depend on how well it's executed by others.

Finally, authority is inconsistent with humanistic–democratic values. Many organizations—especially small ones and those that employ a preponderance of professionals—are organized around participative principles. Authority and control are replaced by openness, trust, and democratic management practices. In such organizations, persuasion is the only viable means to get people to do what you want them to do.

Persuasion Strategies

There are many strategies that can be used to persuade others. Some of the most effective are credibility, logical reasoning, emotional appeals, social proof, and ingratiation.[2]

1. *Credibility.*   You're more likely to persuade people when they like, trust, and have confidence in you. This credibility doesn't arise out of blind faith; it has to be earned. How? One way is by demonstrating competence—by demonstrating knowledge or ability. Another way to gain credibility is by having trustworthy intentions. When your motives are perceived as objective and honest by others, you gain credibility in their eyes. Figure 13.1 summarizes ways you can establish a trust bond with others. A related source of credibility is character—being ethical, industrious, and dependable. Finally, credibility can be enhanced through your personal charisma. If you strike others as friendly, caring, enthusiastic, and positive, people will be drawn to you.

   Credibility is not easy to attain, but it has controllable elements.[3] For instance, it takes time to develop a reputation for competence, but you can help it along by doing things like volunteering for projects that will increase your visibility and allow you to demonstrate your talents. Similarly, you can concentrate on being friendly and thoughtful to others, conscientious in doing your work, and avoiding actions that might give the appearance of a conflict of interest.

2. *Logical Reasoning.*   You're more likely to persuade others when you can cite logical reasons for them to behave as you wish. People seek to be rational. Before they do something, they like to feel certain it's consistent with their goals. If that's not directly apparent, you need to clarify why they should think or act the way you want; that is, you need to be prepared to answer the question "Why?" This can be done by planning ahead and anticipating

---

Trust refers to the overall feeling of safeness that you have with another person. You make "deposits" into an emotional bank account with another person through kindness, honesty, and keeping commitments. But, if you show disrespect, fail to honor commitments, or take advantage of the other person, your trust account becomes depleted. The relationship then becomes degenerative, with hostility and defensiveness making it difficult to build up trust again.

There are six major deposits to build up emotional bank accounts:[4]

- *Understand and honor other peoples' needs and priorities*, which may be very different than our own.
- *Attend to little things*, like showing kindness and being courteous, because they make big positive deposits in relationships.
- *Keep commitments*. Breaking a promise can be a massive withdrawal that may prevent future deposits because people won't believe you.
- *Clarify expectations* so that others don't feel cheated or violated if you don't behave in ways that they assumed you knew they desired, even though they never overtly told you.
- *Show personal integrity* by keeping promises, being honest, fulfilling expectations, and being loyal to all people equally, including those not present.
- *Apologize sincerely when you make a withdrawal* without rationalizing or trying to shift some of the blame to the other.

FIGURE 13.1   Establishing a Trust Bond.

negative responses. You can prepare a number of possible reasons why a particular action is desirable and then advance the one that seems most appropriate for the particular situation. In this way, you make sure that you present the best argument possible.

You do not make an effective argument by using every reason you can possibly think of or find. Any reason you use should meet three tests.[5] First, it must uphold what you're proposing. Second, it must be supportable by the facts. Third, the reason must have an impact on the person you're trying to persuade. The implications of these three criteria are self-evident. Take aim at your target with the precision of a rifle rather than with the overkill of a shotgun. If you're trying to persuade through logical argument, do your homework. Gather the facts to support your argument and, very important, get to know the "persuadees." The best-supported argument can fail if you haven't taken into consideration the goals, needs, and interests of the person you're trying to persuade.

3. *Emotional Appeal.* You might be able to persuade people on the basis of good reasons alone. However, you're more likely to be effective if you also use language that touches their emotions. Therefore, whenever you can, supplement good reasons with appeals to a person's fears, loves, joys, frustrations, and the like.

Why is a combination of logic and emotional appeal more effective than logic alone? The answer is that people can believe in the logic of an argument but still not act on that belief. What they need is a stimulus or kick that will move them from passive to active. An appeal to the emotions can be that stimulus.

4. *Social Proof.* Another way of convincing people to do something we are recommending is to demonstrate to them that others are taking the same action. This "social proof" suggests that others agree with the action and that it is appropriate and socially acceptable.[6] Examples of the effectiveness of social proof in action range from victims rushing to invest with Bernard Madoff because other sophisticated investors had done so, to bartenders priming their tip jars with a few dollar bills to signal to customers that folding money is the appropriate type of tip.

5. *Ingratiation.* Ingratiation is a strategic attempt to get someone to like you in order to obtain compliance to a request.[7] Three common ingratiation tactics are flattery and offering complements, conforming to the other's opinion, and rendering favors to be perceived as helpful.[8]

Persuasion Tactics

Credibility, reason, and emotion are three general strategies for persuading others. There are also four more specific tactics people use for influencing others:[9] active facilitative, passive facilitative, active inhibiting, and passive inhibiting. The first two tactics improve persuasive results; the latter two hinder effectiveness. People rarely use inhibiting tactics deliberately. Rather, these tactics are usually the unintended consequences of poor planning, lack of information, inadequate listening skills, or an inability to assess one's impact on others accurately. They're included here to dramatize how a tactic that might have begun as facilitative can backfire and hinder persuasive efforts.

1. *Active Facilitative.* If you actively engage in behavior that succeeds in influencing another person, you have used an active facilitative approach. Popular examples of this approach are being prepared and organized, stating views with conviction, providing information, asking for information, making recommendations, being willing to negotiate, taking the initiative, and paraphrasing.[10] This approach is an effective means of clarifying facts, correcting mistakes or inaccurate or incomplete beliefs, and modifying priorities.

2. *Passive Facilitative.*   Sometimes the most effective way to persuade another is to do nothing. The passive facilitative approach recognizes that remaining silent, waiting patiently, letting others do the speaking, and similarly passive actions can, at times, be a highly effective means of influence. Victory doesn't always go to the loudest, the longest-winded, or the person armed with the most facts. The astute persuader knows when to say nothing and let someone else take the offensive.

3. *Active Inhibiting.*   What kind of active behavior hinders persuasive effectiveness? Examples include trying to "wing it," stating views tentatively, being unwilling to negotiate, being aggressive, discouraging feedback, discouraging discussion, criticizing, changing the subject, rejecting ideas, and giving advice prematurely.[11] This message should not be lost on those who want to become more effective persuaders: Action, without thought, is likely to be counterproductive.

4. *Passive Inhibiting.*   The final category encompasses failure by omission. Examples are withholding information, not paying attention, being submissive, ignoring others or their ideas, failing to respond with empathy, leaving issues ambiguous, failing to give praise or appreciation, refusing to grant recognition, withholding help or support, failing to ask for help or support, or allowing others to define your role.[12]

Looking at persuasion through the prism of these four tactical categories drives home three points. First, the potential for failure always exists. Even with the best of intentions, you can fall flat on your face. Second, an active approach is not always preferable. At times, purposely "doing nothing" is likely to prove most effective. Third, whether you choose an active or a passive approach depends on whom you're trying to influence. If you have the necessary information about that person's needs, interests, goals, and the like, you can make a better decision about whether to use an active or a passive approach.

Improving Your Persuasive Skills

A review of the oral communication and persuasion research has identified a number of suggestions that can help you improve your persuasive skills. They build and expand upon the strategies and tactics previously discussed.

1. *Establish your credibility.*   Nothing undermines persuasive efforts more than a lack of credibility. People don't want to listen to a person they don't trust and respect. They also won't follow the advice of someone who doesn't know what they're talking about. Start by developing your expertise so that your information is reliable. Then demonstrate your belief and commitment to your suggestions with a dynamic and friendly presentation style.[13]

2. *Use a positive and tactful tone.*   Assume the person you're trying to persuade is intelligent and mature. Don't talk down to that person. Be respectful, direct, sincere, and tactful. The worst thing that will happen if you follow this advice is that the person will respond in an immature manner and your persuasive effort will be for naught. However, you will have advanced your credibility and laid the groundwork for a more effective response next time. On the other hand, if your tone is negative or if you treat people as if they are unintelligent, you risk making them defensive, failing in your effort to persuade, and undermining your credibility for future persuasive efforts. Unless you're a football coach—for whom talking down to players seems to be a role expectation—always speak to those you want to persuade in a tone that shows respect.

3. *Make your presentation clear.*   In the event persuasion is successful, what exactly do you want to accomplish? This delineation of an objective should guide your presentation. That is, before you can convincingly articulate your view to someone else, you need to be clear about what you want. You'd be surprised how many people don't focus on what they want to accomplish before they jump in. This explains why potential "persuadees" are often confused and unclear about what is being asked of them.

   Once your objective is clear, you should present your argument one idea at a time. Don't jump from issue to issue, and avoid unrelated topics. Focus on your end objective, and then present your ideas in a straight path that will lead the person to the conclusion you want and the objective you set.

4. *Present strong evidence to support your position.*   You need to explain why what you want is important. Merely saying that a request is important or urgent is not enough. Demanding compliance because you're the boss has limited applicability, and even if it were appropriate, relying on authority doesn't build credibility. You should demonstrate with strong supporting evidence why someone should do as you wish. The responsibility for building the case lies with you.

5. *Tailor your argument to the listener.*   Effective persuasion demands flexibility. You have to select your argument for your specific listener. To whom are you talking? What are the person's goals, needs, interests, fears, and aspirations? How much does the listener know about the subject you're discussing? Does the person have preconceived views on this subject? If so, how do they align with yours? How does this person like to be treated? What is his or her behavioral style? Answering questions like these can help you define the right persuasion strategy to use.

   Different personal characteristics influence peoples' susceptibility to be persuaded.[14] For instance, research indicates that people with high intelligence tend to be more easily influenced than people with low intelligence when exposed to persuasive communications that rely primarily on strong, logical arguments. However, highly intelligent people are less influenced by persuasive communications that rely primarily on unsupported generalities or false, illogical, irrelevant arguments. High intelligence, in other words, seems to make people more receptive to logical reasoning and less susceptible to flawed logic. People with authoritarian personalities, who believe that status and power differences should exist among people in an organization, are easily influenced by those in authority. In contrast, nonauthoritarian types are persuaded more by facts and credibility. Our overall conclusion, based on this research, is that you should alter your persuasive strategy to reflect the personal characteristics of the subject. Specifically, the higher a person's intelligence level, the more logical and well documented your arguments should be; in addition, you should rely more on facts than on your formal position in attempting to persuade nonauthoritarian types.

6. *Appeal to the subject's self-interest.*   To persuade people effectively, you need to understand what makes them tick. Then you can put yourself in their position when you make a request. An individual's behavior is directed toward satisfying self-interests. You need to appeal to that self-interest by anticipating, before you make any demands, that the subject will ask, "What's in it for me?" Don't assume that other people will do what you want merely because you're a credible person or because you can articulate logical arguments. You also have to motivate people to action by showing them why it is in their best interests to do as you wish.

7. *Use logic.*   A logical, reasoned argument is not guaranteed to persuade the subject, but if you lack facts and reasons to support your argument, your persuasiveness almost certainly

will be undermined. One test of your persuasive skills is your ability to present a logical argument.

8. *Use emotional appeals.*   Presenting clear, rational, and objective evidence in support of your view is often not enough. You also should appeal to a person's emotions. Try to reach inside the subjects and understand their loves, hates, fears, and frustrations. Then use that information to mold what you say and how you say it. The persuasiveness of most television evangelists lies in their ability to understand their audience and to structure their oral presentation's appeal to their audience's emotions.

Applying Persuasive Skills in Formal Presentations

People in organizations often find themselves making formal oral presentations to others. Some examples are sales presentations, requests for project funding, running for office, and supporting a proposal. A study conducted by AT&T and Stanford University revealed that the ability to make effective presentations is the top predictor of success and upward mobility in organizations.[15] Given their importance for your interpersonal effectiveness, personal satisfaction, and career progression, the question is, "How can I make effective formal presentations?"

The success of your public speaking is determined primarily by the time you spend preparing before you step in front of your audience. You want to avoid speeches that are too long, detailed, confusing, vague, boring, or veer off-track. The first step is to determine the purpose of your presentation and the outcomes you want to achieve. Next, you need to mold your message to clarify how what you want will match the needs of your audience. Finally, you want to ensure that the audience will act on your suggestions. Figure 13.2 provides some tips for making formal presentations.

PLANNING AND PREPARING

- **Identify your purpose.**   What is the outcome you want to achieve? *Why* are you giving this presentation: to persuade, explain, instruct, or report? *What* do you want the audience to know or do?
- **Analyze your audience.**   Mold your presentation to fit their specific characteristics. Find out their needs, concerns, and preferred format for presentations by talking to the audience or people who know them.
- **Organize the presentation.**   First, clarify your focus or main point. Second, develop an outline of the presentation's three main parts: the introduction, body, and conclusion. Third, plan the visual aids you need for the audience to understand your points. Following are some guidelines for making each of these components effective.

a. **Introduction**

- **Get the audience's attention.**   Grab the audience with something vitally interesting to them and convince them to listen to you. Give them an interesting story, an example that ties into your focus, a meaningful quotation, a startling statistic, or appropriate humor that makes a relevant point.
- **Increase your credibility**   by relating something about your background and experience that makes you an expert on the topic you are speaking about.
- **Present your agenda,**   keeping in mind the familiar slogan: "Tell them what you are going to tell them, tell them, and then tell them what you just told them."
- **Share what you expect of the audience.**   Tell listeners about the decision, commitment, or actions that they will be expected to perform at the end.

FIGURE 13.2   Tips for Making Formal Presentations.

b. The main message.   Because of the short attention span of most audiences, you need to make your points in the shortest, most interesting way possible. Some suggestions are:

- **Change your pace**   by including appropriate humor, stories, or exercises requiring people to raise their hands or respond verbally.
- **Use repetition**   to make sure the main ideas get through accurately and are remembered. You can talk about them and show visuals, as well as have your audience read handouts and ask questions.
- **Use stories and analogies**   to *associate and connect* your ideas to something the listeners already understand.
- **Change the intensity**   in the pitch, tone, and loudness of your voice to focus audience attention.
- **Get audience involvement.**   Use brainstorming, questions, sharing of experiences, or anything that gets the audience involved.

c. The conclusion.   Your conclusion should repeat your main ideas to reinforce your objectives and expectations for the audience.

- **Practice and visualize success.**   Rehearse aloud at least four or five times in order to check your timing and to make sure your presentation flows and sounds the way you want it to. Then visualize yourself presenting successfully. This will allow you a chance to feel success and become more confident in your delivery.

DELIVERY OF THE PRESENTATION

- **Be enthusiastic.**   Your interest in your topic tends to be contagious. Speak as if you are in a lively conversation with friends, but avoid shouting or preaching.
- **Maintain eye contact.**   Eye contact enhances audience involvement. It makes the audience feel that they are being spoken to personally and that you are sincere. It is most effective to rotate looking at audience members one at a time on a random basis.
- **Use proxemics.**   Use physical space to enhance your presentation. Don't hide behind a podium. Eliminate distracting items from the area. Use a variety of body movements to emphasize key points, build rapport, and signal transitions.
- **Never apologize.**   Don't apologize for anything! The minute you apologize, your ability to influence your audience is decreased.

AFTER THE PRESENTATION

- **Evaluate how you did.**   Immediately after the presentation, ask others who were there to debrief you what went well and where you need to improve. This can help you fine-tune the presentation for future audience, or provide tips for putting together other ones later on.
- **Follow up.**   Send materials you promised the audience as well as reminders of what they have committed to, or you have asked them to do.

FIGURE 13.2   (Continued)

CONCEPT QUIZ

The following 10-question, true–false quiz is based on the previous material. If you miss any of these questions, go back and find out why you got them wrong.

Circle the right answer.

True	False	1.	Authority is an effective means of influencing superiors.
True	False	2.	Oral persuasion seeks to induce others to take action.
True	False	3.	The evidence demonstrates that age and credibility are positively correlated.
True	False	4.	An effective argument should include every possible reason you can find.
True	False	5.	Oral persuasion works best when it focuses on logical reasoning and avoids appeals to emotions and feelings.
True	False	6.	Persuasion encompasses active and passive approaches.
True	False	7.	An understanding of persuasion tactics ensures success.
True	False	8.	You have nothing to gain by talking down to a person you are trying to persuade.
True	False	9.	If a well-thought-out argument works with one person, it is likely to be effective with most people.
True	False	10.	You should rely more on emotions than on your formal position when attempting to persuade nonauthoritarian types.

Answers: (1) False; (2) True; (3) False; (4) False; (5) False; (6) True; (7) False; (8) True; (9) False; (10) False

BEHAVIORAL CHECKLIST

Look for these specific behaviors when evaluating your oral persuasion skills and those of others.

An Effective Persuader:

- Establishes credibility.
- Uses a positive, tactful tone.
- Presents ideas one at a time.
- Presents strong evidence to support a position.
- Tailors arguments to the listener.
- Appeals to the listener's self-interest.
- Makes a logical argument.
- Uses emotional appeals.

ATTENTION!
Do not read the following until assigned to do so by your instructor.

MODELING EXERCISE

The Grade Change

After reading the situation, two students need to volunteer to be actors in the following grade change role-play. The actors should not read the other person's role. The rest of the class will be observers using the observer's rating sheet to provide feedback to the actors after the exercise.

Actors.   Professor Hatch (college instructor) and Dale Dillon (one of Professor Hatch's former students)

Situation.   Dale Dillon has come to Professor Hatch's office. Dale took the professor's course last semester and just received the grade report, which said that Dale earned a C. Dale has come to Hatch's office to persuade the professor to raise the grade to a B.

Dale Dillon's Role.   You are a senior, majoring in management. You carried four courses last semester and also worked 20 hours a week. Your 87-year-old grandmother died last term, and attending her funeral required you to miss a week of class. Your grade-point average, with the C in Hatch's class, is 3.65 (out of 4.0). Hatch's C is the only C on your record. You're disappointed with the grade. You made a B on the midterm and on the final, and a B– on the term paper; however, participation accounts for 20 percent of the grade and Hatch gave you a D in that category.

Professor Hatch's Role.   You pride yourself on being a fair instructor. If you make a mistake, you're willing to correct it. However, you don't think grades should be a political process. In the past 5 years, you've taught about a thousand students and have changed only three grades. In fact, on occasion, you've openly criticized colleagues who make a frequent practice of changing the grades of students who complain.

You perceive Dale Dillon as an exceptionally bright student who wasn't committed to your class last term. You gave Dale a B on the midterm and on the final, and a B– on the term paper; however, participation accounts for 20 percent of the grade and you gave Dale a D in that category. Dale missed 4 of the 30 class sessions, two of them in one week. In contrast, no one else in the class missed more than two sessions. The quality of Dale's in-class contributions was at about the 75th percentile, but the quantity of those contributions was significantly below the class average.

Total Time. 25 minutes (preparation, 5 minutes; role-play, 10 minutes; debriefing, 10 minutes)

OBSERVER'S RATING SHEET

Evaluate Dale Dillon's oral persuasive performance on a 1 to 5 scale (5 being the highest). Insert examples for feedback in spaces between behavioral criteria.

Establishes credibility.   _____

Uses positive, tactful tone.   _____

Presents ideas one at a time.   _____

Gives strong, supportive evidence.   _____

Tailors argument to listener.   _____

Appeals to subject's self-interest.   _____

Makes a logical argument.   _____

Uses emotional appeal.   _____

GROUP EXERCISES

Three different types of exercises are presented in this section. The first is a chance to practice and hone your skills in personal persuasion in a one-on-one situation. The second allows you to practice formal oral presentations to larger audiences. In the third exercise, participants need to persuade others to trust them.

Group Exercise 1: Personal Persuasion

Instructions.   Break up into groups of three. Each group will perform three role-plays, allowing each member a chance to be the persuader, subject, and observer. As the observer, you are to evaluate the persuader's skills using the behaviors identified in the observer's rating sheet.

Group members should discuss current issues until they find several that they disagree on. Then determine two people who disagree on an issue. For the first exercise, one of the two has 10 minutes to try and change the other's mind. The listener should not argue with the persuader, but just actively listen to understand the persuader's position. After 10 minutes, the listener tells the persuader why he or she was or wasn't persuaded to change his or her mind on the issue. Then the observer gives the persuader feedback on the skills identified in the observer's rating sheet. This debriefing from the listener and observer should take about 10 minutes. Group members need to switch roles until each has been the persuader, listener, and observer.

Total Time. 60 minutes (three persuasion attempts, 10 minutes each; three debriefings, 10 minutes each)

Group Exercise 2: Making Formal Persuasive Presentations

Many students steer clear of classes and situations requiring formal presentations. The problem is that most management jobs require them. There is no substitute for experience in honing your formal presentation skills. Consequently, this exercise consists of everyone making and evaluating formal presentations to gain confidence and feedback to become better presenters.

Instructions.   Each class member is to prepare and deliver a 3- to 5-minute persuasive presentation to other class members. Use the following observer's rating sheet as a guide for preparing and delivering your presentation. The topic can be any controversial issue you feel strongly about. After the presentation, the listeners tell the persuader why they were or were not persuaded to accept the presenter's position on the issue. Then they give the speaker feedback on the skills identified in the observer's rating sheet.

Total Time. 30–50 minutes (persuasive presentations, 5 minutes each times the number of group members; debriefing, 5 minutes each)

OBSERVER'S RATING SHEET

For the exercise in which you were the observer, evaluate the persuader on the key oral persuasion behaviors on a 1 to 5 scale (5 being the highest). Write comments in the spaces between checklist items to explain your ratings.

Establishes credibility.   _____

Uses positive, tactful tone.   _____

Presents ideas one at a time.   _____

Gives strong, supportive evidence.   _____

Tailors strong, supportive evidence.   _____

Appeals to self-interest.   _____

Makes a logical argument.   _____

Uses emotional appeals.   _____

Group Exercise 3: Trust Walk

Allowing yourself to be totally dependent on someone else for your physical well-being is an exercise in trust. In this exercise, you will be asked to close your eyes and allow someone else to take you on a 10-minute walk to experience your environment without sight.

Instructions.   Class members should pick a partner that they do not already know very well. Designate a leader and a follower. The leaders have 5 minutes to convince the followers that they can trust them to lead them safely for 10 minutes around campus with their eyes closed.

After the 5-minute persuasion session, the followers close their eyes and the leaders lead them around the campus for 10 minutes before returning to the classroom. During that time the leader's job first and foremost is to maintain the safety of his or her partner at all costs, and second to provide a meaningful experience.

When the dyads return to the classroom, they discuss what they experienced and what they learned about behaviors that enhance or decrease trust. After everyone has returned, the total class shares what they learned about behaviors that enhance or decrease trust. Then the partners switch roles and repeat the exercise.

Total Time. 35 minutes (preparation, 5 minutes; first trust walk and debriefing, 15 minutes; second trust walk and debriefing, 15 minutes)

Summary Checklist

Take a few minutes to reflect on your performance and look over others' ratings of your skill. Now assess yourself on each of the key learning behaviors. Make a check (✓) next to those behaviors on which you need improvement.

I establish credibility.   _____

I use a positive, tactful tone.   _____

I present ideas one at a time.   _____

I present strong evidence to support my position.   _____

I tailor my argument to the listener.   _____

I appeal to the subject's self-interest.   _____

I make logical arguments.   _____

I use emotional appeals.   _____

APPLICATION QUESTIONS

1. In what ways do television advertisements draw on the concepts in this chapter?
2. In what ways do effective persuasion skills parallel the skills necessary to be an effective salesperson?
3. Explain the differences between authority and persuasion.
4. Explain in what situations, and why, you would use each of the four persuasion tactics.

REINFORCEMENT EXERCISES

The following suggestions are activities you can do to practice and reinforce the oral persuasion techniques you learned in this chapter.

1. Persuade a person you know only in passing to lend you $20 for a week.
2. Convince a friend or relative to go with you to see a movie or play that you know the person doesn't want to see.
3. Go into a small retail store. Convince the proprietor, as a condition of purchase, to accept a price below that marked on an item.

ACTION PLAN

1. Which behavior do I want to improve the most?

2. Why? What will be my payoff?

3. What potential obstacles stand in my way?

4. What specific things will I do to improve? (For examples, see the Reinforcement Exercises.)

5. When will I do them?

6. How and when will I measure my success?

Endnotes

1. Otto Lerbinger, *Designs for Persuasive Communication* (Englewood Cliffs, NJ: Prentice Hall, 1972).

2. H. Steensma, "Why Managers Prefer Some Influence Tactics to Other Tactics: A Net Utility Explanation," *Journal of Occupational and Organizational Psychology* (2007), pp. 355–362; Kathleen S. Verderber and Rudolph F. Verderber, *Inter-Act: Using Interpersonal Communication Skills,* 4th ed. (Belmont, CA: Wadsworth, 1986), pp. 163–169.

3. J. Kouzes and B. Posner, *The Leadership Challenge* (San Francisco, CA: Jossey-Bass, 1987).

4. Tony Alessandra and Phillip Hunsaker, Communicating at Work (New York, Simon & Schuster, 1993), p. 169.

5. Stephen R. Covey, *The Seven Habits of Highly Effective People* (New York: Simon & Schuster, 1989), pp. 188–189.

6. R. B. Cialdini, "Basic Social Influence is Underestimated," *Psychological Inquiry*, Vol. 16, No. 4 (2005), pp. 158–161.

7. G. M. Vaughan and H. A. Hogg, *Introduction to Social Psychology*, 5th ed. (Frenchs Forest, NSW: Pearson Education, 2008), p. 196.

8. A. Shankar, M. Ansari, and S. Saxena, "Organizational Context and Ingratiatory Behavior in Organizations," *Journal of Social Psychology*, 134 (1994), pp. 641–648.

9. Ibid., pp. 190–199.

10. Kathleen S. Verderber and Rudolph F. Verderber, *Inter-Act: Using Interpersonal Communication Skills*, 4th ed. (Belmont, CA: Wadsworth, 1986), p. 168.

11. Kenneth E. Hultman, "Gaining and Keeping Management Support," *Training and Development Journal* (April 1981), pp. 106–110.

12. Ibid., p. 108.

13. Ibid.

14. Ibid.

15. Robert E. Coffey, Curtis W. Cook, and Phillip L. Hunsaker, *Management and Organizational Behavior* (Burr Ridge, IL: Austin Press/Irwin, 1994), pp. 210–211.

14

■ ■ ■

Applying Leadership Style

SELF-ASSESSMENT EXERCISE: WHAT KIND OF LEADER AM I?[1]

For each statement, circle the number on the scale that best describes you.

	Strongly Disagree			Strongly Agree	
1. I like to stand out from the crowd.	1	2	3	4	5
2. I feel proud and satisfied when I influence others to do things my way.	1	2	3	4	5
3. I enjoy doing things as part of a group rather than achieving results on my own.	1	2	3	4	5
4. I have a history of becoming an officer or captain in clubs and/or organized sports.	1	2	3	4	5
5. I try to be the one who is most influential in task groups at school or work.	1	2	3	4	5
6. In groups, I care most about good relationships.	1	2	3	4	5
7. In groups, I most want to achieve task goals.	1	2	3	4	5
8. In groups, I always show consideration for the feelings and needs of others.	1	2	3	4	5
9. In groups, I always structure activities and assignments to help get the job done.	1	2	3	4	5
10. In groups, I shift between being supportive of others' needs and pushing task accomplishment.	1	2	3	4	5

Scoring and Interpretation

Leadership Readiness Score: Add the scale values you circled on   _____
   items 1 through 5:

Leadership Style Preference Score:

Task Emphasis Score: Add the scale values you circled on   _____
   items 7 and 9:

Relationship Emphasis Score: Add the scale values you circled on   _____
   items 6 and 8:

Difference between task and relationship scores:

Check the higher score: task _____ or relationship _____.

Adaptability Score: Your score on item 10:   _____

Leadership Readiness.   If your total score on items 1–5 is 20 or more, you are likely to enjoy being a leader. If your total score is 10 or less, at this time in your life, you are likely more interested in personal achievement. If you score in the middle range, your leadership potential could go either direction, depending on events.

Leadership Style.   Your leadership style is suggested by your responses to items 6–10. Check the following totals to determine if you prefer a task-oriented, relationship-oriented, or flexible leadership style.

Your leadership style preference is indicated by whether your task emphasis or relationship emphasis score is higher. The difference between these scores indicates how strong this preference is.

Leadership Style Adaptability.   Your leadership style adaptability is indicated by your adaptability score. A score of 4 or 5 on item 10 suggests that you adapt to circumstances as you see the need.

SKILL CONCEPTS

This chapter and Chapter 15 cover the two primary types of leadership. This chapter focuses on transactional leaders, who get things done through people. They are implementing leaders who apply task and relationship behaviors in a specific leadership style to influence people to do what they want them to do to achieve organizational goals.

Leadership is the ability to influence individuals and groups toward the achievement of goals. How someone accomplishes this is a matter of leadership style. Research has demonstrated that no one leadership style is universally effective and that the most appropriate leadership style depends on the situation.[2] How do you determine the best leadership style to apply? The purpose of this chapter is to share information you need to consider when choosing a leadership style and to help you develop the skills to determine and apply the best style in a variety of situations.

The critical overriding skills for effectively choosing a leadership style are being able to diagnose the situation to determine what behaviors are needed and being able to act effectively in the ways that are most appropriate. Therefore, the primary question you are trying to answer is, "What leadership style works when?" The answer is that it depends on the specific characteristics and behaviors of the leader, the situation, and the followers involved. Let's look at each of these one at a time.

Leader Behaviors and Styles

Although different terms have been used, more than 50 years of research has resulted in a differentiation between leader behaviors that focus on task production and leader behaviors that focus on building positive employee relationships.[3] *Task-oriented behavior* focuses on careful supervision of group members to obtain consistent work methods and explain what activities are needed to accomplish the job. It centers on initiating structure intended to establish defined roles and organizational relationships, channels of communication, and methods of procedure. It includes giving directions and setting goals. Employee-oriented, or *relationship behaviors*, aim at satisfying the social and emotional needs of group members. This type of behavior focuses on showing consideration for the development of friendship, mutual trust, respect, and warmth in the relationship between the leader and followers.[4] Relationship behaviors include maintaining personal relationships with followers by opening channels of communication, providing socioemotional support (psychological strokes), and facilitating behaviors.[5] It includes activities such as listening, providing encouragement, and coaching.

Leadership style can be classified according to the relative amount of task and relationship behavior a leader engages in. As illustrated in Figure 14.1, four combinations of task and relationship behaviors determine different leadership styles.[6]

- *Style 1: High task and low relationship.*   The *telling* style is directive because the leader produces a lot of input but a minimum amount of relationship behavior. The leader defines roles in an autocratic manner and tells people what, how, when, and where to do tasks.
- *Style 2: High task and high relationship.*   The *selling* style is also directive, but in a more persuasive, supportive, and guiding manner. The leader provides considerable input about task accomplishment but also emphasizes human relations in a coaching style.
- *Style 3: High relationship and low task.*   In the *participating* leadership style, less direction and more collaboration exist between leader and group members. This is a consultative or consensus type of leadership in which the leader concentrates on facilitating shared decision making.
- *Style 4: Low relationship and low task.*   In the *delegating* leadership style, the leader delegates responsibility for a task to group members but is kept informed of progress.

When is each leadership style most effective? The answer is contingent on the specific characteristics of the followers and the situation.

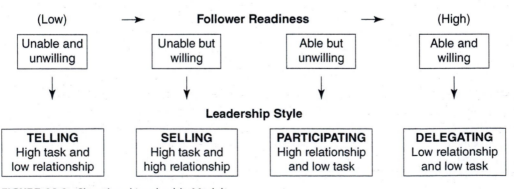

FIGURE 14.1 Situational Leadership Model.

Source: Based on Paul Hersey, Kenneth H. Blanchard, and Dewey E. Johnson, *Management of Organizational Behavior*, 9th ed. (Upper Saddle River, NJ: Pearson Education, 2008), p. 188.

Followers

The situational leadership model of Paul Hersey and Kenneth H. Blanchard states that the most appropriate style of leadership depends on the readiness of the group members.[7] Readiness is the extent to which group members have the ability and willingness to accomplish a specific task. Ability is the knowledge, experience, and skill an individual or group brings to a particular task or activity. Willingness is the extent to which an individual or group has the confidence, commitment, and motivation to accomplish a specific task. It should be noted that readiness is related to specific tasks. A person might be ready for one task but not for another. A continuum of follower readiness can be divided into four levels based on different combinations of ability and willingness.

- *Situation R1: Low readiness.*   When followers are unable and unwilling, the leader should use the directive and autocratic telling style that emphasizes task-oriented behavior.
- *Situation R2: Moderate readiness.*   When group members are unable but willing, the leader should focus on being more relationship-oriented, using a selling style.
- *Situation R3: Moderate to high readiness.*   When group members are able but unwilling, the leader needs to engage in a participative style that provides a high degree of relationship-oriented behavior but a low degree of task behavior.
- *Situation R4: High readiness.*   When followers are able, willing, and confident, the leader should grant these self-sufficient and competent followers considerable autonomy by using the delegating style.

You can benefit from this model by diagnosing the readiness of group members before choosing the right leadership style. As group member readiness increases, a leader should rely more on relationship behavior and less on task behavior. The preceding guidelines for applying the appropriate leadership style for different degrees of follower readiness are diagrammed in Figure 14.1.

Situational Variables

Contingency theories of leadership suggest that variations in a number of situational variables determine the leadership style that is most appropriate for any specific person or group.[8] We believe that the most important contingencies you should consider in addition to follower readiness include the degree of trust in the leader–follower relationship, ethical considerations, the objectives to be accomplished, the task characteristics, the rewards available, and the time requirements.

TRUST.   People will not follow someone they do not trust. Trust provides leaders with respect and the commitment from followers that is necessary for credibility, a key characteristic of effective leaders.[9] Leaders must possess credibility before followers accept their vision and commit themselves to specified goals.

Trust is a willingness to take risks in a relationship based on the positive expectation that another will be ethical and not act opportunistically at your expense.[10] When people trust you, they make themselves vulnerable. People make themselves vulnerable when they disclose intimate information or rely on another person's promises. These risks provide the opportunity for disappointment or to be taken advantage of. It is difficult to get people to follow you if they think they will be taken advantage of.

Five key dimensions underlie the concept of trust: integrity, competence, consistency, loyalty, and openness.[11] Integrity refers to honesty and truthfulness. If people don't think you are truthful, the other dimensions of trust don't matter. Competence encompasses technical and interpersonal knowledge and skills. People are unlikely to listen to or depend on someone whose abilities they don't respect. Consistency relates to reliability, predictability, and good judgment in handling situations. Inconsistency, especially between words and actions, decreases trust. Loyalty is the willingness to protect and save face for others. Openness means that someone will always tell the truth.

OBJECTIVES.   Before you can begin to determine the appropriate leadership style to use, you need to clarify the specific goals and objectives you want to accomplish. The appropriate leadership style will vary according to an individual's or a group's readiness to achieve different objectives.

TASK CHARACTERISTICS.   The degree of clarity and structure in the task that the group has been asked to accomplish also influences the best choice of leadership style. Tasks that are commonly known and specific procedures might not require much task intervention from the leader. On the other hand, unstructured tasks with no prescribed operating procedures might require leaders to help clarify and structure the work and offer hands-on coaching to help followers identify and learn the behaviors that will lead to successful task accomplishment.[12] In all cases, a leader needs to make the paths to goal attainment and resulting rewards clear and unambiguous.

REWARDS.   A leader can increase follower motivation by clarifying how followers can obtain the rewards they desire through successful task accomplishment. Because different people are motivated by different things—for example, intrinsic rewards from the work itself versus extrinsic rewards such as raises or promotions—the leader needs to talk with subordinates to learn which specific rewards they desire. Then the leader's job is to increase personal payoffs of the rewards that the followers desire, contingent on goal achievement.[13]

TIME.   Another important element in the environment of a leader is the time available. In emergency situations, leaders do not have time to seek opinions and suggestions from followers or to use other participative styles. When immediate actions are required, task-oriented behaviors are highly relevant and will most likely be accepted, especially if the leader is trusted. If time is not a major factor in the situation, the leader has more opportunity to select from a broader range of leadership styles.

CONCEPT QUIZ

Take the following 10-question, true–false quiz. The answers are at the end of the quiz. If you miss any answers, go back and check your understanding of the concepts to determine why you got it wrong.

Circle the right answer.

True	**False**	1.	Transactional leaders are concerned primarily with bringing about major changes in organizations.
True	**False**	2.	The most appropriate style of leadership is based on the extent to which group members have the ability and willingness to accomplish a specific task.
True	**False**	3.	Transactional and transformational leaders do the same things but in different ways.

True	**False**	4.	Transactional leader behaviors focus on task production and building positive employee relationships.
True	**False**	5.	Leaders can enhance trust by practicing integrity and being competent, consistent, loyal, and open.
True	**False**	6.	Leaders need to establish trust with followers if they expect followers to commit to their specified goals.
True	**False**	7.	The appropriate leadership style will vary according to how the leader's vision is perceived by the followers.
True	**False**	8.	If a task is clear and structured, leadership is never necessary.
True	**False**	9.	Part of a leader's job is to increase personal payoffs of the rewards that the followers desire, contingent on goal achievement.
True	**False**	10.	When immediate actions are required, a leader's task-oriented behaviors most likely will be accepted.

Answers: (1) False; (2) True; (3) False; (4) True; (5) True; (6) True; (7) True; (8) False; (9) True; (10) True

BEHAVIORAL CHECKLIST

Be aware of these specific behaviors when evaluating your own skills for choosing appropriate leadership styles. Also use them as criteria for providing feedback to others about their leadership style skills.

Choosing An Appropriate Leadership Style Requires That You:

- Establish trust with followers.
- Clarify objectives.
- Check out followers' readiness level (ability and willingness) to achieve specific objectives.
- Clarify and structure the task.
- Explain paths for obtaining desired rewards.
- Clarify the time line for task accomplishment.
- Apply appropriate degrees of task and relationship behaviors.

ATTENTION!
Do not read the following until assigned to do so by your instructor.

MODELING EXERCISE

Leading the Cobra Development Team[14]

Pick volunteers to play the roles of the leader and three employees. Everyone should read the Situation section. Role-players should read their own role, but not the roles of others, and prepare for the role-play. The rest of the class reads all of the roles and reviews the observer's rating sheet.

Actors. Team Leader, Employee 1, Employee 2, Employee 3

Situation. Williams & Associates is a leading advertising firm based in New York City. The firm specializes in the development of advertising campaigns for many *Fortune* 500 corporations. It employs approximately 75 advertising specialists and support staff at its main headquarters.

Williams & Associates faces fierce competition from other advertising firms from around the United States and the rest of the world. Speed and responsiveness to tough customer demands are critical for success in this industry. In the end, however, everything hinges on the effectiveness of advertising campaigns in generating business for their clients. This reality puts tremendous pressure on these firms to leverage every advantage they can find.

Recently, the firm has won a contract to develop an advertising campaign for Cobra Motor Corporation, a new luxury car manufacturer that aims to compete directly with world-class luxury car manufacturers such as Lexus, BMW, Mercedes, Audi, Jaguar, Cadillac, and Lincoln. Cobra is new to the luxury car market, so it needs to establish its name in the highly competitive U.S. market and enhance its name recognition. In the future, Cobra wants consumers to associate its name with the attributes of quality, exclusivity, elegance, performance, and sportiness.

The challenge for Williams & Associates is to create an advertising campaign that will make consumers remember the name Cobra Motor Corporation.

The Leader's Role. You are the leader of the advertising development team that is in charge of the Cobra account. Your task is to lead the various members of your team effectively in completing the task of developing a high-quality advertising campaign for Cobra. Use the most effective leadership style for leading your team through the process of developing the ad campaign.

You have three employees on your advertising development team. Employee 1 is a recent graduate of Billingsworth College with a major in English and no prior work experience. Employee 2 is a seasoned veteran with more than 15 years of experience on the job with your company. Employee 3 has been with the firm for about 3 years now and appears to be highly committed to the success of the firm.

Remember that you want to develop an advertising campaign for Cobra that meets their requirements of establishing the name of the company and getting consumers to view it as a legitimate player in the luxury auto industry. Assess the needs of your employees and the nature of the task. Then match the appropriate leadership behavior (directive, supportive, achievement-oriented, participative) to each employee. Remember that you have only 30 minutes to develop your advertising campaign.

Employee 1's Role. You are one of the advertising specialists on the team that is developing an advertising campaign for Cobra Motor. You are a recent graduate of Billingsworth College, where you majored in English. You were an excellent student in college, maintaining a 3.7/4.0 GPA. However, you have had only one introductory course in advertising, and you have no prior work experience in the business world.

Repeatedly state that you just started and that you don't have a clue what's going on or what you are supposed to be doing. Ask for a lot of clarification on issues the leader brings up, and act confused by his or her explanations. The bottom line is that you need structure and direction from the leader.

Employee 2's Role. You are one of the advertising specialists on the team that is developing the advertising campaign for Cobra Motor. You have more than 15 years of experience on the job, so you are a seasoned veteran. You don't need direction from the leader, because you believe you already know how to perform your job. However, you have a strong need for recognition of your contributions to the project and to the firm in general.

Emphasize repeatedly that you have bent over backward for the firm in the past, but the firm has never shown any appreciation for your contributions. Also state that management has not provided enough support for advertising development teams in the past and that you feel like management doesn't care much about its employees.

Employee 3's Role. You are one of the advertising specialists on the team that is developing an advertising campaign for Cobra Motor. You have been with the firm for about 3 years. You are highly committed to the success of the firm, and you want to excel at your job in order to have a chance of being promoted in the future.

You want the leader to inspire you, to "fire you up," and to lead the team to victory. The bottom line is that you demand strong leadership. State that you expect the leader to communicate a vision or mission for the project to the team. Ask the leader why employees should give 150 percent of their effort to this project. You want your leader to be someone who has a clear sense of goals and who can get others to become committed to achieving those goals as well. Make "Why should we care?" or "Why is this important?" statements during the process.

Observer's Role. Your job is to observe the process and document what the leader does to handle the situation and how employees react to the leader's behavior. Use the observer's rating sheet to provide feedback about how effective the leader was in choosing the appropriate leadership style for each employee.

Questions

1. What were the characteristics of each of the employees and the task?
2. What types of behaviors did the leader use in dealing with each of the employees? Were they appropriate?
3. What suggestions would you make to the leader to enhance his or her effectiveness in this situation?
4. What are the practical implications of this simulation for you as future leaders in organizations?

Total Time. 35 minutes (assigning and preparing roles, 10 minutes; role-play, 15 minutes; answering questions and debriefing, 10 minutes)

OBSERVER'S RATING SHEET

Rate the team leader's skills for applying the appropriate leadership style on a 1 to 5 scale (5 being the highest). Provide specific feedback comments in the space provided under each skill criterion.

Rating	Behavioral Skills
_____	Established trust with followers.
_____	Clarified objectives.
_____	Assessed followers' readiness level (ability and willingness) for achieving specific objectives.
_____	Clarified and structured the task.
_____	Explain paths for increasing desired rewards.
_____	Clarified the time line for task achievement.
_____	Applied appropriate degrees of task and relationship behaviors.

GROUP EXERCISES

Group Exercise 1: Choosing an Appropriate Leadership Style[15]

Task 1 (5 minutes)

Read the following scenario carefully and think about how you would behave if you were a leader in this situation.

You manage an automotive accessories and repair department in a large department store. Large discount chains are squeezing profit margins of department stores, resulting in numerous department store closings nationwide. Auto accessories such as batteries, shock absorbers, and other items always have been a major profit center in your store, generating a large percentage of the store's total revenue and earnings. Total sales of the automotive department have been at a moderate to low level during the winter and early spring, and the rest of the store has been doing even worse.

The salespeople in your department are all fairly young (in their twenties and thirties), and about half are high school graduates. None attended college. All have families with small children. They are paid on an hourly basis, and several have other jobs in their off hours to supplement their income. They get along fairly well at work, but they are so busy and involved with their own families that little social interaction occurs among them outside of work. They are generally experienced, capable, and highly independent.

From your experience, you know that store traffic always increases in the summer, and customers are interested in making sure their cars are comfortable, safe, and reliable for summer vacations. A successful salesperson in this department is one who is up to date on all product specifications, is outgoing and polite to customers, helps customers troubleshoot problems with their cars, and follows up on customer inquiries with an attempt to close each sale. These activities are related directly to the effort and skill of the salesperson. Your store has a reputation for quality products and service, which the store management believes must be maintained. The store manager has emphasized that you must significantly increase the sales of your department or the entire store will be threatened with possible closing. The manager has confidence in you and believes that department managers should have the freedom to lead and motivate their people as they see fit.

Task 2 (15 minutes)

Rate each of the following triads of statements according to how much you agree with them as an appropriate leader behavior by the manager in this situation. For each triad, rate the statement you believe is most appropriate and impactful as a 1. Rate the statement you think is least appropriate as a 3, and rate the other statement as a 2. You must rate all the statements in each triad 1, 2, or 3. No two items in a triad can be given the same rating. Mark your answers in the Your Answer column and complete all five triads of statements. For a given triad of statements, your answers might look like the following:

YOUR ANSWER

1. <u>3</u>

2. <u>1</u>

3. <u>2</u>

Triad I

	Your Answer	Triad Answer
1. Tell salespeople that they must increase sales during the summer.	1. _____	_____
2. Be friendly and encourage followers to keep up the high-quality service they provide.	2. _____	_____
3. Revise the compensation system so that salespeople are paid commissions based on the amount of their sales.	3. _____	_____

Triad II

4. Hold a group meeting with all departmental employees to ask for their ideas on how to increase sales while maintaining quality of service.	1. _____	_____
5. Emphasize appropriate sales techniques and the importance of closing all sales.	2. _____	_____
6. Provide coupons for local grocery stores to salespeople who reach a specific sales goal.	3. _____	_____

Triad III

7. Keep followers informed and let them know you trust them to do a good job.	1. _____	_____
8. Inform the store manager whenever a salesperson reaches a high level of sales or provides outstanding service to customers.	2. _____	_____
9. Closely monitor salespeople to be sure they use effective sales techniques.	3. _____	_____

Triad IV

10. Show concern for the status and well-being of all department employees during this stressful period.	1. _____	_____
11. Recommend a pay increase for an employee whose sales are unusually high.	2. _____	_____
12. Write a letter of commendation for an employee whose sales and service are outstanding.	3. _____	_____

Triad V

13. Conduct a review/training session with salespeople about product characteristics and correct sales techniques.	1. _____	_____
14. Be approachable and sympathetic about employees' problems and concerns.	2. _____	_____
15. Provide coupons for gasoline to salespeople who receive repeated compliments from customers about their good service.	3. _____	_____

Task 3 (30 minutes)

Form groups of three. Discuss your answers to the 15 statements and come to an agreement within your group on the ratings for each statement.

Task 4 (10 minutes)

Discuss your answers with the entire class, relating them to the behavioral guidelines for choosing an appropriate leadership style in this chapter.

Total Time. 60 minutes (task 1, 5 minutes; task 2, 15 minutes; task 3, 30 minutes; task 4, 10 minutes)

Group Exercise 2: Leader Adaptability Exercise[16]

Instructions. Form groups of four to six members.

Step 1 (5 minutes) Assume you are involved in each of the following six situations. Read each item carefully and think about what you would do in each circumstance. Then circle the letter of the alternative action choice that you think would describe most closely your behavior in the situation presented.

Step 2 (20 minutes) Discuss each situation with other group members and reach a consensus for the best alternative.

Step 3 (10 minutes) Check your answers with the diagnosis provided in the Appendix. Discuss why you got any of the answers wrong.

Step 4 (10 minutes) Discuss with the rest of the class what you learned about choosing the appropriate leadership style.

Situations

1. Your subordinates are not responding lately to your friendly conversation and obvious concern for their welfare. Their performance is in a tailspin.
   A. Emphasize the use of uniform procedures and the necessity for task accomplishment.
   B. Make yourself available for discussion but don't push.
   C. Talk with subordinates and then set goals.
   D. Do not intervene intentionally.
2. The observable performance of your group is increasing. You have been making sure that all members are aware of their roles and standards.
   A. Engage in friendly interaction, but continue to make sure that all members are aware of their roles and standards.
   B. Take no definite action.
   C. Do what you can to make the group feel important and involved.
   D. Emphasize the importance of deadlines and tasks.
3. Members of your group are unable to solve a problem themselves. You have normally left them alone. Group performance and interpersonal relations have been good.
   A. Involve the group and together engage in problem-solving strategies.
   B. Let the group work it out.
   C. Act quickly and firmly to correct and redirect.
   D. Encourage the group to work on the problem and be available for discussion.
4. You are considering a major change. Your subordinates have a fine record of accomplishment. They respect the need for change.
   A. Allow group involvement in developing the change but don't push.
   B. Announce the change and then implement it with close supervision.

    C. Allow the group to formulate its own direction.

    D. Incorporate group recommendations but direct the change yourself.

5. The performance of your group has been dropping during the last few months. Members have been unconcerned with meeting objectives. Redefining roles has helped in the past, but now you are noticing that they continually need to be reminded to have their tasks done on time.

    A. Allow the group to formulate its own direction.

    B. Incorporate group recommendations but see that objectives are met.

    C. Redefine goals and supervise carefully.

    D. Allow group involvement in setting goals but don't push.

6. You stepped into an efficiently run situation. The previous administrator ran a tight ship. You want to maintain a productive situation but would like to begin humanizing the environment.

    A. Do what you can to make the group feel important and involved.

    B. Emphasize the importance of deadlines and tasks.

    C. Intentionally do not intervene.

    D. Get the group involved in decision making but see that objectives are met.

Time. 45 minutes (step 1, 5 minutes; step 2, 20 minutes; step 3, 10 minutes; step 4, 10 minutes)

Group Exercise 3: Case of the Tough Assignment[17]

Instructions. Form groups of four to six students. Everyone should read the Tough Assignment situation. Then the group should discuss the questions. Finally, groups can share and discuss their answers with the entire class.

Situation. Ted Wills has been hired as the new supervisor for the parts department of an automobile dealership. During his first day on the job, his manager, Linda Dunn, tells him, "You have a tough assignment. The group you supervise has an active troublemaker who has managed to keep from getting fired because he is the only employee who knows the inventory system. Three other employees follow his lead in consistently finding things to complain about, and the other four employees stay out of trouble by doing only what they are told." Linda handed the personnel files for the department employees to Ted. "The most important thing," Linda continued, "is that you change the sloppy way that work is being done in the department and improve the accuracy in filling parts orders."

    After hesitating a moment, Ted asked, "What was the former supervisor like?"

    "Well," replied Linda. "He had semi-retired on the job and let the employees do what they wanted. He was not concerned about accuracy in filling orders or maintaining the inventory. As I said before, it is a tough assignment, especially since all of our employees have been with the dealership for more than 5 years, and most are friends with the owner."

    Ted smiled. "I guess I have my work cut out for me."

Questions

1. How would you define the leadership problems in this situation?
2. What appears to be the readiness level of the employees?
3. What other situational factors should Ted take into account before deciding on what leadership actions to take? What difference do they make?
4. What leader behaviors would you recommend to Ted? Why?

Total Time. 20–30 minutes

Summary Checklist

Take a few minutes to reflect on your performance and look over others' ratings of your skills in choosing appropriate leadership styles. Now assess yourself on each of the key behaviors for effectively choosing a leadership style. Make a check (✓) next to those behaviors in which you need improvement.

Establish trust with followers.   _____

Clarify objectives.   _____

Assess followers' readiness level (ability and willingness)
for achieving specific objectives.   _____

Decide the best way to clarify and structure the task.   _____

Determine how to explain paths for increasing desired rewards.   _____

Assess how time availability impacts on leadership style options.   _____

Apply appropriate degrees of task and relationship
behaviors for best leadership style.   _____

APPLICATION QUESTIONS

1. When have you performed especially well as a leader? What skills did you apply that made your leadership effective?
2. Think of a time when your leadership attempts were not successful. Why were you not successful? What skills should you develop to be more successful in this type of situation in the future?
3. Think of a group you belong to or have been a member of. What was the leadership style exhibited by the leader of the group? Was it effective? Why or why not?
4. Is ethical leadership behavior something people can learn (or be encouraged to exhibit by the organization) or is it an innate characteristic (e.g., it cannot be influenced by organizational circumstances). Can organizational pressures or incentives (e.g., for profits or cost-cutting) lead to unethical behaviors in leaders who would normally behave ethically? What are the implications for reducing unethical leadership behaviors in organizations (e.g., should organizations focus on devising ways to select only ethical leaders or should organizations focus on reducing pressures and incentives to behave unethically?).
5. Based on your own leadership experiences and what you know about other leaders, what are your five top guidelines for becoming a successful leader?

REINFORCEMENT EXERCISES

1. Interview someone in a leadership position about his or her leadership philosophy and what skills are most important for leadership success. Ask what advice this person would give students about developing their leadership skills.
2. Think of someone you consider a great leader from any area (e.g., military, politics, business, religion, or sports). Research some articles about this leader and determine what skills this person exhibited that made him or her a great leader.

3. Observe a sports team. What leadership behaviors are being used by whom? How would you describe the predominant style of leadership? Is it appropriate for the team situation you observed? To what degree do you think the leadership style influenced the team's outcomes?

4. Read an autobiography about a great leader, such as Martin Luther King Jr., Lee Iacocca, or Eleanor Roosevelt. Then identify why this leader was so successful with reference to the skills in this chapter. Determine what additional factors contributed to this leader's success.

5. Write out a goal statement for a team you are currently participating in as a leader or member. Decide on the best leadership style to obtain commitment to your goals from team members using the skills you have learned in this chapter.

ACTION PLAN

1. Which skills for choosing a leadership style do I want to improve the most?

2. Why? What will be my payoff?

3. What potential obstacles stand in my way?

4. What specific things will I do to improve? (For examples, see the Reinforcement Exercises.)

5. When will I do them?

6. How and when will I measure my success?

Endnotes

1. Adapted from C. W. Cook, P. L. Hunsaker, and R. E. Coffey, *Management and Organizational Behavior*, 2nd ed. (Burr Ridge, IL: Irwin, 1997), p. 465. With permission of the authors.

2. Ramon J. Aldag and Loren W. Kuzuhara, *Organizational Behavior and Management* (Cincinnati, OH: South-Western, 2002), p. 331.

3. Stephen R. Likert, *New Patterns of Management* (New York: McGraw-Hill, 1961), p. 36; Ralph M. Stodgill and A. E. Coons, *Leader Behavior: Its Description and Measurement* (Columbus, OH: Ohio State University, Bureau of Business Research, 1957), p. 75.

4. Andrew W. Halpin, *The Leadership Behavior of School Superintendents* (Chicago, IL: Midwest Administration Center, University of Chicago, 1959), p. 4.

5. Paul Hersey, Kenneth H. Blanchard, and Dewey E. Johnson, *Management of Organizational Behavior,* 9th ed. (Upper Saddle River, NJ: Pearson Education, 2008), p. 105.

6. Ibid. p. 104.

7. Ibid. pp. 133–156.

8. Richard L. Daft, *The Leadership Experience* (Mason, OH: South-Western, 2005), pp. 23–24.

9. J. Kouzes and B. Posner, *The Leadership Challenge* (San Francisco, CA: Jossey-Bass, 1987).

10. D. J. McAllister, "Affect and Cognition-Based Trust as Foundations for Interpersonal Cooperation in Organizations," *Academy of Management Journal* (February 1995), p. 25.

11. P. L. Schindler and C. C. Thomas, "The Structure of Interpersonal Trust in the Workplace," *Psychological Reports* (October 1993), pp. 563–573.

12. F. E. Fiedler, A *Theory of Leadership Effectiveness* (New York: McGraw-Hill, 1967).

13. Robert J. House, "A Path Goal Theory of Leadership Effectiveness," *Administrative Science Quarterly,* Vol. 16 (1971), pp. 371–388.

14. Adapted from Ramon J. Aldag and Loren W. Kuzuhara, *Organizational Behavior and Management* (Cincinnati, OH: South-Western College Publishing, 2002), pp. 313–315.

15. Adapted from Jon P. Howell and Dan L. Costley, *Understanding Behaviors for Effective Leadership* (Upper Saddle River, NJ: Prentice Hall, 2001), pp. 208–210.

16. Adapted from Paul Hersey and Kenneth H. Blanchard, "So You Want to Know Your Leadership Style?" *Training and Development Journal* (February 1974), pp. 36–48.

17. Adapted from Jon P. Howell and Dan L. Costley, *Understanding Behaviors for Effective Leadership* (Upper Saddle River, NJ: Prentice Hall, 2001), p. 51.

15

■ ■ ■

Managing Change

SELF-ASSESSMENT EXERCISE: ARE YOU A CHANGE LEADER?[1]

Complete the following questions based on how you act at work or school. For each item, enter the number that best describes you.

	Disagree			Agree	
	1	2	3	4	5

Score

_____ 1. I have a clear sense of mission for change, which I repeatedly describe to others.

_____ 2. I signal the value of change and improvement with various symbols and statements.

_____ 3. One of my strengths is to encourage people to express frequently ideas and opinions that differ from my own.

_____ 4. I always celebrate the effort to improve things, even if the final outcome is disappointing.

_____ 5. I see my primary job as inspiring others toward improvement in their jobs.

_____ 6. Sometimes I use dramatic flourishes—a brainstorming session, stop work, go to an off-site—to signal an important change to people.

_____ 7. Often I take risks and let others take risks that could be a problem if the idea fails.

_____ 8. I spend time developing new ways of approaching old problems.

_____ 9. I believe in learning from failures.

_____10. I frequently compliment others on changes they have made.

_____11. I am personally involved in several improvement projects at one time.

_____12. I try to be a good listener and be patient with what people suggest, even when it is a "dumb" idea.

_____13. I like to support change efforts, even when the idea might not work.

_____14. I work at the politics of change to build agreement for ideas for improvement.

_____15. I am able to get higher-ups to support ideas for improvement.

_____ **Total Change Leadership Score**

Scoring and Interpretation

Add the numbers you entered for your total change leadership score. Your score indicates the extent to which you are a positive leader force for change. The questions represent behaviors associated with successful change leadership.

60–75: Great—A dynamo for leading change.

45–60: Good—A positive change leader.

30–45: Adequate—You have a typical attitude toward change.

15–30: Poor—You may be dragging down change efforts.

Go back over the questions on which you scored lowest and develop a plan to improve your approach toward change. Discuss your score and your ideas with other students.

SKILL CONCEPTS

It takes more than transactional leadership—as discussed in Chapter 14—to guide an entire organization through major changes. For that task, transformational leaders are needed. They tend to be more visionary and concerned about charting a mission and direction than other types of leaders. These pathfinders are entrepreneurs and charismatic leaders who are concerned about where the organization ought to try to go.[2] How transformational leaders initiate and overcome resistance to change is the topic of this chapter.

Transformational leaders engage in the processes of providing direction, energizing others, and obtaining voluntary commitments to the leader's vision.[3] A transformational leader brings about change by creating a vision and goals and influencing others to support that vision of change and work toward the goals.

Transformational leaders apply the skills you have learned in previous chapters to send effective messages, set goals, clarify expectations, and persuade others to implement desired changes, whether they are changes in the organization's vision, strategy, and culture, or innovation in products and technologies. Research has shown that transformational leadership differs from the transactional leadership discussed in Chapter 14 in four significant ways.[4] It develops followers into leaders, motivates by providing satisfaction of higher-level psychological needs, inspires followers to go beyond their own self-interests for the good of the group, and creates a vision in a way that makes the pain of change worth the effort.

THE PHASES OF PLANNED CHANGE

Planned change progresses through three phases: unfreezing, changing, and refreezing.[5] The first phase, unfreezing, involves helping people see that a change is needed because the existing situation is not adequate. Existing attitudes and behaviors need to be altered during this phase so that resistance to change is minimized. A manager might do this by explaining how the change can help increase productivity. It will also be necessary to convince participants that their social satisfaction will not be lowered or that this cost will be worth some other gain they care about. The manager's goal is to help the participants see the need for change and to increase their willingness to make the change a success.

The second phase, changing, involves moving or making the change. This involves getting participants to let go of old ways of doing things and developing new ones. This is difficult because of the anxiety involved in letting go of the comfortable and familiar to learn new ways of behaving, with new people, doing different tasks with perhaps more complex technology. In more complex changes, several targets of change might need to be altered simultaneously.

The third phase, refreezing, involves reinforcing the changes made so that the new ways of behaving become stabilized. If people perceive the change to be working in their favor, positive results will serve as reinforcement. If they perceive that the change is not working in their favor, it might be necessary for the manager to use external reinforcers, which can be positive or negative.[6] For example, the manager might encourage the employees to keep working at the change by predicting that the desired positive results will occur. A small reward, such as a lunch or an afternoon off, might be awarded when the change has been completed successfully. The goal of this phase of the change process is to cause the desired attitudes and behaviors to become a natural, self-reinforcing pattern.

SKILLS FOR PROMOTING CHANGE

Major change does not happen easily. The change process goes through stages, each of which is important and requires a significant amount of time. Exhibit 15.1 presents an eight-stage sequence

1. **Create awareness of the need to change**
   - Unfreeze current complacency
   - Demonstrate the need for change
   - Create a sense of urgency
2. **Form a guiding coalition**
   - Establish a team of opinion leaders
   - Assess problems and how to approach them
   - Develop a shared commitment for change
3. **Develop a shared vision and implementation plan**
   - Formulate a compelling vision that will aspire people to change
   - Develop strategies for achieving the vision.
4. **Communicate the vision widely**
   - Continually communicate the vision and strategy to all stakeholders
   - Members of guiding coalition model new behaviors
5. **Empower Action**
   - Overcome resistance to change
   - Provide knowledge, resources, training, and necessary authority
   - Create systems and structures to facilitate and reward change
6. **Generate short-term wins**
   - Begin by targeting highly visible projects that can be easily achieved
   - Visibly reward people who achieve wins with bonuses, recognition, and praise
7. **Evaluate changes achieved, consolidate gains, and motivate greater change**
   - Avoid experiencing letdown after achieving short-term change goals
   - Use credibility achieved by short-term wins to consolidate improvements and motivate employees to tackle bigger problems
   - Change systems, structures, and policies that impede change efforts
8. **Make Change Stick**
   - Refreeze new values and beliefs in the culture by rewarding new behaviors
   - Articulate connections between new behaviors and organizational success

EXHIBIT 15.1 Eight Skill Sequence for Planned Change.

Sources: Based on J. S. Osland, D. A. Kolb, I. M. Rubin, and M. E. Turner, *Organizational Behavior: An Experiential Approach*, 8th ed., (Upper Saddle River, N.J.: Prentice Hall, 2007), pp. 637–642; J. P. Kotter, *Leading Change* (Boston: Harvard Business School Press 1996), p. 21; P. L. Hunsaker, *Management: A Skills Approach,* 2nd Edition (Upper Saddle River, N.J.: Prentice Hall, 2005), pp. 481–484, J. P. Kotter and D. Cohen, *The Heart of Change: Real-Life Stories about How People Change Their Organizations* (Cambridge MA: Harvard Business School Press, 2002).

of skills that managers need to apply to bring about planned change successfully.[7] Stages in the change process generally overlap, but skipping stages or making critical mistakes at any stage can cause the change process to fail.

CREATING AWARENESS OF THE NEED TO CHANGE   At stage 1, leaders unfreeze people by establishing a sense of urgency that change is needed. If the organization is obviously facing a threat to its survival, this kind of crisis gets people's attention. Dramatically declining profits and stock prices at IBM in the early 1990s, for example, provided a sense of urgency for all stakeholders. In many cases, however, no current crisis is obvious, but leaders have identified potential problems by scanning the external environment, looking at such things as competitive conditions; market position; and social, technological, and demographic trends. In these cases, leaders need to find ways to communicate the information broadly and dramatically to make others aware of the need for change.

FORMING A POWERFUL GUIDING COALITION   Stage 2 involves establishing a team of opinion leaders with enough power to guide the change process. The critical variable at this point is the development of a shared commitment to the need for and direction of organizational change. Mechanisms such as off-site retreats can get people together and help them develop a shared assessment of problems and how to approach them. It is also important to include all levels of management in this coalition to ensure support from top leaders and enthusiastic implementation from middle and lower managers.

DEVELOPING A COMPELLING VISION AND STRATEGY   Leaders of change need to formulate and articulate a compelling vision that people will aspire to and that will guide the change effort. The vision of what it will be like when goals are achieved should illuminate core values and principles that pull followers together in a common endeavor. Effective visions create passion in followers to achieve specific goals because they can visualize a common contribution to a cause they believe in. Leaders also need to develop the strategies for achieving that vision.

COMMUNICATING THE VISION WIDELY   Leaders need to use every means possible to communicate the vision and strategy to all stakeholders. Transformation is impossible unless the majority of people in the organization are involved and willing to help. This should start with the managers in the change coalition themselves, who should set an example by modeling the new behaviors needed from employees.

EMPOWERING EMPLOYEES TO ACT ON THE VISION   At this stage, people are empowered with knowledge, resources, and discretion to make things happen. Leaders should encourage and reward risk taking and nontraditional ideas and actions. Also, they need to revise systems, structures, or procedures that hinder or undermine the change effort. For example, with the survival of the company at stake, labor and management at Rolls-Royce Motor Company revised hundreds of precise job descriptions that were undermining the change into a new contract and specified that all employees would do anything within their capabilities to support the company.[8]

GENERATING SHORT-TERM WINS   Major change takes time, and a transformation effort loses momentum if no short-term accomplishments can be recognized and celebrated by employees. Consequently, leaders should plan for visible performance improvements, enable them to happen, and celebrate employees who were involved in the improvements. These successes can boost the credibility of the change process and renew the commitment and enthusiasm of employees.[9]

Sometimes small wins can bring about big results. Much like the spread of an epidemic, a tipping point occurs when a few people initiate small changes that produce big positive effects.[10]

CONSOLIDATING GAINS AND CREATING GREATER CHANGE   Stage 7 builds on the credibility achieved by short-term wins to consolidate improvements, tackle bigger problems, and create greater change. Leaders change systems, structures, and policies that do not fit the vision but have not yet been confronted. They hire, promote, and develop employees who can implement the vision and create new change projects. When Rolls-Royce was at this stage, for example, leaders set up "change teams" made up of members who were horizontally cross-trained to perform one another's jobs, and vertically integrated from executives to shop-floor workers, and charged them with communicating and developing new ideas together.[11]

MAKING THE CHANGE STICK   This is the refreezing stage during which new values and beliefs are instilled in the culture so that employees view the changes not as something new but as a normal and integral part of how the organization operates. Old habits, values, traditions, and mindsets are permanently replaced through the processes of emphasizing and rewarding new behaviors.

SKILLS FOR OVERCOMING RESISTANCE TO CHANGE

Excessive or irrational resistance to change can hinder progress and even destroy a change effort. Many times change is resisted even when its benefits clearly outweigh its costs. Why does this happen? The first step in overcoming resistance to change is to understand the overlapping reasons why it occurs. Then, decide on strategies for overcoming resistance to change. The key is to match the demands of a change situation with the best approach to overcoming resistance with minimum disruption.

Sources of Resistance to Change

In general, people resist change because they seek to avoid uncertainty. Past ways of doing things are well known and predictable. Other reasons for resisting change might include the following:

- *Fear of the Unknown.*   Individuals resist change when they are uncertain about how it will affect their well-being with regard to issues such as being able to perform as well as before the change, or losing position, income, status, power, or even their jobs.[12]
- *Selective Perception.*   When changes are initiated, individuals tend to focus on how they will be affected personally rather than seeing the big picture for the entire organization. At other times, change might be perceived as incompatible with personal beliefs and values.
- *Lack of Information.*   People will resist change if they lack knowledge about what is expected or why the change is important. In addition, if people don't have enough information about how to change, they might fear making mistakes, so they will not try.

- *Habits.*   People prefer familiar actions and events, even if they are not optimal. Breaking a habit is difficult because it takes hard work and involves giving up perceived benefits from the habit, even if the new behavior has more desirable consequences.
- *Resentment toward the Initiator.*   If a change seems arbitrary or unreasonable, or its timing and manner of implementation lack concern for the people involved, resentment and anger often are directed toward those initiating the change. People also resent being controlled and losing autonomy, especially when their thoughts and feelings are not considered.
- *Threat to Power Maintenance.*   Changes in decision-making authority and control of resource allocations threaten the balance of power in organizations. Units benefiting from the change will endorse it, but those losing power will resist it, which often can slow or prevent the change process.[13]
- *Structural Stability.*   Managers of organizations create hierarchies, subgroups, rules, and procedures to promote order and guide behaviors. All of these steps are designed to develop consistent, predictable behaviors that resist change.
- *Organizational Culture and Norms.*   Organizational culture establishes values, norms, and expectations to promote predictable ways of thinking and behaving. Organizational members will resist changes that force them to abandon approved ways of doing things.

Strategies to Overcome the Resistance to Change

After you have determined why resistance to change exists, the next step is to determine what strategies you can apply to overcome the resistance. Sometimes you can apply several of the following strategies simultaneously.[14]

- *Education and Communication.*   Even if the consequences of a change generally are perceived as positive, extensive communication will help reduce anxiety and ensure that people understand what is happening, what will be expected of them, and how they will be supported in adapting to change.[15] The objective is to help people learn beforehand the reasons for the change, how it will take form, and what the likely consequences will be.
- *Participation and Involvement.*   Participation increases understanding, enhances feelings of control, reduces uncertainty, and promotes a feeling of ownership when change affects people directly. Encourage those involved to help design and implement the changes in order to draw out their ideas and to foster commitment. It is difficult for people to resist changes that they themselves have helped bring about.
- *Facilitation and Support.*   By accepting people's anxiety as legitimate and helping them cope with change, managers have a better chance of gaining respect and the commitment to make it work. Provide encouragement and support, training, counseling, and resources to help those affected by the change adapt to new requirements.
- *Negotiation and Agreement.*   Using this tactic is often necessary when dealing with powerful resisters, like bargaining units. Bargain to offer incentives in return for an agreement to change. Sometimes specific things can be exchanged in return for help in bringing about a change. Other times, general perks can be distributed widely to help make the change easier to undertake.

- ***Co-optation.***   Co-optation is influencing resistant parties to endorse the change effort by providing them with benefits they desire and opportunities to fill desired roles in the process. This might be accomplished through establishing profit-sharing systems, stock-ownership plans, or opportunities for career advancement.
- ***Coercion.***   At certain times, managers might have to use authority and the threat of negative incentives to force acceptance of the proposed change. For example, if employees do not accept proposed changes, it might be necessary to shut the plant down, decrease salaries, or lay off people.

When Might Resistance to Change Be Helpful?

Resistance to change is not necessarily bad. Resistance sometimes keeps an organization from being whipsawed by capricious ideas for change that, if too frequent, could seem like random chaos, which destroys predictability.[16] Resistance can be a stimulus to dialog and deeper, thoughtful analysis of alternatives and their consequences. Resistance can also provide meaningful feedback to management, for example, that it needs to strengthen its commitment and support, or that training needs to be implemented to overcome ingrained work practices.[17]

CONCEPT QUIZ

Take the following 10-question, true–false quiz. The answers are at the end of the quiz. If you miss any answers, go back and check your understanding of the concepts to determine why you got it wrong.

Circle the right answer.

True	**False**	1.	Co-optation can prevent resistance to change.
True	**False**	2.	Effectively planned change goes through four phases.
True	**False**	3.	Refreezing is necessary to reinforce changes.
True	**False**	4.	People usually have to be forced to change.
True	**False**	5.	Transformational leadership creates a vision that makes change appear desirable.
True	**False**	6.	Only change agents need to understand the underlying reasons for change.
True	**False**	7.	Because the stages of the change process overlap, it is advantageous to skip some in order to expedite change.
True	**False**	8.	All levels of management should be included in planning change.
True	**False**	9.	Offering incentives in return for agreement to change is often necessary when dealing with powerful resisters.
True	**False**	10.	Leaders of change should focus on long-term goals and not worry about the short-term wins.

Answers: (1) True; (2) False; (3) True; (4) False; (5) True; (6) False; (7) False; (8) True; (9) True; (10) False

BEHAVIORAL CHECKLIST

When managing change, an effective leader engages in the following behaviors. Look for them when evaluating your own and others' skills in this area.

Managing Change Requires:

- Sharing a compelling vision and strategy.
- Creating a sense of urgency.
- Forming supportive coalitions.
- Dealing with resistance to change.
- Empowering employees to act.
- Generating short-term wins.
- Institutionalizing changes in the organizational culture.

ATTENTION!

Do not read the following until assigned to do so by your instructor.

MODELING EXERCISE

Multi-Phase Products Company[18]

This role-playing exercise initially involves all class members and gives everyone an opportunity to exert change in one of six groups representing each of the six major activity centers for the Multi-Phase Products Company. Representatives from each group then vie to promote their group's suggested changes and overcome other groups' resistance to reallocating a $500,000 budget. Total time required is about 30 minutes.

Instructions

1. The class is divided into equal groups assigned to the six major activity centers for the Multi-Phase Products Company: Research, Manufacturing, Marketing, Administration, Scientific Instruments Division, and Medical Instruments Division.
2. Everyone should read the background notes on the Multi-Phase Products Company.
3. Group members should read the specific role for their designated group. Do not read the roles for the other five groups.
4. Group members discuss ideas for improving the firm, restoring quality, and selecting an approach that seems reasonable. They also decide what share of a $500,000 quality improvement budget they believe their recommendation merits.

Time for Steps 1 through 4 (10 minutes)

5. Groups select one member to represent their interests as a leader at the task force meeting.
6. The six task force leaders now assemble in front of the room for the task force budget meeting.
   a. Each presents his or her group's recommendations and discusses them with the other five.
   b. The six-person group will then decide on the merits of the six proposals by allocating the $500,000 quality improvement pool of funds the CEO has budgeted for this purpose. The allocation that is finally accepted by the task force group should be proportionate to the perceived value of the six proposals for improving Multi-Phase Products.

Time for Steps 5 and 6 (15 minutes)

> 7. The rest of the class will act as observers. During the role-play, observers rate their group's leader on his or her skills in promoting and overcoming change to your group's proposals using the behavioral guidelines shown on the observer's rating sheet.

Situation.   Multi-Phase Products, Incorporated, is a mid-size firm in the medical and scientific instruments industries that has begun to experience difficulties. The firm is organized along functional lines, and it has two business divisions that produce and sell products. Now 12 years old, the firm currently employs about 700 people. Last year, it generated revenues of $120 million with profits before taxes of $3 million. Now, 3 months into the fiscal year, managers within the firm are troubled by declining profit margins. Three years ago, net profit margins before taxes peaked at 10 percent of gross revenues; this quarter, a loss is projected. Gross margins also have declined (from 55 percent 3 years ago to 40 percent this quarter). In part, this is because of the higher costs involved in introducing a new technology within the Medical Instruments Division. Price points also have eroded in the maturing Scientific Instruments Division, which is facing intensified competition in domestic and foreign markets. In several specific product market areas, customers have the perception that the quality of Multi-Phase products has slipped relative to that of competitors.

Research and Development's Role.   Members of the Research group believe customers perceive that quality is deteriorating because less is being invested to improve on the designs of existing products and to channel funds into developing product possibilities. Complications in the timely movement of designs into production are also evident because of "walls" between the R&D effort at the home office and the two product divisions. To cope with these challenges, some of the plans proposed by the central R&D group are:

- Reengineer the processes for converting ideas into salable products (cost estimate: $25,000) to streamline the flow and cut months out of the normal development cycle.
- Pull back research activities from the two product divisions, involving a reorganization (cost estimate: $80,000).
- Increase the investment in research for five key projects by a minimum of $250,000.

These are just starting points for group discussions and proposals. Your group and spokesperson will need to embellish on these and other alternatives if you are to be successful in negotiating a package of benefits that will improve the performance of Multi-Phase Products.

Manufacturing's Role.   Equipment in the Scientific Instruments Division needs to be updated, as much of it is no longer state of the art. As a consequence, costs are not as efficient as they are for key competitors, and quality is not at the level of consistency expected by customers. The Medical Instruments Division has grown quickly and is limited by manufacturing capacity. Furthermore, a Total Quality Management (TQM) process needs to be applied, led by Manufacturing. To cope with these challenges, some of the plans proposed by Manufacturing are:

- Equipment upgrades for the Scientific Instruments Division are estimated at $200,000, which should cut cost per unit by 7–10 percent.
- Expansion of capacity for the Medical Instruments Division could get by with a minimum of $12,500, although $175,000 is preferred.
- TQM (and reengineering of some production processes) will streamline the flow of work-in-process, cutting inventory and improving quality (cost estimate: $50,000).

These are just starting points for group discussions and proposals. Your group and spokesperson will need to embellish on these and other alternatives if you are to be successful in negotiating a package of benefits that will improve the performance of Multi-Phase Products.

Marketing's Role.   Marketing and the process of order fulfillment is the lifeblood of this business. To provide marketing with more clout in arguing their case that product quality and features are lagging behind rivals, a focus group with a range of customers is believed essential. Beyond that form of marketing research, the company needs to embark on an image-building public relations campaign and add additional sales representatives. To cope with these challenges, some of the plans proposed by Marketing are as follows:

- Conduct customer focus groups to obtain feedback about products and services and to anticipate needs (cost estimate: $50,000).
- Launch quickly a corporate image-building campaign (cost estimate: $100,000).
- Boost sales with additions to the sales force, as experience indicates that the addition of one sales rep increases sales by $4 million (cost estimate: $200,000).

These are just starting points for group discussions and proposals. Your group and spokesperson will need to embellish on these and other alternatives if you are to be successful in negotiating a package of benefits that will improve the performance of Multi-Phase Products.

Administration's Role.   The administrative side of the business (involving principally finance and human resources) is concerned about the effects of declining profitability on systems and personnel. Morale has declined, and turnovers have increased. The information system that links individual work stations companywide needs advanced upgrades. A companywide TQM training program will help increase participation in improving processes and quality and in the process of elevating morale. To cope with these challenges, some of the plans proposed by Administration are as follows:

- An enhanced benefit package, including medical insurance and retirement contributions (cost estimate: $250,000).
- Information system upgrades (cost estimate: $100,000).
- TQM training and process ($75,000).

These are just starting points for group discussions and proposals. Your group and spokesperson will need to embellish on these and other alternatives if you are to be successful in negotiating a package of benefits that will improve the performance of Multi-Phase Products.

Scientific Instruments Division's Role.   Maturing product lines have intensified in this division, with the combination of domestic and foreign rivals squeezing out weaker contenders. This has forced the Scientific Instruments Division to reduce prices; however, without offsetting cost reductions, the net effect is that gross margins and profits are falling. To cope with these challenges, some of the plans proposed by the division are as follows:

- Reorganize to streamline and flatten the structure (with costs for early retirement and lay-off funding), combined with an enhanced cost-management system. The one-time cost of $350,000 is projected to result in savings of $2 million per year.
- Conduct an aggressive ad campaign to increase the visibility of Multi-Phase and the division's product line (cost estimate: $70,000).

These are just starting points for group discussions and proposals. Your group and spokesperson will need to embellish on these and other alternatives if you are to be successful in negotiating a package of benefits that will improve the performance of Multi-Phase Products.

Medical Instruments Division's Role.   The Medical Instruments Division (the newer of the two product divisions) faces higher levels of risk than many businesses. One potential risk is that of lawsuits initiated by customers who claim a product did not function as specified and thus put patients at risk; another risk is that suits initiated by Multi-Phase against firms believed to infringe on their patents might not be successful. The division is concerned about the delay from the Food and Drug Administration (FDA) in approving products judged to be safe—a lengthy process. Managers in the division also are looking to process reengineering as a way of increasing the speed of getting products to market and holding the line on escalating costs. To cope with these challenges, some of the plans proposed by the Medical Instruments Division are as follows:

- Hire a divisional corporate counsel to strengthen legal defenses and aggressively go after firms that appear to be infringing on the division's products (cost estimate: $175,000).
- Design ways of speeding new products through the FDA review process (cost estimate: $80,000).
- Process reengineering to cut out unnecessary activities and speed the cycle of product development to production to markets (cost estimate: $100,000).

These are just starting points for group discussions and proposals. Your group and spokesperson will need to embellish on these and other alternatives if you are to be successful in negotiating a package of benefits that will improve the performance of Multi-Phase Products.

Total Time. 35 minutes (steps 1–4, 10 minutes; steps 5 and 6, 15 minutes; debriefing, 10 minutes)

OBSERVER'S RATING SHEET

Rate your own group's leader on his or her skills in promoting and overcoming change to your group's proposals on a 1 to 5 scale (5 being the highest). Provide comments for specific feedback in the space provided under each skill criterion.

Rating	Behavioral Skills	Person Rated: _____
_____	Shared a compelling vision and strategy	
_____	Created a sense of urgency	
_____	Formed supportive coalitions	
_____	Dealt with resistance to change	
_____	Empowered others to act on the vision	
_____	Generated short-term wins	
_____	Institutionalized changes in the organizational culture	

GROUP EXERCISES

Group Exercise 1: "Reshaping Unacceptable Behaviors"[19]

Actors.   Andre Tate (manager) and Shaheen Matombo (staff member)

Instructions.   Read the situation. Pick two volunteers to play the roles of the manager, Andre Tate, and the staff member, Shaheen Matombo. The rest of the class will act as observers. Specific directions for the role-players and observers follow.

- *Andre Tate, Manager.*   Read your role and prepare to role-play your discussion with Shaheen Matombo. After the discussion, assigned observers will provide feedback on your performance, using the Observer's Rating Sheet as a guide. Do not read the role instructions for Shaheen.
- *Shaheen Matombo, Staff Member.*   Read your role and prepare to role-play your discussion with your manager, Andre Tate. Do not read the role instructions for Andre.
- *Observers.*   Read the case situation and both roles. Then review the behavioral guidelines shown on the Observer's Rating Sheet. During the role-play, rate the person playing Andre Tate on his or her skills in promoting and overcoming change in Shaheen Matombo's behavior.

Situation.   Shaheen Matombo is a single parent who has recently entered the workforce after a difficult divorce. Shaheen has been a member of Andre Tate's staff in a hectic customer-relations office for a utility company for 3 months. Shaheen is often 10–20 minutes late for work in the morning. Today Shaheen enters the office 25 minutes late. Shaheen is obviously flustered and disheveled.

Andre Tate's Role.   The phones start ringing promptly at 8:00. When Shaheen is late for work, you have to answer the phone, and this interrupts your work schedule. This morning you are particularly annoyed. Shaheen is 25 minutes late, and the phones are ringing like crazy. Because you have been forced to answer them, it will be difficult for you to complete an important assignment by the noon deadline. You are getting more upset by the minute.

While you are in the middle of a particularly unpleasant phone conversation with an irate customer, you look out your window and see Shaheen bounding up the steps to the building. You think to yourself, "This is ridiculous. I've got to put a stop to this tardiness. Maybe I should just threaten to fire Shaheen unless this behavior shapes up." Upon further reflection, you realize that would be impractical, especially during this period of retrenchment after the rate hike was turned down. Given the rumors about a possible hiring freeze, you know it might be difficult to refill any vacancies.

Also, Shaheen is a pretty good worker when present. Shaheen is conscientious and has a real knack with cranky callers. Unfortunately, it has taken Shaheen much longer than expected to learn the computer program for retrieving information on customer accounts. Shaheen frequently has to put callers on hold to ask for help. These interruptions have tended to increase an already tense relationship with the rest of the office staff. Shaheen has had some difficulty fitting in socially; the others are much younger and have worked together for several years. Shaheen is the first new hire in a long time, so the others aren't used to breaking someone in. Three of your staff complained to you about Shaheen's constant interruptions. They feel their productivity is going down as a result. Besides, Shaheen seems to expect them to drop whatever they are doing every time a question arises. They had expected their workload to be lighter when a new person was hired, but now they are having second thoughts. In the past, you have had enough time to train new hires, but your boss has had you tied up on a major project for almost a year.

Shaheen enters the office obviously flustered and disheveled. Shaheen's face has "I'm sorry" written all over it. You motion for Shaheen to pick up the blinking phone line and then scribble a note on a tablet while you complete your call: "See me in my office at 12:00 sharp!" It's time you got to the bottom of Shaheen's disruptive influence on an otherwise smooth-flowing operation.

Shaheen Matombo's Role.   Boy, what a morning. Your babysitter's father died during the night, and she called you from the airport at 6:30 AM saying she would be out of town for 3 or 4 days. You tried three usually available backups before you finally found someone who could take Keen, your 3-year-old. Then Shayla, your seventh grader, went through five outfits before she was satisfied that she had just the right look for her first yearbook picture. It's a miracle that Buddy, your oldest, was able to pull himself out of bed after getting only 5 hours of sleep. On top of football and drama, he's now joined the chess team, and they had their first tournament last night. Why did it have to fall on the night before his final in physics? This morning you wished you had his knack for juggling so many activities. By the time you got the kids delivered, you were already 10 minutes behind schedule. Then there was this incredible accident on the expressway that slowed traffic to a crawl.

As you finally pull off the downtown exit ramp, you notice you're almost 20 minutes late for work. "My kingdom for a car phone!" you groan, "Although by now I probably couldn't get an open line into the office, anyway." As you desperately scan the side streets for a parking space, you begin to panic. "How am I going to explain this? Andre will be furious. I'm sure Andre's upset about my chronic lateness. On top of that, Andre's obviously disappointed with my lack of computer skills, and I'm sure the others complain about having to train a newcomer." You're sure that one of the reasons you got the job was that you had completed a computer class at the local community college. Unfortunately, there hasn't been much carryover to the incredibly complex computer program you use at work. It seems to defy every convention of logic.

"What am I going to tell him about my being late for work so often?" Unfortunately, there isn't an easy answer. "Maybe it will get better as the kids and I get used to this new routine. It's just very difficult to get the kids to the bus stop and the sitter, commute 20 minutes, and arrive precisely at 8:00. I wonder if he would allow me to come in at 8:30 and only take a half hour for lunch. Staying late wouldn't work because they close down the computers at 5:00, unless there was some paperwork I could do for half an hour."

Then what about the problems with the computer and the other staff members? "Sooner or later Andre's going to get on my case about those things. Is it my fault I don't think like a computer? Some people might be able to sit down and figure this program out in a couple of hours, but not me. So is that my fault or should someone be giving me more training? I wish the others weren't so cliquish and unwilling to help me out. I wonder why that's the case. It's like they're afraid I'll become as good as they are if they share their experience with me. I wish Andre had more time to help me learn the ropes, but there always seem to be meetings. Well, I'm probably no longer employed. I've never been this late. Maybe I'll be back home full time sooner than I expected."

Total Time. 30 minutes (preparation, 5 minutes; role-play, 15 minutes; debriefing, 10 minutes)

OBSERVER'S RATING SHEET

Rate the skills of the manager, Andre Tate, in promoting and managing resistance to change with the staff member, Shaheen Matombo, on a 1 to 5 scale (5 being the highest). Provide comments for specific feedback in the space provided under each skill criterion.

Rating	Behavioral Skills
_____	Shared a compelling vision and strategy
_____	Created a sense of urgency
_____	Formed supportive coalitions
_____	Dealt with resistance to change
_____	Empowered others to act on the vision
_____	Generated short-term wins
_____	Institutionalized changes in the organizational culture

Group Exercise 2: Improving Performance[20]

Objective.   What would you do as a leader as you encounter changing situations? This role-play gives several members of the class the opportunity to test their approach to promoting change and managing resistance to change.

Instructions.   Two people volunteer to be leaders—one to be the leader for situation A, the other for situation B. Next, everyone reads the background in situation A. Then, leader A conducts a meeting with the class acting as employees for 7–8 minutes to review the issues generated by the grand opening of your computer store. After concluding situation A, leader B will conduct a group discussion with the class acting as employees for 7–8 minutes pertaining to situation B issues.

Situation A.   You are the newly appointed manager of a new computer store, the twenty-first in a fast-growing regional chain. The grand opening just concluded, which turned in better-than-expected sales performance. However, it was a week scarred by confusion and numerous problems serving customers. With two exceptions, the full-time sales-service staff you hired have no previous computer sales experience. You personally did all the hiring 2–3 weeks before the store opened, looking for people experienced in working with computers. The glitches during the last week were a combination of the staff not knowing the technical specifications of inventory items they had not personally used and at times resorting to faking their recommendations to customers—or acting with indifference toward customers. You decide to meet with your entire staff before the store opens on Monday morning to share with them the sales success of the opening week and to begin correcting the types of customer-related problems that caused you to be less than pleased with their overall performance during the opening.

Situation B.   Your store is now into its second quarter of operation. You have hired four more staff members. With a couple of exceptions, the staff have settled into their roles nicely. People have learned the technical side of the business and have generally become versatile across several brands of equipment. They demonstrate a basic knowledge of most software products. Paul, however, continues to generate two to four customer complaints per week, usually about his impatient, condescending attitude in working with customers who lack technical expertise. Samantha has proven to be a capable technician, especially in configuring hardware and installing software, but she is often hesitant to make specific recommendations when serving customers. You have decided to hold your first staff meeting of the quarter to review progress to date and engage your people in a quest for continuous improvement.

Debriefing.   Select a third volunteer to conduct a class discussion of the following questions:

1. What did leader A do that seemed effective? What was not so effective?
2. Which leadership theories seem to have relevance for the way leader A handled the group? What is your assessment of the job maturity of group members in situation A? Did the leader's behavior seem to take this into account? How?
3. What did leader B do that was effective? What was not so effective?
4. Again, what leadership theories appear to have relevance for leader B's handling of the situation? To what degree has employee job maturity changed in situation B? Did the leader seem to take this into account? How?

Total Time. 20 minutes

Group Exercise 3: MediScribe Corporation[21]

Instructions.   Divide into groups of five or six. Read the following case and discuss the questions. Share and discuss your group answers with the entire class.

MediScribe Corporation Case.   MediScribe provides medical transcription, insurance claims, and billing and collection services for doctors, clinics, and hospitals in south Florida. As a production supervisor, Ramona Fossett is responsible for the work of approximately 40 employees, 25 of whom are classified as data-entry clerks. Fossett recently agreed to allow a team of outside consultants to come to her production area and make time and systems-analysis studies in an effort to improve efficiency and output. She had little choice but to do so; the president of the company had personally issued instructions that supervisors should cooperate with the consultants.

The consultants spent 3 days studying job descriptions, observing employees' daily tasks, and recording each detail of the work of the data-entry clerks. After this period of observation, they told Fossett that they would begin more detailed studies and interviews on the following day.

The next morning, four data-entry clerks were absent. On the following day, 10 failed to show up for work. The leader of the systems-analysis team explained to Fossett that if there were as many absences the next day, his team would have to drop the study and move on to another department, as a valid analysis would be impossible with 10 out of 25 workers absent.

Fossett, who had only recently been promoted to the supervisor's position, knew that she'd be held responsible for the failure of the systems analysis. Concerned for her employees and her own job, she telephoned several of the absent workers to find out what was going on. Each told approximately the same story, saying they were stressed out and exhausted after being treated like "guinea pigs" for 3 days. One employee said she was planning to ask for a leave of absence if working conditions didn't improve.

At the end of the day, Fossett sat at her desk considering what could be done to provide the necessary conditions for completion of the study. In addition, she was greatly concerned about implementing the changes that she knew would be mandated after the consultants finished their work and presented their findings to the president. Considering how her employees had reacted to the study, Fossett doubted they would comply instantly with orders issued from the top as a result of the findings—and, again, she would be held responsible for the failure.

Questions
   1. Why do you think employees are reacting in this way to the study?
   2. How could leaders have handled this situation to get greater cooperation from employees?
   3. If you were Ramona Fossett, what would you do now to overcome resistance to change?
   4. What would you do to implement any changes recommended by the study?

Total Time. 20 minutes

Summary Checklist

Take a few minutes to reflect on your performance and look over others' ratings of your skills for promoting and managing resistance to change. Now assess yourself on each of the key skills. Make a check (✓) next to those skills on which you need improvement.

Sharing a compelling vision and strategy   _____

Creating a sense of urgency   _____

Forming supportive coalitions   _____

Dealing with resistance to change   _____

Empowering others to act   _____

Generating short-term wins   _____

Institutionalizing changes in the organizational culture   _____

APPLICATION QUESTIONS

1. Think about changes you have experienced over the last year. Did you initially resist the change? Why or why not? How did you overcome your resistance to the change?
2. Think about a time when you have successfully influenced a change in somebody else or a group. What did you do to bring about this change effectively?
3. Think of a time when you unsuccessfully attempted to change somebody else's behavior. What problems did you encounter? Why were you unsuccessful? What would you do differently the next time?
4. A common resistance to change lies in people's perception of how the change will affect them personally. Take a moment to reflect on a time when you felt that a change in your organization would directly affect you personally. Was your initial reaction correct? What was the outcome of the change?
5. Think of a time when someone in your family initiated a major change. What was the change and who initiated it? Was the change successful or not? Why? What was your part in the change process?

REINFORCEMENT EXERCISES

1. Interview managers at three different organizations about the changes they have implemented. What was their experience in implementing the changes? How did they manage resistance to the changes?
2. Attend an event featuring a well-known motivational speaker. What skills does he or she utilize for getting the audience to change? Note how the speaker utilizes the three-step change process of unfreezing, changing, and refreezing. Discern how the speaker attempts to overcome resistance to change.
3. Nissan is a good example of how a reconstruction of the company's image and functionality was executed effectively by an upper-management-planned change initiative. Check the Business sections of the newspaper, the Internet, or magazines to find similar success stories. See what you can learn about how these companies bring about change.

4. To replace negative old habits with better new habits, it takes at least 21 consecutive and consistent applications of the new behaviors before they become naturally ingrained. Try this theory with a personal vice you currently want to change. Next, apply this procedure to your current work or school situation.

5. Think of a behavior you want to change in your pet. Determine what change principles to apply. Try them out and see what you learn.

ACTION PLAN

1. Which behaviors for promoting and managing resistance to change do I want to improve the most?

2. Why? What will be my payoff?

3. What potential obstacles stand in my way?

4. What specific things will I do to improve? (For examples, see the Reinforcement Exercises.)

5. When will I do them?

6. How and when will I measure my success?

Endnotes

1. Adapted from Richard L. Daft, *The Leadership Experience*, 2nd ed. (Fort Worth, TX: Harcourt College Publishers, 2002), pp. 608–609.
2. Harold J. Leavitt, *Corporate Pathfinders* (New York: Penguin, 1987), p. 3.
3. Warren Bennis and Burt Nanus, *Leaders: The Strategies for Taking Charge* (New York: Harper & Row, 1985), p. 20.
4. Bernard M. Bass, "Theory of Transformational Leadership Redux," *Leadership Quarterly* 6, No. 4 (Winter 1995), pp. 19–31.
5. K. Lewin, *Field Theory in Social Science* (New York: Harper & Row, 1951).
6. Thomas G. Cummings and Christopher G. Worley, *Organization Development and Change*, 5th ed. (St. Paul, MN: West Publishing Company, 1993), p. 63.
7. John P. Kotter, "Leading Change: Why Transformation Efforts Fail," *Harvard Business Review* (March–April, 1995), pp. 59–67.
8. Charles Matthews, "How We Changed Gear to Ride the Winds of Change," *Professional Manager* (January 1995), pp. 6–8.

9. John P. Kotter, "Leading Change: Why Transformation Efforts Fail," *Harvard Business Review* (March–April, 1995), pp. 59–67.

10. Malcolm Gladwell, *The Tipping Point: How Little Things Can Make a Big Difference* (Boston, MA: Little, Brown and Company, 2002), pp. 7–9.

11. Charles Matthews, "How We Changed Gear to Ride the Winds of Change," *Professional Manager* (January 1995), pp. 6–8.

12. C. Argyris, *Personality and Organization* (New York: Harper & Row, 1957).

13. R. M. Kanter, When Giants Learn to Dance: Mastering the Challenges of Strategy (New York: Simon & Schuster, 1989).

14. John P. Kotter and Leonard A. Schlesinger, "Choosing Strategies for Change," *Harvard Business Review* 57 (March–April 1979), pp. 106–114.

15. Jean B. Keffeler, "Managing Changing Organizations: Don't Stop Communicating," *Vital Speeches* (November 15, 1991), pp. 92–96.

16. Margaret J. Wheatley, Leadership and the New Science: Learning about Organization from an Orderly Universe (San Francisco, CA: Barett-Koehler, 1994), pp. 25–99.

17. Mei-I Cheng, Andrew Dainty, David Moore, "Implementing a New Performance Management System within a Project-Based Organization: A Case Study," *International Journal of Productivity and Performance Management*, Vol. 56 (January 2007), pp. 60–75.

18. Adapted from Phillip L. Hunsaker, *Training in Management Skills* (Upper Saddle River, NJ: Prentice Hall, 2001), pp. 390–392.

19. Adapted from David A. Whetten and Kim S. Cameron, *Developing Management Skills*, 5th ed. (Upper Saddle River, NJ: Prentice Hall, 2002), pp. 342–343.

20. Adapted from Phillip L. Hunsaker, *Training in Management Skills* (Upper Saddle River, NJ: Prentice Hall, 2001), pp. 386–387.

21. Adapted from John M. Champion and John H. James, "Resistance to Change," In *Critical Incidents in Management: Decision and Policy Issues*, 6th ed. (Homewood, IL: Irwin, 1989), pp. 230–231.

16

■ ■ ■

Facilitating Teamwork

SELF-ASSESSMENT EXERCISE: WHAT IS MY TEAMWORK STYLE?

For each of the following questions, select the answer that best describes your behavior as a team member.

	Usually	Sometimes	Seldom
1. I seek agreement on a common purpose.	_____	_____	_____
2. I let other members worry about their specific goals.	_____	_____	_____
3. I clarify what each member is accountable for individually and collectively.	_____	_____	_____
4. I focus on home runs versus small wins.	_____	_____	_____
5. I keep my problems and limitations to myself.	_____	_____	_____
6. I respectfully listen to others' ideas.	_____	_____	_____
7. I'm dependable and honest.	_____	_____	_____
8. I don't bug others for feedback on how well I am doing.	_____	_____	_____
9. I offer advice on how group processes can be improved.	_____	_____	_____
10. I give others feedback on their contributions.	_____	_____	_____

Scoring and Interpretation

For questions 1, 3, 6, 7, 9, and 10, give yourself 3 points for Usually; 2 points for Sometimes; and 1 point for Seldom. For questions 2, 4, 5, and 8, give yourself 3 points for Seldom; 2 points for Sometimes; and 1 point for Usually.

Sum up your total points. A score of 27 or higher means you're a good team player. A score of 22–26 suggests that you have some deficiencies as a team member. A score below 22 indicates that you have considerable room for improvement.

SKILL CONCEPTS

Groups and teams are not necessarily the same thing. A group is two or more individuals who interact primarily to share information and to make decisions to help each other perform within a given area of responsibility. Members of a group have no need to engage in collective work that requires joint efforts so their performance is merely the summation of each group member's individual contribution.

It could be worse. Groups often experience process losses that detract from their potential productivity. Such things as poor communication, antagonistic conflicts, and avoidance of responsibilities can cause negative synergy resulting in a *pseudoteam* that produces even less output than the potential of the individual members working alone. Even though members might call themselves a team, they're not. Because it doesn't focus on collective performance and because members have no interest in shaping a common purpose, a pseudoteam underperforms a working group.[1]

What differentiates a team from a group is that members are committed to a common purpose, have a set of specific performance goals, and hold themselves mutually accountable for the team's results. Because of these unique elements, teams can produce positive synergy that enables the overall level of performance to be greater than the sum of individual inputs. The primary force that moves a work group toward being a real, high-performing team is its emphasis on collaborative performance.

"Going in the right direction but not there yet" is the best way to describe a potential team. It recognizes the need for and is trying hard to achieve higher performance levels, but some roadblocks are in the way. Its purpose and goals might need greater clarity, or the team might need better coordination. The result is that it has not yet established a sense of collective accountability. The goal is to become a real team with a set of common characteristics that lead to consistently high performance. We can identify six characteristics of real teams.

CHARACTERISTICS OF HIGH-PERFORMING TEAMS

Studies of effective teams have found that they contain a small number of people with complementary skills who are equally committed to a common purpose, goals, and a working approach for which they hold themselves mutually accountable.[2]

Small Size

The best teams tend to be small. When teams have more than about 10 members, it becomes difficult for them to get much done. They have trouble interacting constructively and agreeing on much. Large numbers of people usually cannot develop the common purpose, goals, approach, and mutual accountability of a real team. They tend merely to go through the motions. Therefore, when designing effective teams, keep them to 10 or fewer. If the natural working unit is larger and you want a team effort, break the group into subteams. FedEx, for instance, has divided the 1,000 clerical workers at its headquarters into teams of 5–10 members each.

Complementary Skills

To perform effectively, a team requires three types of skills. First, it needs people with technical expertise. Second, it needs people with the problem-solving and decision-making skills to identify problems, generate alternatives, evaluate those alternatives, and make competent choices. Finally, teams need people with good interpersonal skills.

No team can achieve its performance potential without developing all three types of skills. The right mix is crucial. Too much of one at the expense of others will result in lower team performance.

Teams do not need to have all the complementary skills at the beginning. When team members value personal growth and development, one or more members will often take responsibility to learn the skills in which the group is deficient, as long as the skill potential exists. Additionally, personal compatibility among members is not critical to the team's success if the technical, decision-making, and interpersonal skills are in place.

Common Purpose

Does the team have a meaningful purpose that all members aspire to? This purpose is a vision that is broader than any specific goals. High-performing teams have a common and meaningful purpose that provides direction, momentum, and commitment for members.

The development team at Apple Computer that designed the Macintosh, for example, was almost religiously committed to creating a user-friendly machine that would revolutionize the way people used computers. Production teams at Saturn Corporation are united by the common purpose of building an American automobile that can compete successfully in terms of quality and price with the best of Japanese cars.

Members of successful teams put a tremendous amount of time and effort into discussing, shaping, and agreeing upon a purpose that belongs to them collectively and individually. This common purpose, when accepted by the team, becomes the equivalent of what celestial navigation is to a ship captain: It provides direction and guidance under any and all conditions.

Specific Goals

Successful teams translate their common purpose into specific, measurable, and realistic performance goals. Just as goals lead individuals to higher performance (see Chapter 4), they also energize teams. Specific goals facilitate clear communication and help teams maintain their focus on getting results. Examples of specific team goals might be responding to all customers within 24 hours, cutting production-cycle time by 30 percent over the next 6 months, or maintaining equipment at a level of zero downtime every month.

Common Approach

Goals are the ends a team strives to attain. Defining and agreeing upon a common approach ensures that the team is unified on the means for achieving those ends.

Team members must contribute equally in sharing the workload and agree on who is to do what. Additionally, the team needs to determine how schedules will be set, what skills need to be developed, how conflicts will be resolved, and how decisions will be made and modified. The recent implementation of work teams at Olin Chemicals' Macintosh, Alabama, plant included having teams complete questionnaires on how they would organize themselves and share specific responsibilities. Integrating individual skills to further the team's performance is the essence of shaping a common approach.

Mutual Accountability

The final characteristic of high-performing teams is accountability at the individual and group levels. Successful teams make members individually and jointly accountable for the team's purpose, goals, and approach. Members understand what they are individually responsible for and what they are jointly responsible for.

Studies have shown that when teams focus only on group-level performance targets and ignore individual contributions and responsibilities, team members often engage in social loafing.[3] They reduce their efforts because their individual contributions can't be identified. In effect, they become free riders and coast on the group's effort. The result is that the team's overall performance suffers. This reaffirms the importance of measuring individual contributions to the team as well as the team's overall performance. Successful teams have members who collectively feel responsible for their team's performance.

OBSTACLES TO EFFECTIVE TEAMWORK

When teams are used appropriately in organizations with supportive internal climates, the results have been predominantly positive. However, a number of obstacles can stand in the way of effective teamwork. Next, we summarize some of the critical obstacles that can prevent teams from becoming high performers. Then we summarize some of the techniques you can use to overcome these obstacles.

A Weak Sense of Direction

Teams perform poorly when members are not sure of their purpose, goals, and approach. Add weak leadership and you have the recipe for failure. Nothing will undermine enthusiasm for the team concept as quickly as the frustration of being an involuntary member of a team that has no focus.

Infighting

When team members are spending time bickering and undermining their colleagues, energy is being misdirected. Effective teams are not necessarily composed of people who all like each other; however, members must respect each other and be willing to put aside petty differences in order to facilitate goal achievement.

Shirking of Responsibilities

A team is in trouble if members exhibit lack of commitment to the team, maneuver to have others do part of their job, or blame colleagues or management for personal or team failures. The result is a pseudoteam—a team in name only and one that consistently underperforms even what the members could accomplish independently.

Lack of Trust

When there is trust, team members believe in the integrity, character, and ability of one another. When trust is lacking, members are unable to depend on each other. Teams that lack trust tend to be short-lived.

Critical Skills Gaps

When skills gaps occur and the team doesn't fill these gaps, the team flounders. Members have trouble communicating with each other, destructive conflicts aren't resolved, decisions are never made, or technical problems overwhelm the team.

Lack of External Support

Teams exist within the larger organization. They rely on that larger organization for a variety of resources—money, people, and equipment—and if those resources aren't there, it's difficult for teams to reach their potential. For example, teams must live with the organization's employee selection process, formal rules and regulations, budgeting procedures, and compensation system. If these are inconsistent with the team's needs and goals, the team suffers.

OVERCOMING OBSTACLES TO EFFECTIVE TEAMWORK

A number of things can be done to overcome obstacles and help teams reach their full potential.

Create Clear Goals

Members of high-performance teams have a clear understanding of their goals and believe that their goals embody a worthwhile or important result. Moreover, the importance of these goals encourages individuals to sublimate personal concerns to these team goals. In effective teams, members are committed to the team's goals, know what they are expected to accomplish, and understand how they will work together to achieve these goals.

Encourage Teams to Go for Small Wins

The building of real teams takes time. Team members have to learn to think and work as a team. New teams can't be expected to hit home runs right at the beginning every time they come to bat. Team members should begin by trying to hit singles.

This can be facilitated by identifying and setting attainable goals. The eventual goal of cutting overall costs by 30 percent, for instance, can be dissected into 5 or 10 smaller and more easily attainable goals. As the smaller goals are attained, the team's success is reinforced. Cohesiveness is increased and morale improves. Confidence builds. Success breeds success, but it's a lot easier for young teams to reach their goals if they start with small wins.

Build Mutual Trust

Trust is fragile. It takes a long time to build and can be destroyed easily. Several things can be done to create a climate of mutual trust.[4]

Keep team members informed by explaining upper-management decisions and policies and by providing accurate feedback. Create a climate of openness in which employees are free to discuss problems without fear of retaliation. Be candid about your own problems and limitations. Make sure you're available and approachable when others need support. Be respectful and listen to team members' ideas. Develop a reputation for being fair, objective, and impartial in your treatment of team members. Show consistency in your actions, and avoid erratic and unpredictable behavior. Finally, be dependable and honest. Make sure you follow through on all explicit and implied promises.

Appraise Group and Individual Performances

Team members should all share in the glory when their team succeeds, and they should share in the blame when it fails. Therefore, a large measure of each member's performance appraisal should be based on the team's overall performance. However, members need to know that they can't ride on the backs of others. Therefore, each member's individual contribution also should be identified and made a part of his or her overall performance appraisal.

Provide the Necessary External Support

Managers are the link between the teams and upper management. It's their responsibility to make sure that teams have the necessary organizational resources to accomplish their goals. They should be prepared to make the case to key decision makers in the organization for tools, equipment, training, personnel, physical space, or other resources that the teams require.

Offer Team Skills Training

Teams, especially in their early stages of formation, will need training to build their skills. Typically, training should address problem-solving, communication, negotiation, conflict resolution, and group-processing skills. If you can't personally provide this kind of skills training for your team members, look to specialists in your organization who can or secure the funds to bring in outside facilitators who specialize in this kind of training.

Change the Team's Membership

When teams get bogged down in their own inertia or internal fighting, allow them to rotate members. To manage this change, consider how certain personalities will mesh and re-form teams in ways that will better complement skills. If lack of leadership is the problem, use your familiarity with the people involved to create teams in which it is highly likely that a leader will emerge.

TEAM PROCESS FACILITATION

Facilitation is the process of assisting a team function effectively. This is accomplished by observing how teams perform internal processes such as goal setting, communicating, decision making, conflict resolution, and problem solving, and then making appropriate interventions to improve the processes.[5] Three of the more critical team processes to observe are role behaviors, communication patterns, and decision-making procedures.

Role Behaviors

There are three types of observable team role behaviors.[6] The first is *task* behaviors that address how the team accomplishes work. Examples are setting agendas, suggesting decision-making procedures, and determining time deadlines. The second is *maintenance* behaviors that focus on meeting members' social and emotional needs. Examples are resolving conflicts, giving recognition, and dealing with difficult behaviors. The third is *personal* behaviors that only serve individual needs and usually interfere with the team's task and maintenance needs. An example is blocking the team's progress by refusing to compromise for the good of the whole because of a personal vested interest.

To increase team effectiveness, facilitators should help members expand their role repertoires. They can also share observations about what roles are impeding the process or are needed to enhance it.

Communication Patterns

One important aspect of team process for facilitators to observe is the pattern of communication: Who talks? For how long? How often? Who talks after whom, or who interrupts whom? What is the style of communication—assertions, questions, tone of voice, and gestures?

Observing these types of communication behaviors can provide clues about who is most influential, whether coalitions exist, and how members feel about each other and about the task. More frequent participators are often more influential, especially if they are assertive, articulate, and repeat their ideas. High-frequency contributors, however, can have their influence diluted by blocking coalitions of two or more members. While all this is going on, more introverted members may feel safer just listening and keeping quiet. The problem is that these members may have the best ideas.

Facilitators can observe and chart these communication patterns and their consequences using a sociogram—a drawing of the team seating arrangement with members' names. Lines can be drawn between members' names whenever they make statements to each other or to the center of the diagram when a comment is directed toward the team as a whole. Each time a member says something, the facilitator can make a mark on the appropriate connecting line and indicate the nature of the statement, for example, an "i" for interrupting, an "e" for encouraging, and a "q" for asking questions.[7] At the end of a team session, the facilitator can report back what has been observed and the team can determine ways to be more effective.

Decision-Making Procedures

The effectiveness of any team decision process depends on the specific nature of the task, the individuals on the team, the existing constraints, and other situational variables. The important thing is to use the most appropriate process. A history of decisions based entirely on self-authorized agendas, for example, may not be in the best interests of total team welfare. Most teams think they reach consensus decisions that are supported by all members, when in fact they are most often made by a minority of influential individuals. Seven common decision-making procedures for facilitators to observe and report back on are summarized in Exhibit 16.1.

Process Interventions

Of course these are not the only processes that can be observed during team interactions. What is important to observe will vary with what the team is doing, its stage of development, its goals and needs, and many other situational factors. Observations about team process provide important data for diagnosing what is needed to increase performance. The next step is to do something beneficial.

Often facilitators can enhance the team process by just reporting what has been observed and letting the team apply the data. Other times appropriate interventions might include suggestions for structural changes such as developing an agenda, setting norms, or assigning task and maintenance roles. Other examples of process interventions could be assigning a moderator to perform a gate-keeping role to improve team communications, or establishing a rational problem-solving process.

Decision Type	Description	Example
The plop	An assertive statement followed by silence.	If a statement such as "I think we need to establish our objectives" is followed by nothing but silence from group members, a nonverbal decision to reject the suggested line of action has been made.
Self-authorized agenda	An assertive statement followed by action implementing the suggestion.	"I think we ought to introduce ourselves. My name is Elena Cortez."
The handclasp	A suggestion made by one person and implemented by another.	Person A says, "I think we should introduce ourselves." Person B replies, "So do I; my name is Howard Johnson."
Minority decision (Does any one object?)	An expressed agreement by a few that meets no resistance from the disjointed or undecided people.	"We all seem to agree with Elena's suggestion," "If no one objects to Howard's plan, let's do it."
Voting	The typical voting system in which the majority wins.	"Let's vote and whoever has the most votes wins."
Polling	Checking with each group member to obtain his or her opinion.	"Let's go around the table and see where individually everyone stands. Elena, what do you think?"
Consensus	Essential agreement by all.	The issue is explored in enough depth that all group members agree that a certain course of action is the best that can be agreed to.

EXHIBIT 16.1   Team Decision-Making Procedures.

Source: Adapted from the *Reading Book (Revised) of the NTL Institute for Applied Behavior Science* (Washington, D.C.: National Education Association, 1970), p. 22.

STAGES OF TEAM DEVELOPMENT

Teams generally pass through life stages similar to people. They are born, grow, and develop, and usually pass away. In order for teams to become stable, cohesive, and effective, members need to resolve issues about goals, power, and intimacy as they progress through several stages of maturation. Bruce Tuckman has developed a research-based model illustrated in Exhibit 16.2, which charts a team's maturation through five developmental stages of forming, storming, norming, performing, and adjourning.[8] Different teams will remain at various stages of development for different lengths of time and some may remain at a given stage permanently, either by design or because the team is "stalled."[9] Awareness of this maturation process can enable leaders and members to facilitate a team's transition through the following five stages of team development.

> *Forming.*   In a newly formed group, uncertainties exist about the group's purpose, structure, climate, and leadership. Members need to clarify team goals, explore relationships, and strategies for addressing the team's task. They also need to clarify that they can satisfy needs for acceptance and personal goal satisfaction. Forming is complete when members commit to team goals and agree about what they have to do to achieve them.

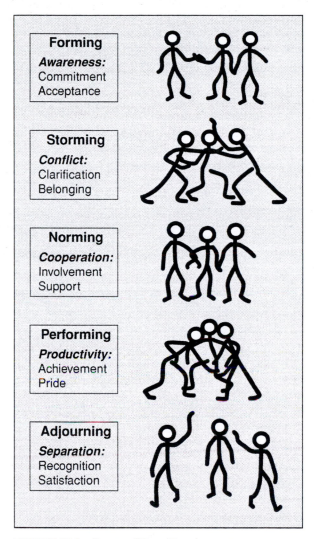

Forming
Awareness:
Commitment
Acceptance

Storming
Conflict:
Clarification
Belonging

Norming
Cooperation:
Involvement
Support

Performing
Productivity:
Achievement
Pride

Adjourning
Separation:
Recognition
Satisfaction

EXHIBIT 16.2   Stages of Team Development.

Storming.   Disagreement is inevitable as members attempt to decide on task procedures, role assignments, ways of relating, and power allocations. Facilitators need to resolve conflicts about power and task structure, work through the accompanying hostility, and develop acceptance and cohesiveness that is necessary to progress to the next stage of cooperation.

Norming.   Norming is the process of establishing a common set of behavioral expectations about how members will treat each other when performing tasks, providing leadership, and relating to each other in general. It is facilitated by promoting open communication and increasing cohesion as members. If successful, increased member involvement and mutual support emerge creating a sense of team harmony.

Performing.   After successful norming, team members are no longer conflicted about acceptance and how to relate to each other. They are committed to the team's mission and can work interdependently to solve problems and achieve mutual goals. Productivity is at its peak. Desired outcomes are achievement and pride. Major concerns include preventing loss of enthusiasm and sustaining momentum. For permanent work teams, this is the desired final and ongoing state of development.

Adjourning.   The adjournment or separation phase occurs when temporary teams like task teams and committees disband after they have accomplished their goals. Feelings about disbanding range from sadness and depression at the loss of friendships to happiness and fulfillment due to what has been achieved. The team facilitator can promote positive closure at this stage by recognizing and rewarding group performance. Ceremonial events bring closure to the desired emotional outcome of a sense of satisfaction and accomplishment.

CONCEPT QUIZ

The answers to the following 10-question, true–false quiz are at the end of the quiz. If you miss any of these questions, go back and find out why you got them wrong.

Circle the right answer.

True   False   1. Groups produce synergy that creates performance that is greater than the sum of the individual inputs.

True   False   2. The best teams tend to be small.

True   False   3. A team will perform effectively if all members have technical expertise.

True   False   4. High-performing teams have a common purpose.

True   False   5. Successful teams translate their vision into measurable performance goals.

True   False   6. Team members must contribute equally in sharing the workload.

True   False   7. Successful teams encourage social loafing by free riders.

True   False   8. If trust is lacking, team members are unable to depend on each other.

True   False   9. Teams should begin by trying to hit singles rather than home runs.

True   False   10. Members should all share the blame when the team fails.

Answers: (1) False; (2) True; (3) False; (4) True; (5) True; (6) True; (7) False; (8) True; (9) True; (10) True

BEHAVIORAL CHECKLIST

Assess the following behaviors when evaluating your effectiveness for facilitating teamwork.

Facilitating Effective Teamwork Requires:

- Establishing and getting commitment to a common purpose
- Task behaviors (e.g., suggesting decision-making procedures, tracking time)
- Maintenance behaviors (e.g., resolving conflicts, giving recognition, building trust)
- Discouraging personal behaviors (ego-centered behaviors that hinder team process)
- Process observation feedback (e.g., both effective and ineffective behaviors)
- Gate keeping (moderating communication patterns)
- Facilitating transition through the five stages of team development

MODELING EXERCISE

Assessing Team Process in a Fishbowl

Objective.   To sharpen observer-facilitator skills of team process behaviors.

Format.   Half the class will be involved in a decision-making exercise while the other half act as observers of the team process. Observers will provide feedback first to the team as a whole and then to team members personally. Decision makers and observers may switch roles and repeat the procedure.

Part I. Team Decision Making and Observations

1. The entire class should form into pairs.
2. One member of each pair participates in the first round of decision-making exercises; these decision makers should form teams of 5–10 members and arrange their seats in a small circle. Their partners are observers for the first round; observers seat themselves opposite their partners around the outside of the decision-making circle. Optimal team size is 6–12 members. In large classes run several exercises simultaneously.
3. The task for the decision-making team is to generate and rank in order the 10 factors that most influence the effectiveness of small teams. They must arrive at one set of prioritized rankings that reflects the team's consensus.
4. Observers view the team's process in general and their partners' behavior in particular. Questions serving as guides for observers' observations are provided on the Observer's Rating Sheet and in Part II, step 5. Observers should remain silent during the decision-making process.

Part II. Feedback and Discussion

5. When the decision-making team completes its task (or after 30 minutes, whichever comes first), the observers provide feedback on the behavior that occurred in the team. Use the Observer's Rating Sheet and the following questions as guidelines:
   a. What things seemed to help the team complete its task successfully? What things seemed to inhibit or hold back the team?
   b. Did the team spend any time discussing how it was going about the task (process issues)? What were the effects?
   c. What communication patterns developed? What were the effects?
   d. What influence structure emerged? Why? What were the results?
   e. What decision-making procedures were used?
6. The observers meet with the team member they observed and provide individual feedback. This is done in dyads.

Part III

With the partners exchanging roles, repeat the procedure for Part I using a different task for the decision-making exercise, such as generating and rank ordering a list of the most important characteristics of effective team leaders.

Part IV

Repeat the procedure for Part II, providing feedback to the new decision-making team.
Note. If there is not enough time for two decision-making exercises, one exercise with a longer observer debriefing accomplishes the goals of this exercise.

Total Time. 40 minutes (Part I, 30 minutes; Part II, 10 minutes)

OBSERVER'S RATING SHEET

Evaluate how well the team and the person you observed applied the following skills during this exercise. Use a 1 to 5 scale (5 being the highest). Enter comments in the spaces between check-list behaviors to explain your ratings.

- Establishing and obtaining commitment to a common purpose.   _____

- Task behaviors (e.g., suggesting decision-making procedures, tracking time, etc.)   _____

- Maintenance behaviors (e.g., resolving conflicts, giving recognition, building trust)   _____

- Discouraging personal behaviors (ego-centered behaviors that hinder team process)   _____

- Process observation feedback (e.g., both effective and ineffective behaviors)   _____

- Gate keeping (moderating communication patterns)   _____

- Facilitating transition through the five stages of team development   _____

GROUP EXERCISES

Three different types of group exercises are presented here. The first one demonstrates the importance of team synergy. The second requires application of team skills to complete a task. The third is a team-building exercise that assesses team strengths.

Group Exercise 1: Naming A to Z Products

Objective.   To demonstrate the importance of team synergy in accomplishing tasks.

Instructions.   Form teams of five to six members. Each team uses all 26 letters of the alphabet to list a product or brand name they have in their possession (e.g., in their backpacks or on their persons). The goal is to see which team can complete the task first. Teams should practice team skills and observe the team process for facilitating task accomplishment and debriefing.

Debriefing.   Use the Observer's Rating Sheet to debrief your team's process.

Total Time. 35 minutes (setup, 5 minutes; exercise, 20 minutes; debriefing, 10 minutes)

OBSERVER'S RATING SHEET

Evaluate how well the team applied the following skills during this exercise. Use a 1 to 5 scale (5 being the highest). Enter comments in the spaces between checklist behaviors to explain your ratings.

- Establishing and obtaining commitment to a common purpose.   _____

- Task behaviors (e.g., suggesting decision-making procedures, tracking time, etc.)   _____

- Maintenance behaviors (e.g., resolving conflicts, giving recognition, building trust)   _____

- Discouraging personal behaviors (ego-centered behaviors that hinder team process)   _____

- Process observation feedback (e.g., both effective and ineffective behaviors)   _____

- Gate keeping (moderating communication patterns)   _____

- Facilitating transition through the five stages of team development   _____

Group Exercise 2: The Card Tower Exercise[10]

This is an inter-team competition exercise. Teams plan and build a card tower in a limited time with the goal of doing better than other teams on three criteria.

Instructions.   Form into five- or six-member teams. Each team receives 100 (5 by 8) index cards, a box of paper clips, and a set of marking pens.

Planning.   Teams have 10 minutes to plan a card tower that will be judged on the basis of three criteria: height, stability, and beauty. No physical work (building) is allowed during this planning period.

Building.   Each group has 25 minutes to construct the card tower using only the materials distributed at the beginning of the exercise.

Judging.   After the instructor numbers the towers, participants mill around and examine them (5 minutes). When you are finished inspecting all of the towers, regroup with your team members and come to a consensus decision as to which tower is the winner (10 minutes). Turn your decisions in to the instructor, who will announce the winner and act as a tiebreaker if necessary. If time is available, and the class wants to know the reasons for the decisions, teams can report how they applied the criteria and why they reached their decisions.

Debriefing.   Teams discuss the following questions and use the Observer's Rating Sheet to debrief their team's process:

During the planning period:

1. What percent of the work did each member contribute on average?
2. Did someone emerge as a leader? What difference did it make?
3. What were the communication patterns?
4. What specific behaviors were helpful? Explain why.
5. What specific behaviors were dysfunctional? Explain why.

During the building period:
Answer the same five questions listed above and compare the similarities and differences between the planning and building periods.

Total Time. 70 minutes (planning, 10 minutes; construction, 30 minutes; judging, 15 minutes; debriefing, 15 minutes)

Group Exercise 3: My Asset Base[11]

Objective.   To help team members get to know each other quickly and to build cohesiveness in the team.

Introduction.   Each of us has an asset base that supports our ability to accomplish the things we set out to do. We refer to our personal assets as talents, strengths, or abilities. When new teams form, one of the first items of concern is getting to know each other and learning what assets each member can contribute to the team.

Instructions.   The following steps will help you assess your own strengths and share them with others to increase the comfort level and provide an understanding of team members' assets.

Step 1 (15 minutes) Individually fill out the following T chart. On the right-hand side of the T, list four or five of your accomplishments of which you are most proud. Your accomplishments should only include things that you can take credit for achieving. When you have completed the right-hand side of the chart, fill in the left-hand side by listing the talents, strengths, and abilities that have enabled you to accomplish the outcomes listed on the right-hand side. Try to be specific in describing which of your assets have enabled you to do what you have done.

Step 2 (15 minutes) If you have already formed teams for class projects, meet with your assigned group. If not, form groups of four to six members. In a round-robin fashion, members share first their accomplishments, and then their talents, strengths, and abilities.

Step 3 (15 minutes) As a group, discuss the following questions.

1. How did your attitudes and feelings toward other members of the team change as you pursued this activity?
2. What does your reaction tell you about the process by which we come to know and care about people?
3. What strengths does your team possess?
4. What areas would you like to increase your team assets in if you had a group research project to complete?

Total Time. 45 minutes

Summary Checklist

Think about your performance working with teams and review others' ratings of your skills. Assess yourself on each of the following key teamwork behaviors. Make a check (✓) next to those behaviors in which you need improvement.

I establish and obtain commitment to a common purpose.   _____

I apply task behaviors (e.g., suggest decision-making procedures,
track time, etc.)   _____

I apply maintenance behaviors (e.g., resolve conflicts, give recognition)   _____

I discourage personal behaviors that hinder team process (e.g., bullying)   _____

I provide process observation feedback   _____

I engage in gate keeping to moderate communication patterns   _____

I facilitate the team's transition through the five stages of development   _____

APPLICATION QUESTIONS

1. Think of a work group, club, or team you currently are in or have been a member of. Was this set of individuals a real team, a pseudoteam, or a group? How do you know?
2. Have you ever been a member of a team that has social loafers going along for a free ride? How did this condition develop? What were the consequences? Was anything done to rectify the situation? If so, what? If not, what should have been done?
3. Contrast a group you have been in whose members trusted each other versus another group whose members did not trust each other. How did these conditions develop? What were the consequences in terms of interaction patterns and performance?

REINFORCEMENT EXERCISES

1. Interview a coach of a sports team about the characteristics of an effective team.
2. Interview a team member of a sports team about what constitutes an effective team.
3. Watch a TV show or movie about a team and determine the team characteristics present. Examples are *Survivor*, *CSI Miami*, *Heroes*, *The A Team*, *Tiger Team*, or *Stargate Atlantis*.
4. Apply your team-building skills to a team you are currently a member of, such as a sports team or a class project team. See what difference you can make in improving your team's effectiveness.

ACTION PLAN

1. Which behavior do I want to improve the most?

2. Why? What will be my payoff?

3. What potential obstacles stand in my way?

4. What specific things will I do to improve? (For examples, see the Reinforcement Exercises.)

5. When will I do them?

6. How and when will I measure my success?

Endnotes

1. A. C. Edmondson and D. M. Smith, "Too Hot to Handle? How to Manage Relationship Conflict," *California Management Review*, Vol. 49, No. 1 (2006), pp. 6–31; A. Edmondson, M. Roberto, and M. Watkins, "A Dynamic Model of Top Management Team Effectiveness: Managing Unstructured Task Streams," *The Leadership Quarterly*, Vol. 14, No. 3, (2003), pp. 297–325; I. D. Steiner, *Group Process and Productivity* (New York: Academic Press, 1972).

2. Jon R. Katzenback and Douglas K. Smith, *The Wisdom of Teams* (Boston, MA: Harvard Business School Press, 1993), pp. 43–64.

3. James A. Sheppard, "Productivity Loss in Performance Groups: A Motivation Analysis," *Psychological Bulletin* (January 1993), pp. 67–81.

4. Fernando Bartolome, "Nobody Trusts the Boss Completely—Now What?" *Harvard Business Review* (March–April 1989), pp. 135–142.

5. A complete description of team facilitation can be found in sources such as R. Sisco, "What to Train Team Leaders," *Training* (February 1993), pp. 62–63; and E. Schein, *Process Consultation* (Menlo Park, CA: Addison-Wesley Publishing Co., 1988).

6. K. D. Benne and P. Sheats, "Functional Roles of Team Members," *Journal of Social Issues*, Vol. 4, No. 2 (Spring 1948), pp. 41–49.

7. D. Ancona, T. Kochan, M. Scully, J. V. Maanen, and D. E. Westney, *Managing for the Future: Organizational Behavior and Process*, 3rd ed. (Mason, OH: South-Western College Publishing, 2005), pp. M-5, 11–12.

8. B. W. Tuckman and M. A. C. Jensen, "Stages of Small Group Development Revisited," *Group and Organizational Studies*, Vol. 2 (1977), pp. 419–427; M. F. Maples, "Group Development: Extending Tuckman's Theory," *Journal for Specialists in Group Work* (Fall 1988), pp. 17–23.

9. K. Vroman and J. Kovacich, "Computer-Mediated Interdisciplinary Teams: Theory and Reality," *Journal of Interprofessional Care*, Vol. 16, No. 2 (2002), pp. 159–170.

10. This exercise is based on *The Paper Tower Exercise: Experiencing Leadership and Group Dynamics*, by Phillip L. Hunsaker and Johanna S. Hunsaker, unpublished manuscript. A brief description is included in "Exchange," *Organizational Behavior Teaching Journal*, Vol. 4, No. 2 (1979), p. 49. Reprinted by permission of the authors.

11. Adapted from D. D. Bowen, R. J. Lewicki, D. T. Hall, and F. S. Hall (eds.), *Experiences in Management and Organizational Behavior*, 4th ed. (New York: John Wiley & Sons, 1982), pp. 14–16.

17

∎∎∎

Valuing Diversity

SELF-ASSESSMENT EXERCISE: WHAT ARE MY ATTITUDES TOWARD WORKPLACE DIVERSITY?[1]

Listed below are 70 words that depict both positive and negative reactions to diversity. Check all the words below that you frequently associate with workplace diversity.

Compassionate	Ethical	Anger	Unfair
Resentment	Wisdom	Insecurity	Progress
Unity	Bureaucratic	Proud	Justified
Stress	Fight	Cooperate	Happy
Support	Listen	Blame	Rivalry
Bad	Fear	Clashes	Confused
Discovery	Sensible	Frustration	Turnover
Stubbornness	Grateful	Unjustified	Harmony
Liability	Team-building	Participate	Asset
Innovation	Expensive	Hopeful	Understand
Useless	Rewarding	Sacrifice	Worthless
Unprofitable	Good	Withdrawal	Patronize
Fair	Pressure	Merit	Enthusiastic
Excited	Collaborate	Unfriendly	Profitable
Disorder	Immoral	Regulations	Useful
Resist	Unnatural	Proper	Disagree
Sleeplessness	Advancement	Enrichment	Apprehensive
Opportunity	Friendly		

Scoring and Interpretation

Give yourself +1 for each of the following words circled: Compassionate, Ethical, Wisdom, Progress, Unity, Proud, Justified, Cooperate, Happy, Support, Listen, Discovery, Sensible, Graceful, Harmony, Team-building, Participate, Asset, Innovation, Hopeful, Understand,

Rewarding, Good, Fair, Merit, Enthusiastic, Excited, Collaborate, Profitable, Useful, Proper, Advancement, Enrichment, Opportunity, Friendly.

Give yourself −1 for each of the following words circled: Anger, Unfair, Resentment, Insecurity, Bureaucratic, Stress, Fight, Blame, Rivalry, Bad, Fear, Clashes, Confused, Frustration, Turnover, Stubbornness, Unjustified, Liability, Expensive, Useless, Sacrifice, Worthless, Unprofitable, Withdrawal, Patronize, Pressure, Unfriendly, Disorder, Immoral, Regulations, Resist, Unnatural, Disagree, Sleeplessness, Apprehensive.

Sum the pluses and minuses. Scores will range from +35 to −35.

This instrument is designed to assess your attitudes toward women, minorities, and others from diverse groups. It taps into five dimensions that represent the range of positive and negative reactions to workplace diversity. These are emotional reactions, judgments, behavioral reactions, personal consequences, and organizational outcomes.

Your result will range from +35 to –35. The researchers categorized individuals by their total scores as follows:

+35 to +11: These are classified as diversity optimists.

+10 to −10: These are diversity realists.

−11 to −35: These are diversity pessimists.

For comparative purposes, the researchers tested this questionnaire on two groups of managers, two groups of employees, and a group of university students. Their scores were (all plus) 8.1, 13.6, 8.7, 9.7, and 5.1, respectively. None of the 40 managers who took the test were classified as pessimists; rather, half were optimists and half were realists. The 116 employees tested closely mirrored the managers, with 46 percent optimists and 49 percent realists. The university sample of 110 students was the least optimistic, with only 35 percent in that category.

If you fell into the pessimistic category, you're likely to have difficulty accepting the increasing diversity in today's workplace. You may want to read more on the benefits of diversity. Some relevant readings include T. H. Cox and S. Blake, "Managing Cultural Diversity: Implications for Organizational Competitiveness," *Academy of Management Executive*, Vol. 5 (1991), pp. 45–56; J. P. Fernandez and M. Barr, *The Diversity Advantage* (San Francisco: New Lexington Press, 1993); and D. A. Thomas and R. J. Ely, "Making Differences Matter: A New Paradigm for Managing Diversity," *Harvard Business Review*, Vol. 74, no. 5 (1996), pp. 79–90.

SKILL CONCEPTS

Understanding how to get along with and manage people who are similar to us are challenges— but understanding and managing those who are dissimilar from us and from each other can be even tougher. As the workplace becomes more diverse and as business becomes more global, managers can no longer assume that all employees want the same things, will act in the same manner, and can be managed the same way. Instead, managers must understand how cultural diversity affects the expectations and behavior of everyone in the organization.

What Is Diversity?

Diversity refers to the array of physical and cultural differences that constitute the spectrum of human differences. Diversity is not a synonym for equal employment opportunity, nor is it another word for affirmative action, though either or both of those may aid diversity. Achieving workforce diversity means hiring and including people with different human qualities, such as age, ethnicity, gender, and race. It is important to remember that diversity includes everyone, not just racial or ethnic minorities.[2]

Workplace diversity was traditionally defined rather narrowly, consisting of a few core dimensions such as the inherent differences of age, ethnic heritage, gender, mental/physical abilities, race, and sexual orientation that have an impact throughout a person's life. These are fixed dimensions that are inborn and readily observable differences.[3] In today's world, most organizations have adapted a more inclusive concept of diversity that includes the whole spectrum of differences between people.[4] Additional inclusive factors include all differences, including dimensions that may change over time, such as work style, military experience, and nationality. These "secondary" dimensions may have less impact than the traditional ones, but they still influence how people think of themselves and how others perceive them.[5] Figure 17.1 illustrates the differences between the traditional and inclusive views of diversity. The challenge is to recognize

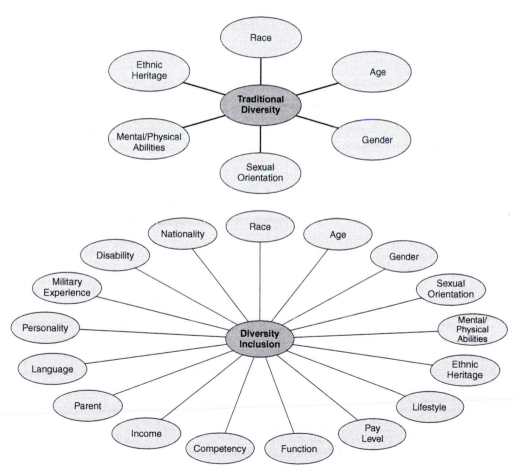

FIGURE 17.1 Traditional Versus Inclusive Views of Diversity.

Source: Based on A. Oshiotse and R. O'Leary, "Corning Creates an Inclusive Culture to Drive Technology Innovation and Performance," *Global Business and Organizational Excellence*, 26, no. 3 (March–April 2007), p. 12; and M. Loden, *Implementing Diversity* (Homewood, IL: Irwin, 1996), p. 14.

that each person can bring value and strengths to the workplace based on his or her own unique combination of diversity characteristics.[6]

The goal of diversity is not diversity for its own sake. Rather, it's to bring in new points of view and ideas. For example, a culturally diverse group that designs a marketing campaign for a new product likely can help develop better plans for reaching different cultural market segments.

How Can Diversity Be Promoted in Organizations?

The origins of diversity training are derived from the civil rights initiatives of the 1960s, specifically affirmative action which involves special efforts to hire and promote disadvantaged groups. Implicit in this approach was the idea that if an organization was proactive, it might avoid government strictures. Furthermore, as women and minorities get better positions in the workforce, others will see that their negative stereotypes were misguided. As those stereotypes crumble, prejudice and discrimination wither. Although prejudice continues to exist, affirmative action has contributed to major gains in opportunities available to women and minorities.[7]

The second approach is diversity management programs. They go beyond affirmative action and entail not just hiring a broader group of workers but creating an atmosphere in which minorities can flourish. A company often lauded for its diversity efforts is Microsoft, which states, "A diverse company is better able to sell to a diverse world." Microsoft places a premium on diversity. For example, it recruits minorities with the aid of black, Hispanic, Native American, and women's groups; donates money and goods to encourage minority education and professional development as well as minority businesses; and supports 13 employee-run diversity groups, including employees with disabilities, women, gays and lesbians, blacks, Hispanics, Native Americans, and Jewish Americans.[8]

North American companies spent from $200 million to $300 million a year on diversity training. A comprehensive review of 31 years of data from 830 midsize to large North American companies found that mandatory programs—often undertaken to avoid liablility in discrimination lawsuits—actually create a backlash against diversity. Successful diversity training is voluntary, provided to make the workplce more inclusive, cater to increasingly diverse customer bases, and promote other business goals. Training programs that work best focus on interpersonal skills, such as those found in this book: mentoring, enhancing self-awareness, self-management, communicating across cultures, and career planning.[9]

What Can Be Done to Facilitate Working with Diverse Others?

Positive actions are available to managers at every organizational level to enhance working with diversity. Some actions that can be applied by everyone are summarized here.

EMBRACE DIVERSITY Successfully valuing diversity starts with accepting the principle of multiculturalism. Accept the value of diversity for its own sake—not simply because you have to. Reflect your acceptance in all you say and do. Managers who truly want to promote diversity must shape organizational culture to allow diversity to flourish.[10]

RECRUIT BROADLY When you have job openings, work to get a diverse applicant pool. Avoid relying on referrals from current employees since this tends to produce candidates similar to your present workforce.[11]

SELECT FAIRLY Make sure your selection process doesn't discriminate. Particularly ensure that selection tests are job-related.[12]

PROVIDE ORIENTATION AND TRAINING   Making the transition from outsider to insider can be particularly difficult for nontraditional employees. Examples of things that can be done to facilitate these transitions include establishing support groups or providing mentoring and coaching.[13]

SENSITIZE ALL EMPLOYEES   Encourage all employees to embrace diversity. Provide diversity training to help all employees see the value in diversity. For example, Digital Equipment Corporation celebrates these differences by sponsoring a calendar of events (e.g., "Black History Month," "Gay and Lesbian Pride Week," and "International Women's Month") and supporting an information network on ongoing discussion groups who meet monthly to discuss stereotypes and ways of improving relationships with those regarded as different.[14]

BE FLEXIBLE   Part of valuing diversity is recognizing that different groups have different needs and values. Be flexible in accommodating employee requests. Some common accommodation examples are flextime, compressed work weeks, job sharing, telecommuting, child-care facilities, and transportation of aging parents to senior citizens' centers.[15]

MOTIVATE INDIVIDUALLY   Investigate the background, cultures, and values of employees. What motivates a single mother with two young children and who is working full time to support her family is likely to be different from the needs of a young, single, part-time employee or an older employee who is working to supplement his or her retirement income. Employees from collectivist cultures are more receptive to team-based job design, group goals, and group performance evaluations than employees from individualistic cultures.[16] On the other hand, avoid being too solicitous of a minorities differences. This can appear patronizing and result in a negative reaction as opposed to the positive one you were trying for. A high-performing black job candidate was not amused and did not accept a job offer, for example, after a white corporate recruiter tapped him on the shoulder and gave him a high-five sign.[17]

REINFORCE EMPLOYEE DIFFERENCES   Encourage employees to embrace and value diverse views. Create traditions and ceremonies that promote diversity. Celebrate diversity by accentuating its positive aspects. Also be prepared to deal with the challenges of diversity such as mistrust, miscommunication, lack of cohesiveness, attitudinal differences, and stress.[18]

CONCEPT QUIZ

Take the following 10-question, true–false quiz. The answers are at the end of the quiz. If you miss any answers, go back and check your understanding of the concepts to determine why you got them wrong.

Circle the right answer.

True   **False**   1. If an organization complies with government affirmative action guidelines, it is doing all it needs to do on diversity.

True   **False**   2. Six core dimensions of diversity are age, ethnic heritage, gender, mental/physical abilities, race, and sexual orientation.

True   **False**   3. The workforce in the United States is becoming more homogeneous.

True   **False**   4. Diverse people should hide their differences and adapt to the dominant culture.

True	**False**	5.	Workers are likely to become more loyal and productive employees when their differences are not merely tolerated but valued.
True	**False**	6.	A diverse workforce enhances an organization's flexibility.
True	**False**	7.	Affirmative action programs have eliminated prejudice from the workplace.
True	**False**	8.	Diversity training programs are only necessary for people who are different.
True	**False**	9.	Diversity means two-way understanding.
True	**False**	10.	Traditional ways of motivation may not be valid for those from other cultures.

Answers: (1) False; (2) True; (3) False; (4) False; (5) True; (6) True; (7) False; (8) False; (9) True; (10) True

BEHAVIORAL CHECKLIST

The following behaviors facilitate working with a diverse workforce. Use them when evaluating your skills and those of others.

To Effectively Work with Diverse Others:

- Sensitize everyone to diversity issues
- Communicate diversity goals
- Embrace (encourage and support) diversity
- Demonstrate your own acceptance of diversity
- Be creative and flexible when dealing with diversity problems
- Motivate according to individual needs
- Reinforce positive and minimize negative employee differences

---

ATTENTION!

Do not read the following until assigned to do so by your instructor.

MODELING EXERCISE

A Problematic Promotion

Instructions. The entire class should read the situation. Then four students should be selected to play the roles of Sam, Charlotte, Harry, and Edgar. Role-players should then read their assigned roles. They should not read the other roles. The rest of the class will be observers. They should read all four roles and review the Observer's Rating Sheet in preparation for observing and critiquing the role-players. During the dialogue, observers should note closely how Charlotte and Harry discuss the issues. What points do they make and what questions do they pose? Be prepared to suggest additional queries and draw conclusions about what arguments the pair makes. Notice what questions they ask of the two candidates and how the candidates respond. There are four actors in this situation.

Sam, an experienced, able technician, has been with Acme Medical Products for 3 years. He's one of the few persons of color working for this company in a technical position. He was a manager at his previous place of employment. Edgar, a well-regarded white technician, has been with the company for 10 years and aspires to management. Charlotte, the division vice president, who is white, is committed to seeing more women and minorities progress at the firm. Harry, the department head, also white, must choose between Sam and Edgar.

Sam was hired 3 years ago at the behest of Charlotte, who thinks, with some justification, that Acme's record of hiring and promoting minorities is poor. In fact, the company was the object of a federal Department of Labor action several years ago, though it was settled by the higher-ups before it garnered too much publicity. Because of a reorganization, a new manager's spot has been created. The question is, who should get it? Charlotte and Harry have a meeting set to discuss the candidates, who at this point have been narrowed to Sam and Edgar. After the meeting, Charlotte and Harry will jointly interview the two contenders, then discuss the results between themselves and try to pick the new manager.

Actors' Roles.   Only to be read by the actor playing the role and the observers. If you are an actor, do not read the other actors' roles.

Sam's Role.   You left your previous employer, where you were a manager, in hopes that you could achieve a similar position with Acme, a larger, more prestigious, and better-paying firm. You were not promised a managerial spot, but certainly you made your aims known in the job interviews and those who hired you didn't discourage you from thinking you had a good shot. It has been 3 years now, and you had hoped you would have been promoted before now. You hope this firm is not the "whites-only boys' club" that it is sometimes made out to be in water-cooler talk around the industry. This new spot ought to have your name on it. If it does not, you will be forced to conclude that you made a mistake in joining Acme. You will probably leave if that is the case, although you are not sure whether you should make that threat at today's interview.

Charlotte's Role.   Being a company officer, you know a lot about Acme. You know that the company historically has not done much to attract and reward minorities, but the Department of Labor threat a few years back did put the fear of God into the top ranks of the firm. Maybe they are not pursuing minorities for the right reason, but at least they are pursuing them. For example, improving the numbers and positions of minorities is a key element of your MBO (management by objectives). So, if Sam and others like him get ahead, you will be rewarded by the company. That is good, but personal gain is not your primary motivation. You genuinely want to see a multiethnic, multicultural workforce because, well, the world is multiethnic and multicultural. You feel the firm must approximate the makeup of its customers if it is going to effectively sell to them. What is more, it is the right thing to do. You were in college during the civil rights movement of the 1960s. You thought that it was a just and righteous cause, and you think fully integrating the workplace is a logical extension of that struggle. Sam is a good man, respected by nearly everyone. The company is unlikely to get a better minority candidate. You have always tried to empower Harry and let him make decisions in his department. In this case, however, he may not understand the "big picture" the way you do, and you may have to overrule him.

Edgar's Role.   You have been with the company for 10 years. You are the senior technician in this department, and you are long overdue for a promotion. This manager's slot rightfully ought to be yours. Sam is a good man, but he is a Johnny-come-lately compared to you. You have worked hard for a decade, enduring sometimes cruel and capricious bosses. You gave up your vacation plans one year to meet a pressing deadline. You have taken special courses to improve your skills. You have made a point of getting along with everyone. You cannot think of a single enemy in the department, remarkable in a company known for the intensity of its infighting.

You hope it does not come down to a racial decision. Because if it does, you will lose; word is the company wants and needs more minority managers. What's more, if it is clearly a racial decision, you will probably leave because you will otherwise be doomed: you can work hard, you can gain others' respect, you can play by the rules . . . but you cannot change your skin color. If the executives turn you down because you are white, you'll have no choice but to go elsewhere—and you think a lot of the other technicians will follow you out the door. In today's interview you hope to show Charlotte and Harry how promoting you is a no-risk move that not only is the right thing to do but will help morale throughout the department.

Harry's Role.   You feel caught in the middle. You are not racist, but you do have an investment in making this department the best it can be. Sam is probably every bit the technician that Edgar is, but Edgar has paid his dues; Sam has not. You suspect Charlotte favors Sam because of some things she has said. But if she forces the issue and orders you to promote Sam, you feel sure there will be a rank-and-file rebellion. She does not realize how tenuous morale is. Edgar is highly competent and well liked, and he has earned his stripes. How can anyone beat those credentials?

Observer's Rating Sheet.   Using the following scale, rate Charlotte's and Harry's application of techniques discussed in this chapter. Also write in comments that will help explain your feedback.

Debriefing.   At the completion of the exercise, provide the role-players with feedback from your observations. Then discuss the following questions as a class:

1. What appeared to be the motivations of each of the four players based on the behaviors you observed?
2. How did those motivations reveal themselves in the discussions?
3. What was not discussed?
4. Whom would you pick for manager? Why?
5. What are the possible repercussions of your decision? How would you deal with them?

Total Time. 45 minutes (preparation, 10 minutes; role-play, 20 minutes; debriefing, 15 minutes)

OBSERVER'S RATING SHEET

Use the following 1 to 5 scale (5 being the highest) to rate Charlotte's and Harry's applications of the techniques discussed in this chapter. Also write in comments that will help explain your feedback.

1	2	3	4	5
Unsatisfactory	Weak	Adequate	Good	Outstanding

Overall, how well did Charlotte: *Rating*   *Comments*

• Embrace (encourage and support) diversity   _____

• Flexibly respond to diversity issues   _____

• Provide orientation and training   _____

• Reinforce value of employee differences   _____

• Sensitize everyone to diversity issues   _____

• Motivate individually for unique needs   _____

Overall, how well did Harry: *Rating*   *Comments*

• Embrace (encourage and support) diversity   _____

• Flexibly respond to diversity issues   _____

• Provide orientation and training   _____

• Reinforce value of employee differences   _____

• Sensitize everyone to diversity issues   _____

• Motivate individually for unique needs   _____

GROUP EXERCISES

In the following three exercises you will be asked to show an understanding of diversity issues. The first exercise involves looking at how prejudices are formed, the second concerns being flexible about employees' needs, and the third entails choosing a work team.

Group Exercise 1: Choosing Music[19]

Step 1. Imagine that you are traveling in a rental car in a city you have never visited before. You face an hour-long drive on an uncrowded highway before you reach your destination. You decide that you would like to listen to the car radio while making the trip.

The rental car has four radio-selection buttons, each with a preset station. Each button plays a different type of music. Button A plays country music, B plays classic rock, C plays classical, and D plays jazz.

Which type would you choose to listen to for the duration of the trip? (Assume you want to relax and stick with one station. You don't want to bother with switching around among stations.)

Step 2. Form four groups, depending on the type of music chosen. In each group, debate the following questions and appoint a spokesperson from within the group to report your answers to the class.

Questions

1. What are your feelings about each of the other three sorts of music?
2. What words would you use to describe people who like to listen to each of the other three forms of music? Specify for each type.
3. Have you listened to enough of the other three types of music to form a valid conclusion about the kinds of people they attract? Why or why not?

Step 3. Have each spokesperson report the responses of his or her group to the questions in step 2.

Step 4. Reconvene as a class and discuss the following questions.
1. What was the purpose of this exercise?
2. What did you notice about the words used to describe the other groups?
3. Upon what sorts of data do you think these images were based?
4. What terms do we normally use to describe such generalized perceptions of other groups?
5. What could be some of the consequences of these perceptions?
6. What parallels are there to other kinds of group differences, such as race, gender, culture, ethnicity, nationality, age, and so on?
7. If an organization was interested in helping employees to value music lovers in the other three genres, what might it do?

Total Time. 50 minutes (setup, 5 minutes; exercise, 20 minutes; questions, 10 minutes; debriefing, 15 minutes)

Group Exercise 2: Diversity in Action

Instructions. Form groups of three. Discuss the workplace problems that each of the following employees might encounter and what you could do (as a senior manager) to help the employees overcome the problems.

Employees.   Lester is a 69-year-old accountant. He's been with your organization for more than 35 years, 22 of which he has been the supervisor of cost accounting. His staff of seven is made up of four women and three men, ranging in age from 23 to 51.

Sonya is the 36-year-old vice president of research and development. She oversees a staff of nearly 20 engineers and designers, only two of whom are female. She's been in her job for 3 months, was hired from outside, and replaced an executive who was widely perceived as a male chauvinist.

Ahman is a recent immigrant from Iran. He is 42, a devout Muslim, with limited skills in the English language. He has an engineering degree from his country but since he's not licensed to practice in the United States, he works as a parts clerk. He is unmarried and has no children but feels a strong obligation to his relatives back in Iran. He sends much of his paycheck to them.

Total Time. 15–20 minutes

Group Exercise 3: Diversity Squares[20]

Instructions.   The entire class participates in the exercise. Pass out the Diversity Squares matrix. This is like BINGO in that you try to complete all five boxes in a row. However, your objective is to complete as many rows as you can in the 30 minutes allotted. Move about the room and try to find people who can answer yes to your questions. Once you have found someone to answer yes to the question, you can cross off the square, placing that person's name or initials in the box. Each person who answers yes to one of your questions can only be used once. Continue to find others until you are able to complete a row.

Do you have any friends who are 10 or more years older than you?	Have you ever worked on a farm?	Do you speak more than one language?	Have you ever worked with anyone with a physical disability?	Have you ever worked with anyone who is a non-Christian?
Have you ever had a roommate of the opposite sex?	Are you of Hispanic or Latin American heritage?	Do you have a family member or friend on welfare?	Do you have friends who are not interested in a college degree?	Do you have a best friend of a different race?
Do you have a friend who is gay, lesbian, or bisexual?	Have you ever been discriminated against because of race or ethnicity?	Have you ever lived outside of your home country?	Have you ever known a convicted felon?	Did a single parent raise you?
Have you ever been sexually harassed at work?	Has either of your parents been in the military?	Are you of Asian heritage?	Are you a vegetarian?	Have you ever had a doctor whose race or ethnicity differs from yours?
Do you know someone with a chronic disease such as cancer or AIDS?	Have you ever dated someone who was less educated than you?	Have you ever been discriminated against because of gender?	Were your parents or grandparents immigrants?	Have you ever had a boss who was younger than you?

Questions

1. How did you feel asking individuals certain questions? What approach did you use to ask the questions?
2. Were some questions more difficult to ask than others? Why?
3. Why did you approach certain individuals for certain questions? Provide some examples.
4. Were you approached by several people about the same question? If so, how did it make you feel? Why did they select you for certain questions?
5. Would some of the questions be more difficult to ask or more likely to offend others if worded in the first person? For example, "Are you gay, lesbian, or bisexual?"
6. What did this exercise make you realize about your own stereotypes and prejudices?
7. What did this exercise make you realize about stereotypes and prejudice in general?

Total Time. 60 minutes (complete the rows, 30 minutes; discussion, 30 minutes)

Summary Checklist

Take a few minutes to reflect on your performance and look over others' rating of your skills in the preceding exercises. Make a check (✓) next to those behaviors you need to improve.

I embrace (encourage and support) diversity.   _____

I recruit broadly.   _____

I select fairly.   _____

I provide orientation and training.   _____

I sensitize everyone to diversity issues.   _____

I am flexible and creative when responding to diversity issues.   _____

I motivate individually based on unique needs.   _____

I reinforce the value of employee differences.   _____

APPLICATION QUESTIONS

1. Does your organization (employer or school) show signs of bias against certain groups of people? What is your first "gut" response to that question? Why do you feel this way?
2. How might a manager's role for promoting diversity change as the organization becomes more diverse?
3. How can more diversity contribute to greater creativity and better problem solving?
4. What diversity programs have you observed at school or at work? Were they effective? Why or why not?
5. What steps could be taken to change these practices? Do you think your organization would be willing to do so?

REINFORCEMENT EXERCISES

The following are suggested activities for enhancing your awareness and reinforcing the techniques described in this chapter for valuing diversity. You may want to adapt them to the Action Plan you will develop next, or try them independently.

1. Ask your minority friends what kinds of biases they perceive in school or in the workplace. Do you agree with their assessments? Even if you think they are wrong or exaggerate the problem, try to imagine yourself in their role.
2. Think of places where you have worked. Were minorities expected to adapt to that culture? Did the employer make any concessions to diversity? If so, what were those efforts? Were the minority employees content? If not, could their discontent have been reduced by more sensitivity by management?
3. Watch the second episode of the television series *The Office:* Diversity Day. How did Michael, the manager, value diversity according to this chapter's behavioral checklist? http://www.tbs.com/video/index.jsp?oid=206532
4. Create a list of suggestions that you personally can use to improve your sensitivity to diversity issues.

ACTION PLAN

1. How can I improve my sensitivity to diversity issues?

2. What will be the payoff for doing so?

3. What potential obstacles stand in my way?

4. What are the specific things I will do to improve my sensitivity?

5. When will I do them?

6. How will I measure my improvement?

Endnotes

1. K. P. DeMeuse and T. J. Hostager, "Developing an Instrument for Measuring Attitudes Toward and Perceptions of Workplace Diversity: An Initial Report," *Human Resource Development Quarterly* (Spring 2001), pp. 33–51.

2. R. L. Daft, *Leadership: Theory and Practice* (Fort Worth, TX: Dryden Press, 1999), p. 302.

3. M. Loden, *Implementing Diversity* (Homewood, IL: Irwin, 1996), p. 14.

4. A. Oshiotse and R. O'Leary, "Corning Creates an Inclusive Culture to Drive Technology Innovation and Performance," *Global Business and Organizational Excellence*, Vol. 26, No. 3 (March-April 2007), pp. 2–21.

5. R. L. Daft, *The Leadership Experience* (Mason, OH: South-Western Cengage Learning, 2008), p. 332.

6. F. Milliken and L. I. Martins, "Searching for Common Threads: Understanding the Multiple Effects of Diversity in Organizational Groups," *Academy of Management Review,* Vol. 21, No. 2 (1996), pp. 402–433.

7. S. Jackson and Associates, *Diversity in the Workplace: Human Resource Initiatives* (New York: Guilford Press, 1992).

8. H. Collingwood, "Who Handles a Diverse Work Force Best?" *Working Woman* (February 1996), p. 23.

9. Shankar Vedantam, "Study: Required Diversity Training Fails," *The San Diego Union-Tribune* (January 21, 2008), p. A5.

10. Charlene M. Solomon, "Communicating in a Global Environment," *Workforce* (November 1999), p. 50.

11. W. B. Johnson and A. H. Packer, *Workforce 2000: Work and Workers in the 21st Century* (Indianapolis, IN: Hudson Institute, 1987); M. Galen and A. T. Palmer, "White, Male and Worried," *Newsweek* (January 31, 1994), pp. 50–55.

12. S. Jackson and Associates, *Diversity in the Workplace: Human Resource Initiatives* (New York: Guilford Press, 1992).

13. J. C. McCune, "Diversity Training: A Competitive Weapon," *Management Review* (June 1996), pp. 25–28.

14. J. Greenberg, *Managing Behavior in Organizations: Science in Service to Practice,* 2nd ed. (Upper Saddle River, NJ: Prentice Hall, 1999), p. 98.

15. I. Harpaz, "The Importance of Work Goals: An International Perspective," *Journal of International Business Studies* (First Quarter 1990), pp. 75–93.

16. G. Hofstede, "Motivation, Leadership and Organizations: Do American Theories Apply Abroad?" *Organizational Dynamics* (Summer 1980), p. 55.

17. J. Bennett, "Corporate Angst' Can Generate Gaffes That Turn Off Coveted Candidates," *The Wall Street Journal* (October 21, 2003), p. D9.

18. T. Cox and S. Blake, "Managing Cultural Diversity: Implications for Organizational Competitiveness," *Academy of Management Executives*, Vol. 5 (August 1991), pp. 45–66.

19. Adapted from D. Bowen et al., *Experiences in Management and Organizational Behavior,* 4th ed. (New York: John Wiley & Sons, 1996), p. 329.

20. This exercise was adapted from J. William Pfeiffer and Leonard D. Goodstein (eds.), *The 1994 Annual: Developing Human Resources* (San Diego, CA: Pfeiffer & Company, 1994).

18

■ ■ ■

Ethical Decision Making

SELF-ASSESSMENT EXERCISE: HOW DO MY ETHICS RATE?[1]

Indicate your level of agreement with these 15 statements by entering the number from the following scale:

1 = Strongly disagree	3 = Neither agree nor disagree	5 = Strongly agree
2 = Disagree	4 = Agree	

_____ **1.** The only moral of business is making money.
_____ **2.** A person who is doing well in business does not have to worry about moral problems.
_____ **3.** Act according to the law, and you can't go wrong morally.
_____ **4.** Ethics in business is basically an adjustment between expectations and the ways people behave.
_____ **5.** Business decisions involve a realistic economic attitude and not a moral philosophy.
_____ **6.** "Business ethics" is a concept for public relations only.
_____ **7.** Competitiveness and profitability are important values.
_____ **8.** Conditions of a free economy will best serve the needs of society. Limiting competition can only hurt society and actually violates basic natural laws.
_____ **9.** As a consumer, when making an auto insurance claim, I try to get as much as possible regardless of the extent of the damage.
_____**10.** While shopping at the supermarket, it is appropriate to switch price tags on packages.
_____**11.** As an employee, I can take home office supplies; it doesn't hurt anyone.
_____**12.** I view sick days as vacation days that I deserve.
_____**13.** Employees' wages should be determined according to the laws of supply and demand.
_____**14.** The business world has its own rules.
_____**15.** A good businessperson is a successful businessperson.

Scoring and Interpretation

No decision is completely value-free. It undoubtedly will have some ethical dimensions. This instrument presents philosophical positions and practical situations. Rather than specify "right" answers, this instrument works best when you compare your answers to those of others. With that in mind, here are mean responses from a group of 243 management students. How did your responses compare?

1. 3.09	**6.** 2.88	**11.** 1.58
2. 1.88	**7.** 3.62	**12.** 2.31
3. 2.54	**8.** 3.79	**13.** 3.36
4. 3.41	**9.** 3.44	**14.** 3.79
5. 3.88	**10.** 1.33	**15.** 3.38

Do you tend to be more or less ethical than the student norms presented above? On which items did you differ most? Your answers to these questions can provide insights into how well your ethical standards match other people with whom you will be working in the future. Large discrepancies might be a warning that others don't hold the same ethical values that you do.

SKILL CONCEPTS

Making the "right" choices in ethics-laden situations is an almost-everyday occurrence for everyone, especially managers today. Ethics is commonly thought of as rules or principles that define right and wrong conduct.[2] Unfortunately, the task isn't as simple as just choosing the "correct" answer. Rather, the decision may involve the many shades of gray between "right" and "wrong." In this chapter, you are encouraged to develop your own ethical decision-making process. You also learn how managers as well as organizations can help or hinder the development of a moral climate.

Why Is Ethics Important?

Ethics is important for everyone, but particularly crucial for managers.[3] One reason is that managers' decisions set the standard for subordinates and help create a tone for the organization as a whole. Second, the behavior of managers is under increasing scrutiny. Because people have more access to information, misdeeds may become quickly and widely known. The reputation of an organization or individual, which may have taken many years to build, can be destroyed in minutes. In addition, today's public has high standards for the behavior of managers and organizations. Customers don't have to tolerate an unethical company; competition allows them to choose the company that best suits their expectations.

Behaving ethically also improves the quality of work life.[4] If employees believe all are held to similar high standards, they likely will feel better about themselves, their colleagues, and their organization. Furthermore, many businesses want employees to behave ethically because such a reputation is good for business (which, in turn, can mean larger profits). Similarly, encouraging employees to act ethically can save money by reducing employee theft, downtime, and lawsuits. Because many unethical acts are also illegal, a firm that allows workers to engage in unfair practices might be prosecuted.

However, the law itself is not an adequate guide to ethics.[5] Some unethical acts—lying under oath or embezzling, for example—are illegal. But many legal acts are potentially unethical, and it is those situations that often pose the toughest choices. For instance, charging a higher price to a naive customer than to a savvy one is not illegal. In fact, it may be seen by some as a smart business practice. But is it ethical? Dismissing an employee for cause is not illegal, but if his poor performance has been tolerated for years and the problem employee will qualify for his pension in a few more months, is firing him ethical?

1. The individual and/or the organization is immature.
2. Economic self-interest is overwhelming.
3. Special circumstances outweigh ethical concerns.
4. People are uneducated in ethical decision making.
5. Possible rewards outweigh possible punishments for unethical behavior.
6. The prevailing attitude is "All's fair in love, war, and business."
7. There is powerful organizational pressure to commit unethical acts.

EXHIBIT 18.1   Why Do Individuals Make Poor Choices on Ethical Issues?

Source: O. C. Ferrell and G. Gardiner, *In Pursuit of Ethics: Tough Choices in the World of Work* (Springfield, IL: Smith Collins Co., 1991), pp. 9–13.

Applying Ethical Guideposts to Decisions

In the final analysis it is individuals who make the decisions, and quite often individuals make poor choices on ethical issues. Exhibit 18.1 provides some of the reasons why this happens in organizations. Consequently, it is important that you develop your own ethical guideposts and decision-making processes to apply for yourself, regardless of the type of organization you are in or who your boss is.

What are the guideposts that you can apply, especially in those "gray" areas where right and wrong are not easily defined? What processes can you follow to enhance your ethical thinking and decisions? Following are some ethical guidelines that can guide your decisions in most situations. If you want more of a cookbook formula, review the step-by-step ethical screening test for individual decision making that follows the seven guideposts.

1. *Understand your organization's policy on ethics.*   Policies on ethics, if they exist, describe what the organization leaders perceive as ethical behavior and what they expect you to do. Understanding your organization's ethics policy will clarify what is permissible and what discretion you have.
2. *Anticipate unethical conflict.*   Be alert to situations that may promote unethical behavior. Under unusual circumstances, even a normally ethical person may be tempted to act out of character. It will be in your best interest to anticipate those unusual situations and be proactive. For example, if an important client has a reputation for cutting corners and putting pressure on your salespeople, you could seek to stifle any unethical temptation by meeting with the customer to tactfully restate the company's ethical credo. You could also give the sales staff helpful advice on how to rebuff questionable overtures and meet goals through ethical means.
3. *Think before you act.*   Ask yourself, "Why am I doing what I'm about to do? What led up to the problem? What is my true intention in taking this action? Is my reason valid? Or are there ulterior motives behind it—such as proving myself to my peers or superiors? Will my action injure someone?" Also ask yourself, "Would I disclose to my boss or family what I am about to do?" Remember, it is your behavior and your actions. You need to make sure that you are not doing something that will jeopardize your reputation or your organization.
4. *Consider all consequences.*   As you ponder your decision, you should also be asking what-if questions. For example: "What if I make the wrong decision? What will happen to me? What will happen to my job? What if my actions were described, in detail, on a local TV news show or in the newspaper? Would that public notice bother or embarrass me or

those around me? What if I get caught doing something unethical? Am I prepared to deal with the consequences?"

5. *Seek opinions from others.* Asking for advice from others you respect is often wise. Maybe they have been in a similar situation and can give you the benefit of their experience. Or maybe they can just listen and act as a sounding board for you.

6. *Do not allow yourself to become isolated.* It is easy to become isolated from what is occurring in the organization. However, if you are a manager you are responsible for being aware of all activities. You can combat isolation by promoting an open-door policy and continually looking for ways to improve ethical behavior.

7. *Do what you truly believe is right.* You have a conscience, and you are responsible for your behavior. Whatever you do, if you truly believe it is the right action to take, then what others will say is immaterial. You need to be true to your own internal ethical standards. Ask yourself, "Can I live with what I have done?"

Ethical Screening

Ethical screening refers to running a contemplated decision through an ethics test. This screening is most relevant when the contemplated action is in that gray area between clearly right or clearly wrong. The following formula provides the basic steps you should take when faced with an ethical dilemma.[6]

Step 1 *Gather the facts.* You should find out the answers to pertinent questions: Does the situation present any legal questions? What are the precedents for this kind of decision? What do our rules and regulations say?

Step 2 *Define the ethical issues.* It may be helpful to talk the situation over with someone to clarify these issues. Such issues might include conflicts of interest, dealing with confidential information, proper use of company resources, or more intangible questions concerning kindness, respect, or fairness.

Step 3 *Identify the affected parties.* Major corporate decisions, such as shutting down a plant, can affect thousands of people. Even a much more modest action, such as hiring or not hiring a handicapped worker, can involve many more people than you might initially think.

Step 4 *Identify the consequences.* Try to predict the consequences for all people involved. Concentrate on the outcomes with the highest probability of occurring and especially those with negative outcomes. Both the short- and long-term results should be considered. Closing an obsolete plant, for example, might create short-term hardships for people laid off, but in the long term the firm may be financially healthier and the employees may find more viable long-term careers.

Do not neglect the symbolic consequences, either. Every action sends a message, good or bad. If you hire a handicapped worker, that act may send a message that is larger and more meaningful than all your words about equal opportunity. It is not just what you say, it is what you do that others will pick up on.

Step 5 *Consider your character and integrity.* Your character refers to the type of person you want to be. So when considering questionable actions, ask yourself the following questions.

    a. What would my family, friends, superiors, and coworkers think of my actions?

    b. How would I feel if my decision was publicly disclosed in a newspaper or e-mail?

    c. Does this decision or action agree with my religious teachings and beliefs (or with my personal principles and sense of responsibility)?

d. Would I want everyone to make the same decision and take the same action if faced with these same circumstances?

e. How would I feel if I were on the other side of this decision?

Step 6 ***Think creatively about alternatives.***   More alternatives can often be identified than just the choice between doing or not doing something. Try to be imaginative when considering options. For example, what could you do if a grateful client sends you an expensive fruit basket that you cannot ethically accept? To keep it would be wrong. But if you returned it, you may appear ungrateful and make the client feel foolish; you could even cause the fruit to spoil.

So, another possibility might be giving the gift to a homeless shelter, then penning the client a thank-you note mentioning that you passed the fruit along to the more needy. You would not have violated your policy or set a bad example for your staff. Meanwhile, you also would have graciously informed the client about your policy and probably discouraged future gift giving.

Step 7 ***Check your intuition.***   Quite apart from the rational decision-making process, you should also ask yourself, "How does this feel in my gut? Will I be proud of myself?"

Step 8 ***Prepare to defend your action.***   Will you be able to explain adequately to others what you are about to do? Will they also likely feel it is ethical or moral? You may want to refer to the ethics check in Exhibit 18.2 when preparing this step.

Principles for Ethical Decision Making

After gathering as much information as possible about the situation through an ethical screening, the decision maker can apply a set of ethical standards to evaluate the options for managing an ethical dilemma. Some of the key principles to apply are:[7]

- *Reliability:*   Keep promises, agreements, and other commitments.
- *Transparency:*   Be honest. Act in a truthful and open manner.
- *Dignity:*   Respect the dignity of all people.
- *Fairness:*   Deal fairly with all parties. Respect the rights of others.
- *Citizenship:*   Act as a responsible member of the community.
- *Responsiveness:*   Be responsive to legitimate claims and concerns of others.

- *Legality test:*   Will I be violating either civil law or company policy?
- *Fairness test:*   Is it fair to all concerned in the short term as well as the long term? Does it promote win–win relationships?
- *Visibility test:*   Would I feel good if my decision were published in the newspaper? Would I feel good if my family knew about it? Will it make me proud?
- *Generality test:*   If everyone in similar position took the same course of action, would I be comfortable with it?
- *Legacy test:*   With respect to my handling of this situation, is this how I want my leadership to be remembered?

EXHIBIT 18.2   Tests for Ethical Actions.

Source: Adapted from K. Blanchard and N. V. Peale, The Power of Ethical Management (New York: William Morrow, 1988), p. 27; R. J. Aldag and L. W Kuzuhara, Organizational Behavior: A Skills-Based Approach (Dubuque, IA: Kendal Hunt, 2009), p. 308.

Making Ethical Decisions in the Global Environment

There are significant variations regarding ethical standards in different parts of the world. Bribery, for example, is illegal in the Unites States, but it is an acceptable practice in many other countries. Four principles for guiding business ethics in a global environment are as follows:[8]

1. *Maintain respect for core human rights.*   Decent working conditions, fair treatment, living wages, etc., should be maintained wherever you are doing business.
2. *Treat organizational values and standards of conduct as absolute.*   Core ethical values and standards should be communicated to all members of the organization worldwide. These standards set the minimum for ethical behavior everywhere.
3. *Respect local traditions.*   Although core human rights and core organizational values set the minimum threshold for ethical behavior, flexibility is needed to adapt to additional ethical standards that are appropriate for specific countries. Sometimes this requires the exercise of moral imagination and flexibility in working out solutions to ethical dilemmas.
4. *Remember that context determines what is right or wrong.*   In many other cultures, actions that are not considered ethical in the United States could be ethical in certain situations. Consequently, it makes sense to let business units operating in foreign environments to fine-tune specific ethical standards.

Encouraging Ethical Behavior in Others[9]

Managers are not only required to behave ethically themselves, but they are also charged with promoting the ethical behavior of others. Some actions you can take to do this are as follows:

- Promote, communicate, and reward ethical behavior as a key value.
- Model ethical behavior yourself. Walk your talk in both public and private.
- Take ethical stands. Speak out against unethical behavior when you see it.
- Give employees ways to voice ethical questions and concerns.

CONCEPT QUIZ

Take the following 10-question, true–false quiz. The answers are at the end of the quiz. If you miss any answers, go back and check your understanding of the concepts to determine why you got them wrong.

     Circle the right answer.

True	**False**	1.	An explicitly written code of conduct reduces ethical ambiguity.
True	**False**	2.	Managers' actions have little to do with how employees behave.
True	**False**	3.	Tasks that are unrealistic and highly stressful may cause unethical behaviors.
True	**False**	4.	A person's values should be considered before being hired.
True	**False**	5.	An ethical corporate culture can lead to long-term success for the company.
True	**False**	6.	In the final analysis, how ethical any decision is depends on the person who makes it.
True	**False**	7.	Some unethical acts are legal.

True	**False**	8.	An organization's culture and structure influence how ethical its employees act.
True	**False**	9.	Business operations in foreign lands often present difficult ethical choices because of differences in cultural norms.
True	**False**	10.	Because ethics are different for different individuals, nothing can be gained by discussing ethical dilemmas with others.

Answers: (1) True; (2) False; (3) True; (4) True; (5) True; (6) True; (7) True; (8) True; (9) True; (10) False

BEHAVIORAL CHECKLIST

The following behaviors are important for ethical decision making. Use them as criteria when evaluating your ethical decision-making skills and those of others.

Ethical Decision Makers:

- Define the ethical issues.
- Gather all pertinent information and seek opinions from others.
- Consider all consequences for all affected parties
- Adhere to their organization's policy on ethics.
- Generate creative alternatives.
- Keep promises, agreements, and other commitments.
- Act in an honest, truthful, and open manner.
- Respect the rights of others and deal fairly with all parties.
- Act as a responsible member of the community.
- Take ethical stands.

ATTENTION!
Do not read the following until assigned to do so by your instructor.

MODELING EXERCISE

Competing Ethical Criteria

Instructions. The entire class should read the following situation. Then two class members volunteer to act out the roles of John Higgins, director of research, and Mary Fernandez, who heads his design team. The role-players read their assigned role only and prepare to explain their position at the forthcoming meeting. Actors should *not* read the other person's role. The remainder of the class reads both roles and reviews the Observer's Rating Sheet. During the role-play, observers rate Higgins's application of ethical decision skills using the Observer's Rating Sheet. Observers should also note what points Higgins and Fernandez make and be prepared to suggest additional arguments and alternatives.

Actors. John Higgins, director of research for Radartec, a major electronics firm. Mary Fernandez, leader of design team charged with developing a critical component for a new radar system.

Situation.[10]   John Higgins appointed Mary Fernandez about 3 months ago to head the design team for a new radar tracking system. The success of the new radar system is crucial to the firm's profitability. The new component has a tight development deadline of 18 months. In fact, the CEO issued a statement indicating that the company's financial future may hinge on the timely development of the new radar.

The CEO's statement also applauded the promotion of Mary Fernandez to a key role. She is a Hispanic female, and the first woman in company history to lead such a unit. The company has traditionally lagged in the hiring and promotion of minorities. Now, more than halfway through the project, certain members of the all-male team have been complaining about Fernandez. The project is on schedule, and no one has faulted Fernandez's technical knowledge. But general criticisms ("She does not know how to lead men" and "She does not understand teamwork") have been made and discussed publicly. The grousing has started to snowball, and recently the pace of work has slowed. Higgins suspects some team members are quietly sabotaging the project.

John Higgins's Role.   You respect and admire Fernandez as an employee as well as a human being. You are sure she has a lot to offer the company as she grows professionally. You do not want to crush her hopes—or stymie her potential—by reneging on this big chance you gave her.

On the other hand, neither you nor the firm can risk having this radar project fail for whatever reason, so you are considering removing her as team leader. You and Fernandez have always gotten along well until now, but you fear that if you take her off the project, she will become embittered and perhaps even file a gender-discrimination lawsuit against you and the company. Furthermore, you feel sure some will see her removal as symbolic of the traditional shortchanging of minorities by the firm.

You feel torn between your responsibility to the company and to a valued employee. You want to explain to Fernandez the ethical quandary you find yourself in and how the economic considerations are at war with the moral ones. Your goal is to try to understand the other person's view and try to perhaps reach an ethical solution that is satisfactory to both parties and the company. You have asked Fernandez to meet with you to discuss a "critical question" relating to her work role.

Mary Fernandez's Role.   The men on the design team have been difficult, almost mutinous, but you think they would be that way with any woman or minority in charge. You are qualified for this job. You have earned it. You want it. You are prepared to endure insults and whatever other hurdles are placed in your way; those challenges are the price pioneers must pay. You owe it not only to yourself but also to other women and minorities to persevere and not let Higgins cave into pressure from the men who are upset because their "white-males-only" club has been disrupted.

If this question is one of ethics, it is a clear issue of fairness and equity, one that can only be resolved by allowing you to complete the job assigned to you.

Total Time. 20 minutes (preparation for role-play, 10 minutes; debriefing, 10 minutes)

OBSERVER'S RATING SHEET

Rate the actor playing Higgins on the application of ethical decision-making skills using the following scale. Write concrete examples in the spaces between the behavioral skills to use in explaining your feedback.

1	2	3	4	5
Unsatisfactory	Weak	Adequate	Good	Outstanding

_____ Defined the ethical issues.

_____ Gathered all pertinent information and sought opinions from others.

_____ Considered all consequences for all affected parties.

_____ Adhered to their organization's policy on ethics.

_____ Generated creative alternatives.

_____ Kept promises, agreements, and other commitments.

_____ Acted in an honest, truthful, and open manner.

_____ Respected the rights of others and dealt fairly with all parties.

_____ Acted as a responsible member of the community.

_____ Took ethical stands.

GROUP EXERCISES

In the three exercises that follow you will be asked to practice ethical decision skills, sharpen your ethical sensitivity, and expand your ethical judgment capability.

Group Exercise 1: West Oceans Bank

Instructions.   The class should divide into trios and then read the following situation. Two trio members volunteer to act out the roles of Carrie Makson, vice president of West Oceans Bank, and Pat Jergen, corporate account executive manager. The role-players should read only their assigned roles and prepare to explain their position at the forthcoming meeting. Actors should *not* read the other person's role. The third person is the observer and should read both roles and review the Observer's Rating Sheet. During the role-play, the observer rates Carrie's application of ethical decision skills using the observer's rating sheet. The observer should also prepare to give feedback to the actors.

Actors.   Carrie Makson, vice president of West Oceans Bank, and Pat Jergen, corporate account executive manager.

Situation.   Pat Jergen, a 20-year banking veteran, is reputed to be the best account executive at West Oceans Bank. Carrie Makson, the bank's vice president, has come across an opportunity to get an enormous new corporate account with Acme Chemical, the world's largest chemical company. This account, if landed and handled properly, could mean an entirely new scope and size of business for the bank. Over the past 5 years, however, Acme has been widely accused of dumping hazardous waste and polluting the environment; it is even on the "most-wanted" list of the Environmental Protection Agency (EPA).

Carrie Makson's Role.   You have been a vice president at West Oceans Bank for 10 years and a friend and admirer of Pat Jergen almost as long. You have recently felt pressure from the board of directors to increase your corporate business, and the Acme account would more than remedy the problem. In addition, you feel your present job has put you on a plateau. Thus, you desperately want this new account not only for the bank's sake but also for the good of your career and Pat's.

You want Pat to personally handle the Acme effort, but you know that he is likely to have major reservations about taking the new account because of Acme's environmental record. You know that Pat feels strongly about the environment; in fact, you once bailed him out of jail after he was arrested in a pro-environment demonstration. Pat almost got fired because his arrest was filmed by a local television station. But you intervened with the CEO and saved Pat's job, arguing that what he did on his own time was not the company's concern. You still believe that, but you wonder: Where do we draw the line? Can an employee legitimately refuse to take an important assignment because of his or her beliefs?

If the Acme Chemical account is not landed because of Pat's personal feelings, the boss will not be so easily placated as he was when Pat was arrested. Meanwhile, you don't quite know how Pat will react. He may be outraged that you would even consider assigning the Acme account to him. Whatever his feelings, you need Pat to complete and manage the deal. But you don't want to order him to do so because he might quit, which would leave you and the company in a pickle. Pat could easily move to another bank, and you are concerned that he might because the environmental issue is so important to him. In any event, the time has come to talk to him.

Pat Jergen's Role.   You rose quickly at the bank from teller to corporate account manager. You know the banking business inside and out and have many contacts in the industry. You have been courted by other banks but you believe in loyalty and you like your job and you like West Oceans. You love the people there and are friendly with Carrie Makson, who helped smooth the waters some time back when you were arrested in an environmental protest. Carrie knows the depth of your commitment to the environment, knows that you ride a bicycle to work, recycle everything, and stay active in environmental politics.

You feel strongly that people need to make sacrifices for what they believe in; not to do so is hypocrisy. In your mind, the environment must come first. Believing that, you know that you sometimes need to take a stand or no one else will.

You've heard some rumors about Acme Chemical being wooed by West Oceans. You hope that doesn't happen, or if it does, that you aren't involved. That would surely put your principles to the test. But, meanwhile, Carrie has asked to see you. Could it be about that?

Total Time. 30 minutes (preparation, 10 minutes; role-play, 10 minutes; debriefing, 10 minutes)

OBSERVER'S RATING SHEET

Rate the actor playing Carrie Makson on the application of ethical decision-making skills using the following scale. Write concrete examples in the spaces between the behavioral skills to use in explaining your feedback.

1	2	3	4	5
Unsatisfactory	**Weak**	**Adequate**	**Good**	**Outstanding**

_____ Defined the ethical issues.

_____ Gathered all pertinent information and sought opinions from others.

_____ Considered all consequences for all affected parties.

_____ Adhered to their organization's policy on ethics.

_____ Generated creative alternatives.

_____ Kept promises, agreements, and other commitments.

_____ Acted in an honest, truthful, and open manner.

_____ Respected the rights of others and dealt fairly with all parties.

_____ Acted as a responsible member of the community.

_____ Took ethical stands.

Group Exercise 2: Mini-Cases[11]

Instructions. Form groups of four to six people. Discuss each of the following mini-cases and arrive at a consensus on the best ethical courses of action for each one. Although some cases have more than one satisfactory solution, and others have no good solutions, you must limit your choices to the options presented. After you have made your decisions, prepare to present and defend them to the class.

Mini-Case 1. You work for a defense contractor that has apparently made a successful bid for a big project. Final approval has gotten bogged down in the government bureaucracy, though it is likely the funds will be allocated; the question is when. You feel you need to get started in order to meet the tight deadline. You start negotiating with a supplier. You decide to tell the supplier:

    a. "Approval is imminent. It is an important deal that will benefit us both in the long run. So, like us, you need to shoulder your share of the startup costs between now and when the contract is okayed. So let's get going on preliminary work without a contract."
    b. "The program is a 'go.' I'll spare you the details."
    c. "Start work now and we will cover your costs when we get the contract."
    d. "The program is almost certain to be approved. Let's quickly put together an interim contract to cover us on the first, tentative phase of the work."

Mini-Case 2. Office supplies are disappearing from the stockroom almost as soon as they're brought in. You're told unofficially that two subordinates, who are well paid and should know better, are taking them for their children's school. Should you

    a. lock up the supplies and issue them only as needed and signed for?
    b. tell the two suspected pilferers that supplies are for office use only?
    c. install video cameras to monitor the stockroom to get proof?
    d. send a reminder to all employees that supplies are for office use only and that disregard for this rule could result in disciplinary action?

Mini-Case 3. Your operation is being relocated. The personnel regulations governing moving expenses, mileage reimbursement, and storage of personal goods are so complex that you fear they may dissuade your "team" from making the move. Relocating without your experienced staff would be difficult for you. Do you

    a. tell the staff the regulations are so complex that you can't go into them now but assure them that everything will work out all right in the end?
    b. not mention the regulations but instead stress the excitement of the move and the importance of the team remaining intact?
    c. present them with a highly simplified version of the regulations and encourage them to come along?
    d. give them a complete copy of the regulations and promise to work with them to get the answers they need?

Mini-Case 4. You make the low bid on an electronics system for the U.S. Army. However, because of staffing problems, you believe it will take you several months longer than your competitor to build the system. When the army asks for further details on the schedule before deciding to whom to award the contract, you

    a. say your schedule will be "essentially the same" as what you believe your competitor's would be?

    b. predict you will complete the job as quickly as your competitor, then tell your engineers they must do it faster than they say it can be done?

    c. sidestep the time issue and instead stress the quality of your firm's work?

    d. admit that your people say you won't meet the competitor's schedule even though you suspect this revelation may cause you to lose points on the evaluation?

Mini-Case 5.   A friend of yours wants to transfer to your division. He is loyal and hardworking, if not exceptionally talented, employee. You have an opening, and one other candidate, whom you do not know, has applied. Do you

    a. select the friend in whom you have confidence?

    b. select the other person, whom you are told is qualified?

    c. request a qualifications comparison from human resources?

    d. ask human resources to extend the search for additional candidates before choosing?

Total Time.   2 hours (presentation of each case, 4 minutes; discussion of each case, 20 minutes)

Group Exercise 3: Anticipating Ethical Conflict

Instructions.   Break into groups of four to five students and study the following situation. Your task is to answer the questions at the end of the case. When you are finished, compare results with the other groups.

Situation.   Jessica has filled an entry-level sales position at Myers Equipment for about 18 months. Her performance has been exceptional. Anna, the inside sales manager and Jessica's supervisor, knows that Jessica is ambitious, a hard worker, and a widowed mother of three who is devoted to her children and gives all her off-hours attention to her family. Anna knows that Jessica not only needs more money but also deserves a promotion.

But the only job opening on the horizon is in outside sales in another unit, which Anna does not supervise. If Anna talked to the outside sales manager about Jessica's work, Jessica would probably get the job. That would be just. It would also make Jessica happy and help her to better provide for her family.

That outside sales slot normally is filled by a more experienced salesperson, although Anna thinks Jessica would grow into the job. However, Anna has other concerns. For one, the new job would put Jessica in with a group of other experienced and extremely competitive salespeople. Anna believes that unit is productive but not well supervised, and she has heard rumors that some outside salespeople use dubious methods to meet their goals. There reportedly have been complaints from customers to the company about the outside sales crew, but nothing has been done because the outside sales force is highly regarded by upper management because of its sales volume. But Anna feels that Jessica, who is young and somewhat naive, would find her peers there to be poor role models with questionable ethics. In turn, Jessica's ethics might be affected.

Anna also fears Jessica would feel intense pressure because of the highly competitive nature of outside sales. Sales goals there are high, and so is the peer pressure as well as management pressure to do whatever it takes to meet those goals.

Jessica has been ethical in all her actions so far. But Anna is worried that in any major conflicts in the new job, Jessica may be tempted to act unethically because of what she observes in her colleagues, the pressure to produce, and the needs of her family.

Jessica, for her part, does not yet know about the opening in outside sales. She knows only that she deserves a break and desperately needs more money. When Anna summons Jessica to her office to talk about this promotion possibility, Jessica hopes that her big chance has come at last.

Questions

1. What questions should Anna ask of Jessica?
2. What questions should Jessica ask of Anna?
3. What safeguards could Anna insist on as a way of protecting Jessica from acting unethically?
4. What could Jessica ask for to reduce the likelihood that time and competitive pressures would be too intense?
5. Does Anna have any options besides promoting Jessica to outside sales or not doing so?
6. In what ways could others help?

Total Time. 45 minutes (preparation, 10 minutes; group discussion, 15 minutes; class discussion, 20 minutes)

Summary Checklist

Take a few minutes to reflect on your performance in the preceding exercises. Assess how your analysis compared to other students (and if you were an actor, how others rated your skills). Make a check (✓) next to those behaviors on which you may need improvement.

I understand defined ethical issues.   _____

I gather all pertinent information and seek opinions from others.   _____

I consider all consequences for all affected parties   _____

I adhere to my organization's policy on ethics   _____

I generate creative alternatives.   _____

I keep promises, agreements, and other commitments.   _____

I act in an honest, truthful, and open manner.   _____

I respect the rights of others and deal fairly with all parties.   _____

I act as a responsible member of the community.   _____

I take ethical stands.   _____

APPLICATION QUESTIONS

1. Describe an ethical situation you've faced recently. How did you handle it? Would you handle it any differently now? How? Why?
2. What questions will you ask yourself when you next encounter an ethical dilemma?

3. Think about managers for whom you worked. Which did you think were highly ethical and which were not? What makes you say this? Did they act differently in similar situations? Why or why not?

REINFORCEMENT EXERCISES

The following are suggested activities for reinforcing the application of ethical guideposts described in this chapter. You may want to adapt them to the Action Plan you will develop next, or try them independently.

1. Check the newspapers and business periodicals for news of a controversial business decision—closing a plant or disciplining an employee for some infraction, for example. List the various alternatives that might have been available and the ethical guideposts that should apply.
2. When your class or school has a speaker or guest lecturer from the business community, ask him or her to describe the kinds of ethical dilemmas faced in his or her business and how they are resolved.
3. When you interview with a corporate recruiter, ask if the firm has a code of ethics and/or ethics training and, if appropriate, to see a copy of the code or a training syllabus.
4. Ask your friends and/or relatives what kinds of ethical situations they run into in their jobs and how they handle them.
5. Search the Internet for company Web sites of interest to you. See whether you can find a published code of ethics for the company. What does that tell you?

ACTION PLAN

1. Which ethical behaviors do I want to improve the most?

2. Why? What will be my payoff?

3. What potential obstacles stand in my way?

4. What are the specific things I will do to improve? (For examples, see the Reinforcement Exercises.)

5. When will I do them?

6. How and when will I measure my success?

Endnotes

1. Adapted from A. Reichel and Y. Neumann, "Attitude Towards Business Ethics Questionnaire," *Journal of Instructional Psychology* (March 1988), pp. 25–33.
2. K. Davis and W. C. Frederick, *Business and Society: Management, Public Policy, Ethics,* 5th ed. (New York: McGraw-Hill, 1984), p. 76.
3. G. Dessler, *Management: Leading People and Organizations in the 21st Century* (Upper Saddle River, NJ: Prentice Hall, 1998), p. 78.
4. T. Kelly, "Ethics Officers Guide Workers to Right Choices," *New York Times News Service* report in *San Diego Union-Tribune* (March 3, 1998), p. C2.
5. K. Durham, "Right and Wrong: What's Ethical in Business? It Depends on When You Ask," *Wall Street Journal* (January 11, 1999), p. R48.
6. Adapted from L. K. Trevino and K. A. Nelson, *Managing Business Ethics: Straight Talk About How to Do It Right* (New York: John Wiley & Sons, 1995), pp. 71–75.
7. Lynn S. Paine, "Ethics: A Basic Framework" (Boston, MA: Harvard Business School Publishing, May 15, 2007).
8. T. Donaldson, "Values in Tension: Ethics Away from Home," *Harvard Business Review* (September–October, 1996), pp. 48–62.
9. Adapted from R. J. Aldag and L. W Kuzuhara, *Organizational Behavior: A Skills-Based Approach* (Dubuque, IA: Kendal Hunt, 2009), pp. 31–13.
10. Adapted from J. R. Boatright, *Ethics and the Conduct of Business* (Upper Saddle River, NJ: Prentice Hall, 1993), p. 1.
11. Adapted from G. Sammet, Jr., *Gray Matters: The Ethics Game* (Orlando, FL: Martin Marietta Corporation, 1992).

19

...

Creative Problem Solving

SELF-ASSESSMENT EXERCISE: HOW CREATIVE ARE YOU?[1]

Circle the 10 words in the following list that best characterize you.

energetic	persuasive	observant	Fashionable	self-confident
Persevering	original	cautious	habit-bound	Resourceful
egotistical	independent	stern	Predictable	Formal
informal	dedicated	factual	open-minded	forward-looking
tactful	inhibited	enthusiastic	Innovative	Poised
acquisitive	practical	alert	Curious	Organized
unemotional	dynamic	polished	Courageous	clear-thinking
helpful	efficient	perceptive	Quick	self-demanding
good-natured	thorough	impulsive	Determined	Understanding
realistic	modest	involved	Flexible	absent-minded
sociable	well-liked	restless	Retiring	

Scoring and Interpretation

For each of the following adjectives that you circled, give yourself 2 points:

energetic	observant	courageous	dynamic
flexible	dedicated	enthusiastic	innovative
persevering	original	perceptive	self-demanding
resourceful	independent	curious	involved

For each of the following adjectives that you circled, give yourself 1 point:

thorough	determined	restless	informal	self-confident
alert	open-minded	forward-looking		

The rest of the adjectives receive no points.

Add up your total number of points:

16–20	Very creative
11–15	Above average
6–10	Average
1–5	Below average
0	Noncreative

SKILL CONCEPTS

Success in any endeavor depends on making the right decisions at the right times.[2] But decision making is just one component of the problem-solving process. Unless a problem has been accurately defined and its root causes have been identified, we are unlikely to make an appropriate decision about how to solve it. Effective problem solvers know how to gather and evaluate information to define and clarify a problem. They know the value of generating more than one action alternative and weighing all the implications of a plan before deciding to implement it. They acknowledge the importance of following through to make sure that changes are effective. This chapter explains how to be a creative problem solver by using the scientific problem-solving process, tapping into individual and group creativity, and applying quality-control techniques.

What Are the Steps for Interpersonal Problem Solving?

Problem solving is the process of eliminating the discrepancy between the actual and desired situation. Defined this way, a problem can be viewed as an opportunity for improvement. If approached with this positive mindset, we are much more likely to be motivated to creatively solve problems than to ignore or avoid them. To solve a problem we need to first become aware of it and acknowledge that it exists. Next, the problem needs to be defined and analyzed. Then alternative solutions need to be generated. Decision making—selecting the best solution from among feasible alternatives—comes next. Finally, the solution needs to be implemented. For optimal problem solving, social scientists advocate the use of the rational problem-solving approach outlined in Exhibit 19.1.[3]

Problem Awareness

Be on a constant lookout for existing or potential problems. Keep channels of communication open, monitor performance, and examine deviations from present plans as well as from past experience.[4] Becoming aware of interpersonal problems is not always easy, however. People may, for example, experience uncomfortable feelings with each other but be confused about what is going on and why. Other times people may hide problems from you because they fear that if they reveal them, you might reject them or think less highly of them.

ESTABLISH TRUST   To obtain active participation from others involved in a problem, you need to ensure that they feel understood and accepted. They need to have confidence that the problem can be resolved and they need to trust that you will see the problem as a learning experience and not as a reason for punishment.[5] People need to feel secure enough with you to acknowledge that a problem exists and to acknowledge their own contributions to it.

Problem Awareness
- Establish trust bond
- Clarify objectives
- Assess current situation
- Identify problems

Problem Definition
- Analyze problems
- Agree on problems to be solved

Decision Making
- Establish decision-making criteria
- Develop action alternatives
- Evaluate alternatives
- Decide on a plan

Action Plan Implementation
- Assign tasks and responsibilities
- Establish implementation schedule
- Reinforce commitment
- Activate the plan

Follow-Through
- Establish criteria for success
- Determine how to measure performance
- Monitor results
- Take corrective action

EXHIBIT 19.1   The Rational Problem-Solving Process.

CLARIFY OBJECTIVES   If you don't know what your objectives are in a relationship, it is difficult to know what your problems are, let alone what to do about them. Therefore, objectives must be set and clarified before a current situation can be assessed. Objectives provide guidelines for your behavior and bases for measuring the effectiveness of your relationship.

ASSESS THE CURRENT SITUATION   The goal of this step is to determine if your needs are being met by the current situation. Does the nature of the actual relationship match the desired one? If not, what are the differences? Mismatches usually show up clearly, but sometimes an inadequate current situation is taken for granted because it is how the relationship has been for so long. If the matching process reveals discrepancies, the next step is to determine why.

IDENTIFY PROBLEMS   Serious mistakes can be made if you react to relationship difficulties before you accurately identify all of the sources of a problem. To identify a problem accurately, it must be understood from all points of view. To get all the relevant information about a relationship problem, all parties must feel free to participate in its identification without fear of being blamed or criticized. If problem solving is perceived as a joint learning experience, people will be much more likely to contribute needed information than if they fear being blamed and punished if the information indicates they have made mistakes.

Problem Definition

If the problem is not defined clearly, any attempt at solving it will be doomed to fail because the parties involved won't really know what they are working on. All of the remaining steps will be distorted because they will be based on insufficient or erroneous information. Lack of information often inhibits the generation of adequate alternatives and the exploration of potentially negative consequences.

All necessary information should be gathered so that all relevant factors can be analyzed to determine the exact problem that must be solved. The goal is to determine the root causes of the problem. Causes should not be assumed; instead, all plausible alternatives should be investigated before settling on the most probable cause(s).

Hasty assumptions can also result in symptoms being mistaken for sources of problems. When symptoms are eliminated, it is often mistakenly assumed that the problem has also been eliminated. If a female worker in the accounting department resigns after only 2 months, it might be assumed that females can't handle the stress of financial statement deadlines, since the male employees have a low turnover rate. The source of the problem, however, may be that the male supervisor harasses female employees.

ANALYZE PROBLEMS   Making sure that the problem is defined accurately and analyzed completely provides a safeguard against incorrect assumptions, treatment of symptoms only, and incomplete understanding. The way a problem is actually defined has a major impact on what alternatives are considered, what decision is reached, and how the action plan is implemented. Failure to define an identified problem accurately can impede consideration and eventual application of the best solution.

Failure to thoroughly diagnose a problem can result from inadequate time and energy available to review all the possible causes and implications. Other times, underlying psychological reasons come into play, such as not wanting to know what the real problems are, fearing that we ourselves are to blame, being concerned that a close associate will be hurt, or anticipating that the problem will prove too enormous for us.

AGREE ON PROBLEMS TO BE SOLVED   If more than one problem has been identified, the next step is to set priorities regarding which problem will be worked on first and which ones will be put aside temporarily or indefinitely. One criterion for rank-ordering multiple problems is how much their solutions will contribute to desired objectives. The most important problems should be dealt with first, even if their solutions seem more difficult.

Decision Making

After the problem has been identified and analyzed, the next step is to develop a course of action that will improve the relationship to an acceptable state. Since there is usually more than one way to solve a problem, it is critical to keep open to all possible solutions and arrive at several alternatives from which to choose.

ESTABLISH DECISION-MAKING CRITERIA   Decision-making criteria are statements of objectives that need to be met for a problem to be solved. Effective criteria should be specific, measurable, attainable, complementary, ethical, and acceptable to those who will implement the decision.

DEVELOP ACTION ALTERNATIVES   Involving all concerned parties in the generation and analysis of alternatives enhances the value, acceptance, and implementation of an action plan. Soliciting feedback to determine if those involved understand the potential benefits and are ready to make the necessary commitment can test acceptance. As many solutions as possible should be generated to avoid picking a premature one that doesn't meet all the long-run criteria.

EVALUATE BENEFITS AND RISKS OF ALTERNATIVES   It is important to look at all the long-run consequences of the alternatives being considered. This is sometimes overlooked because of our tendency to avoid spending extra time and energy and our fear of discovering negative consequences in preferred solutions. Important criteria for evaluating action alternatives are each alternative's *probability of success* and the associated *degree of risk* that negative consequences will occur. If the chance of failure is high and the related costs for an alternative are great, the benefits may not justify its use. Risk can be personal as well as economic—just ask the person whose reputation is on the line or who is soon to undergo a performance review.

DECIDE ON A PLAN   As alternatives are evaluated according to these criteria, many will be clearly unsatisfactory and can be eliminated. Sometimes the evaluation will reveal that one alternative is decidedly superior to all others. At other times none of the proposed action plans will be acceptable, signaling a need to develop additional alternatives. Most often, however, several alternatives will appear feasible, and the best one must be selected. Exhibit 19.2 illustrates a decision-making grid that summarizes the criteria for evaluating alternatives. Such a grid can help visualize which alternative offers the maximum benefits with minimal risks and costs. The decision-making goal is to select the best solution alternative for solving the entire problem without creating any additional negative consequences for anyone else in the organization.

Action Plan Implementation

A decision and an action plan are of little value unless they are effectively implemented. How the action plan is to be accomplished connects the decision with reality. Implementation includes assigning tasks and responsibilities and establishing an implementation schedule.

ASSIGN TASKS AND RESPONSIBILITIES   It is important to clarify both verbally and in writing what each person involved will do to make the new action plan work. To avoid misunderstandings, it is essential to specify who is to do what, by when, and how.

Alternatives		Criteria					
	Benefits	Probability of Success	Costs	Risks	Consequences	Timing
Alternative A						
Alternative B						
Alternative C						

EXHIBIT 19.2   Decision-Making Grid.

ESTABLISH AN IMPLEMENTATION SCHEDULE   To be effectively implemented, all necessary tasks need a specified time schedule for completion. One way to do this is to start at an end point (the date by which the objective should be completed) and work backward. Action implementation steps can be listed in priority order and assigned reasonable time periods for completion, starting with the last step before the objective is accomplished.

Once an action plan is implemented, people often move on to another task. It is of key importance, however, to follow through to be sure that the solution is working effectively and that no additional problems have been created. Follow-through is the final stage of the problem-solving process.

Follow-Through

Following through entails the development and maintenance of positive attitudes in everyone involved in the implementation process. Several guidelines help to establish the positive climate necessary for the implementation steps that follow:

- Visualize yourself in the position of others who are implementing the plan so that you understand their feelings and perspectives.
- Establish sincere respect and concern.
- Make sure necessary resources are available.

After this positive climate has been established, there are several sequential steps in the follow-through process. They include establishing the criteria for measuring success, monitoring the results obtained, and taking corrective action when necessary.

ESTABLISH CRITERIA FOR MEASURING SUCCESS   Unless the circumstances have changed, the criteria for measuring problem-solving success are the time, quality, and quantity goals already developed in the action-planning stage. These criteria serve as *benchmarks* for measuring and comparing the actual results.

MONITOR THE RESULTS   Actual results should be compared with the established criteria. If the new performance meets the criteria, no further action is necessary other than continued monitoring. If the new results do not measure up, the next step is to determine why. Each implementation step may alter the problem situation in unanticipated ways.

TAKE CORRECTIVE ACTION   The problem-solving process is a *closed-loop system*. If performance fails to match the success criteria, the problem needs to be identified by again applying the problem-solving process. For any new corrective action plan, new measures and schedules need to be determined and new data need to be gathered and tested against the criteria.

HOW CAN CREATIVITY BE ENCOURAGED?

For people to creatively solve problems, they have to value new ideas and know how to deal with innovations when they are suggested. The Center for Creative Leadership has determined some of the characteristics of people who can generate creativity in their solutions to problems.[6] The brainstorming technique for stimulating creativity in groups is described in Exhibit 19.3.

To encourage creativity in others you must be willing to *absorb the risks* of failures. You need to allow other people freedom to experiment, expect some errors, and be willing to learn

> Brainstorming is a demonstrated approach for achieving high participation and increasing the number of action alternatives.[7] To engage in brainstorming sessions, people meet in small groups and feed off one another's ideas, which provide stimuli for more creative solutions. Rules for effective brainstorming are:
>
> - Form groups of five to seven people.
> - Different people spontaneously call out ideas, one idea at a time.
> - The goal is quantity and variety of ideas.
> - Be creative and don't worry about practicality—outlandish, far-fetched ideas can be tamed.
> - Don't criticize or evaluate ideas as they are generated.
> - Build on each other's ideas to make combinations and improvements.

EXHIBIT 19.3 Brainstorming.

Source: The brainstorming technique was originally developed by A. F. Osborn, *Applied Imagination* (New York: Scribners, 1957). It has been modified by others over the years.

from inevitable failures. People who are afraid of mistakes restrict the freedom of others to experiment and be creative.

You need to be able to live with *half-developed ideas.* You can't insist that an idea be 100 percent proven before supporting its implementation. You need to be willing to listen to and encourage others to press on with "half-baked" proposals that hold promise. Criticism can kill an innovation.

You need to have a feel for the times when it is best to *stretch normal policies* for the greater long-term good. If you never permit deviation from standard operating procedures, your relationship will make predictable progress and avoid some mistakes, but it will not obtain giant breakthroughs that calculated risk taking can promote.

You need to be a *good listener.* Active listeners try to pull out good ideas and build on suggestions. They do not try to impose their solutions on other people without listening to the other side first.

You *shouldn't dwell on mistakes* or hold the mistakes of others against them indefinitely. Be more future-oriented than past-oriented. Be willing to begin with the relationship as it is today and work for a better future. Learn from experience, but don't wallow in the past.

You should *trust your intuition.* When ideas are presented that seem right to you, be courageous enough to commit to implementing them on the spot without waiting for further opinions or advice.

If possible, try to be *enthusiastic and invigorating.* Encourage and energize others to try out new ideas and behaviors. Use your resources to facilitate others in making improvements.

CONCEPT QUIZ

Take the following 10-question, true–false quiz. Answers are at the end of the quiz. If you miss any, go back and find out why you got them wrong.

Circle the right answer.

True **False** 1. A problem exists whenever the actual situation is not what is desired.

True **False** 2. It is more important to thoroughly analyze a problem than to generate many solutions.

True **False** 3. Dwell on mistakes to enhance creativity.

True	False	4.	The problem-solving process is a closed-loop system.

True   False   4. The problem-solving process is a closed-loop system.

True   False   5. To identify a problem accurately, it must be understood from all points of view.

True   False   6. The last step in problem solving is deciding on the best solution to the problem.

True   False   7. To obtain active participation from others involved in a problem, they need to feel understood and accepted.

True   False   8. If the problem is not clearly defined, any attempt at solving it will be doomed to fail.

True   False   9. People may hide problems even if they want to solve them.

True   False   10. Objectives provide guidelines for measuring the effectiveness of your relationship.

Answers: (1) True; (2) True; (3) False; (4) True; (5) True; (6) False; (7) True; (8) True; (9) True; (10) True

BEHAVIORAL CHECKLIST

The following skills are important to creative problem solving. Use them when evaluating your own problem-solving skills and those of others.

The Creative Problem Solver:

- Establishes trust with involved people.
- Identifies all problems in a negative situation.
- Analyzes problem sources and consequences.
- Decides what to do after evaluating all alternatives.
- Implements the best action plan in a timely manner.
- Follows through by measuring results and taking corrective actions.
- Encourages creativity from participants.

ATTENTION!

Don't read the following exercises until assigned to do so by your instructor.

MODELING EXERCISE

Problems Everywhere[8]

Instructions. The entire class should read the following situation. Next, two people should volunteer to play the roles of Ricky and Lynn. They should read their own roles, but not the other person's role, and prepare for the role-play. The rest of the class will be observers and they should read both roles and then study the Observer's Rating Sheet for evaluating the role-play.

Actors. Lynn Bosco works in the blending department of a large pharmaceutical company. Ricky Thomas is Lynn's supervisor.

Situation.   Lynn works hard but recently can't concentrate very well on the task at hand. At the age of 45, Lynn was divorced after a 15-year marriage. Six months later, Lynn married a 23-year-old aerobics instructor. In the last 5 years, Lynn has twice bid for a higher-paying job elsewhere in the company. In both cases, Lynn was advised that she did not have the necessary educational qualifications for advancement into a skilled trade.

Lynn Bosco's Role.   Your mind is continually wandering to your debts. With easy credit, you have become a chronic borrower. This borrowing is not due to illness, rent payments, or any of the other common reasons people go into debt. You borrow for luxuries like the new Acura you just bought and the jet-ski boat you bought last year. You realize that your work is falling off somewhat but you are absolutely convinced you will get it straightened out soon.

Ricky Thomas's Role.   You have noticed that Lynn's work is beginning to deteriorate. The number of batches Lynn mixes per shift fell from 15 to 11 in the last 6 months, and on several occasions Lynn has scorched a batch. The last time you talked to Lynn about this slump, Lynn responded, "Everything is all right, I'm just a little untracked right now, I'll get it going again." Despite this assurance, however, Lynn's work has continued to be poor. You know about Lynn's bids for other jobs in the company and suspect the problems may be financial. Lynn has always been a good worker up to this point, and you want to keep her if possible. You feel that Lynn is not going to get over these problems without some help. You decide to call Lynn in and see if you can help.

Total Time. 30 minutes (preparation, 10 minutes; role-play, 15 minutes; debriefing, 5 minutes)

OBSERVER'S RATING SHEET

During the role-play, rate the actors' creative problem-solving skills using the following 1 to 5 scale (5 being the highest). Write concrete examples in the space for comments below each criterion skill to use in explaining your feedback during the debriefing.

1	2	3	4	5
Unsatisfactory	Weak	Adequate	Good	Outstanding

_____ Established trust with involved people.

_____ Identified all the problems in a negative situation.

_____ Analyzed problem sources and consequences.

_____ Decided what to do after evaluating all alternatives.

_____ Implemented the best action plan in a timely manner.

_____ Followed through by measuring results and taking corrective actions.

_____ Encouraged creativity.

GROUP EXERCISES

Three different types of group exercise are presented here. First is a short case for you to practice your conceptual problem-solving skills. Second is a role-play to practice your behavioral problem-solving skills in a conflict situation. Third is a brainstorming exercise to flex your creativity.

Group Exercise 1: Dealing with Academic Dishonesty[9]

Objective.   To apply the creative problem-solving process to a current situation familiar to participants.

Instructions.   All steps in this exercise can be conducted by the instructor with the entire class or autonomous groups can apply the process themselves.

Step 1 Read the following description of academic dishonesty.
Step 2 Form groups of five or six members and discuss the case questions in your groups.
Step 3 Groups share their solutions with the entire class.
Step 4 Groups analyze their application of the creative problem-solving process using the Observer's Rating Sheet.

The Problem of Academic Dishonesty.   Someday it will happen to every professor. A student will turn in such an excellent, well-written paper that its authenticity is in serious doubt. Or, during a test, the professor looks up and sees one student copying from another, or from crib notes lying on the floor. Studies show that about 40 percent of students cheat in a given term, and it isn't only the lazy student looking for a shortcut. In fact, overachievers are more likely to cheat than underachievers when a professor springs a test on them and they feel that they're losing control of their ability to prepare for class. For example, a student who is taking 16 course-hours, working 30 hours a week, and still trying to have a social life may not feel adequately prepared for a test and feel pressured to cheat. The question for professors is what to do about it.

It seems unthinkable that a professor would ignore students whispering answers to one another during a test, or obviously copying from crib notes, yet some admit that they frequently overlook such dishonesty. Although cheating rates are rising nationwide, many professors turn a blind eye to it because it puts them in the uncomfortable role of police officer instead of educator. Most universities' academic dishonesty policies scare professors with onerous, ambiguous regulations. Professors typically don't know what to expect of the policies and often avoid dealing with them. Many fear that complex legal proceedings will hurt their reputations and feel that it's their word against the student's. Others have trouble with the penalties. Some believe that lowering students' grades is unlikely to stop them from cheating again, but having them expelled from the university is too severe.

University administrators are worried about these faculty attitudes toward cheating, and some feel that "academic dishonesty is one of the most serious problems facing higher education today." They know that many professors are anxiety-ridden about it and believe that it is reducing the validity of the education students are receiving.

Students at universities with honor codes are much less likely to cheat than those at schools without such codes. Many students report that there is a confusing lack of set rules about what professors define as cheating, which makes cheating seem unimportant. Others, however, report that they rely on faculty to stop their classmates from cheating and express disappointment in the professors who let cheaters get away with it.

Questions

1. What types of student cheating behavior have you observed?
   a. How did you detect the cheating?
   b. Whose responsibility was it to control the cheating?
   c. Was the cheating dealt with? If so, how? If not, why not?
2. Apply the creative problem-solving process to develop an action plan to prevent the problem of academic cheating. Be prepared to present your plan to the class.

Total Time. 85 minutes (group problem solving, 30 minutes; class discussion, 30 minutes; analyzing the problem-solving process, 25 minutes)

Group Exercise 2: The Copying Machine[10]

Instructions.   Divide into trios. Read the situation. Decide who will be the two actors and the observer. The actors should read their roles, but not the other actor's role, and prepare for the role-play. The observer should read both roles and review the Observer's Rating Sheet in preparation for giving feedback at the end of the exercise.

Actors.   Rusty Buchanan (manager of client inquiries), Manny Caputo (manager of documentation)

Situation.   A problem has arisen with the use of the copying machine. In the last 2 weeks, members of two work units have been fighting for the use of the machine they share. Yesterday, the conflict erupted into an argument with yelling and name-calling between workers from each unit. Managers Rusty Buchanan and Manny Caputo have decided to meet and try to solve the problem. They have just entered the conference room, which they reserved for the next 15 minutes.

Rusty Buchanan's Role.   Your unit has extensive contact with the public. You have 10 workers who need to use the machine for routine documentation of their work. Most of the copies are photocopies of signed documents that must be returned to the signer. The original is filed.

Your unit's work is regular, not sporadic, and in the past workers made their single copies throughout the day and returned to their workstations. Your workers need access to the machine throughout the day.

Manny Caputo's Role.   Although your unit has less direct contact with the public, it is responsible for periodically mailing important documents to citizens throughout the state. You have three workers who use the machine for larger work orders.

They need 1–2 hours at a time to complete the copying. Your unit's workflow is sporadic and not predictable, but you have tight deadlines when you do get work.

Total Time. 35 minutes (preparation, 10 minutes; role-play, 15 minutes; debriefing, 10 minutes)

Group Exercise 3: How to Get a Date

Brainstorming groups are encouraged to be freewheeling and radical. Through use of a nonevaluative environment that is intentionally fun, brainstorming encourages involvement, enthusiasm, and a large number of solution alternatives.

Instructions.   Form groups of five to seven people. Complete tasks 1 and 2 below. Then share your solution with the class and discuss what you learned from the brainstorming process.

Task 1.   Take 10 minutes to brainstorm as many ways as you can for a new student on campus to get a date. The goal is quantity and variety of ideas. Assign one person to jot down the ideas on the board or a notepad. Make sure to adhere to the following rules: (1) Spontaneously call out ideas, one idea at a time; (2) be creative and don't worry about practicality; (3) do not criticize or evaluate; (4) build on each other's ideas.

Task 2.   Take 15 minutes to apply the rational problem-solving process in Exhibit 19.1. You have just finished generating a number of alternatives. Your goal now is to evaluate them and decide on the best dating strategy, a practical action plan, and a method for evaluating and enhancing your success.

Task 3.   The decision teams share the answers to the following questions with the class.

- How many ideas did you generate? What were the wildest ones?
- What was your best dating strategy?
- What was your practical action plan?
- What was your method for evaluating and enhancing your success?
- What did you learn about group problem solving?

Total Time. 45 minutes (preparation, 5 minutes; brainstorming, 10 minutes; problem solving, 15 minutes; class discussion, 15 minutes)

Summary Checklist

Take a few minutes to reflect on your performance and look over others' ratings of your creative problem-solving skills. Now assess yourself on each of the key learning behaviors. Make a check (✓) next to those behaviors on which you need improvement.

I establish trust with involved people.   _____

I identify all problems in a negative situation.   _____

I analyze problem sources and consequences.   _____

I decide what to do after evaluating all alternatives.   _____

I implement the best action plan in a timely manner.   _____

I follow through by measuring results and taking corrective actions.   _____

I encourage creativity from participants.   _____

APPLICATION QUESTIONS

1. Explain why it is so important to establish an atmosphere of trust when solving interpersonal problems. Can you cite situations in which you have not trusted others with whom you were involved in solving a problem? Compare these situations with situations in which you have felt trust. Have you ever felt that others distrusted your problem-solving efforts? Why?
2. What four purposes are served by clarifying objectives early in the problem-solving process? Whose objectives should be considered?

3. Explain this statement: "No problem solution can be better than the quality of diagnosis on which it is built."

4. With regard to selecting an action plan, indicate whether you agree or disagree with each of the following statements and why: (1) Experience is the best teacher. (2) Intuition is a helpful force. (3) Advice from others is always beneficial. (4) Experiment with several alternatives.

5. What difficulties might you anticipate when using the rational problem-solving process? Why? What additional difficulties might arise because of personal attributes? Which of these have you experienced? Explain. What were the consequences? How can these difficulties be avoided?

6. How can you encourage creative problem solving by others?

REINFORCEMENT EXERCISES

1. Ask several managers how they make decisions. Compare the answers you receive to the steps in the rational problem-solving model. Also, check the degree of participation that these managers use when other people are involved.

2. Ask some other people to help you solve a problem that you are concerned with. Get their ideas by applying the rational problem-solving model and techniques for enhancing creativity, such as brainstorming.

3. Help someone you know to creatively solve a problem they are having difficulty with by applying the creative problem-solving skills you have acquired from this chapter.

4. Watch a movie or television show, such as *Law and Order, CSI Miami, or Lie to Me*, in which the objective is to solve a crime. Note the problem-solving process that the characters apply and compare it to the creative problem-solving techniques you have learned about in this chapter. What did you learn from this comparison?

ACTION PLAN

1. Which creative problem-solving behavior do I want to improve the most?

2. Why? What will be my payoff?

3. What potential obstacles stand in my way?

4. What are the specific things I will do to improve? (For examples, see the Reinforcement Exercises.)

5. When will I do them?

6. How and when will I measure my success?

Endnotes

1. Copyright © 1981 Eugene Raudsepp. Adapted from *How Creative Are You?* (New York: Putnam, 1981), pp. 22–24.
2. B. M. Bass, *Organizational Decision Making* (Homewood, IL: Richard D. Irwin, 1983).
3. R. E. Archer, "How to Make a Business Decision: An Analysis of Theory and Practice," *Management Review* (February 1980), pp. 289–299.
4. W. F. Pounds, "The Process of Problem Finding," *Industrial Management Review*, Vol. 2 (Fall 1969), pp. 1–19.
5. P. L. Hunsaker and A. J. Alessandra, *The Art of Managing People* (New York: Simon & Schuster, 1986), pp. 224–226.
6. David Campbell, "Some Characteristics of Creative Managers," *Center for Creative Leadership Newsletter*, No. 1 (February 1978), pp. 6–7.
7. Based on A. F. Osborn, Applied Imagination (New York: Scribners, 1957).
8. Adapted from William C. Donaghy, *The Interview: Skills and Applications* (Glenview, IL: Scott, Foresman, 1984), pp. 299–300.
9. The case was prepared based on material appearing in Bridget Murray, "Are Professors Turning a Blind Eye to Cheating?" *APA Monitor* (January 1996), pp. 1, 42; Don McBurney, "Cheating: Preventing and Dealing with Academic Dishonesty," *APS Observer* (January 1996), pp. 32–35.
10. Adapted from Robert E. Quinn, Sue R. Faerman, Michael P. Thompson, and Michael R. McGrath, *Becoming a Master Manager* (New York: John Wiley & Sons, 1990), pp. 297–298.

20

■ ■ ■

Resolving Conflicts

SELF-ASSESSMENT EXERCISE: WHAT IS MY CONFLICT-MANAGEMENT STYLE?[1]

Indicate how often you do the following when you differ with someone by inserting the appropriate number after the statements. Answer as you actually do behave, not as you think you should behave.

5	4	3	2	1
Usually	Quite a bit	Sometimes	Occasionally	Seldom

When I differ with someone   *Points*

Set A:
1. I explore our differences, not backing down, but not imposing my view either. _____
2. I disagree openly and then invite more discussion about our differences. _____
3. I look for a mutually satisfactory solution. _____
4. Rather than let the other person make a decision without my input, I make sure I am heard and also that I hear the other person out. _____

Sum the points for questions 1–4 to get your **Set A score =** _____

Set B:
5. I agree to a middle ground rather than look for a completely satisfying solution. _____
6. I admit I am half wrong rather than explore our differences. _____
7. I have a reputation for meeting a person halfway. _____
8. I expect to get out about half of what I really want to say. _____

Sum the points for questions 5–8 to get your **Set B score =** _____

Set C:
9. I give in totally rather than try to change another's opinion. _____
10. I put aside any controversial aspects of an issue. _____
11. I agree early on, rather than argue about a point. _____
12. I give in as soon as the other party gets emotional about an issue. _____

Sum the points for questions 9–12 to get your **Set C score =** _____

Set D:
13. I try to win the other person over.   _____
14. I work to come out victorious, no matter what.   _____
15. I never back away from a good argument.   _____
16. I would rather win than end up compromising.   _____
Sum the points for questions 13–16 to get your **Set D score =**   _____

Set E:
17. I prefer to avoid the other person until the problem is solved.   _____
18. I would rather lose than risk an emotional confrontation.   _____
19. I feel that most differences are not worth worrying about.   _____
20. I try to postpone discussing the issue until I can think it through thoroughly. _____
Sum the points for questions 17–20 to get your **Set E score =**   _____

Scoring and Interpretation

Total your choices for each set of statements, grouped as follows:

     Set A: (items 1–4):   _____
     Set B: (items 5–8):   _____
     Set C: (items 9–12):   _____
     Set D: (items 13–16):   _____
     Set E: (items 17–20):   _____

Sets A, B, C, D, and E represent the following conflict-resolution strategies:

     A = Collaborating: I win, you win.
     B = Compromising: Both win some, lose some.
     C = Accommodating: I lose, you win.
     D = Competing/Forcing: I win, you lose.
     E = Avoiding: I lose, you lose.

Treat each set separately to determine your relative frequency of use.

- A score of **17 or above** on any set is **high**. When you differ with someone you do these things more often than most people.
- Scores of **8–16** are **moderate**. When you differ with someone you behave in these ways the same as most people.
- Scores of **7 or less** are considered **low**. When you differ with someone you behave in these ways less often than most people.

Everyone has a preferred or habitual conflict-handling style. High scores in a set indicate the strategies you rely on most often (i.e., use the most). Scores do not indicate proficiency at using a strategy. The key thing to consider when analyzing your conflict style is whether it is appropriate for the conflict situations you usually encounter with respect to the outcomes you desire. The five styles and their appropriate uses are explained in the following section on understanding the basic styles of handling conflicts.

SKILL CONCEPTS

Conflict is a natural phenomenon of organizational life, because organizational members have different goals and because organizations are made up of scarce resources. The forces that make politics endemic to organizations also act to create conflict. In addition, contemporary management practices increase the potential for conflict by emphasizing interdependence, coordination, and "we-versus-them" situations. Examples include matrix structures, task teams, participatory decision making, two-tier pay systems, and the restructuring of units to cut costs and increase efficiency. It's not surprising, then, that Tjosvold and Johnson[2] have found that "no skill is more important for organizational effectiveness than the constructive management and resolution of conflict."

Because conflict is natural to organizations, it can never be completely eliminated. That, of course, isn't necessarily bad. Conflict has some positive properties. It stimulates creativity, innovation, and change.[3] If organizations were completely devoid of conflict, they would become apathetic, stagnant, and unresponsive to change. Yet all conflicts are clearly not functional or constructive. When managers talk about conflict problems, they usually are referring to conflict's dysfunctional effects and how they can be resolved. Given this reality, even though conflict management encompasses conflict-stimulation and conflict-resolution techniques,[4] we limit our discussion in this chapter to conflict-resolution approaches and skills.

Resolving Conflicts Relies on Other Interpersonal Skills

Few interpersonal skills draw upon other interpersonal skills the way conflict resolution does. Specifically, resolving conflicts requires the use of goal-setting, listening, feedback, and persuasion skills.

We know that formal goals guide and motivate employees and provide standards against which job performances can be compared. However, they also prevent conflict by reducing ambiguity and sublimating personal interests to the larger goals of the organization. Goal setting establishes specific job-performance standards. These, in turn, make self-serving behaviors and dysfunctional conflicts more visible. As with politics, conflicts are more likely to grow and flourish in a climate of ambiguity, so goal setting lessens the need to use conflict-resolution skills.

Listening and feedback skills are central to effective communication. As we'll show, distortions in communication are a frequent source of interpersonal conflict. The use of listening skills to improve communication clarity and the use of feedback skills to improve accuracy of understanding act to reduce distortions in the communication process.

Finally, persuasion is an interpersonal skill that is closely tied to resolving conflicts. It's a means to get others to do what you desire when you don't have, or don't want to use, formal authority. When two or more parties in an organization disagree, you can use your persuasion skills to resolve their differences. In addition, effective negotiation depends on your ability to persuade others to reduce their demands and to see the merit in your offer.

Key Conflict Management Skills

To manage conflict effectively, you need to know yourself, as well as the conflicting parties; to understand the situation that has created the conflict; and to be aware of your options.

1. ***Determine your preferred conflict-handling style?***   As pointed out in Chapter 2, success in interpersonal relations begins with self-awareness. This appears to be especially true of conflict management. Most of us have the ability to vary our conflict response according to the situation, but each of us has a preferred style for handling conflicts.[5] The questionnaire you completed at the opening of this chapter was designed to identify your

basic conflict-handling style. Take another look at your results. You might be able to change your preferred style to suit the context in which a certain conflict occurs; however, your basic style tells you how you're most likely to behave and the conflict-handling approaches on which you most often rely.

2. ***Be judicious in selecting the conflicts that you want to handle.***   Every conflict doesn't justify your attention. Some might not be worth the effort; others might be unmanageable. Avoidance might appear to be a cop-out, but it can sometimes be the most appropriate response. You can improve your overall management effectiveness and your conflict-management skills in particular, by avoiding trivial conflicts. Choose your battles judiciously, saving your efforts for the ones that count.

   Regardless of our desires, reality tells us that some conflicts are unmanageable.[6] When antagonisms are deeply rooted, when one or both parties want to prolong a conflict, or when emotions run so high that constructive interaction is impossible, your efforts are unlikely to meet with much success, so don't be lured naively into believing that a good manager can resolve every conflict effectively. Some aren't worth the effort. Some are outside your realm of influence. Still others might be constructive and, as such, are best left alone.

3. ***Evaluate the conflict players.***   If you choose to manage a conflict situation, it's important that you take the time to get to know the players. Who is involved in the conflict? What interests does each party represent? What are each player's values, personality, feelings, and resources? Your chances of success in managing a conflict will be greatly enhanced if you're able to view the conflict situation through the eyes of the conflicting parties.

4. ***Assess the source of the conflict.***   Conflicts don't pop out of thin air; they have causes. Because your approach to resolving a conflict is likely to be largely determined by its causes, you need to determine the source of the conflict. Research indicates that although conflicts have varying causes, they generally can be separated into three categories: communication differences, structural differences, and personal differences.[7] Communication differences are those disagreements that arise from semantic difficulties, misunderstandings, and noise in the communication channels. People are often quick to assume that most conflicts are caused by lack of communication. As one author has noted, plenty of communication usually is going on in most conflicts. The mistake many people make is equating good communication with having others agree with their views.[8] That is, people assume that if others don't accept their position, a communication problem must exist. What might at first glance look like an interpersonal conflict based on poor communication is usually found, upon closer analysis, to be a disagreement based on different role requirements, unit goals, personalities, value systems, or similar factors. As a source of conflict for managers, poor communication probably gets more attention than it deserves.

   Organizations, by their very nature, are horizontally and vertically differentiated.[9] Management divides up tasks, groups common tasks into departments, sets up a hierarchy of authority to coordinate departments, and establishes rules and regulations to facilitate standardized practices among departments. This structural differentiation creates problems of integration. The frequent result is conflicts. Individuals disagree over goals, decision alternatives, performance criteria, and resource allocations. These conflicts, however, are not due to poor communication or personal animosities. Rather, they are rooted in the structure of the organization itself. The resources that people want—budgets, promotions, pay increases, additions to staff, office space, influence over decisions, and the like—are scarce, so they must be divided up. The creation of horizontal units (departments) and vertical levels (the management hierarchy) brings about efficiencies through specialization and coordination, but at the same time produces the potential for structural conflicts.

The third conflict source is personal differences. Conflicts can evolve out of individual idiosyncrasies and personal value systems. The chemistry between some people makes it hard for them to work together. Factors such as background, behavioral styles, education, experience, and training mold each individual into a unique personality with a particular set of values. The result is people who might be perceived by others as abrasive, untrustworthy, or strange. These personal differences can create conflict.

5. ***Know your options.***   Thomas[10] identified five conflict-resolution strategies: avoidance, accommodation, forcing, compromise, and collaboration. Each has particular strengths and weaknesses, and no one strategy is ideal for every situation. You should consider each strategy as a tool in your conflict-management "tool chest." Although you might be better at using some tools than others, the skilled manager knows what each tool can do and when it is likely to be most effective.

As we noted earlier, every conflict doesn't require an assertive action. Sometimes avoidance is the best solution—just withdrawing from the conflict or ignoring its existence. Avoidance is a desirable strategy when the conflict issue is trivial, when emotions are running high and time is needed to cool them down, or when the potential disruption from a more assertive action outweighs the benefits of resolution.

The goal of accommodation is to maintain harmonious relationships by placing another's needs and concerns above your own. You might, for example, yield to another person's position on an issue. This strategy is most viable when the issue under dispute isn't that important to you or when you want to build up credits for later issues.

In forcing, you attempt to satisfy your own needs at the expense of the other party. In organizations, this is illustrated most often by a manager using formal authority to resolve a dispute. Forcing works well when you need a quick resolution, on important issues where unpopular actions must be taken, and where commitment by others to your solution is not critical.

A compromise strategy requires each party to give up something of value. This is typically the approach taken by management and labor in negotiating a new labor contract. Compromising can be an optimum strategy when conflicting parties are about equal in power, when it is desirable to achieve a temporary solution to a complex issue, or when time pressures demand an expedient solution.

Collaboration is the ultimate win–win solution. All parties to the conflict seek to satisfy their interests. It is typically characterized by open and honest discussion among the parties, intensive listening to understand differences, and careful deliberation over a full range of alternatives to find a solution that is advantageous to all. Collaboration is the best conflict strategy when time pressures are minimal, when all parties seriously want a win–win solution, and when the issue is too important to be compromised.

6. ***Select the "best" option.***   Given that you're familiar with the options, how should you proceed? Start by looking at your preferred conflict-handling style. (See the Self-Assessment Exercise at the beginning of this chapter.) This makes you aware of the styles with which you feel most comfortable.

Next look at your goals. The best solution is closely intertwined with your definition of best. Three goals seemed to dominate our discussion of strategies: the importance of the conflict issue, concern over maintaining long-term interpersonal relations, and the speed with which you need to resolve the conflict. All other things being equal, if the issue is critical to the organization's or the unit's success, collaboration is preferred. If sustaining supportive relationships is important, the best strategies, in order of preference, are accommodation, collaboration, compromise, and avoidance. If it's crucial to resolve the conflict as quickly as possible, forcing, accommodation, and compromise—in that order—are preferred.

Lastly, you need to consider the source of the conflict. What works best depends, to a large degree, on the cause of the conflict.[11] Communication-based conflicts revolve around misinformation and misunderstanding. Such conflicts lend themselves to collaboration. In contrast, conflicts based on personal differences arise out of disparities between the parties' values and personalities. Such conflicts are most susceptible to avoidance because these differences are often deeply entrenched. When managers have to resolve conflicts rooted in personal differences, they frequently rely on forcing—not so much because it placates the parties, but because it works. The third category—structural conflicts—seems to be amenable to most of the conflict strategies.

This process of blending your personal style, your goals, and the source of the conflict should result in identifying the strategy or set of strategies most likely to be effective for you in any specific conflict situation.

CONCEPT QUIZ

The following 10-question, true–false quiz is based on the previous material. If you miss any of these questions, be sure to go back and find out why you got them wrong.

Circle the right answer.

True   **False**   1. All conflicts hinder organizational effectiveness.

True   **False**   2. Most people have the ability to vary their conflict response according to the situation.

True   **False**   3. Every conflict doesn't justify a manager's attention.

True   **False**   4. Some conflicts are unmanageable.

True   **False**   5. Most conflicts are caused by a lack of communication.

True   **False**   6. Research indicates that paying senior executives high salaries is a major source of conflict.

True   **False**   7. Accommodation requires each party to give up something of value.

True   **False**   8. Forcing is an effective strategy for resolving important issues where unpopular actions need to be implemented.

True   **False**   9. Collaboration is an effective strategy for arriving at an expedient solution under time pressures.

True   **False**   10. Collaboration has been consistently shown to be the most effective resolution strategy.

Answers: (1) False; (2) True; (3) True; (4) True; (5) False; (6) False; (7) False; (8) True; (9) False; (10) False

BEHAVIORAL CHECKLIST

Look for these behaviors when evaluating your own or others' skills at resolving conflicts.

Effective Conflict Resolution Requires:

- Dealing directly with the conflict.
- Assessing the source of the conflict.
- Empathizing with the conflicting parties.
- Using the appropriate conflict-handling style.
- Selecting the most appropriate conflict-resolution option.

ATTENTION!

Do not read the following until assigned to do so by your instructor.

MODELING EXERCISE

New Hire in an Old Culture

Instructions.   The entire class should read the following situation. Then two class members volunteer to act out the roles of Lee Lattoni and B. J. O'Malley. The role-players read their assigned roles only and prepare to explain their positions at the forthcoming meeting. Actors should *not* read the other person's role. The remainder of the class reads both roles and reviews the Observer's Rating Sheet. During the role-play, observers rate Lattoni's application of conflict-resolution skills using the Observer's Rating Sheet. Observers should also note what points Lattoni and O'Malley make and be prepared to suggest additional arguments and alternatives.

Actors.   Lee Lattoni and B. J. O'Malley

Situation.   Lee Lattoni supervises an eight-member cost-accounting department in a large metals-fabricating plant in Albuquerque, New Mexico. Lee was promoted about 6 months ago to this supervisory position after only a year as an accountant. It was no secret that Lee got the promotion predominantly because of education—Lee has a Master of Business Administration degree, whereas no one else in the department has a college degree. The department consists of eight chauvinistic, high-school-educated older males. Lee wants to hire a young female six units short of her bachelor's degree in accounting.

Lee Lattoni's Role.   Your transition to supervisor has gone smoothly; you've encountered little in the way of problems until now.

Business has been prospering at the plant for some time, and it has become apparent that you need an additional cost accountant in the department to handle the increased workload. In fact, it has been on your mind for more than a month. Department members have been complaining about the heavy workload. Overtime has become commonplace, and the large amount of overtime is adversely affecting your department's efficiency statistics. You don't think you'll have any trouble supporting your request for a new, full-time position with your boss.

The search for a new employee should be relatively hassle free, since you already have spotted someone you think can fill the slot nicely. The person you have in mind is currently working in the production control department of the plant.

Unofficially, you have talked with the production control supervisor and the plant's personnel director about moving Regina Simpson, a young clerk in production, into your department. Regina has been with the company for 8 months, has shown above-average potential, and is only six units shy of her bachelor's degree (with a major in accounting), which she has been earning at night at the state university. You're aware that the department currently is made up of older male employees. None of them has a college degree, and the attitude of most members is that advanced education is just a frivolous waste of time. They are a macho, raucous group who tell a lot of chauvinistic jokes but always get the job done well. You know through the grapevine that they get together every Tuesday night for their weekly poker game. You are aware that Regina could have a problem gaining acceptance in this group, but she is certainly a qualified candidate and deserving of the promotion.

You met with Regina earlier in the week and discussed the possibility that cost accounting will have a vacancy. Regina told you that she was interested in the position. After further discussion over lunch—all unofficially—you said that although you couldn't make any promises, you were prepared to recommend Regina for the job. However, you emphasized that it would be a week to 10 days before a final decision and an official announcement would be made.

You are in your office when B. J. O'Malley comes in. B. J. works for you as a cost accountant and has been at the plant for 26 years. You like B. J. but consider him close-minded and the most extreme of the chauvinistic old-timers. If Regina were to join the department, you would expect B. J. to be the least receptive. Why? B. J. was raised in a conservative, working-class family and you've heard him speak disparagingly about "college girls."

B. J. O'Malley's Role.   You are a cost accountant in the plant, working for Lee. You're 58 years old; you were raised in a conservative, working-class family. You have been working at the Albuquerque plant since it opened 26 years ago. You have heard rumors that Lee is planning to bring Regina Simpson, a young, inexperienced college student, into the department. You understand the need to hire another cost accountant—the workload has gotten too heavy and the department's overtime budget has gotten out of hand. But the department is made up of an established group of male employees. None of them has a college degree, and the attitude of most members is that advanced education is just a frivolous waste of time. They're a close-knit group—you've all worked together for years and even socialize together. For instance, the entire group has been getting together every Tuesday night for poker for more than 6 years. Your work group has a lot of fun, you tell a lot of chauvinistic jokes, and take breaks throwing darts at each month's *Playboy* centerfold, but the group always gets the job done properly and on time. You're concerned that Regina will cause problems for your group, and you believe there must be equally qualified and experienced males who could do the job better.

You believe that Lee should be sensitive to your feelings. You're not prejudiced; you just don't want to disturb the camaraderie and efficiency of your department. You want Lee to talk with all department members before making an appointment. You view the department as a close-knit, homogeneous group and you don't want to add any newcomer who won't fit in. In the back of your mind, you know that if all the department members get to vote on who joins the department, a young, inexperienced, female college student who probably will need constant hand holding is unlikely to be hired. However, you also know that if you don't speak up, no one else will. You're upset and have decided to go to Lee's office to let Lee know that you have no intention of working with an uppity, know-it-all college girl who probably doesn't know the first thing about cost accounting.

Total Time. 25 minutes (preparation, 5 minutes; role-play, 10 minutes; debriefing, 10 minutes)

OBSERVER'S RATING SHEET

Evaluate Lee Latoni's conflict-resolution skills on a 1 to 5 scale (5 being the highest). Enter comments in the spaces between checklist behaviors to explain your ratings.

Deals directly with the conflict.   _____

Ascertains the source of the conflict.   _____

Empathizes with the conflicting parties.   _____

Uses the appropriate conflict-handling style.   _____

Selects the most appropriate conflict-resolution option.   _____

GROUP EXERCISES

Group Exercise 1: Crisis at Beacon Lights[12]

Instructions.   Divide into groups of three. One person is to play Jan, the manager. Another plays Chris, the secretary. The third observes. Everyone, including Chris, should read Jan's role, but Jan is not to read Chris's role.

Actors.   Jan and Chris

Jan's Role.   You have been director of personnel for Beacon Lights for 10 years. Just when you thought you had your job down pat, the sky fell in. A strong labor union has been trying to organize your plant, the federal government recently filed a claim against your company for discriminatory hiring practices, the president and vice president of sales were forced to resign last month because of the company's poor performance, and on top of all that, your long-time secretary just died of a heart attack.

A month ago, you hired Chris to replace your secretary. Chris has 2 years of secretarial experience, so you could save some salary money and you think that Chris should have no difficulty picking up the pieces. Chris asked for some temporary help recently, but you can't afford it right now and told her you would keep her informed about the more urgent items you want her to concentrate on first. Your former secretary had no problems getting the job done, and you don't expect that Chris will either.

You have been asked to give a talk at a national convention on a new productivity program your company has pioneered, and you are looking forward to getting away from the office for a few days to catch your breath. You gave your talk to your new secretary, Chris, a couple of days ago so Chris would have plenty of time to get it typed and reproduced.

This morning, you have come into the office to proofread and rehearse your talk prior to catching a plane this evening, and you are shocked to find a note saying your secretary called in ill this morning. You rush over to her desk and frantically begin searching for your paper. You find it mixed in with some material for the quarterly report that should have been sent in 2 weeks ago, a stack of overdue correspondence, and 2 days' worth of unopened mail.

As you dial your secretary's home phone number, you realize that you are perspiring heavily and your face is flushed. This is the worst foul-up you can remember in years.

Chris's Role.   You hear the phone ring, and it is all you can do to get out of bed and limp into the kitchen to answer it. You feel rotten. On the way home last night, you slipped on your son's skateboard in the driveway and sprained your knee. You can hardly move today and the pain is excruciating. You are also a bit hesitant to answer the phone because you figure it is probably your boss, Jan, calling to chew you out for getting behind in your work. You know you deserve some blame, but it wasn't all your fault. Since you began working for Jan a month ago, you have asked several times for a thorough job description. You feel you don't understand Jan's priorities or your specific job responsibilities. You are replacing a woman who died suddenly after working for Jan for 10 years. You were hired to pick up the pieces, but you have found working with Jan extremely frustrating. She has been too busy to train you properly, and she assumes you know as much about the job as your predecessor did. This is particularly a problem because you haven't worked as a secretary for 3 years, and you feel a bit rusty.

Jan's talk is a good example of the difficulties you have experienced. She gave you the talk a couple of days ago and said it was urgent—but that was on top of a quarterly report that was already overdue and a backlog of correspondence, filing, and so forth. You never filled out a report like this before, and every time you asked Jan a question, she said she'd discuss it with you later—as she ran off to a meeting. When you asked if it would be possible to get some additional help to catch up on the overdue work, Jan said the company couldn't afford it because of poor sales. This irked you because you knew you were being paid far less than your predecessor. You knew Jan faced some urgent deadlines, so you had planned to return to the office last night to type Jan's speech and try to complete the report, but 2 hours in the emergency room at the hospital put an end to that plan. You tried calling Jan to explain the problem, only to find out she has an unlisted number.

You sit down and prop up your leg, wincing with pain as you pick up the phone.

Total Time. 30–45 minutes (preparation, 10 minutes; role-play, 10–15 minutes; debriefing, 10 minutes)

OBSERVER'S RATING SHEET

Evaluate Jan's conflict-resolution skills on a 1 to 5 scale (5 being the highest). Enter comments in the spaces between checklist behaviors to explain your ratings.

Deals directly with the conflict.   _____

Ascertains the source of the conflict.   _____

Empathizes with the conflicting parties.   _____

Uses the appropriate conflict-handling style.   _____

Selects the most appropriate conflict-resolution option.   _____

Group Exercise 2: MIS Mumbo Jumbo[13]

Actors.   Jerry and Forrest

Situation.   The product-marketing teams at Salvo, a designer of computer software programs, enjoy developing point-of-sale demo tapes of their new games or programs for use in dealer stores, and the dealers love them. They are filled with sound and color and clever graphics and are successful as a sales tool. The sales staff members use them as demos when they make sales calls and then leave them with the store owners when they make the sale. The marketing people work up an outline for the tapes, based on the product content, and then submit them to a development team member in management information systems to work out displays and graphics before the sound is added and the videotapes are recorded.

It is a complex relationship, but the results have been highly successful. Jerry, in marketing, submitted an outline of a new videotape to Forrest for development. He received a highly technical memo from Forrest in return, explaining why the project wouldn't work as presented. Jerry is accustomed to working closely with his MIS counterparts, and he can't understand why he got a memo instead of a phone call. Furthermore, he can't understand the memo. He decides to go to Forrest's office to straighten things out.

Jerry's Role.   Jerry is energetic, has a good sense of humor, and has a demanding taste for excellence. Jerry knows what a computer can do but is not a programmer or a technician. Jerry is dependent on an MIS counterpart to translate concepts and schedules into working and exciting displays and graphics.

Forrest's Role.   Forrest is new at Salvo and has been assigned to Jerry. Forrest is one of the real experts on computer language and systems, having worked in all of them. For the last 2 years, Forrest was a teacher at a university and has had a difficult time abandoning the teacher image. Forrest spends some time with the other programmers, teaching them the history and usage of systems and computer language (even though they might not use this information at Salvo). He also delights in developing totally new programs to process already-running assignments. Forrest talks and writes in technical language and has great difficulty communicating clearly with nonsystems people. Unfortunately, this attitude, more often than not, comes off as condescending, because Forrest seems incapable of speaking English to other people, preferring to discuss a problem or project in computerese.

Both employees' objective is the same: to carry out the tasks assigned by their managers without disruptive confrontation.

Jerry appears at Forrest's door.

Total Time. 30–45 minutes (preparation, 10 minutes; role-play, 10–15 minutes; debriefing, 10 minutes)

OBSERVER'S RATING SHEET

Evaluate Jerry's conflict-resolution skills on a 1 to 5 scale (5 being the highest). Enter comments in the spaces between checklist behaviors to explain your ratings.

Deals directly with the conflict. _____

Ascertains the source of the conflict. _____

Empathizes with the conflicting parties. _____

Uses the appropriate conflict-handling style. _____

Selects the most appropriate conflict-resolution option. _____

Group Exercise 3: What's the Right Conflict-Management Style?[14]

Instructions. Form groups of three to five members. Each group member is to begin by independently ranking the five alternative courses of action in each of the following four incidents. You are to rank the responses from the most desirable or appropriate way of dealing with the conflict situation to the least desirable. Rank the most desirable course of action "1," the next most desirable "2," and so on, with the least desirable or least appropriate action ranked as "5." Enter your rank for each item in the space next to each choice. Next, identify the conflict style being used with each of the possible courses of action (e.g., forcing, accommodation, avoidance, compromise, or collaboration).

After each person has done this for all four incidents, group members are to compare their answers. Begin with Incident 1. Do you all agree? If not, discuss. Be prepared to defend why you answered as you did. You might want to change your answer as a result of the discussion. After completion of Incident 1, do the same with Incident 2, and so on. Confine the analysis and discussion of each incident to 10 minutes or less.

Incident 1. Pete is lead operator of a production molding machine. Recently, he has noticed that one of the men from another machine has been coming over to his machine and talking to one of his men (not on break time). The efficiency of Pete's operator seems to be falling off, and some rejects have resulted from his inattention. Pete thinks he detects some resentment among the rest of the crew. If you were Pete, you would

a. talk to your man and tell him to limit his conversations during on-the-job time.
b. ask the foreman to tell the lead operator of the other machine to keep his operators in line.
c. confront both men the next time you see them together (as well as the other lead operator, if necessary), find out what they are up to, and tell them what you expect of your operators.
d. say nothing now; it would be silly to make a big deal out of something so insignificant.
e. try to put the rest of the crew at ease; it is important that they all work well together.

Incident 2. Sally is the senior quality control (QC) inspector and has been appointed group leader of the QC people on her crew. On separate occasions, two of her people have come to her with different suggestions for reporting test results to the machine operators. Paul wants to send the test results to the foreman and then to the machine operator, because the foreman is the person ultimately responsible for production output. Jim thinks the results should go directly to the lead operator on the machine in question, because the lead operator is the one who must take corrective action as soon as possible. Both ideas seem good, and Sally can find no ironclad procedures in the department on how to route the reports. If you were Sally, you would

a. decide who is right and ask the other person to go along with the decision (perhaps establish it as a written procedure).
b. wait and see; the best solution will become apparent.
c. tell Paul and Jim not to get uptight about their disagreement; it is not that important.
d. get Paul and Jim together and examine both of their ideas closely.
e. send the report to the foreman and a copy to the lead operator (even though it might mean a little more copy work for QC).

Incident 3. Ralph is a module leader; his module consists of four complex, expensive machines and five crew members. The work is exacting, and inattention or improper procedures could cause a costly mistake or serious injury. Ralph suspects that one of his men is taking drugs on the job, or at least is showing up for work under the influence of drugs. Ralph feels he has some strong indications, but he knows he does not have a case. If you were Ralph, you would

a. confront the man outright, tell him what you suspect and why, and let him know that you are concerned for him and for the safety of the rest of the crew.
b. ask that the suspected offender keep his habit off the job; what he does on the job is part of your business.
c. not confront the individual right now; it might either turn him off or drive him underground.
d. give the man the "facts of life"; tell him it is illegal and unsafe to use drugs, and that if he gets caught, you will do everything you can to see that he is fired.
e. keep a close eye on the man to see that he is not endangering others.

Incident 4.   Gene is foreman of a production crew. From time to time in the past, the product development section tapped the production crews for operators to augment their own operator personnel to run test products on special machines. This put little strain on the production crews, because the demands were small, temporary, and infrequent. Lately, however, the demand for four production operators seems almost constant. The rest of the production crew must fill in for these missing people, usually by working harder and taking shorter breaks. If you were Gene, you would

a. let it go for now; the crisis probably will be over soon.
b. try to smooth things over with your own crew and with the development foreman; we all have jobs to do and cannot afford a conflict.
c. let development have two of the four operators they requested.
d. go to the development supervisor or his or her foreman and talk about how these demands for additional operators could best be met without placing production in a bind.
e. go to the supervisor of production (Gene's boss) and get him or her to "call off" the development people.

Total Time. 40 minutes (discussion, 10 minutes per incident)

Summary Checklist

On the basis of your experiences and observations, assess yourself on each of the key learning behaviors. Make a check (✓) next to those behaviors in which you think you need improvement.

I deal directly with conflicts.   _____

I ascertain the conflict's source.   _____

I try to empathize with the conflicting parties.   _____

I try to apply the appropriate conflict-handling style.   _____

I try to resolve the conflict most appropriately for the specific person   _____
and situation.

APPLICATION QUESTIONS

1. Most people dislike conflict because it is dysfunctional. Do you agree or disagree? Why?
2. When is conflict likely to hinder an organization? When can it help?
3. Is conflict inevitable in organizations? Why?
4. What are the key steps in diagnosing a conflict situation?

REINFORCEMENT EXERCISES

1. Describe, in detail, three recent interpersonal conflicts you have experienced. How did your basic conflict-handling style influence your actions? To what degree do you believe your conflict style is flexible? The next time you find yourself in a conflict situation, (a) be sure to recall your basic conflict style; (b) consider its appropriateness to this specific situation; and (c) if inappropriate, practice exhibiting more appropriate conflict-resolution behavior.
2. Think of a recent conflict you had with a colleague, friend, or relative. What was the source of the conflict? What goals did you seek? How did you handle the conflict? Was it resolved consistently with your goals? Were there other ways of handling this conflict that might have been more effective?
3. Take the role of a third-party consultant for an individual or a group involved in a conflict. Advise the party/parties as to their options. Note how your advice works.

ACTION PLAN

1. Which behavior do I want to improve the most?

2. Why? What will be my payoff?

3. What potential obstacles stand in my way?

4. What specific things will I do to improve? (For examples, see the Reinforcement Exercises.)

5. When will I do them?

6. How and when will I measure my success?

Endnotes

1. Adapted from T. J. Von der Embse, *Supervision: Managerial Skills for a New Era* (New York: Macmillan, 1987); Ralph H. Kilmann and Kenneth W. Thomas, "Developing a Forced-Choice Measure of Conflict Handling Behavior: The MODE Instrument," *Educational and Psychological Measurement* (Summer 1977), pp. 309–325.

2. Dean Tjosvold and David W. Johnson, *Productive Conflict Management: Perspectives for Organizations* (New York: Irvington Publishers, 1983), p. 10.

3. Stephen P. Robbins, "'Conflict Management' and 'Conflict Resolution' Are Not Synonymous Terms," *California Management Review* (Winter 1978), pp. 67–75.

4. Ibid.

5. Ralph H. Kilmann and Kenneth W. Thomas, "Developing a Forced-Choice Measure of Conflict Handling Behavior: The MODE Instrument," *Educational and Psychological Measurement* (Summer 1977), pp. 309–325.

6. Leonard Greenhalgh, "Managing Conflict," *Sloan Management Review* (Summer 1986), pp. 45–51.

7. Stephen P. Robbins, *Managing Organizational Conflict: A Nontraditional Approach* (Englewood Cliffs, NJ: Prentice Hall, 1974).

8. Charlotte O. Kursh, "The Benefits of Poor Communication," *Psychoanalytic Review* (Summer–Fall 1971), pp. 189–208.

9. Stephen P. Robbins, *Organization Theory: Structure, Design, and Applications,* 2nd ed. (Englewood Cliffs, NJ: Prentice Hall, 1987).

10. Kenneth W. Thomas, "Conflict and Conflict Management," in Marvin Dunnette (ed.), *Handbook of Industrial and Organizational Psychology* (Chicago, IL: Rand McNally, 1976), pp. 889–935.

11. Stephen P. Robbins, *Managing Organizational Conflict: A Nontraditional Approach* (Englewood Cliffs, NJ: Prentice Hall, 1974).

12. David A. Whetton and Kim S. Cameron, *Developing Management Skills*, 2nd ed. (New York: HarperCollins, 1991), pp. 438–439. Reprinted by permission.

13. Adapted from Mary Jean Parson, *An Executive's Coaching Handbook*, Copyright © 1986 by Mary Jean Parson. Reprinted with permission of Facts on File, Inc., New York.

14. Adapted from A. Zoll III, *Explorations in Managing* (Reading, MA: Addison-Wesley Publishing Company, Inc., 1974). Based on a format suggested by Allen A. Zoll III. Reprinted with permission.

21

■ ■ ■

Negotiating

SELF-ASSESSMENT EXERCISE: HOW DO I NEGOTIATE?

For each of the following statements, indicate your degree of agreement or disagreement by circling one of the five responses.

SA = Strongly Agree	D = Disagree
A = Agree	SD = Strongly Disagree
U = Undecided	

_____ **1.**	I believe everything is negotiable.	SA	A	U	D	SD
_____ **2.**	In every negotiation, someone wins and someone loses.	SA	A	U	D	SD
_____ **3.**	I try to get as much information as possible about the other party prior to negotiation.	SA	A	U	D	SD
_____ **4.**	The other party's initial offer shapes my negotiating strategy.	SA	A	U	D	SD
_____ **5.**	I try to open negotiations with a positive action such as offering a small concession.	SA	A	U	D	SD
_____ **6.**	I build an image of success by focusing on winning as much as possible in every bargaining situation.	SA	A	U	D	SD

Scoring and Interpretation

For questions 1, 3, and 5, give yourself 5 points for SA, 4 points for A, 3 points for U, 2 points for D, and 1 point for SD. For questions 2, 4, and 6, reverse the scoring; that is, give yourself 1 point for SA, 2 points for A, and so forth.

A score of 25 or above suggests that you have a basic understanding of how to be an effective negotiator. Scores of 19–24 indicate that you have room for improvement. Those who scored 18 or less should find the following discussion and exercise valuable for improving their negotiating effectiveness.

SKILL CONCEPTS

What is negotiation? It's a process in which two or more parties exchange goods or services and attempt to agree upon the exchange rate for them. For our purposes, we also use the term *negotiation* interchangeably with bargaining.

Lawyers and car salespersons spend a lot of time negotiating. So do managers: They have to negotiate salaries for incoming employees, cut deals with superiors, bargain over budgets, work out differences with associates, and resolve conflicts with subordinates.

Bargaining Strategies

The two general approaches to negotiation are distributive bargaining and integrative bargaining.

Suppose you see a used car advertised for sale in the newspaper. It appears to be just what you've been looking for so you go to see the car. It's great and you want it. The owner tells you the asking price, but you don't want to pay that much. The two of you then negotiate over the price. The negotiating process you are engaging in is called distributive bargaining. Its most distinctive feature is that it operates under zero-sum conditions. That is, any gain one makes is at the other's expense, and vice versa. Every dollar you can get the seller to cut from the car's price is a dollar you save. Conversely, every dollar more that the seller can get from you comes at your expense. Thus, the essence of distributive bargaining is negotiating over who gets what share of a fixed pie.

Figure 21.1 depicts the distributive bargaining strategy. Parties A and B represent the two negotiators. Each has a target point that defines what they would like to achieve. Each also has a resistance point, which marks the lowest outcome that is acceptable—the point below which the person would break off negotiations rather than accept a less favorable settlement. The area between their resistance points is the settlement range. As long as there is some overlap in their aspiration ranges, there exists a settlement area where each one's aspirations can be met.

When engaged in distributive bargaining, your tactics should focus on trying to get your opponent to agree to your specific target point or to get as close to it as possible. Examples of such tactics are as follows:

- persuading your opponent of the impossibility of getting to his or her target point and the advisability of accepting a settlement near yours;
- arguing that your target is fair but your opponent's isn't;
- attempting to get your opponent to feel emotionally generous toward you and thus accept an outcome close to your target point.

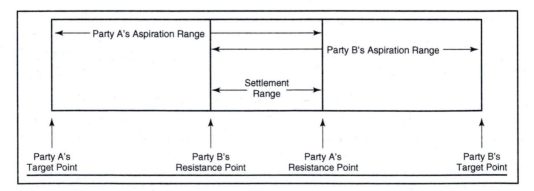

FIGURE 21.1 Staking Out the Bargaining Zone.

Now let's look at integrative bargaining. Assume a sales representative for a women's sportswear manufacturer has just closed a $15,000 order from a small clothing retailer. The sales rep calls in the order to the firm's credit department. She is told that the firm can't approve credit to this customer because of a past slow-pay record. The next day, the sales rep and the firm's credit supervisor meet to discuss the problem. The sales rep doesn't want to lose the business, and neither does the credit supervisor, but he also doesn't want to get stuck with an uncollectible debt. The two openly review their options. After considerable discussion, they agree on a solution that meets both their needs: The credit supervisor will approve the sale, but the clothing store's owner will have to provide a bank guarantee that will assure payment if the bill isn't paid within 60 days.

The sales-credit negotiation is an example of integrative bargaining. In contrast to distributive bargaining, integrative problem solving operates under the assumption that at least one settlement is possible that can create a win–win solution.

In general, integrative bargaining is preferable to distributive bargaining, because the former builds long-term relationships and facilitates working together in the future. It bonds negotiators and allows each to leave the bargaining table feeling that they have achieved a victory. Distributive bargaining, on the other hand, leaves one party a loser. It tends to build animosities and deepen divisions between people who have to work together on an ongoing basis.

Why, then, don't we see more integrative bargaining in organizations? The answer lies in the conditions necessary for this type of negotiation to succeed. These conditions include openness with information and frankness between parties, sensitivity on the part of each party to the other's needs, the ability to trust one another, and a willingness by both parties to maintain flexibility. Because many organizational cultures and interpersonal relationships are not characterized by openness, trust, and flexibility, it isn't surprising that negotiations often take on a win-at-any-cost dynamic.

Guidelines for Effective Negotiating

The essence of effective negotiation can be summarized in the following eight guidelines.

1. *Consider the other party's situation.*   Acquire as much information as you can about your opponent's interests and goals. What are this person's real needs versus wants? What constituencies must your opponent appease? What is this person's strategy?

   This information will help you understand your opponent's behavior, predict responses to your offers, and frame solutions in terms of their interests. Additionally, when you can anticipate your opponent's position, you are better equipped to counter arguments with the facts and figures that support your position.

2. *Have a concrete strategy.*   Treat negotiation like a chess match. Expert chess players have a strategy. They know ahead of time how they will respond to any given situation. How strong is your situation and how important is the issue? Are you willing to split differences to achieve an early solution? If the issue is important to you, is your position strong enough to let you play hardball and show little or no willingness to compromise? These are questions you should address before you begin bargaining.

3. *Begin with a positive overture.*   Establish rapport and mutual interests before starting the negotiation. Then begin bargaining with a positive overture—perhaps a small concession. Studies show that concessions tend to be reciprocated and lead to agreements. A positive climate can be further developed by reciprocating your opponent's concessions.

4. *Address problems, not personalities.*   Concentrate on the negotiation issues, not on the personal characteristics of your opponent. When negotiations get tough, avoid the tendency to attack your opponent. If other people feel threatened, they concentrate on defending their

self-esteem as opposed to solving the problem. It's your opponent's ideas or position that you disagree with, not the person. Separate the people from the problem and don't personalize differences.

5. *Maintain a rational, goal-oriented frame of mind.*   Use the previous guideline in reverse if your opponent attacks or gets emotional with you. Don't get hooked by emotional outbursts. Let the other person blow off steam without taking it personally while you try to understand the problem or strategy behind the aggression.

6. *Pay little attention to initial offers.*   Treat an initial offer as merely a point of departure. Everyone has to have an initial position. These initial offers tend to be extreme and idealistic. Treat them as such. Focus on the other person's interests and your own goals and principles while you generate other possibilities.

7. *Emphasize win–win solutions.*   Bargainers often assume that their gain must come at the expense of the other party. As noted with integrative bargaining, that needn't be the case. Win–win solutions often can be found. However, assuming a zero-sum game means missed opportunities for trade-offs that could benefit both sides, so if conditions are supportive, look for an integrative solution. Create additional alternatives, especially low-cost concessions you can make that have high value to the other party. Frame options in terms of your opponent's interests, and look for solutions that can allow both of you to declare a victory.

8. *Insist on using objective criteria.*   Make your negotiated decisions based on principles and results, not emotions or pressure.[1] Agree upon objective criteria that can aid both parties, and assess the reasonableness of an alternative. Don't succumb to emotional pleas, assertiveness, or stubbornness if the underlying rationale does not meet these criteria.

CONCEPT QUIZ

The following 10-question, true–false quiz is based on the previous material in this chapter. The answers are at the end of the quiz. If you miss any of these questions, be sure to go back and find out why you got them wrong.

Circle the right answer.

True	False	1.	Distributive bargaining is preferable to integrative bargaining.
True	False	2.	Don't plan a bargaining strategy so that you can remain flexible during negotiation.
True	False	3.	When negotiations get tough, the best defense is a good offense.
True	False	4.	Begin negotiations with a tough stance so your opponent won't try to take advantage of you.
True	False	5.	Don't take initial offers seriously.
True	False	6.	Always try for a win–win solution if possible.
True	False	7.	Emotional pleas are just as important as rational criteria in reaching an agreement.
True	False	8.	Making minor concessions can help you achieve a beneficial outcome.
True	False	9.	Don't be provoked by your opponent's attacks and emotional outbursts.
True	False	10.	Integrative bargaining requires openness, trust, and flexibility.

Answers: (1) False; (2) False; (3) False; (4) False; (5) True; (6) True; (7) False; (8) True; (9) True; (10) True

BEHAVIORAL CHECKLIST

Look for these specific behaviors when evaluating your negotiating skills and those of others.

Effective Negotiating Requires:

- Considering the other party's situation.
- Applying a concrete strategy.
- Beginning with a positive overture.
- Addressing problems, not personalities.
- Maintaining a rational, goal-oriented frame of mind.
- Not taking initial offers very seriously.
- Emphasizing win–win solutions.
- Insisting on using objective criteria.

ATTENTION!

The entire class should read the following "situation." DO NOT read the roles following the situation.

MODELING EXERCISE

What's a Fair Pay Increase for Lisa?

Instructions. The entire class should read the following situation. The two people chosen to play the roles of Terry and Dale should not read each other's roles. The remainder of the class can read everything, including the Observer's Rating Sheet for evaluating both participants in the role-play.

Actors. Terry (department supervisor) and Dale (Terry's boss)

Situation. Terry and Dale work for Nike in Portland, Oregon. Terry supervises a research laboratory. Dale is the manager of research and development. Terry and Dale are former college runners who have worked for Nike for more than 6 years. Dale has been Terry's boss for 2 years.

One of Terry's employees, Lisa Roland, has greatly impressed Terry. Lisa was hired 11 months ago. She is 25 years old and holds a master's degree in mechanical engineering. Her entry-level salary was $52,500 a year. She was told by Terry that in accordance with corporate policy, she would receive an initial performance evaluation at 6 months and a comprehensive review after 1 year. Based on her performance record, Lisa was told she could expect a salary adjustment at the time of the 1-year evaluation.

Terry's evaluation of Lisa after 6 months was very positive. Terry commented on the long hours Lisa was putting in, her cooperative spirit, the fact that others in the lab enjoyed working with her, and that she was making an immediate, positive impact on the projects she had been assigned. Now that Lisa's first anniversary is coming up, Terry has again reviewed Lisa's performance. Terry thinks Lisa might be the best new person the R&D group has ever hired. After only a year, Terry has rated Lisa as the number-three performer in a department of 11.

Salaries in the department vary greatly. Terry, for instance, has a basic salary of $77,000, plus eligibility for a bonus that might add another $5,000–8,000 a year. The salary range of the 11 department members is $46,400–71,350. The lowest salary is a recent hire with a bachelor's degree in physics. The two people that Terry has rated above Lisa earn base salaries of $67,700 and $71,350. They're both 27 years old and have been at Nike for 3 and 4 years, respectively. The median salary in Terry's department is $62,660.

Terry's Role.   You want to give Lisa a big raise. Although she's young, she has proven to be an excellent addition to the department. You don't want to lose her. More important, she knows in general what other people in the department are earning and she thinks she's underpaid. The company typically gives 1-year raises of 5 percent, although 10 percent is not unusual and 20–30 percent increases have been approved on occasion. You'd like to get Lisa as large an increase as Dale will approve.

Dale's Role.   All of your supervisors typically try to squeeze you for as much money as they can for their people. You understand this because you did the same thing when you were a supervisor. However, your boss wants to keep a lid on costs.

He wants you to keep raises for recent hires generally in the 5–8 percent range. In fact, he's sent a memo to all managers and supervisors saying this. However, your boss is also concerned with equity and paying people what they're worth. You feel assured that he will support any salary recommendation you make, as long as it can be justified. Your goal, consistent with cost reduction, is to keep salary increases as low as possible.

Terry has a meeting scheduled with Dale to discuss Lisa's performance review and salary adjustment.

Total Time. 30 minutes (preparation, 5 minutes; role-play, 15 minutes; debriefing, 10 minutes)

OBSERVER'S RATING SHEET

Evaluate the negotiating skills of Terry and Dale on a 1 to 5 scale (5 being the highest). Enter comments in the spaces between checklist behaviors to explain your ratings.

	Terry	Dale
• Considers the other party's situation.	_____	_____
• Applies a concrete strategy.	_____	_____
• Begins with a positive overture.	_____	_____
• Addresses problems, not personalities.	_____	_____
• Maintains a rational, goal-oriented frame of mind.	_____	_____
• Doesn't take initial offers seriously.	_____	_____
• Emphasizes win–win solutions.	_____	_____
• Insists on using objective criteria.	_____	_____

GROUP EXERCISES

Instructions.   Divide the class into trios. Two people play the roles and negotiate a settlement, and the third person observes and provides feedback according to the Observer's Rating Sheet. Rotate observer roles for each of the three exercises. Do not read the other person's role when you are playing a role in an exercise. Take 5 minutes after reading your roles to develop your negotiation strategy.

Group Exercise 1: Who Gets the Overtime?[2]

Actors.   Chris Lodge (manager of Unit One in the production supply department) and Lee Deore (manager of Unit Two in the production supply department)

Situation.   Unit One has been working overtime for the past 3 months on a new project, which has caused pressure on the workers, especially because it required a change in the vacation schedule. The project has expanded even more, but Unit Two has been assigned to help out and share the overtime requirements projected for the next 2 months in any way the two managers mutually decide.

Chris Lodge's Role.   You manage 10 people in Unit One in production supply. You've been with the department almost 2 years now and are pleased with your job. Three months ago, your unit was assigned to a new project. It required your people to work a lot of overtime and change vacation plans. Now the project has been expanded and another unit, headed by Lee Deore, who was transferred recently from another branch office, has been brought in to help. Employees will still need to work overtime for at least 2 months.

The people in your unit are tired and are complaining that they haven't seen much of their families during the past 3 months. You believe that Lee's people should assume the major portion of the overtime to give your employees a rest. Your people are burned out and morale is slipping. Lee's people, on the other hand, are fresh and could give you a rest. You have heard, however, that Lee intends to have the new unit pick up only half the overtime.

Your manager has told you that he expects you and Lee to settle the overtime issue and then inform him of your joint decision. On the way to get a cup of coffee, you meet Lee Deore. You decide to bring up the issue.

Lee Deore's Role.   You manage 10 people in Unit Two in production supply. You've been with the agency for just over a year and are generally happy with your job.

Your unit has been assigned to help Chris Lodge on a recently expanded project. The project has required and will continue to require people to work overtime. The project is expected to last at least 2 months.

Your manager has asked that you and Chris work out the distribution of overtime. You like Chris and look forward to working on this project. You believe the overtime should be evenly split between your two units. That way, minimal disruptions will occur in people's schedules as vacations near.

However, you have heard through the grapevine that Chris expects your unit to assume all the overtime. It is Chris's belief that someone else has to take up the slack because Chris's people have done it for the past 3 months. You can sympathize, but you don't want your people to take on all the overtime. Your manager has told you that she expects the two of you to work out the details and inform her of your decision. On the way to get a cup of coffee, you meet Chris Lodge. You decide to bring up the issue.

Total Time. 30 minutes (preparation, 10 minutes; role-play, 10 minutes; debriefing, 10 minutes)

OBSERVER'S RATING SHEET

Enter any comments in the spaces between checklist behaviors. Evaluate the negotiating skills of Chris and Lee on a 1 to 5 scale (5 being the highest).

	Chris	Lee
• Considers the other party's situation.	_____	_____
• Applies a concrete strategy.	_____	_____
• Begins with a positive overture.	_____	_____
• Addresses problems, not personalities.	_____	_____
• Maintains a rational, goal-oriented frame of mind.	_____	_____
• Doesn't take initial offers seriously.	_____	_____
• Emphasizes win–win solutions.	_____	_____
• Insists on using objective criteria.	_____	_____

Group Exercise 2: The Used Car Negotiation

Actors.   Buyer and Seller

Situation.   You are going to negotiate the purchase/sale of a used car. Before advertising it in the local newspaper, the seller took the car to the local Volkswagen dealer, who has provided the following information:

> 2000 Volkswagen Cabrio Convertible GL
>
> Red with white interior and top
>
> Five-speed transmission
>
> AM/FM Cassette, No CD; 80,350 miles
>
> New tires and brakes
>
> No rust; small ding on passenger door
>
> Muffler is loud and will need to be replaced at some point (estimate from dealer is $325)
>
> Kelly Blue Book values for this car in "good condition" are as follows: Retail, $9,500; Private Party, $7,390; Trade-in, $5,580.

Buyer's Role.   You are a second-semester college freshman who has just obtained a part-time job at the Costco located seven miles from campus. This is too far to walk and not located on any bus routes, so you need an economical car that you can afford. It would be nice to have something a little fun and sporty also. The Cabrio that was advertised for $6,995 looks like a pretty good deal, and you would like to buy it right away if possible so that you can stop begging your roommates for rides or to borrow their cars. You have $4,000 in savings and will be obtaining a $3,000 student loan within a week. You have another $500 in your checking account, but you intended to spend most of that on a ski trip with an extremely attractive classmate.

You can't borrow any more money from your parents because they are already forking over the burdensome out-of-state tuition, plus room and board. You have a VISA card but that already has $2,324 outstanding at 23 percent on its $5,000 limit. The Cabriolet is the best deal you've seen, and the car would be really fun to drive.

Your roommate's sister has a 2001 Ford Escort you can immediately buy for $5,490 (the wholesale value). It's a boring, brown, four-door sedan with an automatic transmission and four-cylinder engine with 86,871 miles. The interior has been pretty well trashed but it would be reliable transportation and you could handle it as long as no one sees you in it.

The seller of the Cabrio is a graduating senior you have never met. The reason given for selling the car is that the seller has a good out-of-state job offer and wants a newer car.

Before beginning this negotiation, set the following targets for yourself:

1. The price you would like to pay for the car.   _____
2. The price you will initially offer the seller.   _____
3. The highest price you will pay for the car.   _____

Seller's Role.   You are a second-semester college senior who has just put a deposit down on a perfect 1-year-old 325 Ci convertible, which was just traded in to the local dealer by a well-to-do client who trades up every year. It is jet black with natural brown leather interior and is equipped with the sport package, 17 × 8 style 44 wheels, performance tires, Harman/Kardon sound system, and fully automatic top. You are totally in love with the car and feel you deserve it.

The down payment is $5,000, with steep monthly payments of $1,682, but you have been hired by an out-of-state firm at a good starting salary, so you think you can handle them in a few months. Besides, you want to celebrate your pending graduation and new job, after 4 tough years of study and deferred partying. Right now, however, you are low on cash and stretched on credit, so if you can't come up with the down payment, you will have to borrow at 18 percent. You and your friends are going to pick up the Beemer in 2 hours, so you want to sell your old VW Cabrio before you go.

You advertised the car (which is in particularly good condition) in the newspaper for $6,995 and have had several calls. Most prospective buyers are college students, however, who cannot come up with the cash and want you to take payments. Your only good prospect right now is a freshman you have never met before but who says that if a deal can be reached, cash payment is no problem. You don't have to sell it to this person right now, but if you don't, you will have to pay high interest charges to cover the down payment until you do sell it.

The BMW dealer will only give you $5,580 for the Cabrio because he will have to resell it to a Volkswagen dealer at the wholesale price. The local VW dealer will not give you any more for your car because he just received a shipment of new cars.

Before beginning this negotiation, set the following targets for yourself:

1. The price you would like to receive for the car.   _____
2. The price you will initially request.   _____
3. The lowest price you will accept for the car.   _____

Total Time. 35 minutes (preparation, 10 minutes; role-play, 15 minutes; debriefing, 10 minutes)

OBSERVER'S RATING SHEET

Evaluate the negotiating skills of the buyer and seller on a 1 to 5 scale (5 being the highest). Enter comments in the spaces between checklist behaviors to explain your ratings.

	Buyer	Seller
• Considers the other party's situation.	_____	_____
• Applies a concrete strategy.	_____	_____
• Begins with a positive overture.	_____	_____
• Addresses problems, not personalities.	_____	_____
• Maintains a rational, goal-oriented frame of mind.	_____	_____
• Doesn't take initial offers seriously.	_____	_____
• Emphasizes win–win solutions.	_____	_____
• Insists on using objective criteria.	_____	_____

Group Exercise 3: Neighbors[3]

Situation.   Two weeks ago, Gene Croft bought a house on a double lot in an established neighborhood. He immediately put his 38-foot side yard up for sale at $150,000. Although land-use bylaws normally require a minimum property width of 40 feet, Gene was given special approval by the city's developmental office when he bought the house to subdivide his property. Local residents had attempted to block the subdivision but failed in their efforts. The site currently has no structures but a number of large trees grow on the property. Gene's neighbor, Shawn Johnston, has lived in her home since she inherited it from her parents 12 years ago. Shawn has asked to meet with Gene about buying the side lot. Shawn and Gene have been neighbors for only about 2 weeks and they have not met. Consequently, Gene and Shawn know very little about each other.

Gene's Role.   You and your wife were delighted to be able to purchase such a nice home in an established neighborhood close to the university where your wife is a graduate student. Purchasing the home was a stretch financially because you have only been working for 3 years since graduating with your B.S. degree in management. You were lucky that your parents could loan you the minimal down payment for your house and that your promotion to manager of the flooring department at Home Depot increased your salary enough to meet the bank's minimum qualifications for a 3-year, interest-only mortgage.

You are happy to be in the real estate market, but are worried that you will not be in a position to pay off the balloon payment or qualify for refinancing in 3 years. You are also financially strapped right now: You have a new house payment, no savings account, only one income, and have promised to pay the down payment back to your parents next year when they both will retire. You were very happy that you were given special approval by the city's developmental office when you bought the house to subdivide the property. Your plan is to sell off the side lot to pay back your parents, add a bedroom and family room to your house to accommodate your future family, and ensure that you will be able to retain ownership of your property.

Shawn's Role.   You are upset because if Gene's side lot is sold and a house is built on it, you will likely incur psychological and financial losses. You will lose financially because the market value of your house is likely to decline if a house is built only 8 feet from yours. Zoning laws allow residential homes to be built within 4 feet of the property line. Because the side lot for sale next door is only 38 feet wide, this is likely to happen. The psychological consequences of a house directly next door are the loss of a green area, a pleasant view, and direct sunlight.

Although you cannot afford the $150,000 price, you really want to buy the lot to protect your privacy and property values. Since you have lived in your home for the past 12 years, your property values have tripled, and you have a $100,000 line of credit in the form of a home equity loan if you need it. Other than that, your source of funds consists of a $5,000 money market account and your retirement funds, which you certainly do not want to touch. You are hopeful that Gene will sell you the property and take back the paper, so that you can make him interest-only payments for the next 5 years. At that time maybe the book royalties from the novel you are writing will be sufficient to pay off the loan or secure favorable financing.

You are somewhat anxious about meeting with Gene because he has been a neighbor for only about 2 weeks and you have not met. He and his wife both leave their home early each morning and look like young professionals of some sort. You really hope that they are nice people who will work with you to preserve your tranquility and build a lasting relationship.

Total Time. 30 minutes (preparation, 10 minutes; role-play, 10 minutes; debriefing, 10 minutes)

OBSERVER'S RATING SHEET

Evaluate the negotiating skills of Shawn and Gene on a 1 to 5 scale (5 being the highest). Enter comments in the spaces between checklist behaviors to explain your ratings.

	Gene	Shawn
• Considers the other party's situation.	_____	_____
• Applies a concrete strategy.	_____	_____
• Begins with a positive overture.	_____	_____
• Addresses problems, not personalities.	_____	_____
• Maintains a rational, goal-oriented frame of mind.	_____	_____
• Doesn't take initial offers seriously.	_____	_____
• Emphasizes win–win solutions.	_____	_____
• Insists on using objective criteria.	_____	_____

Summary Checklist

Review your performance and look over others' ratings of your negotiating skills. Now assess yourself on each of the key learning behaviors. Make a check (✓) next to those behaviors on which you need improvement.

I consider the other party's situation.   _____

I apply a concrete strategy.   _____

I begin with a positive overture.   _____

I address problems, not personalities.   _____

I maintain a rational, goal-oriented frame of mind.   _____

I do not take initial offers seriously.   _____

I emphasize win–win solutions.   _____

I insist on using objective criteria.   _____

APPLICATION QUESTIONS

1. Why is integrative bargaining preferable to distributive bargaining? Why don't we see more integrative bargaining in organizations?
2. Think of a recent negotiation you have participated in with your boss, significant other, parents, or roommate. Which of the negotiation behaviors did you successfully apply? How could those negotiation behaviors you did not use have helped?
3. How do you know when you are involved in distributive bargaining? What is your objective? What tactics would be most appropriate?
4. How do you know when you are involved in integrative bargaining? What is your objective? What tactics would be most appropriate?
5. You are representing your company in an important negotiation. After being stuck in a stalemate for several hours, your counterpart misquotes and misrepresents you on a number of earlier statements. After you correct the record, your opponent loses his temper and aggressively slanders your character in front of others on your negotiating team. What should you do? Why?

REINFORCEMENT EXERCISES

1. Negotiate with a professor to raise the grade on an exam or paper on which you think you should have received a higher grade.
2. The next time you purchase a relatively expensive item (e.g., automobile, apartment lease, appliance, jewelry), negotiate a better price and gain some concessions such as an extended warranty, smaller down payment, or maintenance services.
3. Negotiate a more favorable set of task assignments for yourself with your roommates or significant other.
4. Research collective bargaining negotiations in the news media when they occur (e.g., baseball player strikes, union strikes, individual sports celebrity salary negotiations,

plea bargains). What type of negotiation is going on? What skills and tactics are being applied?

5. Research international crisis negotiations in the news media when they occur (e.g., trade negotiations, military or hostage crises, political party bargaining). What type of negotiation is going on? What skills and tactics are being applied?

ACTION PLAN

1. Which behavior do I want to improve the most?

2. Why? What will be my payoff?

3. What potential obstacles stand in my way?

4. What specific things will I do to improve? (For examples, see the Reinforcement Exercises.)

5. When will I do them?

6. How and when will I measure my success?

Endnotes

1. R. Fisher and W. Ury, *Getting to Yes: Negotiating Agreement without Giving In* (New York: Penguin Books, 1986).

2. Adapted from W. C. Morris and M. Saskin, *Organizational Behavior in Action* (St. Paul, MN: West Publishing Company, 1976), pp. 177–180.

3. The situation is based on Exercise 7.1, "Can We Make a Deal?" in L. W. Mealiea and G. P. Lastham, *Skills for Managerial Success* (Chicago, IL: Richard D. Irwin, 1996), pp. 291–292.

Part 7

■ ■ ■

Integrating Exercises

In this, the last chapter of the book, you won't be exposed to any new skills. The objectives here are to give you an opportunity to try out a number of skills you have learned and to help you summarize those skill areas where you need to concentrate in the future.

SKILL ASSESSMENT REVIEW

You undoubtedly have mastered most of the skills presented in this book. However, if you're like most people, your skills in some areas are still not as good as you want. It's now time to review those areas of improvement in order to identify action plans for the future.

Look back through the Summary Checklists in Chapters 3–21. Make a list of all those skill techniques where you made a check mark. Do you see any patterns to your deficiencies? In a paragraph or two, summarize any insights you have drawn from reviewing those areas in which you have shown deficiencies.

Now review your Self-Awareness Profile in Chapter 2. Write a paragraph summarizing your learning style, interpersonal needs, assertiveness level, Big Five personality factors, and cognitive style. What insights into the sources of your deficiencies do these sentences give you?

INTEGRATIVE EXERCISES

In the real world, interpersonal activities don't come neatly separated and packaged into topics like goal setting, listening, and delegating. In practice, the interpersonal skills you've read about in this book overlap greatly. For instance, goal setting and feedback go hand in hand; so do running a group meeting and managing conflict. More complex situations often require all of the interpersonal skills you have learned. For example, a performance-appraisal review typically requires multiple skills, including sending, listening, feedback, persuasion, goal setting, coaching, counseling, mentoring and, sometimes, problem solving, conflict management, ethical decision making, and working with diverse others.

The following exercises require the application of a number of the interpersonal skills you've previously practiced. These exercises give you opportunities to determine how well you've assimilated the skills and how effectively you can integrate them into more complex situations requiring multiple skills.

ATTENTION!
Read the following instructions and background information, but DO NOT read the roles until assigned by your instructor.

Integrating Exercise 1: Chris Amon and Lee Petty

Instructions.   Break into groups of two. Decide who will play the role of Chris Amon (the manager) and who will play Lee Petty (the employee). Both individuals should read the following background information and then their own roles, but not the other person's role. Exhibits are located at the end of this exercise.

Actors.   Chris Amon and Lee Petty

Situation.   The Sloane Company, headquartered in New York, produces and markets four major brands of cosmetics. The marketing function is organized as shown in Exhibit 1, with product managers reporting to brand managers. This exercise involves a meeting between

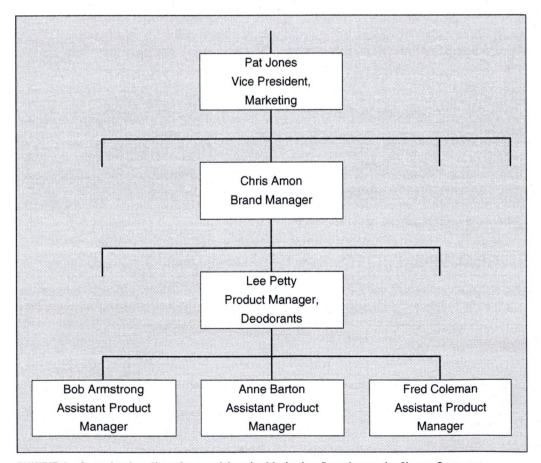

EXHIBIT 1   Organization Chart Summarizing the Marketing Function at the Sloane Company.

Chris Amon, the brand manager, and Lee Petty, one of Chris's three product managers. Both came to the Sloane Company after receiving an MBA from the Amos Tuck School of Business at Dartmouth College. Chris has been with Sloane for 10 years. Lee has been with Sloane for 4 years.

An important event in the relationship between brand managers and product managers is the performance review, which is supposed to occur every 3 months. The fourth such meeting every year is also the annual salary review. Because of Chris Amon's rather hectic travel schedule during the past few months, 6 months have elapsed since Lee Petty's last review, which was also the annual salary review session. Lee's salary was raised 14 percent.

The most recent review was a positive one, with no corrective action suggested. During the interview, Lee asked Chris if it would be possible to trade weekend work for longer vacation time. Lee felt the company's vacation policy favored high-seniority employees too much. (See Exhibit 2.) After checking with the vice president of human resources, Chris reported back to Lee that such a trade was impossible because it might set a precedent that would upset the vacation benefits structure. The vice president of human resources did, however, assure Chris that the entire benefits structure at the Sloane Company would be reviewed.

Now read your role. **Remember not to read the other person's role!**

Lee Petty's Role.   Your immediate supervisor, Chris Amon, has returned from extended overseas travel and is now catching up on a backlog of administrative duties. Among these are long-overdue reviews of the product managers. Chris has been a good boss during the past 2 years since you were promoted from assistant product manager and has been particularly supportive of you, but he has a tendency to dump things in your lap and not be around to follow through.

During the past 6 months, for instance, Chris tried to pass two projects on to you and your group of three assistant product managers. Each happened to come at a bad time for your group, but Chris was out of town at these times and didn't realize that your group was particularly busy while other groups were running slack. Chris was reasonable when you pointed this out and quickly reassigned the projects, but you felt a little bad because you always try to cooperate. If Chris had been in the office more, these projects—which weren't particularly interesting or challenging—automatically would have gone to less-busy product managers.

Number of Years of Service	Vacation
Less than 1 year	None
1–5 years	2 weeks
6–7 years	3 weeks
8–9 years	4 weeks
10–15 years	5 weeks
Over 15 years	6 weeks

EXHIBIT 2 Vacation Policy of the Sloane Company.

You suspect that Chris tends to think of your group first because you have the best track record. On the one hand, this is flattering; on the other hand, your group is, in effect, being penalized for being good by getting saddled with extra projects that are just busywork. The other product managers seem a little jealous of what you've accomplished. One is a Harvard MBA and the other a Wharton MBA, and some rivalry has always been evident. In fact, you feel that they have at times gone beyond kidding around and have tried to undermine you in the eyes of higher management. In addition, they are eager to ask for help from you and your group but seldom give you credit or return the favor when you need help. This is an organization in which the rewards flow from producing, not from cooperating. When your rivals take the credit after you helped them out, you get hurt.

The other product managers have gone beyond exploiting you and your group and have tried to undermine you by making nitpicking complaints to higher management about your attempt to build a little flextime into an overly rigid organization. Your group always gets the job done, even if it means working evenings and weekends. Other groups miss deadlines because they like to keep to a 9-to-5 schedule. You occasionally return the favor to your assistant product managers by being flexible when they have something special to do outside the office. Such flexibility is inconsistent with company policy, which was developed for the hourly workers. Thus, when the assistant product managers have received your approval to take time off, they leave an official message in the office saying they are "working at home," "visiting the agency," or something similar. You wish you didn't have to do things this way, but the company's inflexible policies on time off leave you little choice. The rules were written for secretaries and others who must consistently be available during the hours the office is open; you think they should not apply to professionals such as the assistant product managers.

The animosity of the other product managers and their groups is particularly bothersome as you contemplate your upcoming performance review with Chris because of a strange occurrence in your office over the weekend. You came in to catch up on some work last Saturday and made a phone call to the home of an advertising agency executive. She was busy when you called, and her husband said she would call back in 15 minutes. While you were waiting, you wrote a quick letter to Leslie, with whom you have been romantically involved for the past 6 months, but who, unfortunately, lives in Boston.

When you had almost finished the second page of the letter, your fountain pen hemorrhaged and spoiled the page. You rewrote the page and had finished the letter by the time your call was returned. You had forgotten about this event until Monday morning.

Monday started off badly. You were menaced on the subway by two adolescent thugs, then you had to wait forever for a new and obviously incompetent waitress to serve you breakfast. When it finally arrived, you found you had been given an onion bagel instead of your usual plain bagel, but you were already late, so you didn't dare send it back and wait for another one. Because you didn't want to taste your breakfast all day, you bought a pack of Dentyne (you were shortchanged!) and chewed a piece as you walked to your office.

When you sat down at your desk and wanted to discard your gum, you looked in the wastebasket for a piece of paper to wrap the gum in. There was one crumpled piece of paper, the second page of your note to Leslie, which you remembered discarding the previous Saturday. You opened it up to place the used gum in it and saw the number "1990" written in ballpoint pen on the back. This was puzzling. You were sure you began with a clean sheet, and the office had been locked from the time you left on Saturday until your arrival Monday morning.

You then reread the other side and became concerned. If a rival product manager photocopied that page, in your distinctive handwriting, the information could be used to discredit you. The text of what you wrote is shown in Exhibit 3.

. . . and it's probably OK with them.

I'm delighted you can get the time off work to meet me in San Diego. We'll have a hotel to stay in, a rental car, and an expense account. All I have to do is register for the convention. We can skip out every day since it's a bullshit convention anyway. You'll love Black's Beach. And a friend of mine has an 18-foot Hobie Cat that we can take out whenever we want.

I'll be calling you next week when I'm in Boston. I hope

[Note writing stopped at this point because of a large ink blot; the page was obviously crumpled before the ink had dried.]

EXHIBIT 3   Text of One Page of Lee Petty's Letter.

It was poor judgment on your part to express in writing a practice that is fairly common among junior-level marketing people at Sloane. The company's vacation policy is so unreasonable that people have to bend the rules a little to adapt. Product managers do a lot of traveling. A key source of information about new developments by competitors is the components manufacturers. For instance, Sloane first found out its major competitor was planning to launch an aerosol antiperspirant from the aerosol-valve manufacturer. Thus, someone from Sloane almost always attends trade meetings and conventions. Because these events are often held at vacation resorts, attendees often manage to budget a lot of leisure time during the event.

The convention in San Diego you referred to in your letter is put on by the Cosmetics Chemicals Manufacturers Association. You have little interest in or knowledge of chemistry but a strong interest in San Diego, where your friends live. You wrote a routine memo to get the trip approved. The request was approved without question.

You don't feel at all guilty about asking to go to a convention that you're not interested in. It's a standard prerequisite of the job, and people informally told you of this benefit during your callback interview. However, you're a little worried that some rival product manager might have seen the page and mentioned it to Chris to make trouble for you.

You flushed the paper and the gum down the toilet last Monday morning. You never did figure out why someone would write "1990" on your sheet of paper.

Chris Amon's Role.   You have been back in town for only a week after an extensive travel schedule to explore new overseas opportunities for the brand. You are now catching up on your backlog of administrative duties, which include the (now quite late) reviews of your three product managers.

Overall, Lee Petty has been doing a good job. A creative, conscientious, and hard worker, Lee has consistently exceeded your expectations since being promoted by you from assistant product manager 2 years ago. Lee's group is the best of the three; they take new problems in stride and have consistently improved their performance.

You have received some mild complaints about Lee's cooperation with other product managers. When other groups need help, for instance, Lee's group is seen as reluctant to provide it, despite their obvious wealth of talent and energy. On one occasion, another product manager made a mistake that was costly and a little embarrassing to the company. This mistake easily could have been avoided had Lee given him some key information.

During the past 6 months, Lee was reluctant to take on two general assignments that directly concerned the brand. Lee's complaint was that the assignments were routine and uninteresting and would divert the group's energy from some more challenging tasks that needed to be tackled and were more directly concerned with the group's product. You didn't push the point, because one other group was slightly less busy during that period, but one of the other product managers made a joking comment about favoritism that has bothered you. The joke concerned the fact that you and Lee are the only two Tuck graduates in the company.

Some resentment is also mounting regarding Lee's group bending the rules on attendance. Lee has been an outspoken critic of the company's vacation policy. Rumor has it that Lee compensates informally by allowing the assistant product managers extra time off under the guise of "working at home," "working over at the agency," or "checking out point-of-purchase displays." You haven't yet said anything to Lee about this. The group always gets its work done and often works evenings and weekends when necessary. However, you have been criticized by your own boss for your laxity in bringing Lee's group into line: There is resentment of Lee's group's privileges among employees who are made to conform to a 9-to-5 schedule.

What bothers you most about your upcoming interview, however, is evidence you found that Lee apparently has arranged a de facto vacation in southern California at the company's expense. In an atmosphere in which there is already talk of favoritism toward another Tuck graduate, there is some risk that this could blow up on you.

You were in the office last Sunday, catching up on your paperwork. You needed some market data for the past 5 years and didn't want to wait until the next day to ask Lee for them, so you used your master key and went into Lee's office and looked them up in a three-ring binder. You needed a piece of paper on which to copy down the numbers but didn't want to go into Lee's desk; you already felt a little uncomfortable invading Lee's office when no one was around. You spotted a crumpled piece of paper in the wastebasket, so you uncrumpled it and started writing on it.

For some reason, you stopped writing and turned it over. You immediately recognized Lee's elegant handwriting on the Sloane Company stationery. It was obviously the second page of a letter. It apparently had been discarded after Lee's fountain pen had leaked. Absentmindedly, you read the page, even though something inside you told you that you should not. You threw the page back in the wastebasket and left the office. The text of that page is shown in Exhibit 3.

Reading that page made you angry. Lee had asked to attend a cosmetics-chemicals convention in San Diego during May. The request seemed odd, because Lee knows nothing about chemistry and has never before shown any interest in the chemicals that go into the product line. Although your boss was skeptical, you trusted Lee and approved the request. Now you are in a quandary. You don't want to admit to having snooped around a subordinate's office over the weekend, much less to having rummaged through a wastebasket and then reading personal mail. On the other hand, you don't feel you can let Lee's duplicity go unchallenged.

Instructions for Role-Play Exercise.   After you have read the background information, your role, and are prepared to act out your role in the exercise, advise your partner. When both actors are ready, begin the role-play. It begins by Chris calling Lee to arrange a location for the meeting.

Instructions for Evaluation Feedback.   After the exercise is completed, evaluate your own behavior and that of your partner on the following evaluation forms. Then partner A shares his or her self-evaluations, one item at a time. Partner B responds with his or her rating of partner A to confirm or provide feedback about discrepancies to partner A. Then the process is reversed: partner B shares self-ratings and partner A confirms and explains why there are discrepancies.

Total Time.   60 minutes (preparation, 15 minutes; role-play, 30 minutes; debriefing, 15 minutes)

EVALUATION SHEET FOR CHRIS AMON

Evaluate Chris Amon's interpersonal skills on a 1 to 5 scale (5 being the highest). Enter comments to explain your ratings in the spaces between checklist behaviors.

Interpersonal Skill	Rating
Sending Effective Messages	
Provided all relevant information.	_____
Was honest.	_____
Used multiple channels.	_____
Was complete and specific.	_____
Used "I" statements to claim message as own.	_____
Was congruent in verbal and nonverbal messages.	_____
Used language the receiver could understand.	_____
Was credible—knew what he or she was talking about and seemed reliable.	_____
Was warm, friendly, and dynamic.	_____
Obtained feedback to ensure understanding.	_____
Listening	
Maintained eye contact.	_____
Used appropriate head nods and facial expressions.	_____
Avoided distracting actions or gestures.	_____
Asked appropriate questions.	_____
Paraphrased using his or her own words.	_____
Avoided interrupting the speaker.	_____
Did not overtalk.	_____
Made smooth transitions between speaker and listener.	_____
Read nonverbal signals.	_____

Providing Feedback

Supported negative feedback with hard data.	_____
Focused on specific rather than general behaviors.	_____
Kept comments impersonal and job-related.	_____
Ensured clear and full understanding by the recipient.	_____
Directed negative feedback toward controllable behavior.	_____
Feedback reflected past performance and future potential.	_____

Goal Setting

Identified an employee's key job tasks.	_____
Established specific and challenging goals for each key task.	_____
Specified deadlines for each goal.	_____
Allowed the subordinate to actively participate.	_____
Prioritized goals.	_____
Rated goals for difficulty and importance.	_____
Built in feedback mechanisms to assess goal progress.	_____
Committed rewards contingent on goal attainment.	_____

Persuading

Established credibility.	_____
Used a positive, tactful tone.	_____
Presented ideas one at a time.	_____
Presented strong evidence to support a position.	_____
Tailored arguments to the listener.	_____
Appealed to the listener's self-interest.	_____
Made logical arguments.	_____
Used emotional appeals.	_____

Resolving Conflicts

Dealt directly with the conflict.	_____
Ascertained sources of conflict.	_____
Empathized with the conflicting parties.	_____
Used appropriate conflict-handling style.	_____
Selected the most appropriate conflict-resolution option.	_____

Coaching

Asked questions to help discover how to improve.	_____
Was positive rather than threatening.	_____

Accepted mistakes and used them to learn.   _____

Modeled qualities expected.   _____

Negotiating

Considered the other party's situation.   _____

Addressed problems, not personalities.   _____

Maintained a rational, goal-oriented frame of mind.   _____

Insisted on using objective criteria.   _____

EVALUATION SHEET FOR LEE PETTY

Evaluate Lee Petty's interpersonal skills on a 1 to 5 scale (5 being the highest). Enter comments to explain your ratings in the spaces between checklist behaviors.

Sending Effective Messages

Provided all relevant information.   _____

Was honest.   _____

Used multiple channels.   _____

Was complete and specific.   _____

Used "I" statements to claim message as own.   _____

Was congruent in verbal and nonverbal messages.   _____

Listening

Maintained eye contact.   _____

Used appropriate head nods and facial expressions.   _____

Avoided distracting actions or gestures.   _____

Asked appropriate questions.   _____

Paraphrased using his or her own words.   _____

Avoided interrupting the speaker.   _____

Did not overtalk.   _____

Made smooth transitions between speaker and listener.   _____

Read nonverbal signals.   _____

Creative Problem Solving

Established trust with involved people.   _____

Identified all problems in the situation.   _____

Analyzed problem sources and consequences.   _____

Decided what to do after evaluating all alternatives.   _____

Planned to implement the best action plan in a timely manner.	_____
Planned how to measure results and take corrective actions.	_____
Encouraged creativity from participants.	_____
Established trust with involved people.	_____
Identified all problems in the situation.	_____
Analyzed problem sources and consequences.	_____
Decided what to do after evaluating all alternatives.	_____
Planned to implement the best action plan in a timely manner.	_____
Planned how to measure results and take corrective actions.	_____
Encouraged creativity from participants.	_____

Persuading

Established credibility.	_____
Used a positive, tactful tone.	_____
Presented ideas one at a time.	_____
Presented strong evidence to support a position.	_____
Tailored arguments to the listener.	_____
Appealed to the listener's self-interest.	_____
Made logical arguments.	_____
Used emotional appeals.	_____

Politicking

Framed arguments in terms of organizational goals.	_____
Projected right image.	_____
Gained control of organizational resources.	_____
Developed powerful allies.	_____
Supported boss.	_____

Negotiating

Considered the other party's situation.	_____
Addressed problems, not personalities.	_____
Maintained a rational, goal-oriented frame of mind.	_____
Insisted on using objective criteria.	_____

Questions

1. What was the solution arrived at in your interview? How did each party feel as a consequence?
2. How many people role-playing Chris confronted Lee at the outset with the evidence? Why or why not?

3. How many of those who played Lee initiated the discussion by confessing their actions? Why?
4. How many of you were able to focus on the other person's interests? What facilitated this?
5. Does Chris have a responsibility to correct the rip-off? Explain.
6. For those playing Lee, how effective were your persuasion efforts?
7. Did Chris approach this situation as a coaching, conflict-resolution, or team-building dilemma?
8. What creative problem-solving skills did Chris demonstrate?
9. How did the two parties negotiate?

Integrating Exercise 2: Team Meeting Demonstration

Effective meeting facilitation requires the application of most of the skills covered in this book. Some additional meeting skills are summarized in the Concepts section below. The purpose of this assignment is to increase your proficiency in applying your interpersonal skills in planning and conducting a meeting.

Directions.   Form teams of five to six members. Each team will choose a significant meeting topic that all members are interested in. Suggestions are planning an event such as a class-related company visit, an awards banquet, or a concert or benefit event. Or the meeting could address a current problem that needs to be solved, such as how to complete a team project or research paper, establish a new student organization, or change university rules to allow alcohol to be served at student events. Then the team will hold a demonstration problem-solving (decision-making) meeting, which will be observed and evaluated by the rest of the class and the instructor. The meeting guidelines provided below and in related skill chapters previously read should be followed.

Concepts.   Managers typically spend between 25 and 30 percent of their work time in meetings.[1] The higher up the corporate ladder managers climb, the more meetings they attend. Chief executives have been found to spend 59 percent of their time in scheduled meetings and another 10 percent in unscheduled meetings.[2]

Many of the hours you'll spend in these meetings will be in nonleadership roles. You'll participate, but it won't be your responsibility to run the meeting. Preparing and contributing appropriately will be your responsibilities. Other times, you'll be the person in charge. You'll choose who will attend. You'll set and control the agenda. Most important, what you do or don't do will largely influence the meeting's effectiveness.

In this exercise, you will apply your interpersonal skills to make a meeting as effective as possible. The 12 most important behaviors that you should demonstrate when conducting a meeting are summarized below.

1. *Prepare a meeting agenda.*   Clarify what is to be done at the meeting and what decisions are to be made. Determine who should attend to optimize meeting effectiveness. Prepare the agenda.
2. *Distribute the agenda in advance.*   If you want to be sure that specific people attend your meeting and that they do their homework beforehand, get your agenda out well in advance of the meeting. What's an adequate lead time? That depends on such factors as the amount of preparation necessary, the importance of the meeting, and whether the meeting will be

recurring (e.g., every Monday at 8:30 AM) or is being called once to deal with an issue that has arisen and will be repeated only under similar circumstances.

3. ***Consult with participants before the meeting.***   Unprepared participants can't contribute to their full potential. It is your responsibility to ensure that members are prepared. What data will they need ahead of time? Do they have those data? If not, what can you do to help them get them?

4. ***Get participants to go over the agenda.***   The first thing you should do at the meeting is have participants review the agenda. Do modifications need to be made? If so, make them. Clarify the issues that you plan to discuss. After this review, get participants to approve the final agenda.

5. ***Establish specific time parameters.***   Meetings should begin on time and have a specific time for completion.[3] It is your responsibility to specify these time parameters and hold to them.

6. ***Maintain focused discussion.***   It is the chairperson's responsibility to give direction to the discussion; to keep it focused on the issues; and to minimize interruptions, disruptions, and irrelevant comments.[4] If participants begin to stray from the issue under consideration, the chairperson should intercede quickly to redirect the discussion. Similarly, one or a few members cannot be allowed to monopolize the discussion or to dominate others. Appropriate preventive action ranges from a subtle stare, a raised eyebrow, or some other nonverbal communication, on up to an authoritative command such as ruling someone "out of order" or withdrawing someone's right to continue speaking.

7. ***Encourage and support participation by all members.***   To maximize the effectiveness of problem-oriented meetings, each participant must be encouraged to contribute. Quiet or reserved personalities need to be drawn out so that their ideas can be heard.

8. ***Maintain an appropriate level of control.***   The style of leadership can range from authoritative domination to laissez-faire. The effective leader pushes when necessary and is passive when appropriate.

9. ***Encourage the clash of ideas.***   You need to encourage different points of view, critical thinking, and constructive disagreement. Your goals should be to stimulate participants' creativity and counter the group members' desire to reach an early consensus.

10. ***Discourage the clash of personalities.***   An effective meeting is characterized by the critical assessment of ideas, not attacks on people. When running a meeting, you must quickly intercede to stop personal attacks or other forms of verbal insult.

11. ***Exhibit active listening skills.***   Model the listening skills discussed in Chapter 6. Active listening reduces misunderstandings, improves the focus of discussion, and encourages the critical assessment of ideas. Even if other group members don't exhibit good listening skills, if you do, you can keep the discussion focused on the issues and facilitate critical thinking.

12. ***Bring proper closure.***   Close a meeting by summarizing the group's accomplishments; clarifying what actions, if any, need to follow the meeting; and allocating follow-up assignments.[5] If any decisions have been made, identify who will be responsible for communicating and implementing them.

Grading criteria for this assignment are based on the previous skill chapters and the behavioral guidelines discussed above. Make sure you cover all of the behaviors in the three meeting phases of planning, process, and debriefing.

Time Requirements.   The meeting should run at least 25 minutes, but no longer than 30 minutes, start to finish.

Meeting Debriefing. During the exercise, the instructor and class members acting as observers evaluate the team members conducting the meeting on the skill dimensions on the following evaluation sheet. After the meeting is over, the observers give the team leader and members feedback on their skill performance during the exercise.

EVALUATION SHEET FOR TEAM MEETING DEMONSTRATION

Evaluate the team members' interpersonal skills during the meeting demonstration on a 1 to 5 scale (5 being the highest). Enter comments to explain your ratings in the spaces between checklist behaviors.

Meeting Facilitation

Prepared and distributed agenda in advance. _____

Participants were prepared for the meeting. _____

Established time parameters. _____

Maintained focused discussion. _____

Encouraged everyone to participate. _____

Encouraged clash of ideas. _____

Discouraged clash of personalities. _____

Made a proper closure. _____

Goal Setting

Identified tasks. _____

Established specific and challenging goals for each key task. _____

Specified deadlines for each goal. _____

Allowed others to actively participate. _____

Prioritized goals. _____

Rated goals for difficulty and importance. _____

Built in feedback mechanisms to assess goal progress. _____

Committed rewards contingent on goal attainment. _____

Listening

Maintained eye contact. _____

Used appropriate head nods and facial expressions. _____

Avoided distracting actions or gestures. _____

Asked appropriate questions. _____

Paraphrased using his or her own words. _____

Avoided interrupting the speaker. _____

Did not overtalk.   _____

Made smooth transitions between speaker and listener.   _____

Read nonverbal signals.   _____

Providing Feedback

Supported negative feedback with hard data.   _____

Focused on specific rather than general behaviors.   _____

Kept comments impersonal and job-related.   _____

Ensured clear and full understanding by the recipient.   _____

Directed negative feedback toward controllable behavior.   _____

Feedback reflected past performance and future potential.   _____

Working with Diverse Others

Embraced diversity.   _____

Sensitized everyone to diversity issues.   _____

Was flexible.   _____

Motivated individually.   _____

Reinforced productive differences.   _____

Resolving Conflicts

Dealt directly with the conflict.   _____

Ascertained sources of conflict.   _____

Empathized with the conflicting parties.   _____

Used appropriate conflict-handling style.   _____

Selected the most appropriate conflict-resolution option.   _____

Coaching

Asked questions to help discover how to improve.   _____

Was positive rather than threatening.   _____

Accepted mistakes and used them to learn.   _____

Modeled qualities expected.   _____

Negotiating

Considered the other party's situation.   _____

Addressed problems, not personalities.   _____

Maintained a rational, goal-oriented frame of mind.   _____

Insisted on using objective criteria.   _____

FUTURE ACTION PLANS

As a result of the Skill Assessment Review at the beginning of this chapter, and the feedback you have just received after the integration role-plays, which behaviors do you still want to improve in the future?

1. Which behaviors do I want to improve in?

2. Why? What will be my payoff?

3. What potential obstacles stand in my way?

4. What specific things will I do to improve?

5. When will I do them?

6. How and when will I measure my success?

Endnotes

1. Edward A. Michaels, "Business Meetings," *Small Business Reports* (February 1989), pp. 82–88; Edward Wakin, "Make Meetings Meaningful," *Today's Office* (May 1991), pp. 68–69.
2. Henry Mintzberg, *The Nature of Managerial Work* (Englewood Cliffs, NJ: Prentice Hall, 1980).
3. Daniel Stoffman, "Waking Up to Great Meetings," *Canadian Business* (November 1986), pp. 75–79.
4. Ibid.
5. Ibid.

APPENDIX

Exercise Guidelines and Materials

This appendix provides general guidelines for exercise participants about how to perform role-plays, observe, and give feedback. It also contains some exercise debriefing notes for the class to refer to after completing some of the chapter exercises. The *Instructor's Manual* provides specific guidance and materials for the instructor when conducting and debriefing the chapter exercises. The *Instructor's Manual* also contains additional exercises, reinforcement exercises, and supplementary lectures.

There are two types of exercises: modeling exercises and group exercises. Modeling exercises are done in front of the class. They provide an opportunity to observe participants performing specific skill behaviors and to learn from that observation. Sometimes students are more comfortable playing the role in a triad instead of in front of the entire class. If students are hesitant to volunteer for a modeling role-play in front of the class, triads can be used. After observers have debriefed the role-plays, a class discussion of the most common areas of strength and weakness can be conducted.

Group exercises are done in small groups and provide opportunities for all members to practice and obtain feedback on their interpersonal skills. Groups may consist of dyads, triads, or more, depending on the particular exercise. Following are some general guidelines for participating and observing the exercises. More specific guidelines are often provided with individual exercises.

GUIDELINES FOR ACTORS

Actors in a role-play read the background information on the exercise and their own role. They do not read the other actors' roles—doing so will lessen the effectiveness of the exercise. The role description establishes your character. Follow the guidelines it establishes. Don't change or omit the facts you're given, but feel free to behave in ways that you feel would be relevant. Remember that role-playing is acting, so you need to project yourself into the character you are portraying and act out your thoughts and feelings as if you were in the real situation.

Once you are familiar with the role, review the relevant skills on the Observer's Rating Sheet and plan how you can demonstrate them in the role-play. These are the behaviors that you are seeking to model correctly. They are also the behaviors that observers are rating and will provide you feedback on at the end of the exercise.

After an exercise has been completed, the actors will evaluate their performance of the relevant skills on the Observer's Rating Sheet. Then the class observers will compare their ratings and discuss the participants' performance, starting with the strong points and followed by areas that could be improved.

GUIDELINES FOR OBSERVERS

If you're an observer in an exercise, you should read everything pertaining to the role-play: the situation, all roles, and the Observer's Rating Sheet. Your job is to note the role-players' effective and ineffective application of the relevant skills and then offer feedback based on these observations in a constructive manner so that the role-players and class members can learn from the exercise. During the time the role-players plan and organize, observers should review the behavioral criteria and think about how to perform the exercise if they were in the actor's role. During the role-play, observers evaluate the actor's skills using the observer's rating sheet and make notes of examples of particularly good behaviors and those that need improvement to share during the debriefing. During the debriefing, observers provide examples of effective skill applications and constructive feedback about how to improve.

DEBRIEFING INSTRUCTIONS

After the role-play exercise is completed, the debriefing starts by having the role-players evaluate their own behavior on the Observer's Rating Sheet that follows the exercise. The observers then provide their ratings of each role-player's skill behaviors. This will confirm or provide feedback about discrepancies regarding self-perceptions. After the first role-player has shared and received feedback, the process is repeated for other role-players if they are also applying relevant behavioral skills.

STUDENT-CREATED SCRIPTS

As an option to any of the group exercises in the skill chapters, students can create their own scenario and scripts for a 5-minute role-play demonstrating application of relevant chapter skills. Another alternative is to have half the class create and demonstrate role-plays in which actors demonstrate the right way to apply skills and the other half of the class demonstrates the wrong way. While actors in one group are demonstrating either the right or the wrong way, the other groups can act as observers and identify which of the behaviors in that skill are correctly applied or violated for debriefing.

CHAPTER EXERCISE MATERIALS

Following are debriefing notes, suggested answers, and answer keys that support the exercises in Chapters 8 and 14. A guide to keeping journals about what you learn in the exercises is also provided. A guide to e-mail etiquette and alternative exercises, cases, and suggestions are provided for each chapter in the *Instructor's Manual*.

ATTENTION!

Do NOT look at anything in the following section until told to do so by your instructor.

Chapter 8: Communicating across Cultures

GROUP EXERCISE 1: DEBRIEFING NOTES   Cross-cultural conflicts are examples of different action chains based on cultural "recipes" that have a sequence of actions leading to a particular goal. In this case, the action chains didn't match. Yoshio and Chip come from cultures that have different ways of expressing discomfort. Chip's background is white working class, and he expresses conflict directly, immediately, and verbally. Yoshio tries to be quiet or give an apology. Because they have different "scripts" about conflict, they didn't pick up each other's cues very well.

Language is central to culture and identity. Language is a core part of who you are, a boundary between groups. Both these students generally pick friends who come from their own cultural and language background. In this case you could see how language differences created friction and distance between the roommates.

It may be difficult to "talk out a problem directly" when the other person comes from a culture where you don't do that.

GROUP EXERCISE 2: SUGGESTED ANSWERS

1. Instead of: That's not the point.
   Use: That's an interesting point. That's another good point.
2. Instead of: I think we should.
   Use: I have one possible suggestion. What do you think of this idea?
3. Instead of: What do you think, Mr. Cato?
   Use: Does anyone else have any suggestions? Have we heard all the opinions?
4. Instead of: Those figures are not accurate.
   Use: I have some other figures here. Those figures may be slightly old.
5. Instead of: You're doing that wrong.
   Use: I would do it like this. Have you tried doing it this way?
6. Instead of: I don't agree.
   Use: I have another idea. What do you think of this idea? May I make a suggestion?

GROUP EXERCISE 3: CLEANING THE VAN CASE—POSSIBLE ANSWERS

The Americans probably thought/felt:

- Why clean the van when it doesn't need it? Stupid. Illogical. Make work. Waste of time.
- Cleaning the van that thoroughly is overkill anyway—who cares if a camp van is super clean and shiny every day?
- Why are the men students sitting around making the women and American students work? Not *fair.*
- Unreasonable expectations of hard labor.
- Don't feel like a real member of this group.
- Isn't this a day off?
- He's belittling us, singling us out, punishing us, on a power trip.
- If he's treating us like that, I'm not going to "behave."
- If you don't agree with something it is okay to refuse to participate.
- Japanese are rigid, stupid, arrogant (men), humiliatingly obedient (women).

The Japanese senior male students may have thought/felt:

- Responsible for these American kids learning how to behave appropriately in Japan.
- We had our turn at the bottom of the heap—our senior year is a time to enjoy a few privileges.
- Everyone has their jobs, their roles. Women cook and clean. Men are responsible for the whole program.
- Each group has tasks to do and it is important that they do it seriously and well.
- Maturity means following form without asking childish questions.
- Outward cleaning is connected to inner purity of motive, heart.
- Japanese are doing more than their fair share of the work.
- Americans are lazy and soft. Self-indulgent. Challenging authority when they are newcomers who know nothing.

The Japanese woman student may have thought/felt:

- Important to do assigned work without complaining.
- May have just expected Americans to show up and work.
- Have to show Americans the right attitude, the right way to do things.
- Quiet humbleness is the right attitude to take.

- Didn't want to interfere with men's roles as leaders.
- (If she was unhappy with situation) didn't want to instigate conflict with the leaders in front of the Americans.

Chapter 14: Applying Leadership Style

ANSWER KEY AND RATIONALE FOR GROUP EXERCISE 2: LEADER ADAPTABILITY EXERCISE

Situation 1.   A. Emphasize the use of uniform procedures and the necessity for task accomplishment. Rationale: This action (HT/LR) provides the directive leadership needed to increase group productivity in the short run.

Situation 2.   A. Engage in friendly interaction but continue to make sure that all members are aware of their roles and standards. Rationale: This action (HT/HR) will best facilitate increased group maturity. Although some structure is maintained by seeing that members are aware of their roles and standards, increased consideration is shown by friendly interaction with the group.

Situation 3.   D. Encourage the group to work on the problem and be available for discussion. Rationale: This action (HR/LT) allows the group to derive its own solution to the problem but makes the leader available to act as a facilitator in this process if necessary.

Situation 4.   C. Allow the group to formulate its own direction. Rationale: This action (LT/LR) would maximize the involvement of this mature group in developing and implementing the change.

Situation 5.   C. Redefine goals and supervise carefully. Rationale: This action (HT/LR) provides the directive leadership needed to increase group productivity in the short run.

Situation 6.   D. Get the group involved in decision making but see that objectives are met. Rationale: This action (HT/HR) best facilitates beginning to humanize the environment. Some structure and direction from the leader are maintained, and socioemotional support and group responsibility are increased gradually by moderate involvement in decision making. If the group handles this involvement well, further increases in socioemotional support become more appropriate.

A GUIDE TO KEEPING JOURNALS

Keeping a journal of your key interpersonal experiences should be a continuing exercise. It is perhaps one of the most important exercises you can do.

Why?

Taking the time to think and write about your interpersonal experiences increases the likelihood that you will be able to look at them from different perspectives and learn from them. Putting experiences into words shifts emotional reactions into more objective analyses. Reviewing entries provides a valuable autobiography of your evolving thinking about interpersonal relations and significant events in your life.

Reviews may also enhance your understanding of your own behavior and stimulate thoughts concerning new ways of behaving that you may want to try out. Journal entries can provide a repository of ideas that you may later want to use more formally for papers, pep talks, or speeches. Your journal will help you develop an agenda for personal growth in future interactions. It will save time, help you avoid missing opportunities, and help you achieve your goals.

When?

Write your journal entries as soon as possible after each class session. You should not write journal entries during group meetings because it detracts from the process. Briefly jotting down key words or phrases to serve as a reminder for later reflection can be helpful, however, if done discreetly and briefly.

What?

Try to recapture what happened and why it was significant to you. Include your reactions, feelings, and ideas for application relevant to the interpersonal skills being experienced in the interaction. You can learn from both good examples and bad ones. As a general guide, journal entries should cover:

- What happened
- The consequences of the interaction
- Your feelings and reactions
- Insights you gained
- Plans for applying your insights in the future

In addition to what you learned about the specific skills being focused on during a specific class session, your journal entries can help you track your interpersonal development in general and facilitate the preparation of agendas for future meetings. As you review your journal, make some decisions on what you want to accomplish in the next class meeting. Each weekly log should conclude with a practical agenda for the next class meeting. Make your entries relatively brief and concrete. Ask yourself whether you can use what you write at the next meeting. For example, you might include the following:

- *Experiences:*   "Jane ignored me the whole meeting. In general she seems indifferent toward me. Check to see what is going on."
- *Behaviors:*   "I asked John a lot of questions but really did not make much of an effort to understand him. I noticed during the week that I do that quite a bit. I think others should challenge me more when I act like that."
- *Feelings:*   "I've been on a high from the last meeting; everyone in the group contacted me, but no one dealt with me as if I were a 'case,' even though I cried. I don't want to be a blubbering slob, but I want to be able to cry at times without feeling I'm betraying my manhood."
- *Tracking Establishing and Developing Relationships:*   For instance, you might write in your log: "I don't talk to Jane at all, because I think she is rather indifferent to me and I'm attracted to her. I don't like this combination."

In general, your interpersonal entries should help you determine what you want to work on, how you can put effort into achieving your goals at each meeting (e.g., not avoiding people who seem distant to you), and keep track of your progress. Some participants keep excellent logs but then fail to use this material in the class meetings. If you are having difficulty using your log material, perhaps it would help to share this with others and let them help you introduce the material into class discussions.

How?

How much you write and how you write it is up to you. Journals are for your own learning, so different people will use different styles. Writing as freely as possible about your own involvement helps you learn about yourself (e.g., what you said or did, why, consequences, etc.). Not feeling involved, or holding back when you want to act, are also worth exploring. Try to determine what implicit assumptions, feelings, underlying motivations, and so on, seem to be "causing" your feelings, thoughts, and actions.

Your journal will be useful for your learning to the extent that you are really searching as you write, and being as open and honest as possible. Explore your feelings, perceptions, evaluations, and questions as much as you can. The journal gives you a chance to reflect and experience more fully and deeply than you may have been able to at the time of the events. It is your private diary for your use only. Be as honest with it as you can.

JOURNAL ENTRY EXAMPLE

Following are some examples of some journal entries related to the interpersonal skill of leadership. They provide a variety of experiences and applications.

- I went skiing this weekend and saw the perfect example of a leader adapting her leadership style to her followers and situation. While putting on my skis I saw a ski instructor teaching little kids to ski. She did it using the game "Red Light, Green Light." The kids loved it and seemed to be doing very well. Later that same day, as I was going to the lodge for lunch, she was teaching adults, and she did more demonstrating than talking. But when she talked she was always sure to encourage them so they did not feel intimidated when some little kid whizzed by. She would say to the adults that it's easier for children, or that smaller skis are easier. She made the children laugh and learn, and made the adults less self-conscious to help them learn too . . .

- Today may not exactly be a topic on leadership, but I thought it would be interesting to discuss. I attended the football game this afternoon and could not help but notice our cheerleaders. I was just thinking of their name in general and found them to be a good example (of leadership). Everyone gets rowdy at a football game, but without the direction of the cheerleaders there would be mayhem. They do a good job of getting the crowd organized and the adrenaline pumping (though of course the game is most important in that too!). It's just amazing to see them generate so much interest that all of the crowd gets into the cheering. We even chant their stupid-sounding cheers! You might not know any of them personally, but their enthusiasm invites you to try to be even louder than them. I must give the cheerleaders a round of applause . . .

- I've been thinking about how I used to view/understand leadership, trying to find out how my present attitudes were developed. It's hard to remember past freshman year, even harder to go past high school. Overall, I think my father has been the single most important influence on my leadership development—long before I even realized it. Dad is a strong "Type A" person. He drives himself hard and demands a great deal from everyone around him, especially his family and especially his only son and oldest child. He was always pushing me to study, practice whatever sport I was involved in at the time, and get ahead of everybody else in every way possible.

INDEX